CHINA FEVER

CHINA FEVER

Fascination, Fear, and the World's Next Superpower

Frank S. Fang

Stone Bridge Press • Berkeley, California

Published by
Stone Bridge Press
P. O. Box 8208
Berkeley, CA 94707
TEL 510-524-8732 • www.stonebridge.com • sbp@stonebridge.com

Printed in the United States of America.

2011 2010 2009 2008 2007   10 9 8 7 6 5 4 3 2 1

LIBRARY OF CONGRESS CATALOGING-IN-PUBLICATION DATA

Fang, Frank S.
China fever: fascination, fear, and the world's next superpower / Frank S. Fang.'
  p. cm.
Includes bibliographical references and index.
ISBN 978-1-933330-55-6 (cloth)
  1. China—Economic conditions—2000- 2. China—Economic policy—2000- 3. Democratization—
China. 4. Political culture—China. I. Title.
HC427.95.F363 2007

  330.951—dc22
            2007014398

Table of Contents

To the memory of Mancur Olson who believed that "Just as the great fighter is looking for the jugular, the great scientist is looking for areas where there can be breakthrough—for areas where strong claims are in order."

Acknowledgments

"The role of the economist, at base, must be that of attempting to understand a certain type of human behavior and the prediction of the social structures that are emergent from that behavior. Ultimately, the economist must hope that his simple truths, as extended, can lead to 'improvement' in the structure of these institutions, through the ability of institutions to modify the conditions of human choice. But improvement must remain his secondary and subsidiary purpose; he verges dangerously on irresponsible action when he allows his zeal for social progress, as he conceives this, to take precedence over this search for and respect of scientific truth." This was written by the 1986 Nobel Prize Laureate James M. Buchanan in his 1979 book titled *What Should Economists Do?*

James Buchanan is the very first Institutional Economist I'd like to thank because his brilliant ideas on Economics Methodology and New Political Economy have been an inspiration for my research during the last twenty years. Specifically for the study of China, Buchanan's inspiration for me is to go beyond both journalistic and academic common sense and add a micro-scrutiny for human behavior, a beyond-evolutionary institutional analysis for political dynamics, and a subjectivist perspective for market and political processes. As for a historical, cultural, and cognitive addition to the study of China, Douglass C. North, the 1993 Nobel Prize Laureate, is the second Institutional Economist I am indebted to. I am fully aware that neither of them may agree with the conclusions in this book, yet their "bring theory into research" approach deserves a great deal of my appreciation and acknowledgment. Mancur Olson (1932–1998), to whom this book is dedicated, was another luminous Institutional Economist whose academic legacy is beyond natural boundary. "Olson-style logic" exemplifies how powerful it is when theory is added into social studies—the logic of collective actions, and the logic of distributional coalitions. All of their stimulations make new ideas in this book both simple and straightforward. And as John M. Keynes said, the difficulty only comes from escaping the old habitual modes of thought.

I'd like to thank my friends in Beijing, many of who influenced me one way or another during 1982–1994 (the brainstorming of this book started in 1995) when I spent some of the best of my time there as a student and scholar. They are Jiang Hong, Guan Shan, Fan Gang, Sheng Hong, Zhang Yuyan, Mao Yushi, Zhang Shuguang, Liu Shijin, Tang Shouning, and Liu Wei. All of them were key contributors when I had the opportunity to moderate those "roundtable conferences" for "Modern Institutional Economics and China's Reform" in Beijing during 1990–1994. Some of them may not even realize their ideas had actually made an impact on me. Of course, if this book contains any mistaken viewpoints, the blame should be on myself only. Flaws are definitely unavoidable as it is one of the first attempts by an institutionalist like myself to be totally un-evasive on China's political-economic institutions, even though this book is at the same time a challenge for all institutionalists to open-mindedly address China's institutional structure both positively and normatively.

In addition, I feel grateful to mention Zhang Weiying, Xiang Bing, Wang Dingding, Ye Hang, Wei Seng, Deng Zhenlai, Ling Yifu, Hu Peizhao, Wang Jun, and Hou Ling, whose books, articles, or personal contacts help keep me up-to-date with the development in China.

I also wish to thank my father Fang Lijun, my mother Ji Huizhen, my wife Lucy (Zhou Yan), my son Jimmy, my daughter Erin, and my sister Fang Shaoshan. They give me the ultimate motivation for this book. Without any of them, this book is simply not possible. This book is also for the memory of my brother Fang Shaopeng.

Chris Robyn, my editor, is "the man" behind this book. Readers who find this book of any value should thank him who took on this project almost at the first sight of my book proposal. I'd also like to thank Peter Goodman, Linda Ronan, and Ari Messer of Stone Bridge Press for their assistance.

Frank S. Fang
Chicago, 2007
Institutional Economics Center
(www.ieCenter.org, ChinaFever.ieCenter.org)

Introduction

At the dawn of the twenty-first century, the rise of China is one of the top stories in magazines, the internet, and the subject of endless articles, commentary, and opinion pieces in newspapers around the world. "China fever" is everywhere. More and more people—many with no background whatsoever with China—now want to learn Chinese: to stay competitive.

China, like a gigantic magnetic field, draws attention, company investment, and every country's resources. In the U.S., IBM is sourcing its components from China, Freeborders is outsourcing its software solutions to China, Motorola is offshoring its production to China, and Microsoft is offshoring its R&D to China. Starbucks is making mergers and acquisitions in China, Goldman Sachs is investing, Morgan Stanley is scooping up property deals, Merrill Lynch is betting on the securities market. GM is selling into China, and Wal-Mart is selling in China and buying from China. For many companies, the option is clear: go "China" or go bankrupt. Amidst these "Big Ten Businesses," Washington is debating its trade policy with China, frustrated over its trade deficit with China, pressuring China to appreciate its currency and to protect intellectual property, and mulling over the challenge and potential threat from China.

In early 2007, when China used a ground-based, medium-range ballistic missile to destroy one of its own weather satellites, the move was immediately seen, theoretically, as putting low-orbiting American spy satellites in danger, an idea unheard of a decade ago. America was supreme in space, but here comes China. Its anti-satellite test made China the third country with such capability and quickly set off a wide range of concerns and anxiety in the West—a sure sign that China now commands the world's attention.

On February 27, 2007, China's Shanghai composite index plummeted from 3,049 to 2,771 points (about 9 percent or $108 billion in value) on profit taking. The worst one-day fall in a decade immediately created a domino effect felt around the world. The U.S. stock market saw its worst day since the Sept. 11, 2001 terrorist attacks. The Dow Jones Industrial Average fell more than 400 points, the Nasdaq composite index fell nearly 100 points, and the S&P 500 index fell by 50 points; all were down by more than 3 percent. Germany's DAX and France's CAC 40 index also fell by around 3 percent. This "China impact" is a sure sign of China's psychological hold on the rest of the world. Though China is generally viewed favorably, there is still a strong sense of unease, misinformation, and outright distrust of China's economic and military ambitions. Questions arise over the safety of Chinese-made products and foodstuffs, including pet food, tires, and massive recalls of toys made in China. With the world looking to the Beijing Olympics in 2008, there are even questions about whether a proposed boycott of the Games will have any impact on China's relationship with Sudan, or even its own reputation on the world stage with regard to the Taiwan issue, the Tibet issue, political and religious persecution, and general state of human rights.

At the same time, China is rising domestically and internationally with more shining stars: basketball star Yao Ming; 110-meter hurdle superman Liu Xian; Olympic diver Guo Jingjing, movie icon Zhang Ziyi; and also its richest businesswoman, Zhang Yin, who edges out even Oprah Winfrey in personal wealth. New "Bizocrat" Huang Guangyu tops the *Forbes* 400 richest Chinese list; and China internet pioneer Jack Ma forced eBay to retreat in its attempt to "make it" in the China market.

As products labeled "Made in China," "Designed in China," and "Printed in China" are shipped to every corner of the world, Chinese companies are flexing their muscle in international business: Legend became Lenovo through a "Snake Eats Elephant" story; Huawei is daringly changing the playing field of the global telecommunications market. CNOOC, China's largest oil company, made a highly controversial move to acquire UNOCAL and is continuing to work with other Chinese oil companies to acquire energy resource assets all over the world.

Meanwhile, software leader Neusoft and numerous companies from Wenzhou are staging a Chinese version of outsourcing and offshoring. Electronics giant Haier, auto parts maker Wanxiang, machinery maker Sany, shipping concern CIMC, and toolmaker Techtronic are all slowly but surely elbowing their way into the U.S. marketplace. As big SUVs grow out of favor with American drivers, Chinese auto companies—Geely, Chery,

Changfeng, and Zhongxing—are already seen as the next wave of foreign imports to invade (and further weaken) the American auto market.

In the new millennium, Chinese language and culture are going global. Confucius Institutes are being established outside of China. Learning Chinese has become a big fad in the new century. China Central Television (CCTV), Phoenix, Dongfang, and Hunan satellite coverage is spreading Chinese culture around the globe.

China vaults onto the world stage with the 2008 Summer Olympic Games in Beijing, a stellar opportunity for the Chinese to showcase their economic boom and stunning cultural glory. China's breakneck growth is taking millions of farmers out of poverty. Its doubling-up of its GDP three years' running is pushing millions of urban residents into a new middle class. Millions of Chinese, made newly rich, are now touring everywhere in their own country and all around the world. In Hong Kong, even after the formal handover from Britain to China in 1997, mainland visitors were looked upon with disdain as backwoods cousins. Now, many shops have difficulty coping with this new wave of tourists, flush with cash, who have as much buying power as their jet-setting European or Japanese predecessors. With potentially the world's largest consumer population, (1.3 billion), the world's largest mobile phone population (461 million), the world's second-largest internet population (137 million), and the largest television audience (350+ million households), China is at the epicenter of the world's new economic order.

Nevertheless, China is not God. Wealth spawns greed. Boom generates transgression. China is a country not only gravely plagued by rampant corruption, State-Owned Enterprise (SOE) inefficiency, distribution-driven overheating, piracy and intellectual property violations, healthcare crisis, and degenerate social mores, but is also dangerously troubled by crime and social unrest, unemployment and income disparity, environmental degradation, and vulnerability to international economic shock. To some China observers, this is a huge, unfathomable mystery: a global-scale business gold-rush built atop a deep-rooted and corrupt government; an unprecedented economic mega-boom coupled with a stiff authoritarian regime; open ambition underscored by a troubled civic culture; and a rich cultural tradition riding on the shoulders of an intractable non-democratic orthodoxy. Every bizarre combination seems to exist in China, defying all explanation.

It is not capitalism, but "Socialism with Chinese Characteristics." You can do what you like, as long as you do not upset the government. There is a line that must not be crossed, yet that line is not clearly delineated. This is the focal point of the "China puzzle": with the social and political crises in its economic rise, why is the Chinese government not collapsing? Why is economic liberalization showing no sign of political democratization? In short, if the situation in China is really so bad, then why does there continue to be China fever?

No matter what your occupation, what happens in China will affect you. Maybe not tomorrow, but soon. It is important to understand the historical processes at work and how they affect what is happening in China today.

For those who wish to see China adopt Western-style democratic change, the problem is not only about the specific mechanism of China's political culture and the logic of democratization, it is also about the contexts of "public choice" in Western democracy and the perception of democracy's "moral superiority." For those who predict China's coming collapse, what needs to be explained is how China's "Dynastic Cycle" fits into its current institutional setting. For those alarmed by the "China threat," what needs to be defined is China's role as a defense "border expansionist." For those puzzled by China's economic boom, what is needed is a solid explanation of China's economic growth and a discussion of why this is, in fact, a long-term opportunity. Finally, for those who see China as a (re)emerging empire, the pressing issue is the still as-yet undefined and unrecognized nature of the unique challenges to the American century and beyond.

1

America's "China Fever"

Scrambling for China Action

China is the big show today. The country's economic transformation began around 1978, continued into the beginning of the new millennium, and, rather than slowing, continues to accelerate at a blistering pace. Looking at the broader background of this economic wonder, we see that China is undergoing a triple transition: from a planned economy to a market economy; from a traditional agricultural society to a modern industrial society; and from an autocratic "Family Rulership" to an authoritarian "Party Rulership." China's triple transition also happens at a time when globalization is poised to catch a new wave: the industrial revolution enters an informational stage and various civilizations become more culturally distinct in the process of an unprecedented worldwide integration. These two pairs of triple mega-trends come together to form a "perfect storm" in China, causing drastic changes domestically, and in turn producing front-page headlines around the world leading to both fascination, and fear, of having to deal with this new mega-economy. Perhaps nowhere else is this China fever felt so strongly as in the United States, where, depending on who you ask, the U.S. and China can work together or are headed for a collision course.

For every five human beings on earth, one is currently experiencing

China's economic boom on Chinese soil: three of the other four are jockeying for a front row seat to what is potentially the biggest modernization transformation in human history. The scale, scope, and strength of China's growth clearly cannot be explained as another Asian tiger economic take-off. Certainly a rising China is the latest international juggernaut in a long series of great powers, starting with Portugal, Spain, The Netherlands, Great Britain, Germany, Japan, and the United States.[1] To some, China is the biggest opportunity in their lifetime. To others, China is a riddle that needs to be demystified.

After President Richard Nixon's strategy-over-ideology effort in 1972, the United States and the People's Republic of China announced on December 15, 1978, that the two governments would establish diplomatic relations effective January 1, 1979. This period also marked the beginning of China's reform and opening to the world. The coincidence of these two events magically binds the two countries onto a track of globalization, crafting a macro shockwave in the decades that followed.

The real "China fever" did not come until 1992, when China's helmsman Deng Xiaoping made a policy-making tour to southern China and proclaimed a bold shift toward genuine market liberalization. Deng had once famously stated: "It doesn't matter if it's a black cat or a white cat; it's a good cat as long as it can catch mice." Subsequent to the 1989 Tiananmen crackdown, Deng's "Good Cat" philosophy attained a new meaning: Party-leadership is the core of the "Four Fundamental Principles," and as long as the Party is in control, everything from foreign investment to free market can be incorporated into "Socialism with Chinese Characteristics."

Japan and Germany took the lead by expanding their business interests in China. Soon the American embassy in Beijing was crowded with group after group of U.S. businessmen who were afraid of falling behind. Deng set the ball rolling for China fever. Americans jumped on the China bandwagon and the American fascination with China started. If America's globalization has to be summarized in a single word, that word is "China."

China imports technology and exports labor. China imports jobs and exports deflation. China imports inspiration and exports ambition. This is the most captivating trading scheme in China's industrialization. As a competitive service provider, the biggest manufacturing hub, and the third greatest manufacturing power in the world (after the U.S. and Japan), China is at the very core of globalization.

To most Americans, the China story is no longer far away on the other side of the earth. Its so-called "peaceful rise" exists not only in newspapers, magazines, books, radio, television, or web pages. People can see and feel it in their everyday lives: from the clothing on their backs, sports, movies, shopping, and job security, to international trade, business competition, classroom and conference discussions, policy debates, and politics at the local and national level. More and more U.S. businesses are talking about having a "China plan," being sensitive to the "China effect," developing a "China-first" strategy, being "China ready," and knowing the "China price" (the two most-feared words for American manufacturing industries).

Americans are also debating China's role as a "must play" partner in the international arena, and asking, "Is the new century really a "Chinese Century," following on the heels of the "American Century?" Is America in decline? Is the hype surrounding "China fever" justified, or is it a fad, another unique fascination similar to the Japan-hype of the 1980s?[2] Willing or not, Americans are bombarded by tons of information on China every day. China's business is now America's business. America's business in China is also China's business.

Despite all the words of caution and high business "transaction costs," an increasing number of U.S. companies are clamoring to join the China gold-rush with unreserved optimism. As investment return remains whopping *and* stable over the years, American businesses' confidence in the country continues to soar. Billions of dollars of hot money—be it venture capital, speculative capital, or production capital—is circling in Chinese skies ready to drop in for the kill. It's about the jaw-dropping low-cost offers. It's about the heart-pounding market magnitude. It's about the mind-blowing environment of friendly people and policies. It's about the best bet in an economy booming at a 10 percent annual rate.

Motorola, the number one foreign company in China and the world's second-largest cell phone maker after Nokia, is now claiming a quarter of China's handset market with sales of more than $10 billion. With over 461 million users, China now has the largest mobile phone population in the world. Motorola's ambition is to outpace the nearly 30 percent annual growth rate of China's handset market. The company recently introduced a new global "flagship store" in Shanghai, and plans to roll out similar stores in Beijing, Guangzhou, and Chengdu. Following the launch of fifty smaller Motorola-branded retail locations operated by local partners throughout China, this flagship retail footprint aims at taking back maket share from China's homegrown rivals like Ningbo Bird and TCL Communication Technology Holdings. Several hundred stores may open in the next few years also to compete with Nokia (the second-largest foreign company in China with near 30 percent share in the mobile phone market) and Samsung.

Motorola's largest handset production base is in the Tianjin "Binhai

New Area." Set up in 1992, the base recently celebrated the production of its 200 millionth handset. Motorola also has sixteen R&D offices in five Chinese cities, employs about 2,000 Chinese engineers, and has an accumulated investment of about $500 million since 1993. Among many of the new gadgets developed there, the A780 cell phone allows users to write on the screen with just a finger rather than a stylus. Another phone can scan contact information from business cards with a built-in camera. Motorola Ventures, the venture investment section of the company launched in 1998, has invested in six high-tech companies so far, looking to play a bigger role in the country's high-tech boom. After making the country its global base for production and research, Motorola plans to establish a corporate finance firm in Tianjin to serve Motorola's seven affiliates in China, taking deposits and offering lending and corporate financing as well as consulting services.

RR Donnelley, the first U.S. company to provide commercial print and print-related services in China, acquired Asia Printers Group Ltd. with $95 million in cash to expand its China-Based Book Production Platform. Asia Printers Group employs approximately 1,400 people in locations that include Dongguan, Guangdong, and Hong Kong. RR Donnelley entered China in 1993 through a joint venture agreement with the Shenzhen Petrochemical Holding Co., Ltd. In 2001, RR Donnelley formed a second joint venture with the Shanghai Press and Publications Administration. Mark A. Angelson, RR Donnelley's Chief Executive Officer, believed that "the acquisition also adds China-based capabilities to our Global Capital Markets financial printing business, which will enhance our ability to sell to a broader client base in the Asia capital markets."[3] China was the inventor of movable-type printing in the eleventh century, some 400 years before the Gutenberg process in Europe. As the Chinese government continues to foster an attractive business environment, RR Donnelley is contributing "Printed in China" alongside the monikers "Made in China" and "Designed in China."

General Motors' business in China is thriving in spite of its misery in the U.S. domestic auto market. As the world's largest automaker and the third-largest foreign company in China, GM generated 45 billion yuan in sales from China for 2005, easily surpassing rivals Volkswagen AG and Hyundai Motor Co. In addition, China and other overseas factories accounted for more than half of GM's total output of 9.2 million vehicles in 2005. As the number one foreign automaker in the country, GM sees stronger-than-expected prospecs, with a 30 percent annual growth potential and a 12.5 percent stable share in the country's quickly growing auto market. While its U.S. sales languish amid fierce competition, China is emerging as one of GM's biggest and most profitable markets.

GM's flagship joint ventures with Shanghai Automotive Industry Corp. Group (Shanghai GM), and minivan and commercial joint venture SAIC-GM-Wuling, both experiencing startling expansion, are outshining the overall auto market in China. GM is now selling vehicles under four major brands: Buick, Chevrolet, Cadillac, and Saab, through Shanghai GM, which plans to manufacture hybrid gas-and-electric powered vehicles by 2008 as part of the effort to shift into next-generation technologies that might help reduce the environmental impact of increased vehicle use. GM also builds luxury cars in China, hoping to profit from the Chinese new rich; and plans to put more than 8 billion yuan ($1.31 billion) every year into research, upgrades, and production expansion.

Compared with GM, Ford is a relative latecomer (1997) to the China market. With its catch-up psychology, Ford is poised to be firm and aggressive for China growth. Sales of Ford-brand vehicles in China rose 46 percent to 82,225 units in 2005, beating the industry-wide sales growth of about 14 percent. Sales in 2006 almost doubled, far exceeding GM and the average industry growth rate for commercial vehicle and passenger car sales. The Ford Focus, launched in September 2005, has been the major growth force of Ford's joint venture with its Japanese affiliate Mazda Motor Corp. and China's Changan Automobile Group. The Focus hatchback model was launched with great success in 2006. Sales of the Ford Transit, a commercial vehicle model made with Jiangling Motor Corp., rose significantly, as did sales of Ford's "Premier Auto Group" brands, namely Volvo, Jaguar, and Land Rover. Good news in the sales front makes Ford's $1 billion expansion plan in China promising.

China's 7.2 million annual new vehicle sales also attracted the German-U.S. automaker DaimlerChrysler. In September 2006, DaimlerChrysler opened its first factory in Beijing to produce Mercedes-Benz E-Class and Chrysler 300C sedans, as well as Mitsubishi's Outlander sport utility vehicles. The deal, partnered with state-owned Beijing Automotive Industries Corp., is part of the company's $1.9 billion investment plan in China.

DaimlerChrysler also invested in Beijing-based truck maker Beiqi Foton Motor Co., China's largest light-duty truck maker. DaimlerChrysler AG's Chrysler Group and China's Chery Automobile Co. will join forces to build small cars to be sold worldwide. DaimlerChrysler also set up a joint venture to manufacture Mercedes-Benz vans with the Fujian Auto Industry Group and Taiwan's China Motor Corp. Before the merger with Daimler-Benz AG, which lasted from 1998-2007, Chrysler was the first

Western company to produce vehicles in China when it opened a joint-venture "Beijing Jeep" factory in 1983.

Asia Pacific R&D Ltd., a research and development subsidiary of microchip giant Intel, now operates in Shanghai's Zizhu Science Park. The company hired as many as 1,000 staff from the growing pool of technical talent in China. In March 2006, Intel opened its second chip testing and assembly plant in Chengdu, capital of Sichuan Province.

Intel has invested almost $1.3 billion in China so far, including a $200 million investment in Intel Capital's China Technology Fund. Intel Capital, one of the largest worldwide corporate venture programs investing in the technology segment, mainly invested in the fields of mobile telecom, broadband, software application, and semiconductor design. Since 1998, Intel Capital has invested in more than fifty companies in China, including UTStarcom and Sohu. A recent investment of $40 million in China's Neusoft Group Ltd. takes shared control of China's biggest outsourcer and one of the country's largest software houses with Philips Electronics and Toshiba Corp.

Intel will also enter into the inexpensive PC market, as well as helping to provide internet access and education in China's rural areas in a five-year project supported by the Chinese government. It will build a $2.5 billion plant in Dalian to produce microchips beginning in 2010. In a market share battle with Intel in China, Advanced Micro Devices (AMD) Inc., the world's number two maker of microchips, has scored its latest victory in a deal to supply China's second-largest PC maker, Founder Technology, with chips of the AMD64 processor. AMD's first major victory dates to 2004, when it signed a deal to supply chips to Lenovo Group Ltd., the world's third-largest PC maker and China's dominant player in the PC industry.

As the world's second-largest PC market, China is expected to overtake the United States as the world's biggest PC consumer market by 2010. A few years ago, Intel took 90 percent of the market share in China, while AMD held less than 5 percent. Now it's a 70/20 percent race.

Meanwhile, Dell China Co. Ltd, the China subsidiary of Dell Inc., is planning to more than double its production capacity in China through the opening of a second factory in Xiamen. Dell's Xiamen operations produce over 3.5 million personal computers a year, generating annual revenue of around $5 billion. Dell recently overtook Tsinghua Tongfang to rank third, with a 10 percent share, after Lenovo and Founder, in China's personal computer market. The company also has design and research labs in Shanghai, and a technical support facility in the northeastern city of Dalian.

Larry Dickenson, Boeing's longtime head of its Asia Pacific sales team and newly appointed top salesman for the commercial airplane division, keeps a thick scrapbook of photos of himself at ceremonial events with China's leaders, many of which date back more twenty years. Outside his office, displays of valuable gifts from Asian airlines and governments include a huge Buddha from China and a model of the fifteenth-century sailing ship of Chinese maritime hero Zheng He.[4] Boeing started to sell airplanes to China in 1972, when it blazed a trail of sales hot on the heels of Nixon's historic visit. Once Airbus stepped into the China market, however, Boeing started to suffer from missed opportunities and complacency. Ten years ago, more than eight out of ten commercial jets flown in China were Boeing planes. Now only about six out of ten are. Airbus's share of new airplane deliveries to China rocketed from 18 percent in 1993 to near 70 percent in 2006.[5] Boeing is also facing China's high-flying ambition of building its own airliners in the near future.

David Wang was recruited from General Electric to become president of Boeing China to turn things around. Boeing bounced back strongly with the sale of sixty of its new 787 jets to Chinese airlines in 2005, and a big order for eighty Boeing 737s accompanied Chinese President Hu Jintao's visit to the U.S. in 2006. Boeing has also worked together with China's aviation industry for more than thirty years. Today, major parts and assemblies of thousands of Boeing airplanes are built in China. Examples include the 737 horizontal stabilizers from Shanghai Aircraft Corp., 737 vertical fins from Xian Aircraft Corp., 737 tail section modules from Shenyang Aircraft Corp., and 757 empennages, aft fuselage sections, and rudders from Chengdu Aircraft Corp.

In 2006, the San Francisco Bay Area-based company eBay was second among consumer auction sites in China with about 28 percent of the market, versus about 58 percent for Alibaba's Taobao.com. Alibaba started in 1999 as a B2B website, and in 2003 it founded Taobao.com for the consumer market, offering a free auction service, which proved to be a huge blow to eBay. With a $1 billion investment, Yahoo quickly took 40 percent control in Alibaba and transferred all of its existing China operations to Alibaba in 2005.

Alibaba also launched a new web-based business software company, Alisoft, in 2007. As the battle intensified, eBay reluctantly dropped transaction fees from its basic C2C services. When eBay was wondering if it was too late to compete with Taobao, here came Paipai.com, a newcomer owned by China's dominant instant messaging firm Tencent. Within a matter of months, Paipai.com saw its share of revenues leap from zero to 14 percent. Alibaba's outspoken Jack Ma claimed that eBay had made too many mistakes in China, and that it was hard for eBay to wrest market share from local firms: "Strong dragons can hardly defeat local snakes." In December 2006, eBay closed its main auction site in China and entered into a joint venture with the Beijing-based Tom Online, a move viewed by some as a retreat, and by others a lesson from Yahoo China.

America's leading financial institutions have bet billions on the country's financial future by acquiring minority stakes in China's state controlled banks, many of which recently restructured through stock offerings in Hong Kong in an effort to stand clear from the shadow of mountains of bad loans. Their initial public offerings (IPOs) sold like the proverbial hotcakes, which made every pre-IPO investment everybody's jealously guarded secret.

In the Bank of China's initial public offering, the world's eighth-richest man, Saudi Prince Alwaleed bin Talal, grabbed one-fifth of the $2 billion in shares. Bank of America paid $3 billion for a 9 percent stake in China Construction Bank, valued at $9 billion after its IPO. Goldman Sachs Group Inc., American Express Co., and German Allianz AG sank a total of $3.8 billion into China's largest lender, the Industrial & Commercial Bank of China (ICBC), capturing a 10 percent stake to mark the largest ever one-off investment by foreign investors in China's financial sector.

Goldman Sachs's $3 billion investment turned into $7.4 billion within one year, when in October of 2006 ICBC made the biggest IPO debut in history.[6] Morgan Stanley, which has a 35 percent stake in China International Capital Corp. (with former Premier Zhu Rongji's son Zhu Yunlai as chief executive) since 1995, acquired China's Nan Tung Bank, the first among its U.S. peers to establish an onshore commercial banking platform in China.

Citigroup increased its stake in China's Shanghai Pudong Development Bank to 19.9 percent, the maximum allowed for a single foreign holding (combined holdings are limited to 25 percent). Citigroup has also won the bid to buy a near $3 billion stake in Guangdong Development Bank, after a lengthy battle with France's Societe Generale and Chinese insurer Ping An Group that involved high-level political backing.

China's property market is sizzling. In 2005 alone, foreign institutions spent $3.4 billion purchasing property in every major city in China. The government's measures of higher land-use fees, taxes, and down payments to cool surging investment did not appear to lessen foreign investors' appetites. Morgan Stanley plans to triple its investment in the Chinese real estate markets to $3 billion. Citigroup's property unit, Citigroup Property Investors, plans to increase its investment tenfold to $800 million in the next three years. To catch up with Morgan Stanley and Goldman Sachs, Citigroup spent $50 million in 2005 to buy a 75 percent stake in Yongxin Group, a developer in Shanghai. The company's plan now is to buy office, retail, and industrial properties, and to invest in residential projects in secondary cities, where housing prices have more potential to rise.

Currently, competition is focusing on the eastern part of China, mainly the coastal Bohai Bay, Pearl River Delta, and Yangzi River Delta regions. Class A office yields are 7 percent in Shanghai, compared with 4.5 percent in the United States, 4 percent in London, 3.5 percent to 4 percent in Hong Kong, and 3.5 percent in Tokyo.[7]

Wal-Mart, which opened its first outlet in China in 1996, is poised for major expansion. "We're going to be growing in all directions. Wal-Mart's China operations could be as big as its U.S. business in twenty years," confirmed Joe Hatfield, chief executive of Wal-Mart Asia, while touring stores in Shenzhen, Wal-Mart's China headquarters.[8] Wal-Mart added twenty stores in 2006 and plans to hire 150,000 people in China over the next five years, five times the number it currently employs. Stores in China draw 1.2 million people per month, and the world's biggest retailer and largest company is constantly on the lookout for new locations.

Domestically, the United States generated 80 percent of Wal-Mart's $312 billion in sales, but slowing growth and rising opposition to the huge footprint of Wal-Mart stores on the local landscape has made international expansion all the more appealing. China relaxed rules for foreign retailers at the end of 2004, making it easier to expand. Now Wal-Mart is eyeing Taiwan-owned Trust-Mart's 100 stores in China to expand in the fast-growing inland provinces. In early 2007, Wal-Mart purchased a 35 percent stake in Trust-Mart's operator, Bounteous Company, Ltd. (BCL). An outright acquisition of Trust-Mart would bounce Wal-Mart to number one top foreign retailer in China.

Wal-Mart is not the only retailer from America. In May 2006, Best Buy Co., the largest U.S. electronics retailer, acquired a 51 percent stake valued at $180 million in privately held Jiangsu Five Star Appliance Co., currently China's fourth-biggest electronics retailer with 136 stores in eight provinces but with a plan to open up to 1,000 new stores in three to five years. Best Buy also opened its first store in China, in downtown Shanghai, and is aiming at capturing China's consumer electronics market, where sales are projected to grow by more than 10 percent annually to reach $100 billion in 2010.

The ambition of Caterpillar Inc., the world's largest construction machinery manufacturer, is to be the industry leader in the China market. Selling products to China as early as 1975, Caterpillar expected sales in China to quadruple from 2.5 percent to 10 percent of Caterpillar's total sales by 2010.[9] As it expanded to own fourteen production plants in China, the company decided to move its Asia Pacific headquarters to Beijing from Tokyo.

Caterpillar's latest facility is in Suzhou Industrial Park, where wheel loaders will be manufactured and exported to other countries in the Asia Pacific region. Its largest and oldest facility in China is in Xuzhou, where Caterpillar has been making excavators, motor graders, and tractors since 1994. The company has recently completed a remanufacturing plant in Shanghai, looking to assist China to develop a remanufacturing industry that recycles old components into "like-new" products.

IBM recently relocated its global procurement headquarters from New York to Shenzhen, where a procurement center has been operating for more than a decade. This is the first time the company moved a major division's headquarters to China to both benefit from lower costs and gain market share. IBM also moved its Asia Pacific office from Tokyo to Shanghai not long ago. As China becomes the core of IBM's technology supply chain, it plans to open more offices in second-tier Chinese cities in the coming years to add to its twenty-two offices and near 10,000-strong workforce in China.

IBM is also partnering with U.S. investment bank Lehman Brothers to launch a $180 million fund that will target publicly and privately held companies in technology, financial services, Bio-tech, and communications. Following IBM, Texas-based Electronic Data Systems (EDS) Corp. plans to double its workforce in China to 2,000 by the end of 2007. EDS posted $1.37 billion revenue in Asia last year, near 20 percent of which came from China, with operations in Beijing, Chengdu, Guangzhou, Hong Kong, and Shanghai. It has invested $50 million in China over the past three years, and will spend more through both organic growth and acquisitions over the next few years.

EMC, the world's largest provider of data storage and information management solutions, plans to invest $500 million in China within five years, much to be spent on a research and development center in Shanghai that will provide software solutions for the global market. Starting from Beijing ten years ago, EMC invested about $150 million in the country between 2001 and 2005, competing with companies such as Hewlett-Packard, IBM, and Hitachi.

Globally, EMC has more than twenty research and development facilities, including four in India. While India has been the primary choice for software development offshoring in Asia, a talent shortage and rising costs have driven many companies to tap China's competitive talent pool. The

Shanghai research and development center will be one of the largest, with a work force growing to 500 people by 2008. China's IT market is growing "substantially faster" than other parts of the world, generating increasing demands for information storage and management, and driving EMC's annual sales in China to grow by forty-five times compared to ten years ago.

FedEx Corp. announced a $400 million agreement in 2006 to boost its presence throughout China and Asia by taking full control of a 50 percent joint venture begun in 1999 with the Tianjin Datian Group. Meanwhile, FedEx Express, the cargo airline division of FedEx Corp. and the world's largest express transportation operator, starts additional weekly all-cargo flights to and from China, bringing its total to thirty, more than any other U.S. airline. United Parcel Service Inc. also expanded its air operations in China. It operates 75 facilities, deploys more than 1,400 vehicles, and employs more than 4,000 people. The company recently opened its first retail centers with two UPS Express stores in Shanghai. DHL, the first international express company to enter China in 1980, continues to maintain its market leadership position with a 40 percent market share. The company's twenty-year successful partnership with Chinese Sinotrans has led to DHL-Sinotrans' average annual growth rate of 35 to 45 percent in the past few years.

United Airlines launched its first nonstop daily flight between Washington and Beijing on March 29, 2007, a move potentially worth $200 million a year. China and the United States signed an agreement in 2004 to increase the number of passenger and cargo flights allowed for Chinese and U.S. carriers from fifty-four per week at that time to 249 in stages over the next six years. Under a new agreement reached during the biannual U.S.-China Strategic Economic Dialogue in May 2007, passenger flights between the U.S. and China will more than double by 2012. U.S. carriers will be able to operate twenty-three daily round-trip flights (up from ten). China can also schedule the same number of flights to the United States.

Viewing China both as a market and as a technology and manufacturing center that benefits global sales, General Electric Co. expects revenues in China to double to $10 billion over the next five years. The company secured a contract from China's National Development and Reform Commission to develop water and energy-related technology, and to provide training for up to 2,500 Chinese managers and government officials during the same period. GE has about 13,000 employees in China, and is expanding a Shanghai research center that employs 2,000 Chinese engineers. GE expects to produce new power generation, coal gasification, water filtration, and other products. Its focus on growth for solar and other renewable energy sources will have far-reaching implications for China's expeted energy crunch and pressing environmental issues.

Dallas-based microchip giant Texas Instruments has been growing at a 20 percent pace in the China market during the last few years. China's semiconductor market is worth nearly $50 billion. Asia accounted for over 40 percent of the company's more than $12 billion in semiconductor revenue in 2005, with China as one of the company's fastest growing markets. The company makes chips for everything from flat-panel TVs to calculators, and is the world's leading producer of chips for cell phones. It controls half of the global share for the 3G WCDMA (third-generation "wideband code division multiple access") chips, amounting to $1 billion, with a client list that includes Nokia, NEC, and Sharp. With broadband, 3G telecom, and digital TV driving the China market in the near future, Texas Instruments' dominance in the global market for WCDMA chips allows it to compete with Qualcomm, Freescale Semiconductor, Inc. (the former chip-making unit of Motorola), and China's home-grown 3G standard TD-SCDMA ("time division/synchronous code division multiple access" developed by Datang and Siemens, produced by Spreadtrum Communications).

Google China is seeking to double or triple its 100 employees and will open the firm's second research center in Shanghai in 2007. Kaifu Lee, head of Google China, expects to double the number of Chinese sites using its advertising services by the end of 2007. With 23 percent market share, Google is still far behind China's search leader Baidu (58 percent market share).

According to investment bank Piper Jaffray, China's internet users are expected to conduct 816 million searches daily in 2007, while annual revenues from advertising on search sites could reach $1 billion by 2010. To gain more popularity in the Chinese market, Google used the new brand name "GuGe" or "Valley Song" that draws on Chinese cultural traditions. The name of its competitor "Baidu" references a line in a classical poem referring to a very large number, echoing Google's creative misspelling of Googol (10 to the power of 100). Google has further penetrated the market through a partnership with China Mobile, the world's largest mobile telecommunications carrier, and by acquiring a stake in the burgeoning entertainment download site, Xunlei.com, China's version of YouTube.

In 2004, Las Vegas Sands became the first Nevada-based operator to open a casino in Macau, which reverted from Portugal to China in 1999. Sands Macau was expanded in 2006 to become the world's largest casino in terms of table games. Macau is one of the fastest-growing gaming markets in the world. Macau's $5.8 billion gaming revenues (vs. Las Vegas's $6 billion) is predicted to surpass Las Vegas in total revenues by 2008. The number of tourists visiting Macau reached 18.7 million in 2005, of which 56 percent (10.5 million visitors) were from mainland China. Sands' success quickly drew Wynn, the Venetian, MGM, and Mirage to join the games in Macau, which is expected to double Macau's tourist visitors to thirty million per year by 2010.

With its booming tourism trade and the upcoming 2008 Olympic Games, China is Asia's hottest spot for hotel development. According to Lodging Econometrics, of the 386 hotels being actively pursued throughout Asia, 188 are in China, 25 in Beijing alone. Marriott International Inc., Hilton Hotels Corp., and Starwood Hotels & Resorts are all active players in China. Hilton Hotels Corp. plans to double its five hotels to ten in the next several years, extending its presence to Shanghai, Macau, Xiamen, Anhui province, and Shanxi province. Starwood Hotels & Resorts Worldwide, Inc. has expanded its portfolio in China significantly in the last two years. It operates twenty-six hotels in mainland China, Taiwan, and Macau, has twenty-seven new hotels under construction, and has become one of the largest international hotel operators in China.

U.S.-based RTKL Associates Inc. was picked as one of the eighteen companies to consult on and design the five-function zones (a high-tech zone, a port logistics zone, an airport logistics zone, a central business district, and a resort area) for the Binhai New Area in the northern port city of Tianjin. The Binhai New Area, about four times bigger than Shanghai's futuristic Pudong New Area, is known as a national pilot reform base (including a program for trading the yuan, China's currency, freely). China intends to turn the Binhai New Area into its third economic engine, following Shenzhen and Pudong, the economic powerhouses of the country's southern and eastern coastal areas respectively. After offering supply chain consulting services in its Shanghai office from 2005 on, Wisconsin-based trucking company Schneider obtained its license to establish a domestic business in China in 2007. Schneider National has business in more than thirty countries, and is now the only North American big trucker in China. Schneider Logistics (Tianjin) will bring an advanced operating model, innovative technology, and leading supply chain practices to offer transportation and logistics services from the Northern Binhai region.

According to China's National Development and Reform Commission, U.S. enterprises have already invested $5 billion in twenty Sino-U.S. joint oil and gas exploration projects in China. Crude oil output of China's offshore oil projects, in which U.S. oil companies are taking part, reached 15.53 million tons in 2005, accounting for 56 percent of the total output of China National Offshore Oil Company (CNOOC), the country's offshore oil and gas giant. Anadarko Petroleum Corp. and Ultra Petroleum Corp. are among many U.S. oil companies that hold a financial and logistical stake in China. China consumed 317 million tons of oil and imported 136 million tons in 2005. As China recently began filling its newly built strategic oil reserves, its oil imports are expected to multiply in the coming years. China, self sufficient in oil until 1993, is now the world's second-largest oil consumer (the United States is the largest).

In Walt Rostow's historical model of economic growth, traditional society, preconditions for take-off, take-off, drive to maturity, and high mass consumption are the five basic stages. In China, these five stages appear to happen all at once across its vast and heterogeneous land. Never before in the history of mankind have we seen economic development happening on such a massive scale. Everything in China is taking off, moving rapidly toward mass consumption.

Many more U.S. companies are scrambling for China action:

- Starbucks has become a common fixture in buildings in almost every big city in China.[10] The company intends to create a thousand stores in China as part of its march to hit 40,000 stores worldwide.

- McDonald's Corp. will open 100 new restaurants in China every year, beginning in 2007. As demand for cars in China spirals upward, half of the new locations will have drive-through facilities supported by new partner China Petroleum and Chemical Corporation (Sinopec), which currently has over 30,000 service stations and adds about 500 new ones annually. McDonald's currently operates 762 locations across China. Rival KFC has over 1,700, and plans to open 100 drive-through locations in the next three years. (KFC's parent company Yum! also operates 230 Pizza Hut outlets in China.)

- Procter & Gamble Co. is among the first group of U.S. companies to transform R&D investment in China from an initial focus on adapting to the Chinese market to developing products for global sales. When P&G opened a research center in China in 1988, there were only two dozen employees studying Chinese consumers' laundry habits and oral hygiene. Today, the U.S. consumer-products giant runs five R&D facilities in China. Some 300 P&G researchers work on innovations for everything from Crest toothpaste and Oil of Olay face cream to a new grease-fighting formula for Tide laundry detergent.[11]

- Mary Kay Inc., like thousands of other American companies, is banking on China's growing middle class and its insatiable hunger for foreign products. The Dallas-based $2.2 billion cosmetics giant operates in thirty-six countries, arrived in China in 1995, and has since recruited 400,000 Chinese beauty consultants.[12] Mary Kay adapts its products to Chinese culture, which values smooth white skin as the essence of beauty. The high-risk entrepreneurship of Mary Kay saleswomen, who buy their product wholesale from the company and resell it at a profit, mirrors the new "sink or swim" economy in China.

The World Competitiveness Year Book, issued by the International Institute for Management Development, raises China's competitiveness ranking among the world's sixty biggest economies from thirty-first in 2005 to nineteenth in 2006. It also ranks China's "government efficiency" at seventeenth and China's "economic performance" in third place to recognize the 25 percent share of the Chinese contribution to total global economic growth.

According to the World Bank, China is now ranked fourth out of 175 nations for its efforts to increase the ease of doing business in the country. China had reduced the time to register a business from forty-eight to thirty-five days (some places have a seven-day fast track program) and cut the minimum capital required from 947 percent to 213 percent of income per capita.

China also established a credit information registry for consumer loans: 340 million citizens now have credit histories. The country's stock markets are also back on track for a new boom. During the period 2005–2007, the Shanghai index shot up from 1,000 to over 5,000. During 2006, key indexes shot up more than 130 percent to new highs. There is even a structural labor shortage, especially on the management level, in many areas. U.S. private equity firms are scouring all over China for acquisitions, as venture capital for China hit a record of $4 billion in 2005. U.S. banks are licking their lips at the nearly $4 trillion in savings by the Chinese (U.S. household debt is about $12 trillion). Many banks are also vying for a slice of China's bourgeoning credit card, mortgage, and wealth management business.

Is this the "China hype" that people are talking about? Are the U.S. businesses simply chasing the "China bubble" with irrational exuberance? Is China's 10 percent annual growth sustainable? Where is the "political risk" those China observers have been touting for so many years?

The Cultural Push

As business with China keeps hitting new highs, U.S. colleges are seeing an unprecedented boom in the study of Chinese language and Chinese history, economics, culture, and society. In 2004, Democratic Senator Joseph Lieberman and Republican Senator Lamar Alexander introduced a bill calling for the U.S. to spend $1.3 billion over five years on Chinese-language programs.

In 2005, the College Board surveyed high schools to find out if they should offer the new Advanced Placement (AP) language courses for Chinese. Board officials expected a few hundred schools to express interest in each new language program. More than 2,400 high schools indicated their intention to build Chinese programs to levels where students could take the AP exam. The College Board quickly decided to offer an Advanced Placement test in Chinese. The first exam for the Advanced Placement Chinese Language and Culture (commonly known as AP Chinese Language and Culture or AP Chinese) was administered in May 2007. The Asia Society has also set a goal of getting 5 percent of the U.S. student population into Chinese classes by 2015.

In September 2005, the University of Oregon and Portland Public Schools won a $700,000-a-year grant from, of all places, the U.S. Defense Department to immerse 1,500 students from kindergarten through college in Mandarin Chinese.[15] The program goal is for students to attain an advanced level of proficiency in Mandarin Chinese, and to present opportunities to connect with communities of Chinese speakers through service learning, internships, and "externships" in China.

In Chicago, the "Chinese Connect" program, supported both by local government and the Chinese government, is the largest public school Chinese program in the nation. High school students in Washington, D.C. participate in an eight-week Chinese language and cultural studies program named "The China Challenge." The Chinese government has actively instituted a "soft power" cultural diplomacy program. By 2010, 100 Confucius Institutes, which offer Chinese language teaching for foreigners, will be established worldwide: many will be in the U.S.

While many Americans stay in China for an English-teaching job, a growing number of U.S. students go to China to learn Chinese. Statistics from the China Scholarship Council (CSC) show that 141,000 overseas students from 179 countries and regions came to China to study in 2005, up 27.28 percent from the previous year, including 86,679 to study Mandarin Chinese. The number of U.S. students in China has grown from less than 100 in the early 1980s to more than 10,000 currently. To them, study in the ancient country is no longer just a cultural experience: it is an integral part of their future professional careers, either in China or back home in the U.S.

As one of the six official languages of the United Nations, Chinese is the most widely spoken first language in the world. According to forecasts by the World Intellectual Property Organization, Chinese will top English as the most-used language on the internet by 2007. As the learning of Mandarin Chinese has been put on the fast track, the shortage of Chinese teachers becomes a problem. But this is just one sign of the language-learning fever. The growth potential of the tremendous interest in Mandarin Chinese appears to be forming a wave that will impact many people in the near future.

More than a hundred and fifty years ago, many Chinese came to America as coolies, or were used for "bitter labor." For the last thirty years, thousands of Chinese came to America mostly for graduate studies in various subject areas. During the years of "Ping Pong Diplomacy," Chinese three-time world champion (1961, 1963, and 1965) Zhuang Zedong and the Chinese table-tennis delegation visited the U.S. in April 1972. In 2002, Yao Ming came to America. The Houston Rockets made the seven-foot-six-inch Chinese Basketball Association (CBA) center and Chinese Olympic team member Yao Ming their first pick in the 2002 NBA draft. Americans were stunned by Yao. In the game against the Los Angeles Lakers on November 17, 2002, he scored twenty points in perfect nine-for-nine shooting and two free throws against one of the best teams in the NBA. TNT channel basketball analyst and former NBA star Charles Barkley bet his colleague Kenny Smith before the game that Yao would never score nineteen points in a game that season; if he did, Barkley said he would "kiss Smith's ass." Barkley was later forced to honor his bet by kissing the hindquarters of a donkey that Smith brought into the studio.

"Man, I Just Wish China Could Export Cheaper Gas to Us"

Many Chinese joke that, in terms of raw dollars, Yao Ming is by far the largest single item that China has ever exported to the U.S. In comparison, the Chinese need to export a few million pairs of shoes in order to buy a Boeing jet. Most of the goods from China are small items that Americans use in their daily life, but they are just as visible. At Amazon.com, a reader from Orange County, California expressed his take on "Made in China":

> So you complained that Chinese products are flooding the U.S. market and the world? Easy, don't buy them, don't use them. Why don't

you blame those importers? Why do you go to Wal-Mart and other super stores? Does your income (mean you) could really afford not going to these stores or 99 cents stores buying cheaper goods for your family? Could you really afford not doing so? We need cheap goods, because nowadays most families who claim themselves middle class in America are burdened with outrageous health insurance, car insurance, property taxes, income taxes, miscellaneous monthly payments, high gas prices. We pumped ourselves to get used to driving V8 big SUVs, luxurious cars, big mortgages, re-financing, remodeling your homes . . . so how much you left after all of these expenses? That's why you go to Wal-Mart, and go to elsewhere buying cheap goods to get by. Why you still want to complain? . . . You watched a stupid TV reporter ambushed a family just stepped out of Wal-Mart with a stupid question:

Q: "Hi, folks, I see you bought two bicycles made in China? Why you bought them?"

A: "Because they're so cheap, and my kids need them to ride to school."

Q: "But do you know how much the Chinese workers in the bike factory got paid each hours? Seventy-five cents! And you think it's fair?"

A: "Oh yeah? That's great! They got the jobs and we got the cheaper bikes. What's wrong with it?"

So you got the picture? 1.5 billion people in China . . . they all need a job, no matter how low the wages might be, at least they could make some money. Without those factories, exporters, importers, they got nothing. You think 75 cents an hour is outrageously low? No, man, it's better than nothing! You complained that those factories hire under-aged children to work long hours? So you would rather those kids to spend day after day in the garbage dumps trying to find some cans, plastic bottles, even food? You think those poisonous garbage dumps are healthier than the factory environment? And they could get what? $6.75 an hour? To them, even one cent an hour is better than nothing, and to you, that's why you got the cheaper goods for your families and making you a proud father and mother! You should send "thank you" letters to China, India and all the countries that make your life much, much easier. I just wish China could export cheaper gas to us, and that would really make my day.[16]

In 2005, Wal-Mart bought $18 billion in goods from Chinese manufacturers, which happens to account for more than 10 percent of total U.S. imports from China. Although it's a matter of free-market competition, the tone made by the individual, above, could still anger many of those who lost their jobs or businesses due to Chinese imports. China not only sells everything that Wal-Mart can buy for its "everyday low price," China also attracts lots of U.S. companies like Wal-Mart to expand their business in its huge domestic market.

Many U.S. companies will not just use China as a low-cost procurement or manufacturing location. They also look to build a local brand and a local reputation. Both contribute to the "import job, export deflation" trading scheme for China. Cheaper goods and raw components from China help keep U.S. inflation under control. But the other side of the story is loss of jobs, hollowing-out of the manufacturing sector, and possibly lowering wages in the United States. The consequences, however, are dramatically different from one group to another. The majority of American owners or shareholders may gain, while some American workers may lose. Consumers are generally happy, while many workers are discontented. Career changes may not be easy for some people, even if they are willing to accept lower pay. Consumers who don't lose their jobs or businesses benefit most.

Globalization doesn't mean everything is win-win for everyone. Somebody somewhere is going to pay sometime. When economic logic prevails, social problems may be behind the scene. Therefore, when China exports deflation, it may also export unemployment and business challenges. Consider the following:

A CEO sits in his office one day, and begins to examine the situation in his company. His number one competitor sells its products and services for lower prices, is able to provide 24-hour customer service, and lately has been offering a slew of innovative new products. The CEO has read his competitor's annual report, and noted that they were profitable again this year. The competitor's revenues are the same as the CEO's company, but its costs are lower. Meanwhile, the CEO's company is unable to raise prices, can't afford to offer 24-hour customer service, and the competitor is starting to take market share at every turn. And, by the way, the CEO's company lost money again this year. The CEO continues to ponder . . . "Both companies have similar transaction volumes. How does my competitor do it? Why are they able to offer lower prices, better service, and do it profitably?"

Meanwhile, Wall Street is demanding that the CEO's company become profitable—not a year from now—now! What is the CEO going to do? How is the CEO's company going to reduce costs so it can be profitable, and begin to invest more capital in research and development, sales, and marketing?

The first step this CEO takes is to hire away one of his competitor's senior managers to learn his competitor's secrets. Once the new manager is on board, the CEO finds out how his competitor is doing so well. The answer is baffling . . . he learns that its executives aren't more educated than his, it doesn't spend any more money on marketing activities, and its existing products are not any better. Each company has about the same number of salespeople, they get mentioned the same number of times in trade articles, and they look similar in many respects. Only one thing seems to be different . . . all of the competitor's non-core activities are outsourced, and 60 percent of its remaining staff is located offshore, in India and China.[17]

To many CEOs and business owners, the current China fever is neither fad nor hype. Not knowing "the China price" may spell big trouble for a company. Competitors can set up significant bases of operation from which they can compete in the American market. One can always choose to ignore China, but at one's peril. One characteristic of contemporary globalization is the mobility of products, technology, and capital—compared with the relative immobility of labor due to immigration restrictions and cultural barriers.

Even though U.S. workers may be much more productive, when a U.S. company is deciding whether to locate a new factory in the U.S. or in China, it is easy logic to see that the difference in productivity will rarely be as great as the wage differential. In manufacturing, the hourly rate in the U.S. is typically more than $20; in China, it's less than $1. That's why many exporters who investigate the China market shift the production to China. In recent years, wage increases in China outpaced those in the U.S. But it will take time for China's manufacturing hourly rate to get to even 20 percent of the U.S. rate.

In 2006, only 1.6 million jobs were available for the 4.13 million new college graduates in China. The over-supply of the Chinese talent pool kept salary raises in check, and helped China remain competitive. Over 800 million Chinese people live in rural areas. The migration of China's rural labor force to manufacturing jobs will mitigate any steep rise in low-skilled wages. This is why production offshoring, service outsourcing, and component offshore sourcing are no longer an option, but a necessity. This is why China is on everyone's map during the "global labor arbitrage."

Now, whenever competitiveness is mentioned, new technologies and a large amount of capital are invariably involved. But China is a developing country, and in developing economics, the concept of competitiveness does not refer to capital or technology. It refers to the production of the same products with lower costs, or to the production of more or better products with the same costs, and of course, in a stable and friendly business environment. A lot of Asian and African countries have much lower labor cost than China, but few U.S. investors dare venture there. America's advantage is technology. High labor cost doesn't prevent it from being the world's second-largest exporter behind Germany, also a high labor cost country. Yet high labor cost does make shifting low-tech and non-core technology products abroad much more attractive to U.S. manufacturers. The mobility of products, technology, and capital—compared with the relative immobility of labor—makes global equilibrium of wages and living standard inevitable.

China has over 1,200,000 IT professionals and is adding about 400,000 technical graduates each year. China ranks No. 1 in the world (followed by India and the U.S.). U.S. market investigation company International Data Corporation predicted that until 2009, China's IT services market would grow at 18.5 percent annually to $11.6 billion, as the global outsourcing market is expected to hit $1 trillion by 2008. China's Ministry of Commerce will launch a project with an annual budget of at least 100 million yuan ($12.5 million) to set up ten bases for service outsourcing over the coming three to five years. It hopes to persuade 100 multinational corporations to transfer their partial outsourcing businesses to China, as well as to create 1,000 large-scale international service outsourcing enterprises.

Even some of India's offshoring giants are offshoring themselves into China to take advantage of its comparatively low labor costs—typically half those of India. In 2002, Tata (TCS) opened an office in Hangzhou, where it employs 350 people and plans to quadruple the staff in the next few years. TCS also signed a deal with Microsoft and three other Chinese companies to create a software joint venture that would supply IT outsourcing services and employ 5,000 people outside Beijing. TCS will hold a 65 percent stake in the joint venture, TCS (China) Co., while three Chinese companies— Zhongguancun Software Park Development Company, Uniware Company, and the Tianjin Huayuan Software Area Construction and Development Company—will hold 25 percent, and Microsoft the remaining 10 percent.

In early 2007, TCS received a multi-million dollar contract to implement an international trading system for China Foreign Exchange Trade System. Infosys hired 360 people in Shanghai Pudong Software Park, opened a campus in Hangzhou to accommodate the expansion, and will hire as many as 10,000 people in China in the next few years. Wipro has

100 people in Shanghai and Beijing and also plans to expand.[18] When salaries in India are jumping at 20 percent or more annually, China's low cost advantage becomes attractive, especially in its Western region. One of India's big-four IT-outsourcing companies (along with Tata, Infosys and Wipro), Satyam Computer Services Ltd.'s new strategy is to hire new staff in smaller cities to avoid wage inflation. It plans to increase its staff in China to 3,000 by the end of 2008 (from 300 in 2006), adding strength to its research centers in the large Chinese cities of Shanghai, Dalian, and Guangzhou.

Trading with China, sourcing from China, out-sourcing and offshoring to China, and investing in China are not short-term tactics; many U.S. companies simply can't afford to not do it. China's annual economic growth averaged 9.6 percent during the last twenty-eight years, the country has drawn $620 billion foreign direct investment into its orbit as of 2006. In 2003, China overtook the U.S. ($53.1 billion) to become the largest recipient of foreign direct investment (FDI) in the world, attracting $53.5 billion.[19] Since then, China remains one of the top three most attractive investment destinations in the world.

In 2005, total inward FDI reached $60.3 billion, and exceeded $63 billion in 2006. FDI has made China the world's largest manufacturing hub. Today foreign direct investment accounts for more than 50 percent of China's manufactured exports and 80 percent of its high-tech exports. China, in 2005, also replaced the United States as the world's largest exporter of technology goods, notably in the InfoTech sector, concentrating on notebook computers, display units, mobile phones, CD/DVD players, and other telecom products. During the 2006 year-end holiday, American consumers lined up early in the morning to scoop up cheap computers and electronics: $4.99 for a digital phone with answering machine, $15.99 for a DVD player, $99.99 for a 20-inch LCD TV, and $299 for a laptop. Only China can make such prices possible for holiday-shopping consumers to whom saving means spending less from credit cards rather than putting money aside for future use.

According to China's Commerce Ministry, mainland China's 100 largest exporters in 2004 were electronics manufacturers: fifty-three were foreign-invested companies, twenty-one were Taiwanese. In the fast-growing mobile phone business, a total of 304 million mobile phones were produced in China in 2005, 36.8 percent of the world's total. The number of exported mobile phones and the export turnover of $20,635 billion represent a 45+ percent year-on-year increase. The market share of mobile phones under foreign brands rose to nearly 60 percent, while that of mobile phones under domestic brands went down from 44.5 percent in 2004 to 40 in 2005. Of the sixty-five mobile phone manufacturers in China, thirty-one are domestically funded, and thirty-four are foreign-funded. China exported 228 million mobile phones in 2005, of which only 13.2 million phones, or 5.8 percent, were domestic brands.

Acquisitions make up a large portion of the foreign investment flowing into China, which, overall, amounted to $60.3 billion in 2005. Private equity investment in China is yet another hot topic. Thanks to a rash of IPOs, privatizations, mergers, and takeovers, opportunities for private-equity investors in China have never looked better. As the government strives to remove impediments to foreign investors, growth in this area increases its pace. In 2003, private equity in China exceeded $1 billion for the first time, reaching $1.57 billion, up from $350 million in 2002.

Success stories, hard to come by a couple of years ago, are now easy to find. Carlyle Asia Venture Partners' $8 million investment in online travel company Ctrip.com International ballooned to $100 million when the company went public in November 2003. And International Data Group (IDG) raked in a 1,900 percent profit on its stake in online auction company EachNet when it was bought by eBay Inc. for $200 million. IDG now has more than 100 investments in China. When Shanghai chipmaker SMIC raised $1.7 billion in an IPO in 2004, it became a big payoff for investors Goldman Sachs, Morgan Stanley, and San Francisco-based Walden International.[20] The state-owned banks' IPO spree also brought huge profits for these investors.

Blaming "People's Money"

In America, private cars are a major source of pollution. Who would have thought international trade would add to the problem in some parts of the country? In Southern California, the area near the Long Beach and Los Angeles harbors, the nation's busiest port complex, is now known as the "diesel death zone." The adjacent ports are the main hub for cargo to and from the Far East and handled more than $200 billion in trade in 2005. Air pollution caused by the ports, rail lines, and roadways that move goods around the state is responsible for 1,500 premature deaths, thousands of cases of asthma, and other health problems statewide each year.

With the amount of goods entering California ports expected to triple in fifteen years, cargo ships, which use high-sulfur fuel, have received little pollution regulation and are expected to contribute 80 percent of the diesel pollution in the state by 2020. California's Air Resources Board now has plans with long-term goals and strategies to roll back air pollution levels from cargo movement to what they were five years ago.

China's trade volume with the U.S. swelled to $285.3 billion in 2005 from $2.4 billion in 1979. With only a fraction of the size of Japan's economy, China surpassed Japan to be the world's third-largest trading nation by increasing its international trade more than its GDP. In 2006, China exported $762 billion and imported $660 billion in total goods and services. It is expected to outdo Germany to be the number two trading nation in 2007. China also overtook Japan as the world's largest trade surplus country, with a record surplus of $177+ billion in 2006 (from $26 billion in 2004 and $101 billion in 2005).

China is now the second-largest U.S. trading partner (overtaking Mexico), the second-largest source of U.S. imports (after Canada), and the third-largest U.S. export market (surpassing Japan). During the last ten years, U.S. exports to China and imports from China maintained a consistent 20 percent annual increase. American exports to China have been growing five times faster than U.S. exports to the rest of the world. The biggest export gainer, the U.S. agriculture sector, more than tripled its exports during the last few years. The slower pace in the tech sector, comparatively speaking, makes the U.S. almost look like a "third world" country. U.S. imports, however, far exceed its exports in absolute terms.

The U.S. is China's number one export destination, but the U.S. is still far behind Japan, South Korea, or even Taiwan as China's leading import supplier. China continues to be the country with the largest trade imbalance with the U.S., overtaking Japan's position in 2000. In 2005, for example, U.S. imports from China were $243.5 billion (about 36 percent of China's total) while exports to China were only $41.8 billion (about 6 percent of China's total imports), making the trade deficit with China $201.7 billion, about 28 percent of the total U.S. trade deficit—nearly equal to the combined U.S. trade deficits with Japan, Canada, and Mexico.

The trade deficit with China is $233 billion of $737 billion total in 2006. To hear some critics of U.S. trade with China tell it, "China and its army of low-wage workers laboring long hours are like a giant vacuum cleaner sucking up American jobs, American factories, American dollars and ultimately American prosperity, and transplanting them across the Pacific."[21] The American Federation of Labor-Congress of Industrial Organizations (AFL-CIO) said China's practices of using child and forced labor and firing workers who attempt to form independent unions keep the wages of Chinese factory workers as low as 15 cents to 50 cents per hour, a level that encourages U.S. companies to close factories in this country and move their production to China.[22] U.S. steel manufacturers claim losing over three million manufacturing jobs directly related to China and its export subsidies since 2000. Job losses and lower wages may also generate adjustment costs totaling $50 billion per year.

On the other hand, however, international trade makes America $1 trillion richer every year, and more can be gained if free trade prevails.[23] According to a Morgan Stanley report, American consumers saved $100 billion by purchasing "high-quality yet inexpensive Chinese goods" in 2004.

Looking at the top ten imports from China directly indicates what types of U.S. companies are struggling or have been forced out of business during the last few years:[24]

1. Electrical/computer machinery and equipment
2. Power generation equipment
3. Toys and games
4. Furniture
5. Apparel
6. Footwear
7. Iron and steel
8. Plastic goods
9. Leather and travel goods
10. Auto accessories and parts

The machinery, furniture, textile, and auto parts sectors have been hit hard—thousands of U.S. companies have shut down or shifted production to China in recent years. Even more shocking, China, having taken control over almost all low-end products, has started to move aggressively into high-end and luxury products, a move unthinkable years ago, with China's "brand identity" virtually nonexistent.

China is the United States' largest foreign supplier of textiles and apparel, accounting for one-third of total imports in 2005 ($16.8 billion). According to the U.S. Commerce Department, U.S. textile and apparel imports from China were 43.7 percent higher in 2005 than they were in 2004 (compared with an 8.3 percent growth in total U.S. imports of these products from the world), largely due to the fact that U.S. textile and apparel quotas on Chinese goods were eliminated in January 2005 because of China's accession to WTO.

Even though China agreed to restrict its textile and apparel exports to the United State from January 2006 through the end of 2008, emotions continue to run high as far as jobs are concerned. "China is much more of a threat than an opportunity right now," said Representative Robin Hayes, a

North Carolina Republican whose district includes textile makers harmed by imports. "You can never be tough enough on the Chinese."[25] Some worry that China's export of flowers, especially from Yunnan Province, may have a significant impact on domestic florists and the U.S. flower business in the coming years.

There is no blame for China's cheap labor, and we simply can't blame labor being too expensive in the U.S. Logically, many blame the trade deficit with China on the value of the yuan or the renminbi (literally "people's money"), China's currency. In 1994, China devalued its currency from $1 for less than 6 yuan to $1 for a little over 8 yuan. In July, 2005, China took a step forward in its move toward a market economy by increasing the value of its currency by 2.1 percent and abandoning its decade-old fixed exchange rate to the U.S. dollar in favor of a managed float system that links to a basket of world currencies. China's most strenuous critics in the United States demanded that Beijing increase the value of its currency by at least 10 percent. Some critics even contend that China's central bank buys most of the foreign currency that flows into the country to keep the yuan artificially low by as much as 40 percent.[26]

Senators Charles E. Schumer (D-NY) and Lindsey O. Graham (R-SC) pushed a bill that would impose across-the-board punitive tariffs of 27.5 percent against Chinese imports if China failed to substantially raise the value of the yuan. The motion was dropped when the yuan appreciated from 8.2 to 7.9 during 2006. But the issue heated up again after the Democrats took control of the U.S. Congress in the 2006 mid-term election, even as the yuan overtook the value of the Hong Kong dollar to its decade-high mark of 7.8 in early 2007. In mid-2007, Senators Baucus, Grassley, Schumer, and Graham pushed for new legislation aimed at correcting China's currency-fixing practices.

The reasoning of value depreciation of the U.S. dollar is: if the same amount of U.S. dollars exchanges for less than a foreign currency, foreigners will buy more of our goods since the same U.S. goods now become cheaper in terms of that foreign currency. At the same time, Americans will buy fewer foreign goods since they now become more expensive in U.S. dollars. The net result of these will turn trade deficit into trade surplus over time.

This theory, unfortunately, isn't supported by U.S. experience with its major trading partners. While the U.S. dollar depreciated against Japanese yen, Canadian dollars, and Euros in recent years, the U.S. trade balances with Japan, Canada, and the EU haven't seemed to improve. Part of the problem is that the theory assumes that demands are sensitive to price changes everywhere. If U.S. consumers simply don't care about minor price changes, and foreign consumers buy fewer American products, dollar devaluation will end up increasing the U.S. deficit since U.S. exports may now result in fewer dollars, while imports result in more dollars. But if the U.S. dollar devalues so much that it forces demand to adjust to price changes, the U.S. may run into possibly bigger problems: inflation at home, and an economic downturn in foreign countries. Both scenarios were proven during the inflation of the Nixon era, and by the sluggish growth in Japan during the 1990s and Europe in recent years.

In China's case, its currency policy is meant not only to favor exports, but also to foster economic stability. A sharp appreciation of the yuan would hurt its export sectors, which in turn could reduce jobs and lower wages in related sectors, causing social unrest. Regardless of U.S. pressure, Chinese officials insisted on a gradual approach for its currency policy because they view economic stability and avoiding a hard landing as critical to sustaining social and political stability.

The other side of the reality is: while the trade deficit continues to soar, the U.S. economy still keeps its own pace, and unemployment is well under control. After the Chinese receive U.S. dollars from exports, they invest in America's equity and treasury bills. They have over $1 trillion in foreign reserves, around 50 percent[27] in U.S. government bonds. We buy more of their goods, and they buy more of our assets and debt. They produce and export more goods, and we issue more debt and print more money. It appears to be a great deal, yet the problem is not so much a yuan issue as it is a U.S. domestic issue of debt economy and federal fiscal irresponsibility.

The often neglected side of the deficit issue is, with so many U.S. companies investing in China's assembly factories, as much as 30 to 40 percent of imports from China are simply U.S. companies shipping their goods back to the U.S. In 2005, 58 percent of China's exports were created by foreign companies; and 50 percent of the trade surplus was derived from foreign companies. The fundamental reason for the steadily rising trade surplus lies in global trade patterns with the U.S. and European countries consuming goods processed in Asia.

The sharp increase in U.S. imports from China is largely the result of movement in production facilities from other Asian economies to China, especially from Japan, Singapore, Taiwan, and Hong Kong. For example, with a 19.6 percent share of total shipments in 2000, Japan was the largest foreign supplier of U.S. computer equipment, while China ranked fourth with a 12.1 percent share. In just five years, Japan's ranking fell to fourth, the value of its shipments dropped by over half, and its share of shipments declined to 7.8 percent in 2005. During the same period, Singapore and Taiwan also experienced significant declines in their computer equipment shipments to the United States. In 2005, on the other hand, China became the largest supplier of computer equipment with a 45.4 percent share of total U.S. imports. While U.S. imports of computer equipment from China rose by more than 300 percent over the past six years, total U.S. imports of computer equipment from the world rose by only 15 percent.

Because U.S. trade data attributes the full value of a product to the final assembler, Chinese value-added contribution is over-estimated. As the last link in a long chain of value-added production, China has the largest scale of assembly manufacturing plants in the world—but its total manufacturing output remains behind the U.S. and Japan. Clearly, when international production is organized vertically in the new globalization era, rather than horizontally as was common in the past, deficit data from bilateral trade conceals multilateral information. The multilateral evidence is: while China's share of the U.S. trade imbalance has risen from nothing to about 25 percent during the last two decades, the share by related East Asian economies has actually declined, from 52 percent in 1985 to 40 percent in 2004.[28]

In *A Year Without "Made in China"* (2007), author Sara Bongiorni entertains readers with how her family embarked on a year-long boycott of Chinese products. Her common-sense label-checking exercise was simply awkward and misguided: how could she know whether China was the final assembler or only one assembler among millions of items and goods sold in the U.S. market? Furthermore, how could she avoid buying things with even a small percentage of their components coming from China? An exercise in futility? Perhaps. A more grave question is: why are we still naïve when the world economy has changed so much that very likely the U.S. will be forever surpassed as the manufacturing powerhouse it once was.

Unless the United States Congress moves from protectionist rhetoric to protectionist legislation, there is no reason to expect the dollar to slide significantly against the Chinese yuan—at least not by 40 percent in the short term. But if protectionist legislation is passed in Congress, U.S. consumers will have to absorb the price increases that would come with the importation of Chinese goods. A pop in rising prices and inflation would mean tighter money and higher interest rates, which would in turn hurt the already slow housing market and other consumer spending. Meanwhile, if the Chinese retaliate against U.S. legislation, either through tariffs or quotas, more than a few American laborers will be put out of work. Such a downward spiral in living standards is something most Americans don't want to see: "Exchange rate changes are not the answer to American trade deficits and Asian trade surpluses."

Today's major distortion in the world's financial system is America's saving deficiency, large fiscal deficits by the Federal Government, and meager household savings—coupled with a virtually unlimited dollar line of credit on which to borrow from the rest of the world. Heavy U.S. borrowing in international markets is then transferred in terms of real resources by foreign countries running trade surpluses with the United States. The U.S. current account deficit forces Canada and countries in Asia, Europe, and now even in Latin America, into current account surpluses."[29]

A natural tendency of the trade deficit issue is to make foreigners into emotionally appealing scapegoats for America's economic problems. This was true for Japanese auto imports in the 1970s. When a devil has to be found, the ideal devil is a foreigner. While the U.S. blames "people's money," the Chinese government blames U.S. export restrictions on technology products for a widening trade surplus with the U.S. In 2005, the amount rejected due to export restriction for potential military use adds up to about $12.5 million, accounting for only a small fraction of the total exports of about $41 billion. However, the dollar value of products subject to export control and other potential related exports could be much larger.

To U.S. exporters, China is among the most open and has the lowest import tariff of the world's developing countries, especially after its accession to the WTO. Its ratio of imports to GDP is also higher (thus more open) than that of the U.S., Japan, and countries like Argentina, Brazil, and India. On the other hand, Washington's visa policy toward China becomes a significant deterrent to Chinese who want to buy goods and services in the United States. According to a 2006 annual report by the American Chamber of Commerce, 44 percent of U.S.-funded companies surveyed said they lost significant sales because of U.S. visa policies.

The U.S., by refusing to buy less and rejecting the idea of selling more, has generated a trade deficit. The U.S. shifts production of labor-intensive projects and non-core technology to China, and imports the finished goods back home. The U.S., at the same time, goes out of its way to keep high-tech and other vital technology from being exported to China, then makes trade deficit an issue. Americans know that, and the Chinese know it too. It would be nice to shift low-tech production abroad and move the U.S. working class up at the same time. But advanced as the U.S. is, this is still not possible. Social and personal reasons dictate that there is always a group of people who can't afford education and will always stay at the bottom, relying on their physical labor for a living. Fortunately, lots of non-manufacturing services, snow-plowing for example, can't be off-shored or outsourced. Americans have reasons to remain positive—only if the immigration policy stays favorable to workers, and the culture of debt economy begins to change.

The Game Logic of Trade Politics

On August 5, 2005, Wall Street witnessed the best stock IPO of 2005, the second-best foreign IPO ever, and one of the top 20 IPOs of all time. Shares of China's No. 1 search engine Baidu.com rocketed 354 percent to $122.54 on its first day debut.[30] The company's 4.04 million American shares were priced at $27, which were boosted from the earlier range of $19 to $21 and $23 to $25. Yet it opened at $66, briefly dipped to $60, and then ran as high as $151 during the shortened trading hours. A tsunami of retail interest boosted the speculative fever, resulting in a first-day trading volume of more than 22 million shares–more than five times that of its float.

Five-year-old Baidu.com is the most frequently used search engine in China, where internet search users will grow at an annual rate of 30 to 50 percent to near 200 million in 2008, from 115 million in 2005. At the time of its IPO, Baidu.com was the second-largest website in China, and the sixth-largest website globally measured by user traffic. Its net revenues have grown twelve-fold over the past few years, to $15.46 million in 2006 from $1.3 million in 2002, a pace that is enough to impress even Google. Only during the internet bubble of 1999 to 2000 could investors have seen such an instant wonder. But with hundreds of listed companies with the word "China" in their names, China is now the new "dot-com" on Wall Street. The stock's frenzy certainly comes from the fact that investors are fueled by the online potential of China. But Wall Street's game logic of trading is "concept play." In Baidu.com's case, it is a combination of "China concept," "Google concept," and "small float concept" at work simultaneously—a big case of "the Buy China Syndrome."

Washington politics in international trade has its own game logic. As China's ballooning exports have brought home billions of U.S. dollars and other foreign currencies, China's global trade surplus and foreign currency reserves reached an all-time high. By the end of February 2006, China's foreign currency reserves reached $853.7 billion, surpassing Japan's $850 billion to become the world's largest foreign currency reserves holder. Its reserve grew over $1 trillion (40 percent of China's GDP) in late 2006, making China the largest holder of U.S. government debt, enough to lower U.S. long-term interest rates by 1.5 percent.

China's purchases of U.S. government bonds funds a chunk of the huge federal budget deficit and helps keep interest rates low in the U.S., a boon to American home-buyers and other borrowers. This has come to be known as a "reverse Marshall Plan." During the recovery era after World War II, the Marshall Plan provided loans for European countries to pay for the imports required to rebuild war-torn economies. Such loans enabled U.S. exports, thereby assisting to provide jobs to demobilized U.S. soldiers and workers laid off from wartime industries. Today, to help sustain its massive exports to the United States, China recycles the resulting dollar inflow in the form of loans and asset purchases. Here, the developing nation lends to the developed: money flows in the reverse direction.[31]

As the United States has run consistent and increasing trade deficits over the last thirty years, the growing fear of losing jobs is now fueled by the concern of a severe international economic crisis should countries like China begin to dump the dollars they hold from trade surplus. In fact, speculation that China will diversify its foreign reserves into other hard currencies has already fueled a further decline in the value of the U.S. dollar. China will set up an institution to better manage its reserves, but it won't risk devaluing its reserves by declaring a radical policy shift now.

Yet, if there is a trade war or other political crisis between China and the U.S., the Chinese could suddenly reverse policy and start dumping U.S. assets and place their reserves in other currencies. Though the interest rate impact by the Chinese debt funding may be small, the psychological effect of a move by the Chinese may far exceed any single factor calculation. The consequence could be a huge blow to the U.S. economy by sending both short-term and long-term interest rates up sharply. An editorial cartoon in the *Washington Post*, printed during the visit of Hu Jintao in 2006, revealed the troubling implication of this dependency. In the cartoon, President George W. Bush says, "I'm the leader of the most prosperous and powerful nation in the world today." Hu Jintao responds: "I'm the Repo Man."[32]

The dependency, luckily, is not at all one-sided. When about 80 percent of its gross domestic product comes from foreign trade, China is not going to risk its trade relationship with the U.S. In fact, the Chinese government has been very deliberate in presenting a good image to the world. In advance of President Hu's visit, a group of 100 Chinese business executives headed by China's vice-premier Wu Yi traveled to thirteen American states hard hit by the offshoring of jobs to China. This "checkbook diplomacy" trip resulted in $16.2 billion in orders from more than 100 contracts for U.S. aircraft, auto parts, computer software, telecommunication equipment, grain, and cotton.

In the contract with Boeing alone, China placed orders for eighty Boeing aircraft valued at $5 billion. China has purchased more than $37 billion in Boeing planes over the years, and in the next fifteen, its demand for new aircraft may reach an astounding 2,000 planes. China also seeks to cut back its export tax rebates, especially on resource-intensive sectors such as textiles and metals. The rebates became an increasing burden on the coffers of China's central bank when the rebates reached 1.19 trillion yuan during the period 2001 to 2005. This "checkbook diplomacy" was repeated with the purchase of $5.3 billion in goods from U.S. firms during the U.S.-China Strategic Economic Dialogue in May 2007.

Trade politics in Washington are played in a different way. Traditionally, protectionism comes from domestic producers who manage to lobby successfully. In recent years, however, globalization has significantly changed the landscape of this playing field. As more producers jump on the bandwagon of offshore sourcing and outsourcing, they themselves become increasingly dependent on imports. Their stake in the game of trade politics is climbing. And, unlike the diverse and large number of consumers, it is cost effective for them to organize to lobby in the same way as those producers who are hurt by imports. The recent decline in U.S. protectionism reflects this new reality in trade politics. Any legislation against Chinese imports will trigger a crisis. China doesn't respond well to threats. And U.S. importers and exporters are also deep in the game now.

A good example of trade politics is the "export control" front. In 2005, concerned that China was using U.S. civilian technology to expand its military know-how, the Bush administration floated plans to limit technology sales to China by requiring special licenses to export some items, background checks on customers, and undertaking broader oversight of transactions. A list originally containing hundreds of exports that would be more closely regulated (including aircraft parts, computer chips, and machine tools) was shortened to forty-six items, according to a revised draft of the proposed regulations. The final list of newly controlled categories in 2007 was reduced to 20 from 27 originally proposed. This scaling back is a partial concession to exporters, such as Intel and Boeing—companies that opposed the original proposal because they rely on Asia as a growth engine for sales, and, as noted earlier, have invested heavily in assembly, research, and testing operations in China.

Among items that would be subject to new export-licensing requirements are nuclear materials, lithography equipment, digital-radio receivers, cameras, radar technology, and rocket-propulsion systems. Some of the items taken off the original list include aircraft engines, bayonets, bearings, boring equipment, mining equipment, and virtual-reality systems. The computer, aviation, and machinery industries, represented by groups such as the Coalition for Employment Through Exports and the Association for Manufacturing Technology, lobbied against the plan because compliance would have hurt their ability to sell to China.[33] U.S. exporters see such plans as "irrational" restrictions born out of "irrational" fear. In reality, ideological differences and fear of China as a potential threat remain the greatest concern of the United States.

Guarding the "Secret Recipe"

Each year, more than 1.5 million Americans visit China either for tourism or business. While the "Yangzi River Three Gorges Tour" and the "Ancient Capital Xian Tour" are popular in recent years, many first-time visitors still love to go to the Great Wall near Beijing. Right at the foot of the Great Wall is a fast-food restaurant called "Mc-Tucky." There you can find fried chicken, hamburgers, French fries, and soft drinks. Probably only after you finish your food do you realize that you didn't notice whether the restaurant is McDonald's or Kentucky Fried Chicken. The decor looks like both, which is confusing. In case you hadn't already figured it out, the restaurant chose this name because it serves food from both McDonald's and Kentucky Fried Chicken. In Chinese it's called *Mai Ken Ji*, which is rendered somewhat awkwardly into the anglicized: "Mc-Tucky."

Piracy, counterfeiting, reverse engineering, other forms of intellectual property, theft of foreign products or service brands—all are widespread in China. Counterfeits make up an estimated 15 percent of all products made in China —about 8 percent of China's GDP. According to estimates by the International Intellectual Property Alliance (IIPA) in 2005, China's piracy rate in motion pictures is 93 percent, records and music 85 percent, business software 88 percent, and entertainment software 92 percent. Estimates by the U.S. Trade Representative's office in 2005 showed that 85 to 93 percent of all sales of copyrighted products in China were pirated. Nine out of ten DVDs sold in China are illegal copies, according to the Motion Picture Association of America, costing Hollywood $2.3 billion a year in lost revenue.

China also accounts for a significant share of imported counterfeit products seized by U.S. Customs and Border Protection: $64 million or 69 percent of total goods seized in 2005, about 80 percent of the more than 14,000 shipments of counterfeit goods seized in 2006. This is what is called "faked in China." Washington believes Beijing could open the door to billions of dollars of increased U.S. exports through tougher enforcement of laws on piracy and counterfeiting, which yearly cost U.S. businesses an estimated $250 billion, enough to erase the U.S. annual trade deficit with China.

Piracy also damages China's own movie industry. In 2005, over half of the $2.7 billion loss to moviemakers in China was carried by the Chinese industry itself. DVDs typically cost less than one yuan to produce, and are sold for three to ten yuan each. Unauthorized airings of films by the country's TV stations cause more than $7.5 million a year in losses.

Even crooks get ripped off in China. When investigators searched the house of Shenyang's former mayor, they found $6 million worth of gold bars, 150 Rolex watches, and what they thought was a treasure-trove of antiques. The gold and Rolexes were real, but the antiques turned out to be fake.

China has no tradition of intellectual property protection in the sense of a market economy. Instead, it has a long history of being a "Secret Recipe" culture—the owners of any business secret bear all the burden of its protection, and other people can rightly benefit from the secret if and when it is revealed. There was simply no government regulation that enforced intellectual property rights (IPR) for both protection and punishment, both in China's imperial past or in its recent economic boom.

This partially explains the long-term stagnation of scientific and technological innovation in China over the past two to three centuries. People simply won't spend years devising new ideas, technologies, or drugs when they can cheat or steal from others without much cost and risk. When copycat operations can duplicate products at a fraction of the cost, there's no incentive to innovate.

For years, 99 percent of Chinese companies never applied for a patent. Recently, no one was found eligible for the "China Science and Technology National Award" for three years running. In May 2006, the scandal of fake chip research by Chen Jin, the former head of Shanghai Jiao Tong University's Microelectronics School, turned a national hero into a national shame overnight. The government swiftly issued a regulation on scientific misconduct in November 2006. The scandal was a shock to many, yet, culturally, it was no surprise at all.

There is, interestingly, a similar situation on the other side, in the U.S. In cases when the creation of a certain product involves the use of many techniques and components patented by different people, it can be expensive to negotiate with all patent holders. A product potentially in great demand thus may not be produced because costs associated with negotiation and license fees are too high, resulting in a typical "lose-lose" situation: the would-be manufacturer loses, the patent holders lose, and hungry consumers lose.

When one browses the massive patent list of the U.S. Patent Office website, it pays to bear in mind that when the patent holders act solely to maximize or protect their own interests above all else, they win nothing, and everyone else loses. This is known as "The Tragedy of the Anticommons,"[34] a type of market failure that exists as the polar opposite of counterfeiting and other intellectual property violations. The sense of favoring American brands over other countries' products makes America the biggest victim for IPR in China now. You can bet that pretty much anything that can be Americanized is already Americanized in China, much in the way that Russian culture influenced China in the 1950s. The "Backdorm Boys" is a good example. Two regular Chinese art students made a crude home video lip-synching to the Backstreet Boys on the internet. This caught on big across China and was even shown on American television in 2005. It won the pair endorsement contracts and TV appearances. Motorola even used the video for its commercials in China.

The Chinese versions of "American Idol," called "Super Girl" (or "Super Female Voice") and "I Love Real Men," attracted an unprecedented TV viewership. China also had its own version of "The Apprentice." Donald Trump was all too happy to exclaim: "Copying is the greatest form of flattery." Many TV programs in China today have American roots. There are struggling musicians who wish their albums would be pirated, if only for the chance to gain greater name recognition. But the owner of the British Rock Point Inn and Cob Gate Fish Bar felt "I have been Shanghaied" after learning her fish-and-chip shop was replicated in a copycat "English Town" called "Thames Town" at Songjiang, Shanghai.

When Hu Jintao visited the U.S., he jokingly said: "If I were not serving in this office, I would certainly prefer to go into one of the coffee shops run by Starbucks." Though "electoral democracy" is still a taboo, China's enterprise reform, or corporatization, is actually modeled after America's public companies. When the Chinese learn English, they usually don't learn British English, they learn American English. It's no longer a surprise to see a Chinese third grader who can speak English with American visitors. In fact, the number of Chinese people who can speak or who are learning English actually exceeds the number of native English speakers in the U.S., even as the U.S. population has reached 300 million.

American products are good, but in many cases they are just too expensive, especially to low-income Chinese workers and farmers. To many Chinese businesses, part of their low cost advantage comes from the fact that they spend only about one-third the amount that similar-sized American businesses spend on hardware and about one-sixth as much on software. There is a "price elasticity" issue here. That is, when American goods are too expensive, people will not buy them, or will buy less expensive substitutes. But if they are cheap and still have American brand names, it will be a different story. This is when piracy and counterfeiting kick in. Most estimates of IPR loss didn't account for "price elasticity." Studios such as Time Warner and Fox have realized that if they don't make low-priced offerings to the Chinese, they won't make any sales. In 2006, both started to release movies on low-priced DVDs soon after their theatrical release. Charging $1.25 to $3.00 per disc and selling a few thousand movies is better than selling none and allowing pirated movies to proliferate.

Nevertheless, China's violation of intellectual property rights is a scorching topic in the U.S. because it involves the entire pantheon of goods and services (software, music, movies, books, clothes, handbags, shoes, watches, auto parts); relates to too many aspects of IPR (copyright, trademarks, trade secrets, patents); the potential loss is too big (measured by billions, even taking "price elasticity" into account); the cost for U.S. companies to combat the infringement is too high; and the violations are too common in all social strata.

No wonder when Microsoft takes a realistic approach to deal with business in China, it immediately draws criticism. But Microsoft still managed to see significant return on its investments in China from its pragmatic policies. In 2006, it signed deals worth more than $1.5 billion with a handful of China's largest PC makers to pre-load Windows into their products. Considering Microsoft has earned less than $200 million in China over the last decade, those deals meant a lot. The company simply doesn't want to see itself losing ground to Linux in the China market.

In other cases, Cisco Systems sued Huawei in 2002 for allegedly stealing Cisco's router technology; and General Motors took Chery to court in 2004 for allegedly copying a GM design for Chery's popular QQ compact. In both cases, the companies settled out of court.

In fact, the majority of IPR lawsuits in China involve Chinese firms, especially for trademark infringement. For the central government, it still cares about international image, long-term interest in innovation, and IP protection both at home and abroad. For local governments, the logic is simply to use their resources to lessen benefits gained by copycat producers, distributors, and consumers, at least in the short run. This lack-of-incentive logic also holds, given that piracy and counterfeiting of domestic products (liquor, cigarettes, food, even eggs) have long been a nightmare in China. Even though the problem is more about economic justice than economic efficiency, the lack of incentives and high "enforcement cost" prevent local governments from taking serious action. Their long list of priorities causes them to rely more on a "fire alarm" approach than on a "police patrol" approach, even for major cases, as when hazardous products cause death.

In May 2006, four people died from using a fake drug produced by the Qiqihar No. 2 Pharmaceutical Co., Ltd. in northeast China's Heilongjiang Province. The drug company was forced to shut down and their drugs were banned from sales nationwide. Recently, fake and poor quality rabies vaccines—even powdered infant formula—have appeared on the market. Many mainland Chinese buy goods from Hong Kong because Hong Kong products can be trusted. In 2007, many Chinese domestic and export goods, such as tainted pet food, toxic toothpaste, defective tires, and toys contaminated with lead paint, gave rise to serious concerns about China's manufacturing, quality control, oversight, and accountability.

Currently, China wants to stop pirating through administrative and civil charges rather than criminal action, but it did pledge to lower the threshold for criminal prosecution of major IPR violations. Severe penalties do work to combat counterfeiting items with the Chinese Olympic mascots and logo for the 2008 Games in Beijing. Like previous host cities Sydney and Athens, Beijing created a special legal framework to protect Olympic logos and symbols for licensing and sponsorship fees to pay for much of the cost of the Games. Under a 2004 decree, piracy and counterfeiting can result in up to ten years in prison.

The Chinese government stepped up to adopt the so-called "China's Action Plan on IPR Protection 2006" to create a national IPR strategy. "Service centers" were set up in fifty cities to handle piracy complaints, and 300,000 government employees and inspectors were enlisted in anticounterfeiting campaigns. The Shanghai city government ordered a cleanup of the infamous Xianyang market in 2006, long known as the center of counterfeit luxury goods in Shanghai. Similarly, Beijing's Silk Street Market is popular with tourists and well known for selling pirated purses, wallets, and other items at cheap prices.

Similar markets in big cities and trade shows on local and national scales will be targeted for IP violations. There was a "100-day campaign," from July 15 to October 25, 2006, to crack down on pirated products.

More than 880,000 state workers, market supervisors, and members of the judiciary were involved in the campaign, and more than fifty-eight million illegal publications were confiscated, four pirate DVD production lines were seized, and 10,000 cases of intellectual property theft were investigated. In east China's Fujian Province, state workers seized 34,900 pirated preschool education books worth 140,600 yuan. In the southwest municipality of Chongqing, more than 10,000 pirated audio and video products were seized. A pirate CD maker and smuggler, Lin Yuehua, was sentenced to life imprisonment in south China's Guangxi Zhuang Autonomous Region, and four million yuan worth of personal property was confiscated. In central China's Henan Province, Wang Fengjuan was given ten months imprisonment and fined 20,000 yuan for pirating a Chinese dictionary.

The government is now building an online anti-piracy platform that will effectively identify the authenticity of a product or software package. Starting in July 2006, the government has been fining distributors of illegally copied music, movies, and other material over the internet by as much as 100,000 yuan. Those who create Chinese subtitles for American TV shows and make them for free download over the internet may now face consequences even when they are not doing it for profit. The online video gaming industry expects to attain a 35.5 percent annual rate of growth before 2010 with the government strengthening intellectual property protection. At the end of 2005, China's online game users totaled 26.34 million people, up 30.1 percent, and the industry posted 3.77 billion yuan in revenue, up 52.6 percent.

Sleek high-rise buildings, new roads, majestic bridges, and modern airports don't really mean innovation. Beijing realized that its failure to protect intellectual property rights will hold back its entire economy in the long run. During the last ten years, China had a sevenfold increase in patent filings. It is now ranked fifth in patent filling, ahead of Germany and behind Japan, the U.S., the European Patent Office, and South Korea.[35] Despite its IPR laws, many in place as early as in 1991, and all the progress thereafter, China is still known as the "Heaven of Piracy" due to legal enforcement issues. The U.S. is pressing through bilateral talks and through the World Trade Organization for tougher action.

China Fever vs. China Threat

On August 14, 2001, only 27 days before the September 11 terrorist attacks, there was a dramatic "War with China" story on the internet:

On the first day of World War III, the United States lost two-thirds of its military and nearly half its population, yielding superiority to communist China. U.S. orders of the day were of high alert, and there is simply no evading the fact that we were not ready.

The Chinese rain of missiles on U.S. installations and homeland cities was a military masterpiece. The People's Liberation Army Second Artillery Corp achieved complete surprise, armed only with a small force of more than 300 tactical and ten strategic missiles.

Defenseless against the attack, U.S. forces in Hawaii, Alaska, South Korea, and Japan were quickly overwhelmed by the guided warheads of the Chinese missiles. The bombs plunged out of the inky blackness of space, striking within seconds of each other. The rain of death fell swiftly upon a sleeping America with precise and devastating accuracy.

In a span of little more than thirty minutes, China wiped out Los Angeles, San Francisco, Seattle, San Diego, Chicago, Washington, Boston, New York, Hawaii, Manila, Seoul, Taipei, and Tokyo.

"China sank five U.S. carriers, seven Ohio-class submarines, vaporized more than 200 MX and Minuteman missiles, and destroyed more than 800 combat aircraft, including fifteen B-2 strategic bombers. The strikes also killed more than 100 million people without the loss of a single PLA soldier.

The Second Artillery succeeded by striking key U.S. bases, warships, and air fields with a swift and bold attack. The attack left China with ten remaining strategic missiles and nearly 300 tactical missiles, holding the devastated U.S. homeland hostage to another strike.

Despite the calls to retaliate, sending the scattered remains of U.S. nuclear forces against China would not stop another attack on America, nor would it stop the PLA generals who ordered the first.

There is no question that the U.S. strategic missiles could devastate the Chinese homeland. However, killing hundreds of millions of innocent Chinese citizens would do little to deter the warlords in Beijing from launching the second wave of ten missiles while remaining hidden inside bomb-proof tunnels.

China's sudden and brutal attack forced America to surrender on Beijing's terms. In little more than forty-eight hours, China won World War III. [36]

This fantasy fairy-tale is surely more devastating than a Chinese online story "The Battle in Protecting Key Oil Routes," which imagines a sea engagement near the Strait of Malacca (which links the Indian and Pacific oceans). The Chinese navy destroys an entire U.S. carrier group. The story-teller argued that this may not be fiction because right now the U.S. has no missile defense in the area and is testing only a limited system that might stop one or two missiles. But the un-raised and un-answered question here is: Why did the Chinese attack first? Or, what do the Chinese gain from a war that eliminates nearly half the population in the U.S.?

Game theory or interactive decision theory would give us some hint of the answer. Game theory is the study of any situation in which two or more people make decisions that affect each other. In an attempt to maximize his return, each individual must take into account what the other is likely to do, either simultaneously or in succession. The game here is called the "nuclear button" game.[37] Suppose your children (Charlotte 9, Owen 13) were each given charge of a different country, and each commanded a strong force of nuclear missiles. Suppose whichever sent the missiles out first would destroy the other country and enjoy peace and prosperity. Here is a dialogue between you and two kids, Owen and Charlotte:

You: What would you do, Owen?

Owen: I'd wait for a little while.

You: Why?

Owen: Um . . . to see what happened.

You: But while you were waiting, Charlotte might seize the opportunity to wipe you out.

Charlotte: I'd send the missiles off straight away.

You: Is that nice?

Charlotte: No, but I don't trust Owen.

You: OK. But suppose you had armies instead of missiles. Whoever moved first was bound to win in the end because of the advantage of surprise, but could expect to lose half their army and some of their cities in the course of the war.

Charlotte: I'd still move as soon as I could. Otherwise Owen's side might.

You: What if the situation were like this: You both have powerful armies and missiles. If one side starts a war and the other side is a bit slow to respond, then the first side will probably win, and if it is lucky will suffer much less damage than the second side. But if one side starts a war and the other side is ready, both will be completely wiped out.

Owen: It would be better to not start a war.

Charlotte: Yes, but I would be on guard all the time in case he did start one.

You: Yes. Well, that's the way it is at the moment.

The logic of this game is simple enough that even kids can figure it out. They can all understand that an intentional first strike would end up with "mutual assured destruction." Albert Einstein put it this way: "I know not with what weapons World War III will be fought, but World War IV will be fought with sticks and stones." The famous nineteenth century German general, Baron Von Cluasewitz, called it the "Fog of Battle."

The idea of game theory is so powerful, both in logic and empirical evidence, that major contributor, Thomas C. Schelling professor of the University of Maryland, was awarded the Nobel Prize in Economics in 2005. Schelling showed that "a party can strengthen its position by overtly worsening its own options, that the capability to retaliate can be more useful than the ability to resist an attack, and that uncertain retaliation is more credible and more efficient than certain retaliation." After World War II, pioneer of game theory John Von Neumann strongly recommended that the U.S. launch a nuclear strike at Moscow. But his idea of a "preventive war" was rejected due in part to the "uncertain retaliation" from the former Soviet Union. The usefulness of retaliation was proven true when both the U.S. and the former Soviet Union developed long-range nuclear weapons, but agreed not to develop defensive weapons during the Cold War. According to the Nobel Committee, these insights formed the theoretical underpinnings for the strategy of nuclear deterrence and "proved of great relevance for conflict resolution and efforts to avoid war."

If "Nuclear War with China" is just a fictional story like *2013: World War III* (2004), *China Attack* (2000), and *Dragon Strike* (1999), there are serious discussions that actually turn the fever of the China threat into the flavor of the month. Here is a short list of some with catchy titles:

- *The Coming China Wars: Where They Will Be Fought and How They Can Be Won* (2006)

- *Showdown: Why China Will Fight the United States* (2006)

- *America's Coming War with China: A Collision Course over Taiwan* (2006)
- *China: The Gathering Threat* (2005)
- *The China Threat: How the People's Republic Targets America* (2002)
- *China Threat: Perceptions, Myths and Reality* (2002)
- *Seeds of Fire: China and the Story Behind the Attack on America* (2001)
- *Hegemon: China's Plan to Dominate Asia and the World* (2000)
- *Red Dragon Rising: Communist China's Military Threat to America* (1999)
- *The Coming Conflict with China* (1998)

Some of these predicted that a war with China would start in a year, some said within four years, some expected it to happen between 2005 and 2010; others foresaw it to occur any time soon, still others argued that the war with China began already without anyone realizing it. According to these "China war talks," the war can be a hot war, cold war, or nuclear war; and it can be over economic competition, oil, Taiwan, or any unexpected crisis.

In a recent article titled "War with China?"[38] William S. Lind of Free Congress Foundation refutes Robert D. Kaplan's ideas in "How We Would Fight China," published in *Atlantic Monthly,* June 2005. Kaplan sees the twenty-first century being defined by a new Cold War and a potential hot war between China and the United States, rather than the clash between states and non-state forces. Kaplan asserts how the U.S. could use naval power to contain a rising China within the framework of a Bismarckian Realpolitik over the issue of Taiwan.

But "Few in Washington understand why China is so adamant about Taiwan remaining officially part of China. The reason is China's history, throughout which her greatest threat has not been foreign invasion but internal division." Of course, China might not be able to successfully fight a sea and air war with America. What will China do if the U.S. sends its carrier battle groups to intervene? Lind proposes that China will do something Kaplan does not mention: "She will go nuclear at sea from the outset . . . what if a Chinese ballistic missile popped a nuke say, 100 miles from an advancing American carrier battle group? No one gets hurt, but the message would be loud and clear: keep coming and you're toast. . . . If we kept coming anyway and the Chinese did nuke a carrier, we would immediately face an asymmetrical situation. How would we respond? By nuking a Chinese carrier? China doesn't have any. If we drop a nuke on

Chinese territory, we have initiated a strategic nuclear exchange. Is Taiwan worth Seattle or Los Angeles?"

Lind believes there are influential voices in Washington that want a war with China; and in George W. Bush's Washington, the rule seems that we will make any blunder we can make. "I regard a war with China—hot or cold—as perhaps the greatest strategic blunder the United States could make, beyond those it has already made. The end result would be the same as that from the twentieth-century wars between Britain and Germany: it reduced both to second-rate powers. In the twenty-first century, the real victors would be the non-state forces of the Fourth Generation, who would fill the gap created by the reduction of both Chinese and American power."

"Nuking a carrier" is an interesting thought, but that doesn't mean the U.S. can't do something similar. Nevertheless, everything is still within the "Nuclear button" game logic. On July 16, 2005, the most inflammatory comments by a senior Chinese general in ten years were widely reported in American media. General Zhu Chenghu, who had a reputation as a hawk in Chinese military circles, said China was prepared to initiate non-conventional warfare over Taiwan: "If the Americans draw their missiles and position-guided ammunition into the target zone on China's territory, I think we will have to respond with nuclear weapons. Because war logic dictates that a weaker power needs to use maximum efforts to defeat a stronger rival, we Chinese will prepare ourselves for the destruction of all of the cities east of Xian," he said. "Of course, the Americans will have to be prepared that hundreds of cities will be destroyed by the Chinese." General Zhu later indicated that he expressed a private opinion, and believed war was unlikely to happen. Of course, for those sensation-catching journalists eager to report his inflammatory comments, the damage had been done.

Regardless of what's being said and done about the "Taiwan issue," the whole thing is just another game. Politicians in Taiwan play it to strengthen political position. China's military plays tough to influence popular sentiment. Taiwan's president Chen Shui-bian uses this "independence card" to divert popular attention whenever he is in political trouble. Isolated in international politics, he attempts to make more room for Taiwan's international status by adopting a gradual approach. He could also take some daring steps before the 2008 Beijing Olympic Games in the hope that China won't react violently and risk the Games.

As a small island, Taiwan exports more goods to mainland China than the U.S. does every year. If anything happens, a simple economic blockade will force the other's hand. This is just one of the ancient Chinese war tactics: "Besieging without attacking" (*wei er bu gong*). Nobody is going to be happy about this, but the mainland can simply use this tactic, and war is avoidable. The local dialect in Taiwan is also the dialect in southern Fujian province across the strait.

Taiwan declaring independence will bring an economic breakdown, political crisis, a leadership nightmare, and social chaos. In July 1995, China launched a belligerent one-week military exercise in the Taiwan Strait to protest the visit of Taiwan's then president, Lee Teng-hui, to the United States. Even though Lee's visit was an "unofficial" one (he was traveling to Cornell University, his alma mater), Taiwan's stock market plunged by more than 35 percent, and its currency fell to a four-year low. China's similar actions in early 1996 drove people on the island to line up at banks to change their money into U.S. dollars, which depleted its foreign exchange reserves at a rate of $300 million to $500 million per day.

On the mainland side, a military solution to Taiwan will easily destroy the fruits of its open policy; its hard-built international image will be demolished; and the American market and China's relations with the U.S. will be in jeopardy. No matter how noisy it is from both sides, this is a "lose-lose" situation that all parties must avoid. The development of electoral democracy in Taiwan will actually keep its politicians busy with internal cleavages rather than making any other decisive moves toward formal independence.

There are good reasons why U.S. business leaders choose to ignore all the "war talk" by the "China hawks" in Washington or elsewhere. China says that its grand strategy is to foster favorable conditions for continuing its modernization, while reducing the risk that others will decide that a rising China is a threat to be countered.[39] As China's near-thirty-year-long reform policy creates a low-cost, mass consumer structure that will remain competitive and attractive, American businesses will continue to benefit from doing business with China for years to come.

"China didn't seek hegemony in the past. It is not doing so in the present. Neither will it do so in the future." This is China's official position. Americans may not accept this no matter how many times it has been assured by the Chinese. But the "war talk" appears to be noise rather than any sound prediction, not to mention America's anti-terrorism effort, which calls for maximum international coalition. In recent years, China has shown its good faith in Middle East peacekeeping, as well as during the Iran and the North Korea nuclear crises. China is more of an "economic powerhouse" than a "war machine" if we look carefully into its "credit history." China is historically a defensive border expansionist, not an aggressive overseas expansionist. It is now more interested in selling than in fighting. Unlike Christian evangelism, Buddhist culture is more fervent in advocating the "Middle Way." China's double-digit growth in military spending during the last decade has more to do with its history than with its future.

The challenge from China's economic ascendance is not a business one. U.S. companies have the advantage of significant flexibility in basic organizational freedoms to trade and invest. Unlike European companies that are perhaps at the greatest disadvantage because of inflexible regulatory structures (especially with regard to labor), U.S. companies can quickly adjust themselves. All they need is time and a change of mindset. Though often charged with "corporate greed" from the labor front and from the ideologues, the latter's non-material orientation doesn't automatically let it stand on any moral high ground either. Indeed, the "culture of greed" could be much more dangerous to America's future.

The challenge from China's rise is not merely economic. As shown above, trade deficit, though not the end of the world, reflects bigger problems. The flow of trade represents the "tail of the dog," as U.S. Federal Reserve Chairman Ben Bernanke once explained. The U.S. became a debtor nation again in 1987 and has been the world's largest debtor nation since. The international debts of the U.S. total more than $8 trillion and are growing. The federal budget deficit started to soar again after the Republicans took office. What Americans need to focus on is fiscal responsibility in both public and private sectors.

The challenge from China's economic success is not a military one; it simply does not fit into China's grand strategy—even though China may seek to exploit U.S. vulnerabilities, complicate U.S. intervention, and counterbalance U.S. interests if the U.S. continues to over-stretch itself in a unilateral manner. The key factor behind China's "charm offensive" lies in its "soft power."[42] And the China Challenge is in fact much more fundamental. China fever is one part of China's economic miracle, and the economic miracle is only one part of the "China miracle."

How can one capture today's China in words? It is a country in constant motion, defying the laws of economic gravity, reaching out insistently around the world for raw materials to fuel its growth, eating up its land and its past, enticing outsiders to help it achieve new levels of wealth and power, opening up class fissures that were thought to be closed, testing the limits of rapid urban growth while giving its people chances for self-exploration and intellectual transformation they have not known for over half a century.[40]

2

The Chinese "Cult of Face": Economic Miracle and National Psychology

The Culture of Shame and Fear

In April 2006, an email exchange between an administrative assistant and her boss was widely circulated in China via the internet. The incident, now known as "EMC's Email Gate," started when Soon Choo Loke, then president of EMC China, returned to his office late one Friday evening to find himself locked out. The Singaporean executive fired off a peremptory email to his secretary, Rebecca Hu, who unexpectedly fought back with a blistering reply. This minor dispute blew up into a public relations fiasco and ended with Loke's resignation.[1] The email exchange was later published by the influential newspaper *Beijing Youth Daily* and became the talk of the nation:

```
From: Loke, Soon Choo
Sent: Saturday, April 08, 2006 1:13 AM
To: Hu, Rui
Cc: Ng, Padel; Ma, Stanley; Zhou, Simon; Lai, Sharon
Subject: Do not assume or take things for granted
```

Rebecca,
I just told you not to assume or take things for
granted on Tuesday and you locked me out of my office
this evening when all my things are all still in the
office because you assume I have my office key on my
person.

   With immediate effect, you do not leave the office until you have checked with all the managers you
support. This is for the lunch hour as well as at
end of day, OK?

When she came back to work the next Monday, Rebecca copied her
reply, along with Loke's original email (note the original email was cc-ed to
four other people), to all of EMC's staff in China:

From: Hu, Rui
Sent: Monday, April 10, 2006 13:48 PM
To: Loke, Soon Choo
Cc: China All (Beijing); China All (Chengdu); China
All (Guangzhou), China All (Shanghai); Lai, Sharon
Subject: FW: Do not assume or take things for
granted

Soon Choo,
First, What I did is absolutely right. Out of concern for security, I locked the door. It is not that
it didn't happen here things got lost. If it happens, I can't afford to take the responsibility.

   Second, you have your own key. You forgot to take
it with you and now you blame others for it. The
reasons for this incident are all from yourself and
don't shift your own mistakes to others.

   Thirdly, you don't have rights to control my private time. I work here for 8 hours a day. Please remember lunchtime and the hours after work are all my
private time.

   Fourth, since I joined EMC, I have been working
diligently to fulfill my responsibilities. I worked
overtime too many times without complaint. But if
you ask me to work overtime for things that are not
part of my job description, I simply can't do that.

> Fifth, our relationship is that of a supervisor and a subordinate, but please pay attention to the way you speak. This is the most fundamental courtesy of human being.
>
> Sixth, let me emphasize here, I didn't assume anything or take anything for granted. I don't have the time or necessity to do that.

Someone forwarded the email to a friend outside the company, and during the next few days, the email exchange was circling around other companies in China, apparently reaching thousands of people, some of whom posted it on online forums, which in turn generated heated discussions as in any online debate. By the end of April, Rebecca had left EMC in what the company described as a "personal decision." The *Beijing Youth Daily* tracked down Rebecca and interviewed her. She complained that all the publicity was making it difficult for her to find a new job. By early May, the story had been repeated in hundreds of newspapers, news websites, blogs, and discussion forums in China. And the debate went on and on:

> "It is indeed a heroic action of Hu Rui who stood up to her abusive boss and defended her rights. What a shame that an internationally renowned company like EMC placed an arrogant, discriminative and abusive employee on its management team. If EMC does not do something to make it right, it will be costly for EMC not only on its image but also its long-term interest in China. This incident should be an alarm to any companies that the days that Chinese employees' rights can be ignored are over. Chinese, particularly the young generation, have increasingly becoming conscious about their rights and demanding respect from their employers, thanks to the Western countries' persistent protests on Chinese human rights condition. If there is evidence that Hu Rui was fired because of her email, then Hu Rui will have a claim against EMC for wrongful termination. Hats off to Hu Rui!"

> "Soo Choo has had multiple run-ins with his senior staff. Lots of turn-overs were caused by his paranoid, totalitarian management style. EMC is better off without him."

> "While Rebecca has the right to respond to that email in the way she responded, she does not have to cc all other office regions, to make a

huge deal out of it. . . . This is very damaging to the company's image. Rebecca's behavior costs company reputation."

"Everybody takes in shit from people above. That's life. If you want to break the rules, you'll have to face the consequences, like what Rebecca is facing now, unable to get a new job."

"This stubborn secretary's email is like a shot in the arm. It's exciting. Seeing how she told off her boss, we can imagine doing the same. That feels wonderful!"[2]

The whole story swirls around the idea of "right and wrong" and "rights and obligations." Yet the real controlling forces under the surface remain untouched. The truth is: the EMC boss made a big mistake by cc-ing several other staff on his original email to the secretary, which essentially turned a private scolding into a public humiliation. Hence, the point of the story is not about "who is right" or "who has the rights." It is about "face," about honor, about a Chinese defending her dignity even when it ultimately cost her her job.

What exactly is this much-talked-about "face" to the Chinese? As an illustration in point, we can take a look at India's experience in the Olympic Games. India is almost as big as China in many aspects. If China is the manufacturing powerhouse of the world, India is its counterpart in the service sector. With over 1.1 billion people, India is the second most populous country in the world and the world's largest democracy. It is also one of the largest economies in the developing world and one of the few nations to possess nuclear weapons. In many areas, India is not far behind China. Yet many people notice that during the six most recent Olympic Games, India, shockingly, managed to win only one bronze medal in Atlanta (1996), one bronze medal in Sydney (2000), and one silver medal in Athens (2004), while China has been consistently one of the top medal gainers, with thirty-two medals in Los Angeles (1984, China's first appearance after 1949), twenty-eight in Seoul (1988), fifty-four in Barcelona (1992), fifty in Atlanta (1996), fifty-nine in Sydney (2000), and sixty-three in Athens (2004).

India's sports fans seem resigned to blame their over-indulgence in Cricket in terms of lack of sponsorship and relative lack of media coverage. In China's case, however, the secret of success is a simple one: heavy investment and huge incentives from businesses and all levels of government. The Chinese see sports not only as a big industry, but also as an expression of national pride and honor in the international arena. Deep in every Chinese athlete's soul, there is only one motto: *wei guo zhen guang* (compete for the nation's pride). Even in the absence of material incentives, this motto can be carried into all levels of sports competition, in which it becomes personal honor, family pride, and the community's reputation.

In fact, this sense of pride goes beyond sports. It is a deeply rooted concept in China's history, nurturing the grandeur of a tradition in the vast and resource-rich Middle Kingdom.[3] In essence, "Face" is a distinctive manifestation of high self esteem, a personal or collective emphasis on fame, image, dignity, pride, and a unique appreciation of interdependence, reciprocity, trust, connections, obligation, reputation, and credit in a specific social setting. It is the "art of relationships" with a dual focus on relation-based honorable pride (*mian zi*) and family-based social connections (*guanxi*).

The dominant importance of honor reflects the fear of shame. Shame is a feeling of anxiety about being criticized or laughed at, a feeling of embarrassment in response to the opinions or disapproval of others, and a feeling of personal or collective inadequacy as perceived by one's own peers. In China, shame is much more than just feelings. It is a relation-oriented psychological response that works as a controlling force in people's lives. Shame mirrors the prevailing significance of honor, and both shame and honor take primary positions in Chinese society.

This relation-oriented psychology comes from a family and clan-kinship setting. Wherever people go, they represent their families and their ancestors; they do not merely represent themselves as individuals. People must always act honorably, so that the honor of their family is upheld. Shameful deeds are covered up. And if someone is badly shamed and the shame cannot be hidden, then it is revenged (such as in the above email story). In extreme cases, the only other way out is suicide (which unfortunately does happen occasionally in cases of rape).

The reasoning of right and wrong is also used as a tool to restore honor and remove shame. Sometimes, people even use lies instead of reasoning between right and wrong. The culture of shame doesn't think of lies as being "right" or "wrong." The key question is: "Is what is done honorable?" If a lie protects honor, then it is fine. If a lie is told for other selfish reasons, then it is shameful. When people debate ethics, they are unconsciously doing their best to determine if things are honorable or not. If honor is brought back and shame is taken away, just like in the EMC email debate, they feel "like a shot in the arm. It's exciting. . . . That feels wonderful!" When shame rests upon the person's group rather than upon the individual, such feeling becomes much more powerful, for it is the whole group that will suffer. This is how a small email fight within a foreign company can turn into a national sensation.

Traditionally, Chinese culture is more of a mix of "shame-based" and "fear-based" culture. As it exposes itself more to the Western ideas of science and democracy, those "right and wrong" elements of Western "guilt-based" culture are added into the cultural mix.[4] Of course, the guilt concept also exists in China, but it is not the controlling factor or first response to actions. The reasoning of "guilty or innocent" and "right or wrong" is used more as a tool to restore honor and remove shame, which is very different from the West, where being innocent or right is self-justified and shame is not a major concern.

In China, the structure of society is based around the group relationship mentality rather than on the individual. In "Super Girl," the Chinese version of "American Idol," for example, the competition is intense, yet the show can contain over three full hours of emotional mutual consoling between singers, between hosts and singers, and between judges and singers. Nearly half of the girls can sing English songs and appeal to Western sensibilities, yet their response to winning and losing is totally Chinese.

A judge named Wu Qixian is as tough as Simon Cowell, but you won't find him fighting with other judges. Everyone is so cooperative that it is less of a competition and more of an encounter group. Everyone is working to assuage the shame from the outright elimination, which, strangely enough, takes more time on the show for the losers than for the winners. The 2007 show "Happy Boys Voice" exhibits similar patterns.

The 2006 reality show "Win in China," a Chinese version of "The Apprentice," is even more intriguing in this regard. More than 12,000 people applied for a spot on the show, from which 108 people were selected—most of whom were startup owners rather than job-seekers. Through rounds of real project presentations, twelve were picked to compete for the CEO position of a company and 10 million yuan (about $1.2 million) worth of stock. These twelve finalists were divided into two teams and were put to the test in seven real-life competitive business situations, after which a member of the "losing" team would be eliminated.

At the first elimination round, the judge clearly stated, "You are now not working as a team anymore, and you are supposed to fight for yourself to avoid elimination." To make absolutely sure, the judge asked "Is this understood?" to which all six members of each team replied "Yes" before they began to speak for themselves. Surprisingly, the first to speak chose to blame himself for his team losing and unambiguously offered to eliminate himself. This occurred before an audience of millions on Chinese national television.

This is the polar opposite of a similar situation on American television, where contestants can't wait to blame others for their team losing. Perhaps even more shocking was that two other team members immediately stepped forward to condemn themselves and volunteered to leave, though the remaining three team members kept silent. The Chinese simply can't "shamelessly" speak for themselves, let alone even conceive of attacking others, even when their own elimination is at stake. In the end, all three judges spent most of the time coaching everyone, including the team leader, who offered to leave, even saying: "You can't be a good CEO unless you have a heart to fire people." If there are any catchphrases for this Chinese reality show, "You're fired!" is not one of them.

In fact, the competition is not even a "win-lose" zero-sum game. While the winner got 10 million yuan, the runner-up pocketed 7 million and the following three contestants got 5 million each. Such an arrangement is not an exception. China's TV Golden Eagle Awards, for example, are not arranged in an American style "nominee-winner" fashion. Nominees are already winners who are awarded, but among these, the "best" is then selected by specialists for the highest award. In addition, Audience's Favorite Actor/Actress is also decided by viewer votes. Everybody, then, is a winner. The "best" is always hailed, yet at the same time "Face" will always be given to those who "lose" so as to avoid disharmonious tension (*mo bu kai main zi*). This interdependent "Cult of Face" is so deep-rooted in the national psychology that even Western-style elections are not accepted in non-political affairs.

Loyalty is seen as honor in China's "shame-based" culture. In the Chinese language, nation (*guojia*) doesn't only mean nation, it means both the motherland (*guo*) and the family (*jia*). Regardless of your citizenship, when you are ethnically Chinese, you are culturally expected to be loyal to the motherland. And the Chinese take pride in their loyalty. The most disgraceful name "*Han jian*" (traitor) would be given to whoever betrayed the motherland. Political dissidents are absolutely not tolerated. In June 2006, a composer named Shi Zhangyuan from China's rural west was acclaimed a hero by China's national television. Shi composed an award-winning song: "Singing Happiness Falling All Over the Slopes of the Hills" in 1959, and has composed more than 2,000 songs in spite of his living in stark poverty throughout his life. No one ever questioned the irony between the songs he composed and the reality in which he lived; it is the loyalty and persistence in his optimism that are honored.

On the other hand, betrayal within China's "shame-based" culture is an unforgivable crime. In 1989, former Chinese Communist Party General

Secretary Zhao Ziyang openly expressed emotion and sympathy for the student hunger strikers in Tiananmen Square, putting the role of the Party in the whole affair in doubt. Zhao further gave away the secret on Party agreement and Deng's final say on key decisions after his retirement. Zhao, handpicked by Deng to a position of leadership, was instantly purged and put under house arrest, living in obscurity until his death in 2005. Only in private, however, did Deng's daughter and other party elites chastise Zhao's "shameful" act and disloyalty to Deng. His appeal to be free from house arrest was of no avail even after Deng's death in 1997. A Chinese saying goes: "Rather make mistakes in ideological thinking than in organizational loyalty." Zhao was seen as lacking the political wisdom to avoid both mistakes. In the end, his removal was less severe than that of many of his predecessors.

"Guilt-based" culture depends more on legalistic sanction. "Shame-based" culture depends more on relational sanction. Paternalism and hierarchies based on power, status, age, and gender provide some of the basic mechanisms. In ancient China, regional warfare between clans, states, and kingdoms often started because someone caused another group shame. Frequently, only the skillful intervention of a third party could end such discord. Many regional and national rulers gained fame and reputation from their skill at ending such conflicts. Some rulers crushed all of the tribes or small kingdoms and made them submit to their rule. Peace was maintained by force. But old conflicts and animosities flared again once the controlling power was removed and freedom returned.

The dependence on an external, outside "power" for social order also comes from a "fear-based" culture. China's fear-based culture was rooted in the agrarian Middle Kingdom and reflected a fear of the natural world, the elements, and for nomadic invaders from the north. In ancient China, these events were the basis for attempts at divination and a way to explain the spiritual or "supernatural" forces at work in the world. People saw their lives depend on their interaction with the spiritual world, which was filled with gods, demons, spirits, ghosts, and, of course, their own ancestors. They believed they must coexist harmoniously with these unseen powers by appeasing them with respect and by living quietly—with fear. They attributed floods, droughts, earthquakes, meteorites, meteor showers, comets, thunder and lightning, crop failure, locusts, famine, epidemics, defeat in wars, and even death—all to the spiritual world.[5]

The seventh month of the Chinese lunar calendar is known as "Ghost Month," when the gates of hell open and the dead walk among the living. People are supposed to please the ghosts by burning paper effigies and offering them food and other daily items. This is a time for families to avoid moving house, couples to postpone their wedding plans, tourists to shy away from beach resorts, and young people to wind down their usually frenzied nightlife. Ghost Month can be a slow business season in some places even today.

In ancient times, controlling resources and tax revenue turned the state from the demand side to the supply side. The size of the kingdom was determined by power, resource potential, and cultural connections. The process is a result of both "spontaneous order" and "collective control." This "Transaction Cost Theory of Political Entrepreneurship"[6] helps explain the rise and fall of kingdoms in pre-dynastic China.

To deal with supernatural powers, rituals or systems of appeasement were established, and rulers or witches came to the forefront to control these systems. They made themselves look like the only ones who could understand and communicate with supernatural powers. People needed to live in safety with powers around them, so rulers controlled people through fear. Chinese history is replete with examples of how rulers made up stories, and used charms and other methods to gain control over people and over powers of the state. In so doing, the use of superstitious ideology saved the rulers.

Fear versus power is the paradigm for the ancient Chinese. Supernatural powers are often regarded as having their own particular character and a will of their own, which can take various forms, such as ghosts, animal-spirits, demons, ancestors who live around people, spirits in trees and rocks, totems, and taboos. People gain extraordinary power, either through incarnation (*tou tai*, a bodily manifestation of a supernatural being at birth) or through philosophical study and appreciation of China's martial arts (*taiji, gongfu, qigong*). Heaven and men are interactive, and men should respect and follow the will and arrangement of heaven to avoid disaster.

It is here that Chinese rulers found the use of the Confucian "five cardinal relationships" (*wu lun*), in part making Confucianism the "state religion" of imperial China. The so-called "five cardinal relationships" are: father and son, ruler and minister, husband and wife, elder brother and younger brother, and relationships between friends. Specific duties were prescribed to each set of relationships. Filial devotion to emperors and parents (*zhong xiao*) is considered among the greatest of virtues, and must be shown toward both the living and the dead. With a top-down hierarchy, it is no wonder that nearly all of Chinese history is one of emperors, kings, generals, and ministers (*di wang jiang xiang*).

Mao Zedong thought himself a "savior" from Heaven—like a god who deserves total loyalty and respect. For decades after his death, China struggled to reverse Mao's God-like image. Coincidentally, only a few weeks before Mao's death in 1976, China experienced a devastating earthquake at Tangshan, east of Beijing, which killed more than a quarter of a million people. According to Chinese superstition, natural calamities are a portent of imminent change in the structure of China's leadership.

After Mao's former private doctor Li Zhisui moved to the United States, he sensationally exposed Mao living the life of an emperor in his biography *The Private Life of Chairman Mao.* In 1995, only weeks after he announced in an interview that he was going to write another memoir, Li was found dead in the bathroom of his son's house. Is it from the swiftness of divine retribution (*bao ying*), or a judgment by Heaven? Nobody knows.

But the Chinese believe in fate and proper respect. Even Wang Chong, a philosopher during the Han Dynasty, who famously attacked superstition, believed in fate. According to the Chinese zodiac, 2007 is the year of the Pig, which coincides with the element of gold in the rotation of the five elements (gold, wood, water, fire, and earth) for the twelve zodiac signs. Thus, the combination of the "Golden Pig" is said to be blessed with exceptional wealth, happiness, and prosperity, which could very well turn 2007 into a baby boom year. As the Chinese saying goes: "Truth lies only in the eyes of the believers" (*xin ze you, bu xin ze wu*).

Gunpowder is one the "four great inventions" of ancient China, along with the magnetic compass, papermaking, and movable type printing. Instead of being used as a weapon outright, gunpowder was discovered by alchemists and used as fireworks to chase away demons and ghosts. The practice of Feng Shui (literally, "wind" "water") is the study of geomancy: the subtle but powerful relationships that exist among the human, natural, and supernatural worlds.

The dragon is another auspicious symbol of power in China, one quite different from the Western concept of the fire-breathing monster. Chinese people often use the term "Children of the Dragon" as a sign of ethnic identity. The dragon was also the symbol of the emperor of China, and it was strictly forbidden to disfigure or desecrate the depiction of a dragon. When an advertising campaign by shoe company Nike featured the American NBA player LeBron James slaying a dragon, it was immediately censored by the Chinese government after public outcry over "disrespect" toward the dragon. Recently, a Shanghai professor's alleged suggestion that the dragon should no longer symbolize China stirred up fiery debate and aroused strong objections from the public.

The "Mandate of Heaven" (*tian ming*) is the most important Chinese concept of legitimacy used to support the rule of the kings of the Shang

Dynasty, and later the emperors of China right up until the decline of the Qing Dynasty in the late nineteenth century. The emperor, or "Son of Heaven" (*tian zi*), represented the will of Heaven, and whatever he said was a "sacred edict" (*shen zi*). The emperor made laws according to the will of Heaven and could choose to change or follow conventions. It is believed that Heaven would bless the authority of a just ruler, but would be displeased with an unwise ruler—thus signaling that the mandate to rule had expired.

Again, this is quite different from the European notion of "Divine Right," which legitimized the unwise ruler instead of providing for an overthrow. In China, a "legitimate" emperor need not be of noble birth. Legitimacy comes from the mutual filial nature of the government, not from the formation of the government. The Confucian classic, the *Book of Mencius*, stated: "Between father and son there should be affection, between ruler and minister there should be righteousness, between husband and wife there should be proper distinction, between elder and younger there should be proper order, and between friends there should be faithfulness."

Government officers are supposed to "take care of people like treating their own children" (*ai ming ru zi*). It was wrong to revolt, but the Mandate of Heaven would pass when a revolt was evidently successful. "The emperor is like a boat, the people are like water; water can keep the boat afloat or overturn it." The logic is: "If you steal a needle, you are a thief; if you steal the state, you are the king." But "You are a hero only if you win; you are a thief if you lose." The system is essentially an arrangement in which one family controls many families. It requires a lot of power and a lot of merit to hold it together. The Mandate of Heaven is therefore defined by both power and merit.

Early China's agrarian society also promoted interdependence to a much larger degree than did a hunting-herding-fishing society such as ancient Greece.[7] From this perspective, the "book culture" of the Confucian ethos was only a world view that reflected and was upheld by Chinese "reality culture." Confucian "book culture" became part of the "reality culture" only when it reinforced the Chinese way of thinking (or the built-in national psychology), which in turn justified the interdependent ethics and Chinese social practices. The impact of "book culture," however, has often been overemphasized because those who were involved with it were often a small group of enlightened gentry class administrators and bureaucrats.

The "shame-honor" and "fear-power" psychology gradually evolved into a mix of "shame-based" and "fear-based" culture until "guilt-based" Western culture challenged its existence. In the light of the "shame-honor" and the "fear-power" cultural psychology, the Chinese "Cult of Face" maintains the concept of Face (*lian mian*) and its connections to power (*guanxi*), which is a manifestation of Chinese interdependence and is expressed through multiple levels of relationships. Favors, blessings, filial piety, and loyalty are the key components of Chinese interdependence.

Personal satisfaction is always obtained by connection-based interdependence, which in turn nurtures national psychology in a tradition that is rich in "big family" passion, yet weak in external pursuit.[8] This is one reason that China was always content with its own material affluence and never became an aggressive overseas expansionist. It also explains why the Chinese are more stable in personal attachment and are less likely to seek help from psychologists; why the Chinese are much less anxious over personal independence or individualistic confrontation; are readily satisfied with limited material achievement (*zhi zhu chang le, ji liu yong tui, jian hao jiu shou*); and readily share personal success within their social connections (*yi jin huang xian, rong gui gu li*).

Interestingly, even in contemporary China, connection to power is viewed as an honor and can be proudly talked about in public. People are not ashamed of patronage and nepotism. "Face" is something really serious. It is always a big deal when you "hurt the Chinese people's feelings." This means the Chinese are sensitive to shame and honor and readily take things personally.

They often show the world their craziness with all-or-nothing efforts in, for example, applying to host the 2000 and 2008 Olympic Games, as well as gaining membership in the WTO (a firmly committed fifteen-year effort). Pride and connection are two sides of the same coin of "Face." Foreigners are frequently amazed by how the Chinese "want Face" as well as how they use personal connections to achieve personal goals. This is the Chinese way of flexibility and practicality in making exceptions to the rules of any business or political game. The Chinese don't trust rules as much as connections. Respect is paid to "real" people rather than to "unreal" rules. And rules should always allow flexibility and exceptions given a specific context or connection. If there is anything that's unique about the Chinese, the "Cult of Face" is at the forefront.

Chinese "shame" points to both "fame" (honor, *mianzi*), "favor" (connections, *guanxi*), and "faith" (trust and credit, *kekao*), just like Chinese "fear" points to both "fate" (Heaven's arrangement, *tianming*) and "force" (official power, *shili*). The Chinese "Cult of Face" suggests a combination of "Five Fs" (fame-favor-faith-fate-force) in the context of its shame-based and fear-based culture.[9] With "faith" at the center, "fame-favor-faith-fate-force" is a cultural "Magic Chain" that dictates every aspect of Chinese daily life, especially in economic and political domains. It is also like a "civil religion" that is practiced through the usages of its language. Modern standard Chinese, known simply as *Putonghua*, or Mandarin, abounds with phrases and idioms containing the word "face" which carry all aspects of meanings related to fame and favor. Below is a list of commonly encountered expressions with Chinese pronunciation (*Pinyin romanization*), and meaning:

Phrases and idioms concerning fame (honor):

- Blacken one's face (dishonor, discredit, disgrace; *wang lian shang mo hei*): He blackened your face just for his own credit.

- Caring for one's face (too proud; *ai mian zi, chen mengmian, zhuang mengmian, gu chan mian, timian, zou mianzi*): He couldn't manage to apologize simply because he cares too much for his face.

- Face project (a project showing merit; *mian zi gong chen*): China's space program is more than just a face project.

- Gain face (add pride, gain pride; *zhang lian, gei lian shang zhen guang*): Liu Xiang's performance at the 110-meter hurdles gained face for the Chinese.

- Get one's face back (make it up, get reputation back; *wan hui mian zi*): He tried so hard to get his face back only to find that no one really cares.

- Lay out one's face (put up air; *bai pu*): He laid out his face to show his seniority.

- All of one's face has been lost. (Shameless; *lian dou diu guang le*): All of his face has been lost due to the shameful deed.

- Faking a big face by beating one's face swollen. (Try to keep false honor. *da zhong lian chong pang zi*)

- No face to see parents. (Too shameful to face up. *wu yang jian jiang dong fu lao, mei lian jian die niang*)

- Men can't live without face, trees can't live without bark. (Only reputation matters. *ren hou lian, shu hou pi*)

- Where do you want him to put his face? (How can he take such humiliation? *ni rang ta ba lian wang na ge?*)

Phrases and idioms concerning favor (connections):

- All for one's face (all for one's sake; *kan zai ni de mian zi shang*): He wouldn't be able to get the business license were it not for his dad's face.
- Big face, old face (leverage, influence, weight; *mian zi da, lao lian*): You've got a big face for the favor. He should be able to make it by his old face.
- Care for another's face (be accommodated, *jian qingmian*): He is not a person who doesn't care for another's face.
- One plays red face, the other plays white face. (Good guy, bad guy; good cop, bad cop; one plays tough, the other plays nice in dealing with a third party; *yi ge chang hong lian, yi ge chang bai lian)*

Phrases and idioms related to both fame and favor:

- All about face (a face issue related to fame and favor, different from "about face" which means a total change of attitude or viewpoint; *mian zi wen ti*): The debate gets personal and now it's all about face.
- Break one's fake face (expose, reveal the truth; *cou chang gui lian, se xia jia mian ju*): You broke his fake face by telling everybody his real intention.
- Change one's face (blow up; *bian lian, fan lian, fan lian bu ren ren*): Rebecca changed her face when her boss openly insulted her in an email.
- Face-off (confrontation, *si puo lian pi*): A military face-off between the U.S. and China over Taiwan is unlikely to happen.
- Give face to, take care of one's face (give a favor to, show respect to; *shanglian, gei mian zi, bu bo ta mian zi, zhao gu mian zi, bukan sen mian kan fu mian*): In Chinese banquet culture, guests are considered not giving face to the hosts when they refuse to drink up the liquor or wine.
- Hurt one's face (disrespect, damage one's image; *sang mian zi*): He wouldn't do something like that to hurt your face.
- Leave face for someone (not to make someone lose face; note that it is not the same as save face; *liu dian mian zi*). To leave face for you, he didn't argue too much.

These phrases and idioms are deeply ingrained on the Chinese psyche. They offer a look at the workings behind the Chinese belief system. The dynamics of their use reflects how this cultural psychology evolves. Through these expressions, the Chinese "Cult of Face" provides a tool by which we can better understand why and how culture matters. In the case of the Olympic Games, considering other neighboring countries like Japan who hosted the 1964 games in Tokyo, and South Korea who hosted the 1988 games in Seoul. It would be "no face" if China can't do the same as early as possible. Hence, the 2008 Olympic Games in Beijing will be a grand event in which China will not only do everything to ensure its success, but also fight for number one status in the total medal count.

From Lord Macartney to "EP-3"

In September 1792, George Macartney led the first British trade mission to China. He set out from Portsmouth and sailed toward the Middle Kingdom. The Macartney mission, comprising 700 people in three ships, marked the first official contact between Britain and China in modern history. Building on his earlier diplomatic success in negotiating with Catherine II for an alliance between England and Russia in 1764, Macartney hoped this trip would accomplish what King George III expected to see: expansion of trade relations between Britain and China, acquisition of a small unfortified island in eastern China, and establishment of a permanent British embassy in Beijing.

At that time, trade between Britain and China was limited by the Qing Dynasty to the southern port of Canton (Guangzhou). Even though direct oceanic trade between China and Europe began earlier in the sixteenth century, British traders were late followers compared with the Portuguese, the Spanish, and the Dutch, who usually brought silver from the Americas to exchange for Chinese silk. With the ongoing industrial revolution at home and Britain's increasing presence in India, Macartney seemed to have every reason to believe that the Chinese emperor would be interested in Britain's "technological marvels" at the time: telescopes, clocks, barometers, air guns, and even a hot-air balloon. All these amazing gadgets of Western scientific progress, along with a large delegation of diplomats, businessmen, soldiers, scientists, painters, a watchmaker, a gardener, five German musicians, two priests, and a pilot for the hot-air balloon, arrived in the Pearl River delta after nine months at sea.[10]

Macartney couldn't imagine that all the presents he brought were not to be seen as gifts from a diplomatic equal, or tokens of respect from what was one of the most powerful nations in the world, but as tribute from Western barbarians. What was waiting for them in China was not the ministry of foreign affairs, but the "Tribute Reception Department" of the

Qing court. Dramatically, after Macartney finally reached Beijing, both sides started to fight over disagreements on ritual issues of the "kowtow," the Three Kneelings and Nine Prostrations dictated by court protocol, and what Macartney had prepared to do: tip his hat, go down on one knee, and even kiss the emperor's hand, if required.

It didn't take too long for Macartney to realize that China was no Russia, and the Qing emperor, Qianlong, was no Catherine II. In fact, Qianlong was not impressed by the "tributes" at all, and found the idea of "kissing the emperor's hand" ridiculous. The gift of elaborate mechanical clocks, furthermore, infuriated the emperor because the Chinese do not give clocks as gifts: the pronunciation of "sending clocks" is exactly the same as "paying tribute to the dead." Qianlong was known as one of the greatest emperors in Chinese history and the longest-reigning emperor in China.[11] His nation seemed strong and wealthy enough to out-dazzle even the best Britain could offer. His famous "sacred edict" to the British king was ready long before he even met Macartney:

> Our dynasty's majestic virtue has penetrated unto every country un-
> der Heaven, and kings of all nations have offered their costly tribute
> by land and sea. As your ambassador can see for himself, we possess
> all things. I set no value on objects strange or ingenious, and have no
> use for your country's manufactures. This then is my answer to your
> request to appoint a representative at my court, a request contrary
> to our dynastic usage, which would only result in inconvenience to
> yourself.[12]

Of course, this emperor could never realize that his 1793 edict would set in motion a series of events that would completely change the course of China's modern history. Since official trade channels weren't going anywhere, and since the huge demand in Europe for Chinese goods, such as silk, tea, and ceramics, could only be met if British merchants funnelled their silver into China, while profiteering British traders started to smuggle large quantities of opium into China. This "opium-for-silver" trading scheme was so powerful that even Charles Elliot, the Chief Superintendent of Trade and British Minister to China, got himself involved in helping British merchants smuggle opium to Canton. In 1839, the Qing government reacted by destroying over 20,000 chests of British opium, and later blockaded the port from European ships. Britain then decided to open China to trade by force. The great British merchant companies of the nineteenth century became some of the world's largest drug traffickers.

In 1840, Britain launched what would be come known as the "Opium

War" against China, and the long isolation of the Middle Kingdom became history. China's military was no match for the British. After a series of defeats and humiliating treaties, such as the Treaty of Nanking, signed with Britain and other Western Powers, including the United States and France, the Qing government still tried to maintain the illusion of greatness and rejected overtures that would have expanded trade.

Pressured by the Western powers, China finally began to receive foreign diplomats in 1873. Guo Songtao was sent to London, where he became the first Chinese ambassador. The Macartney mission has often been seen as a prime example of an unsuccessful collision between two civilizations, a failure on China's part to maintain its empire and recognize the power of a different culture (which came from the sea rather than from the other side of the Great Wall), or a critical miscalculation by one of its greatest emperors. More importantly, it forced China to face a totally new and assertive global system set in motion by the Western enlightenment and expressed through trade, colonialism, war, political and economic revolution, and innovation in science and technology.

Since 1840, China has been struggling with internal and external crises, torn between national independence and social development, and divided by its cultural legacy and modernization efforts. As for the events that are most unforgettable to the Chinese and still have impact on China's future policies, internally it is the Cultural Revolution (1966–1976); externally they are the First Sino–Japanese War (1894–1895), in which China's first modern navy fleet was destroyed by Japan while the island of Taiwan was ceded to Japan in the "unequal" Treaty of Shimonoseki; and the Second Sino–Japanese War (1937–1945), known in China as the "War of Resistance," during which the Nanking Massacre occurred—one of the most horriffic crimes against humanity in recorded history.

Japan's invasions are in fact the most egregious of all "face-losing" events for the Chinese. "March of the Volunteers," a popular song during the War of Resistance, became the national anthem of the People's Republic of China. Anti-Japanese sentiment remains so instinctive that even relatively minor offenses involving visitors from Japan can lead to heated or even violent reactions. Disputes over the Diaoyu or Senkaku Island group northeast of Taiwan, lead to strained relations between China and Japan. In 2006, a scare over contaminated, American-branded but Japanese-manufactured cosmetics in China turned into a PR nightmare that erupted in full-scale rioting and the destruction of several stores in Shanghai. When former U.S. Secretary of Defense Donald Rumsfeld addressed a meeting of defense ministers in Singapore in June 2005, he came up with the question: "Since no nation threatens China, one wonders: why this growing investment (in military)?" To the Chinese, it's not about "future threat," it's about history, it's about "never again," and it's about "face." Their feet have been held to the fire for so long that they now usually respond better in the absence of external pressure than in the presence of it.

When Richard Nixon prepared to "induce change" to China in 1970, he laid out two options to the Chinese leaders: send an emissary to Beijing or receive a Chinese representative in Washington for more thorough talks. The Chinese reply in the Warsaw meeting was: "If the U.S. Government wishes to send a representative of ministerial rank or a special envoy of the United States President to Peking . . . the Chinese Government will be willing to receive him." As James H. Mann[13] observed in his book *About Face: A History of America's Curious Relationship with China from Nixon to Clinton*: "Thus in the earliest days of the Nixon era was established the pattern that China would follow for decades in dealing with American leaders. American politicians regularly sought permission to visit China. The Beijing leadership could either grant the invitations or hold them in abeyance, depending on which option would be better for China. The handling and scheduling of presidential candidates, ex-presidents, opposition party leaders, and out-of-office politicians was to become an important component of China's handling of America."[14]

On July 9, 1971, when U.S. Secretary of State Henry Kissinger landed in Beijing for his important mission, John Holdridge, one of the aides who accompanied Kissinger on the trip, was pulled aside by Huang Hua, then China's ambassador to Canada. Huang wanted to make sure that Kissinger was going to shake China's Premier Zhou Enlai's hand because the Chinese could never forget former U.S. Secretary of State John Foster Dulles's refusal to touch Zhou's hand in Geneva eighteen years before. Of course, Kissinger, who told Nixon that the mission was "the most important communication that has come to an American president since the end of World War II" had no intention of imitating Dulles. When Zhou appeared, Kissinger extended his hand. What Huang Hua was actually trying to do was make sure that Kissinger made the gesture first. This defining moment became one of the most frequently mentioned anecdotes by the Chinese.

The Chinese "Cult of Face" is the key to understanding all these events. However, it is a difficult game to play. The early years of the relations between China and the U.S. were characterized by high level contacts between the top leaders rather than ordinary citizens. In May, 1988, U.S. ambassador to China Winston Lord made an unusual move, to appear at Peking University (commonly called Bei Da) to give a speech. Lord was a diplomat but also a Sinophile. He took part in one of the "political salons" organized by Wang Dan, who later became one of the leaders of the 1989 student movement. At a time when Chinese intellectuals were eager to promote political liberalization as a means of deepening ongoing economic reform, Lord's involvement with the students, as the ambassador of a foreign state, was deemed wholly inappropriate, so much so that he deserved a warning.

In February 1989, President George H. Bush planned to host a large banquet on his visit to China after he attended Emperor Hirohito's funeral in Japan. Lord decided to put Fang Lizhi, the astrophysicist and dissident scholar, on the guest list. The Chinese side was unhappy about this and sent a protocol officer to express their concerns. But it was taken by Lord as a low-level complaint that, frankly, he could ignore. After Bush flew to Tokyo, Lord got a phone call from Chinese Vice Foreign Minister Zhu Qizhen. Zhu's message was straightforward: if Fang Lizhi attended the banquet, Chinese President Yang Shangkun and Premier Li Peng would not attend. After rounds of intensive talks, both sides reached a compromise: Fang could attend the banquet, but would be seated in a distant table out of sight of the Chinese leaders.

On the evening of February 26, 1989, the banquet was held smoothly at the Great Wall Sheraton Hotel in northeastern Beijing. Fang didn't speak to the media at all. In fact, he never made it to the banquet. He was physically blocked by Chinese secret police from entering the hotel. While Lord was unfortunate enough to take all the blame from Washington, he still forcefully argued that it was the Chinese who had misbehaved and owned him an explanation. The American side continued to be puzzled by why the Chinese leaders should feel so threatened by a "mild-mannered professor," without realizing it is again not about "threat" but about "face."[15]

On April 1, 2001, a United States Navy EP-3 surveillance plane collided with a Chinese F-8 fighter jet, killing the Chinese pilot in China's own airspace above its claimed 200-mile Exclusive Economic Zone. The Chinese claimed that their "national feelings" were badly hurt by America's refusal to apologize or even show appreciation that the damaged U.S. plane was able to use a nearby Chinese airport for an emergency landing. The reaction in China was similar to what happened after the U.S. bombing of the Chinese Embassy in Belgrade in 1999. With all the technological might of the United States, the Chinese simply could not believe that the bombing was an accident. Both the Belgrade embassy bombing and the EP-3 story are frequently quoted as evidence of the recent rise of Chinese nationalism, which is not at all misplaced but definitely misinterpreted: it is nationalism when it happens to any other country, yet the China-can-say-no reaction can only be explained by its "face culture" in the context of its previous historical humiliation. If the history of China in the nineteenth and twentieth centuries is a history of "losing face," China in the twenty-first century will be a history of "getting face back."

Getting Face Back

One hundred and eighty-five years after Emperor Qianlong's 1793 edict, China opened its doors to the world in 1978. This time it was a proactive move from inside rather than a passive reaction to pressures from outside. And the "edict" now is totally different: "Poverty is not socialism. To get rich is glorious." Immediately, the world started to witness an unprecedented economic miracle characterized by prolonged and rapid economic growth, large-scale urbanization, explosive foreign direct investment, huge outflow of low-priced manufactured and high-tech goods, and an increasingly open and receptive domestic market. The momentum of China's economic boom caught the United States and much of the rest of the world unprepared. It also poses a series of questions to Western mainstream ideology, which tends to link China's kind of economic development to democracy and liberal capitalism.

What has really happened in China? How can China achieve such development within less than thirty years under a Communist regime? Is the development sustainable? Why do we even care? Is there something wrong with Western theory or something still not right with the Chinese reality? Is China's experience just a case of "development without progress?" Is it the same old China with its "mental Great Wall," which had failed miserably during the previous two centuries? What, exactly, is the nature of the challenge to the U.S. and the rest of the world?

Many people are familiar with this story: Solemnly and slowly, with his fingers extended, Napoleon Bonaparte outlined a great stretch of territory on a map of the world. "There," he growled, "is a sleeping giant. Let him sleep. If he wakes, he will shake the world." The sleeping giant was, of course, China. Today, every Chinese is proud of the French Emperor's prophecy.

Napoleon is not the only one who predicted the ascendancy of China. Writing in the 1960s, renowned world historian Arnold Toynbee also speculated on China playing a role in world politics: "By the year 1840, China had been, for 2,061 years 'the Middle Empire' of her own East Asian world, and, in this role, she had given her world long-lasting unity and peace. In the twentieth century of the Christian era, unity and peace were the crying needs of the global world that had been brought into existence by Western technology's feat of 'annihilating distance.' If a 'Middle Empire' was now needed as a nucleus for political unification on a global scale, China was the country that was designed by history for playing this part of world-unifier once again, this time on a literally world-wide stage."[16]

Toynbee's conclusion was based on intuition from his life-long research of world history and cultural changes. At the time he said this, there seemed to be no supporting evidence whatsoever. But recent development in China suggests that Toynbee's "world-unifier hypothesis" may be something to pay attention to.

So just how big is China? With more than 1.3 billion people, the People's Republic of China (PRC) is the world's most populous country. For every one American, for example, there are 43.3 Chinese. Each year, nearly ten million people are added to its population, almost a half of the total population of Australia. Independent estimates of China's population are near 1.5 billion, which makes the "unaccounted for" population almost equal to the entire population of Brazil. Even though China is the forth largest in terms of territory (after Russia, Canada, and the U.S.), it has only 7 percent of the world's arable land to feed one-fifth of the world's population. It is the world's most cosmopolitan and geographically diverse country when one takes into account the two factors of population and geography. With more than 5,000 years of history, it is arguably the oldest continuous civilization in the world. All these features boil down to a strong tension between "centralism" and "localism" that has a far-reaching effect on shaping its national policy throughout its history.

Unlike developing countries that experienced "growth without development," China's economic boom goes with significant social changes. To measure such success, an index called the "National Power Composite" was created by Chinese scholars. It consists of such factors as technology, human resources, capital, natural resources, military power, GDP, international influence, and government regulatory effectiveness. According to the "Global political and security report 2006" produced by the Chinese Academy of Social Sciences (CASS), China's leading academic and research organization, as measured by its own National Power Composite, China's overall national strength ranked sixth among the world's major powers,[17] up from ninth in 1990, eighth in 1995, and seventh in 2000.[18]

The United States, Britain, Russia, France, and Germany are ahead of China; and Japan, Canada, South Korea, and India rank below China.

The United States, according to the report, enjoys absolute superiority in all factors of the index. However, an earlier report by CASS predicted that, by the year 2020, China would enter into the top three in terms of the "National Power Composite,"[19] and the gap between the U.S. and those behind it will narrow substantially. The report also foresees that by the year 2020, China's urbanization rate will increase from the current 36 percent to 55 percent, with a capacity to accommodate an urban population of 700 to 750 million. China's eastern coastal areas will have gone though three "zero growths:" zero growth rate of the natural population in 2010; zero growth rate of natural resource and energy consumption in 2015; and zero growth rate of environmental degradation in 2020. China's central and Western regions will achieve these three "zero growth" rates in the next fifteen to twenty years.

Currently, in terms of military power, China possesses nuclear weapons capability and has the largest army in the world. It is not the world's most advanced army, however. While China's military power is growing, it ranks far behind that of the U.S. According to U.S. estimates, China's military budget—the second largest in the world at $81.5 billion (the Chinese official figure is $30 billion)—pales in comparison to U.S. military spending of $518.1 billion in 2005. In 2007, the number might be as high as $100 billion (the Chinese official figure is estimated as $45 billion). To put it another way, China's military spending, in per capita terms, is just one seventy-seventh that of the U.S.

The "8th Wonder"

How did China overtake one country after another in the "National Power Composite" during the last thirty years? Compared with the "National Power Composite," the GDP (Gross Domestic Product) focuses on measuring a nation's economic performance. It is the total market value, either at current prices (nominal GDP) or at constant prices of a specific year (inflation-adjusted real GDP), of final goods and services produced within the borders of a nation in a given period of time. GDP is a widely accepted economic indicator; even though it ignores such factors as non-market transactions, underground economic activities, the value of leisure, ecological costs, production rather than consumption bias, and measuring government spending at cost rather than at value.

China is the world's largest developing economy in terms of GDP. It was the fourth largest in the world in 2006 with approximately $2.5 trillion, up from sixth place in 2004. It leap-frogged France and Britain and now has Germany ($2.8 trillion) and Japan ($4.6 trillion) in its sights. When measured by Purchasing Power Parity (PPP), China was the second largest in the world in 2005, with a GDP of $8.572 trillion.[20] According to the World Bank's PPP estimate, by the year 2020, China will be the number one economy in the world, followed by the U.S. and Japan. The calculations usually don't account for the "black and gray" markets that are estimated at around 15 percent of China's GDP. Local government officials are suspected to substantially overestimate economic performance figures in a manner tantamount to "fraudulent window-dressing." Yet there is also evidence they may underestimate to avoid higher tax by the central government. In addition, local statistics were believed to insufficiently reflect the situation of the non-state-owned sector.

During the past twenty-eight years, China enjoyed an average annual growth rate of about 9.6 percent, a record rate of growth for an industrializing country; it matches or exceeds those best growth periods in Japan, South Korea, Singapore, Taiwan, and Hong Kong.[21] By the U.S. Federal Reserve's estimate, the average level of productivity or output per worker (the most important determinant of living standards) grew at 6.5 percent per year between 1978 and 1989, and 9 percent per year from 1990 to 2005.[22] A 3 percent productivity gain in the U.S. economy is often considered strong.

If China maintains a conservative annual growth rate of 7 to 8 percent, which is more than double the U.S. growth rate, average personal income in China will also be catching up quickly. This is what is known as the "power of compounding," or what Albert Einstein called the "8th Wonder of the World": the growth rate required to double a GDP in ten years is approximately 7.2 percent. To put it differently, China's GDP growth at the rate of 10 percent will need only 7.2 years before doubling. This is also known as the "Rule of 72," and it is exactly what happened in China. Calculated in 1990 U.S. dollars, its economy doubled in size from $141.5 billion in 1978 to $291.1 billion in 1986, doubled again to $619.8 billion in 1994, and doubled for the third time to $1.3 trillion in 2003.[23]

While China managed to increase its GDP tenfold in less than thirty years (1978–2006), there is also a clear pattern of doubling up about every eight years. With the nearly 10 percent annual growth between 2003 and 2005 and over 10 percent growth in 2006, it could double for the fourth time in 2011. Putting it in perspective, for a modern economy to double its GDP once, Britain took fifty-eight years (from 1780), the United States took forty-seven years (from 1839), Japan thirty-three years (from the

1880s), Indonesia seventeen years, and South Korea eleven years.[24] China is one of very few countries in the history of the modern world that takes about eight years to double its GDP three times in a row, and is the only one that has done so after 1970. Its GDP is expected to outdo Germany to reach $3.2 trillion in 2010, with a $2,400 per capita GDP.

Due to the effect of its "one-child policy," China's per capita GDP enjoyed a much higher growth rate than that of India ($1,700 vs. $700 in 2005). It is estimated that the birth of an additional 400 million Chinese (roughly the U.S. and Mexico population count combined) has been prevented since the one-child policy was implemented thirty years ago. This makes it possible for China's real per capita GDP in 2005 to be nine times that of 1978 (although this also resulted in the birth of 90 million children with no siblings). In comparison, many countries in Latin America achieved only 10 percent growth during the same thirty-year period.

The power of compounding means that small differences in growth rates can cause very large differences in gross and per capita levels of output over a short time (between China and India), and that large differences in gross per capita output can be eliminated much more quickly than is often imagined (between China and the U.S.). Even though China has a much larger population, its per capita GDP can catch up from one-twenty-fifth to one-quarter that of the U.S. in thirty years. During the height of the Ming Dynasty 500 years ago, China's GDP was around 40 percent of the total GDP of the world, and its per capita GDP led the world. From the sixteenth century forward, China's per capita GDP began to lag behind that of the developing world. But at the beginning of nineteenth century, China's GDP was still about one-third of the total world GDP. Looking ahead into the twenty-first century, the tide is changing in favor of China again.

China's economic expansion that saw its GDP rise by around 10 percent in recent years has been powered by its high domestic savings rate (in the form of enterprise retained earnings and public savings). After averaging 40 percent or so of GDP for most of the 1990s, the savings rate has grown over the past couple of years to over 50 percent of GDP. This is an unprecedented number, and while a portion has been invested abroad in U.S. Treasury bonds (thus funding the U.S. current account deficit and keeping U.S. interest rates low), the vast majority has been invested in the domestic Chinese economy, which is why it makes many believe that China's spendthrift savings culture contributes a lot to its current economic miracle.

In 2005, *The Wall Street Journal* interviewed ten recipients of the Nobel Prize in Economics. Two questions pertained to China. The first question was: "Seventy-five years from now, the largest economic entity in the world is likely to be the United States, the European Union, or China?" Here are the responses from the Nobel Prize laureates.[25]

Kenneth J. Arrow: "Unless there are fundamental changes in economic growth situations, China will be the largest economic entity in the world in seventy-five years' time."

Ronald H. Coase: "China will surpass the United States and the European Union in seventy-five years' time. I firmly believe that."

Milton Friedman: "China."

Lawrence R. Klein: "Seventy-five years later, the largest economic entity in the world will likely be China."

Harry M. Markowitz: "China."

William F. Sharpe: "The probability of China being the top country economically is 50 percent, European Union is 30 percent and the United States is 20 percent."

Robert M. Solow: "Based upon economic value, it may be China."

The second question was: "Which country or region has the most rational economic policies right now?"

Kenneth J. Arrow: "Good policies are one thing, but the effects are something else. We must say that based upon experience, the economic policies in the China-Taiwan area and Korea are against the standards of economics, but their policies are really reasonable."

Harry M. Markowitz: "America's 'Free Market' is the best policy, followed closely by China."

Joseph E. Stiglitz: "Based upon the overall economic performance, China is obviously the best, and it has also shown excellent economic management abilities during the East Asian financial crises. From the viewpoint to economic growth rate and flexibility, China has been highly impressive."

On the other hand, U.S. Treasury Secretary Henry Paulson believed that China faces important "downside" risks and is unlikely to overtake the United States as the world's largest economy (with a GDP of nearly $13 trillion): "China's remarkable success since market reforms began in 1978 has led many to predict that its meteoric growth will continue indefinitely—that we can extrapolate its future growth from its past performance—as if China has somehow found a way to immunize itself from business cycles and all other economic problems."[26]

In the sense that China cannot defy economic gravity, this statement could be true. Considering China's reliance on U.S. consumption and the many gaps in economic performance, university, science, and innovation between China and the U.S.,[27] it can be argued that it is indeed unlikely for China to overtake the U.S. economy in the near future. However, a consumer-led U.S. downswing of its debt economy can hurt China's exports to the U.S. as much as it can hurt America itself. The appreciation of the Chinese yuan and the depreciation of U.S. dollar may well shorten the time for the Chinese economy to catch up. Also, when the U.S. was catching up with Great Britain in the nineteenth century, its GDP growth rate was under 4 percent, compared with China's over 9 percent in the last thirty years.

There is simply no reason for the U.S. to take China's social problems for granted by always assuming a "coming collapse." But "economic gravity" is not the only gravity a country may face. Whether China will surpass the U.S. not only depends on if China can go on rising, but also depends on whether the U.S. continues to sink in the ongoing Iraq quagmire, squandering on average $8 billion per month. In the U.S. war on terror, there won't be any room for mistakes or miscalculations. America will have to stand the test from both "the clash of civilizations" and "the challenge of globalization" in the new century. Production is not the only factor determining a country's economic power; economic growth relies on production as much as on how domestic distribution and military reach are institutionalized.

The First-World "Bizocrats" of China

The expansion of China's economy lies not only in stunning statistics; it also manifests itself on people's faces and on the skylines of their cities. When you plan your first visit to China, prepared to be dazzled by its frenzied pace, hyperactive streets, crowded stores, colorful nightlife, and seemingly never-ending construction. Every year, almost half of all concrete used in construction worldwide is poured in China.

Massive infrastructure projects are coming to Beijing, notably the series of new metro lines, the airport light rail line, new expressways, and new sports facilities. Eager to reach out to the world, Beijing is being made over for the Olympics in what can only be described as a "pedal to the metal" approach. The 2008 Games has turned much of the city into a raucous construction zone. Visitors, some to their great disappointment, will find many traditional courtyard houses (*si he yuan*) and quaint alleyways (*hutong*) that had characterized most of the ancient areas of the city, razed, replaced by grandiose real estate projects. By 2008, $40 billion will be spent for a new Beijing, three times that of Athens's infrastructure spending for the 2004 Games. Among the building projects that take one's breath away are the new National Stadium, the National Swimming Center, the new CCTV building, and the Grand Theater: the new architectural wonders of China.

Qianmen Avenue, running through one of Beijing's most historic districts, is being transformed into a massive pedestrian thoroughfare with restaurants and stores along its length. Elsewhere, China's old-fashioned department stores, which never had much going for them except for their historic, Soviet-era architecture, have been replaced by glass-walled supermarkets and gleaming new multilevel shopping malls, jam-packed by customers with deep pockets, while family shoppers swarm through and stuff their purchases into shiny new cars. Sound familiar?

The Olympics have fired up China's impulse to impress the world with its economic success, in whatever way possible and by whatever means necessary—even when historic preservation must be compromised. With all the changes, the streams of bicycles with blue-jacketed workers that once characterized Beijing's rush hour are found only in memory. Today, Beijing's wide new boulevards and ring roads are choked with privately owned cars. As many people own larger apartment homes, the much-envied new rich are increasingly seen in their Mercedes-Benz and BMW automobiles. Beijing set an ambitious 245-day "blue sky" target for 2007 after beating the annual good-air-quality day target of 238 days in 2006. The city is ready to embrace its new glory in 2008. A campaign to replace poorly translated English street signs is already underway, and despite the horrendous traffic congestion, the city is ready to embrace its newfound place on the world's stage in 2008.

In Shanghai, streets are lined with trees, and flowers are neatly planted along major thoroughfares. While bicycles still zoom around Shanghai, a common scene is skyscrapers towering over bustling streets lined with expensive stores and shopping malls. Shanghai, always China's cosmopolitan jewel, is getting a twenty-first century makeover. Its neon lights glow twenty-four hours a day.

Big, powerful, and rich, Shanghai is home to one of the world's tallest hotels, China's trendiest restaurants, Asia's largest shopping mall, and some of China's most luxurious stores. There are hundreds of major buildings underway and one of them, the Shanghai World Financial Centre, will be 492 meters (1,615 feet) tall, over 300 feet taller than the Empire State Building. Shanghai boasts 4,000 buildings over fifteen stories: New York City has half that many.

What really sets Shanghai apart from the rest of the world's major cities, however, is that almost all of Shanghai's big towers have been built since 1990. In 2010, the "new Shanghai" will host a World Expo expected to attract seventy million visitors from inside China and across the globe.[28]

The Yangshan deep-water port in Shanghai's Nanhui District is the largest port project ever built in China and is the largest port project currently under construction in the world. The Lingang Industrial Area enjoys a status of "Free Port" (referred to as "Bonded Port" in Chinese), where bonded manufacturing inside the port area is allowed; and with the combined functions of the export processing zone, free trade zone, and bonded logistics park, it offers one of the most open and most favorable manufacturing regions in China. When the port is completed in 2012, Shanghai will overtake Singapore as the world's number one port and will be in a much better position to compete against Taiwan's Kaohsiung, South Korea's Busan, and Japan's Yokohama. China's "eco-city" Dongtan is also close to Shanghai. While Beijing remains China's cultural capital, Shanghai is without question the face of future China. In June 2007, the Hangzhou Bay Bridge was completed and stands as the world's longest sea-crossing bridge, a 36-kilometre-long (22.5-mile-long) road links Cixi City in Zhejiang province with Jiaxing City to the north, shortening the journey between Shanghai and the major port of Ningbo by 120 km (75 miles).

In China's southern Guangdong Province, Shenzhen, the first "Special Economic Zone" and one of Deng Xiaoping's signature projects in the early 1980s, is known as a veritable Mecca for high-tech workers in China. Twenty years ago it was a small village surrounded by marshland. In recent years, it has experienced an increase of more than one million permanent residents. Shenzhen now leads the country in terms of population density, with 4,239 people per square kilometer for a population of nearly nine million.

Shenzhen has the fourth-largest container port in the world and the third-largest port in China. Futian Free Trade Zone, Shatoujiao Free Trade Zone, and Yantian Port Free Trade Zone form one of the business manufacturing sectors in China. Shenzhen is China's "Dodge City," the hustler capital of New China, a classic frontier town, a place on the make, unashamedly *nouveau riche*, with an average age of less than thirty. The city is home to the world's biggest golf club, the opulent and breathtakingly large Mission Hills. Its 180 holes spread out over ten courses, each designed by a different top golfer. Shenzhen also reportedly has 120,000 sex workers, making it China's vice capital.[29]

China has more than 160 cities with populations over one million, far exceeding the sum of those in the U.S. and Europe. For the urbanization rate to rise from 20 percent to 40 percent, Britain took 120 years, France 100, Germany eighty, the United States forty, the Former Soviet Union thirty, Japan thirty, and China took twenty-two. Growth, furthermore, along China's coastal cities, is staggering:

- In 1980, China established Special Economic Zones in Shenzhen, Zhuhai and Shantou in Guangdong Province and Xiamen in Fujian Province, and designated the entire island province of Hainan as a Special Economic Zone.

- In 1984, China further opened fourteen coastal cities to foreign investment: Dalian, Qinhuangdao, Tianjin, Yantai, Qingdao, Lianyungang, Nantong, Shanghai, Ningbo, Wenzhou, Fuzhou, Guangzhou, Zhanjiang, and Beihai.

- In 1985, the Chinese government decided to extend its open door policy to a wider range of coastal areas: the Yangzi River Delta, Pearl River Delta, Xiamen-Zhangzhou-Quanzhou Triangle in south Fujian, Shandong Peninsula, Liaodong Peninsula, Hebei, and Guangxi.

- In 1990, the government decided to open the Pudong New Zone in Shanghai to overseas investment, and opened more cities westward along the Yangzi River.

- In 1992, China started to open a number of border cities, and all the capital cities of inland provinces and autonomous regions. In addition, fifteen free trade zones, thirty-two state-level economic and technological development zones, and fifty-three new and high-tech industrial development zones had been established in large and medium-sized cities countrywide.

- In 2006, China decided to expand its opening-up strategy for three coastal and three inland areas. The coastal areas are the Pearl River Delta, the Yangzi River Delta, and the Bohai-rim Region around the Tianjin-based Binhai New Zone. The inland areas are border cities and provinces in the northwest, northeast, and southwest of China. The three coastal areas are mainly being opened as sea routes that will take advantage of industry in other coastal port cities, depending primarily on overseas investment, international industry transfer, and developing processing and manufacturing industries. The opening-up of China's southwest will rely chiefly on the China-ASEAN free trade area; the northwest region will take advantage of the Shanghai Cooperation Organization; and the northeast will rely on economic cooperation with Russia, South Korea, and Japan. The opening-up of the three inland areas is in line with China's plan to develop the western part of the country and revitalize northeast China as well as other old industrial bases.

This is arguably the largest well-planned economic development rollout in human history and an economic mega-boom of the highest order. One outcome is the rise of a new class of entrepreneurs—"Bizocrats"—and a group of large firms that are active in the international business arena. Today, business revenue of the top 500 Chinese enterprises accounts for more than 70 percent of China's GDP.

Baosteel Group Corp., China's biggest steelmaker, topped the list of 500 companies with 176 billion yuan in sales in 2005. Among the 100 largest multinational corporations from emerging markets, fifty are from China. Ten Chinese companies were listed in the *Fortune* Global 500 in 2000. In 2006, the number increased to nineteen. Sinopec, China's largest company, is number twenty-three on the list. Companies considered "world class" include Lenovo (formerly Legend), Haier, Huawei, and Hong Kong's Hutchison Whampoa. More are on the horizon. In 2005, twenty-eight Chinese companies were listed in *Forbes* Global 2000. PetroChina ranks fifty-two among "The World's 2000 Largest Public Companies," and it ranks No. 2 in Asia's Fabulous Fifty Companies, right behind Toyota. Both Warren Buffett's Berkshire Hathaway and Harvard University's $29.2 billion endowment have invested in PetroChina.

While multinational corporations poured in billions of dollars, euros, and yen to expand in China, Chinese companies are going overseas on a buying spree to win access to raw materials, technology, and consumer brands. They also seek a way into new markets that could help them realize their growth aspirations. So far, mining, oil, and gas assets have dominated their acquisitions list. But the range of assets has been getting wider with the help of cheap financing from Chinese state-owned banks and being in a great position to cut costs at acquired companies by shifting the manufacturing to mainland China.

In 2005, China's investment in foreign countries soared by 123 percent to $12.3 billion, raising Chinese investments abroad to a total of $57.2

billion. The top investment destinations were Hong Kong, the United States, Japan, and Russia, half of which were invested in mergers and acquisitions. More than 9,000 Chinese companies set up operations in more than 170 countries around the world. As new rules effective May 2006 encourage companies and individuals to make investments overseas for the first time, total outlay by Chinese companies on foreign deals may grow in the next few years.

The Chinese need to go abroad for resources to feed their industrial machine and to scale up the talent and research they can't find at home. China-driven resource prices have already helped countries like Australia experience its longest period of economic boom since federation in 1901. The value of Australian mineral exports to China has risen almost tenfold in the past decade, from about $1 billion in 1996 to at least $8.5 billion in 2005.

Flush with cash and in command of the world's lowest-cost manufacturing plants, China will buy into the industries in which it already competes heavily, particularly electronics, auto parts, appliances, textiles, and apparel. In these industries, acquiring global supply chains can confer big advantages, especially for low-cost players. The Chinese understand that buying assets abroad is not equal to operating in world markets. The key is to set up interactive operations around the world.

The pace at which Chinese companies are learning and catching up could soon alter the playing field of international business. Boston Consulting Group, in a recent review of 515 Chinese mergers and acquisitions since 1986, found that 223 deals involved Chinese companies acquiring foreign operations with a total value of about $18 billion. Other categories included 186 deals of purchasing stakes in foreign companies, 76 deals of buying out the mainland assets of a foreign joint-venture partner, and 30 deals of Chinese investment in foreign assets in the country. After China joined the WTO in 2001, Chinese M&A transactions took on a more outward appearance with stronger government support. Some of the major M&A transactions and market expansions include:

- Beijing-based Lenovo Group Ltd. (formerly Legend) China's biggest computer maker, bought a controlling stake in IBM's PC operations for $1.75 billion in 2004, a deal considered a "snake eats elephant story."

- Huawei Tech., the No. 1 telecom equipment maker of China, passed a significant milestone in 2005 when international sales revenue surpassed domestic sales for the first time. The firm has products in over 100 countries worldwide. Huawei's presence in the U.S. through its subsidiary FutureWei is the biggest threat to Cisco Systems. Huawei's international expansion has been considered the most game-changing factor in the telecom supply market in the past five years. Its no-holds-barred expansion found other global telecom suppliers doing little more than watching in stunned silence. Nearly half of Huawei's global workforce of 44,000+ focuses on R&D, and it's boosting its software development team into the service giant India.

- ZTE (*zhongxin*), Huawei's local rival, with about 40 percent of Huawei's sales or $2.6 billion in 2005, is also beginning to move aggressively outside China. ZTE is looking to international acquisitions to help it close the gap with Huawei.

- Huizhou-based TCL Corp. snapped up French Thomson's television brand to create the world's biggest TV manufacturer with the venerable brand name RCA. The company also took over Thomson's DVD player operations and Alcatel's mobile phone unit, all within six months during 2003 and 2004.

- China National Petroleum Corp. (parent of New York Stock Exchange-listed PetroChina), Sinopec (an oil-and-gas company), and CNOOC (an offshore driller) have each invested billions in oil-and-gas projects in Africa, Southeast Asia, and Latin America.[30] These three state oil companies now have interests in nearly twenty African countries, from Libya in the north, to Nigeria in the west, Angola in the south, and Ethiopia in the east. Sinopec also holds a 51 percent stake in the Iran oil field at Yadavaran. On June 23, 2005, the China National Offshore Oil Corporation, through its Hong Kong subsidiary, made huge waves by bidding to buy the U.S. energy company UNOCAL for $18.5 billion. On August 2, 2005, CNOOC withdrew its bid due to U.S. concerns for the national security of one of its key strategic resources.

- Shanghai Automotive Industry Corp., one of China's largest carmakers, bought a 48.9 percent stake in Korean truck maker SsangYong for close to $500 million in 2004. In October 2006, the company launched its first own-brand car, the unintentionally hilariously named "Rongwei," based on technology from the once-dominant British carmaker Rover.

- The Nanjing Automobile Corporation also adopted the "lift and shift" approach. Its bid over Britain's troubled MG Rover Group Ltd. was accepted in July 2005. The company plans to build MG-brand cars in Oklahoma, becoming the first Chinese carmaker to assemble cars in the United States. It will locate its headquarters in Oklahoma City with assembly and distribution in Ardmore, and research and development facilities at the University of Oklahoma in Norman.

- Fuyao Group Glass Industries Co. Ltd., China's biggest auto glassmaker, is set to bid for the North American glass-making assets of Ford Motor Co. The bid would mark another effort by the Chinese auto industry to expand overseas by buying distressed assets from a foreign firm.

- Geely Automobile Holdings Ltd. plans to sell cars in the United States as early as 2008. It is now also considering making cars in the U.S. as an option for market entry. In 2006, it exported nearly 20,000 cars to developing countries, and expects to double its exports in 2007. It also partners with Britain's Manganese Bronze Holdings Plc to produce around 40,000 cars annually—about 10,000 of the London cabs and 30,000 limousines or sedans in Shanghai.

- Following Geely, Hunan-based Changfeng Motors Group displayed its five-passenger Liebao at the 2007 Detroit auto show. Changfeng, state-owned and with a minority stake by Mitsubishi, could enter the U.S. market as soon as 2008. Zhongxing Automobile also had a number of vehicles on display, and it plans to begin selling in the U.S. as early as the end of 2007.

- Great Wall Motors entered the European market with a shipment of 500 sport utility vehicles to Italy in 2006. Great Wall is also looking for distributors for its Hover SUV in Spain and Greece. The Hong Kong–listed company is among the Chinese carmakers planning to sell vehicles in European and U.S. markets.

- The first Chinese vehicle exporter, Chery Automobile, will set up a joint venture in Chery's home city of Wuhu with Johnson Controls Inc. of the United States to make auto interiors. Chery is also working out a deal with DaimlerChrysler to make subcompacts in Wuhu for the American market. In 2007, Chery produced its one-millionth automobile, and will reach sales of one million annually by 2010.

- Brilliance China Automotive Holdings Ltd., the domestic partner of BMW AG, will export 158,000 Zhonghua-brand sedans to Germany within five years. The move comes after Brilliance broke into more than twenty-three overseas markets with thirty-three dealers in Africa, North and South America, and the Middle East.

- Global scale has motivated Hangzhou-based auto-parts maker Wanxiang Group to buy more than ten overseas companies in the last few years, including NASDAQ-listed Universal Automotive Industries Inc.

Wanxiang Chairman Lu Guanqiu's goal is to combine international and domestic resources to speed up development. Wanxiang America is now operating in Elgin, Illinois. Wanxiang America's president Ni Pin is just as ambitious; his goal is to build Wanxiang into one of the world's biggest auto-parts companies.

- As China's leading maker of refrigerators, air conditioners, and washing machines, Haier is actively expanding its international markets. It invested more than $40 million in a refrigerator manufacturing plant in Camden, South Carolina, and built it into the Haier America Industrial Park. In 2005, Haier Group also took part in the bidding war over Maytag Corporation. With an annual production capacity of over 120 million, China is the world's largest base for air conditioner production. Its air conditioner market is now dominated by Haier, Gree, and Midea, whose market share is a combined 56 percent. In 2006, the export of China-made air conditioners exceeded domestic sales for the first time since the country started to export air conditioners sixteen years ago.

- As the world's largest producer of microwave ovens and one of China's largest air-conditioner exporters, Galanz exemplifies China's production model for home electrical appliances. Its ability to disperse into over 130 countries makes it another big success story in the international market.

- Hunan-based privately owned Sany Corp. plans to build a plant in the United States, potentially becoming the first Chinese machinery maker to assemble equipment in the U.S. Sany will initially invest $9 million in the U.S. plant, rising to $50 million three years later.

- China International Marine Container (CIMC), a shipping container and semi-trailer company, is already selling in the U.S. CIMC's subsidiary, Vanguard National Trailer Group, bought Indiana company HPA Monon and created hundreds of jobs. The company uses a U.S. name and many people aren't aware that it's Chinese owned.

- Techtronic, a power tool maker that competes with Maryland-based Black & Decker, started out as a contract manufacturer with factories in China. Techtronic has branched out and acquired older appliance and power tool brands, and makes private label tools for Home Depot. The company has 11 percent market share and is gaining on Black & Decker's.

- China Mobile, the world's largest mobile phone company with more than 300 million subscribers across the mainland, made its first overseas acquisition in early 2007 by buying an 89-percent stake in Pakistan's Paktel, a company owned by Luxembourg-based Millicom International Cellular.

- The Industrial and Commercial Bank of China (ICBC), the country's biggest lender, is expanding its overseas services and gaining a larger market share in Europe. By the end of 2005, ICBC created 106 branches around the world and established ties with 1,165 banks in 114 countries and regions.

- China's National Council for Social Security Fund selected Citigroup Inc. and Northern Trust Corp. as custodians for the fund's overseas investments, which could be up to 20 percent of its total assets of 230 billion yuan.

- China's first qualified domestic institutional investor (QDII) fund, managed by Hua An Fund Management Co., Ltd., will invest in stocks, bonds, real estate investment trusts, and other mainstream financial products in international markets such as New York, London, Tokyo, and Hong Kong. China launched the QDII scheme in July 2006, allowing domestic institutions and residents to buy financial products overseas via mainland commercial banks and other financial institutions.

As companies prosper, more and more entrepreneurs and businessmen are getting rich. And the wealthiest get more wealthy as the nation's economy continues to boom. While Hong Kong's Li Ka-shing still tops *Forbes*'s The World's Richest People (Li ranked No. 10 in 2006), Hong Kong is no longer the only place that produces business tycoons. Claimed to be the richest teacher in China, Yu Minhong's success story is one of the biggest in the country. When Yu began to make his hard-earned money from teaching TOEFL, GRE, and GMAT test preparations in the 1980s, the school he founded consisted of merely three teachers, a few administrative staff, and some street boys who helped claim territory for its "ad posts" on public bulletin boards in west Beijing. The waves of Chinese students going to America for graduate studies gave Yu solid footing, while the country's open-door policy sharpened his vision for the growth potential of an English language and test preparation provider.

At first, Yu was like a shy college kid; the status of a private school was still in the gray area of government policy. Yu's New Oriental Education & Technology Group Inc. took off in 1993, and Yu quickly moved into teaching practical English in 1996. New Oriental is now the largest provider of private educational services in China, based on the number of program offerings, total student enrollment, and geographic presence. It is also expanding into the professional certification preparation field, which includes preparation for the PRC bar exam, and the CPA and civil service exams.

When the company's IPO landed on Wall Street in September 2006, Yu's three-teacher school had become a little empire with 1,700 trained instructors, 375,000 annual enrolled students for test preparation, 497,000 annual enrolled students for foreign language learning, and two million registered online users through a network of 25 schools, 111 learning centers, and 13 bookstores in twenty-four cities. Since 2004, New Oriental's revenues have increased at an annual compounded growth rate of 32 percent to $96.1 million; net income totaled $6.2 million. With an initial market capitalization of $529 million, Yu is surely a new star among China's bizocrats, many of whom now take on the new mission of balancing investor-expected growth with quality brand names customers expect.

New Oriental is only one of the many successful Chinese companies making a splash on Wall Street. While New Oriental and other big names like China Life and PetroChina chose to list on the New York Stock Exchange, many more are listed on Nasdaq. In fact, Chinese companies are the Nasdaq's biggest source of new listings and they appear undaunted by stricter legal requirements. Twenty-nine firms from mainland China and fifty firms from Hong Kong place China third behind first-place Israel and second-place Canada in having the most non-U.S. listings on the Nasdaq index.

With more than 300,000 millionaires in the country, the Chinese are now looking to stories of billionaires for inspiration. According to *Forbes*, China was home to three billionaires in 2004, ten in 2005, and fifteen in 2006. With more than 100 new faces, the total wealth of the 400 richest Chinese soared 51 percent from $18 billion in 2004, to $26 billion in 2005, to $38 billion 2006. The minimum wealth required to make the list was $100 million—$38 million more than in 2005.

Forbes found that more than a quarter of the top forty Chinese are under age forty, an average age much younger than that of America's richest. "Business—stock listing—wealth" is the pattern for many Chinese all-first-generation *nouveau riche*. The top five all have companies listed on the prestigious Hang Seng index, Hong Kong's leading stock market listing; and sixty-five of the top 100 companies now have a major foothold in international stock markets.

Among the 400 richest Chinese, half are from China's most developed regions: sixty-six from Guangzhou and the Pearl River region, followed by Zhejiang with forty-seven, Shanghai forty-six, and Beijing forty-two.

Huang Guangyu (Wong Kwong Yu), the thirty-eight-year-old native of Shantou and owner of electrical-appliance giant Gome Electrical Appliances, led the 2006 list with a net worth of $2.3 billion. Huang is seen by many as the "new" Li Ka-shing, also from Shantou. The richest man on the 2005 list, Rong Zhijian, who runs Citic Pacific, one of China's most successful conglomerates, dropped to third place with a net worth of $2 billion. Other big names include Ma Huateng of Tencent (also a native of Shantou, runs qq.com), Shi Zhengrong of Suntech Power, Lu Guanqiu of Wanxiang Group, William Ding Lei of Netease.com, Chu Lam Yiu of Huabao International, Chen Lihua of Fu Wah International HK Group, Lin Li of Ping An Insurance, Zong Qinghou of Wahaha Group, and Lan Shili of China East Star Group.[31]

It was a national sensation when China's "2006 Hurun Millionaire Report" revealed that a female paper recycling entrepreneur, worth an estimated 27 billion yuan ($3.4 billion), topped the list. Zhang Yin, the first woman to be named China's wealthiest person, is also the world's richest self-made woman, surpassing Oprah Winfrey, J.K. Rowling, and Martha Stewart. Zhang was ranked as the fifth-richest by *Forbes* by a different calculation. Her company, Nine Dragons Paper, listed in Hong Kong in March 2006, buys scrap paper from the U.S. and processes it into boxes and other packaging products in China.

Among the ten richest people on Hurun's list, seven have their companies listed in Hong Kong. Hurun's report also shows China's billionaires club is growing fast with fifteen members in 2006. Several female executives joined the ranks of the prosperous and powerful, accounting for 6 percent of the top 500. *Fortune* magazine has Baosteel Group chairman Xie Qihua and Lenovo CFO Mary Ma in its top ten ranking of China's most powerful international businesswomen.[32] China's richest mostly live in Guangdong or Zhejiang provinces, and often are active in real estate as six out of the top ten are from that industry. Huang Guangyu is ranked second with $2.5 billion. Rong Zhijian, who topped *Forbes* magazine's 2005 list, was sixth with $1.8 billion—but came in first on Hurun's "China Power List."

Ironically, the *Fortune* and *Forbes* lists were once seen as a "death list" in China. Some on the list, especially those whose fortunes were related to real estate, became "automatic" targets of tax fraud investigations or corruption crackdowns—and some ended up in jail. To be rich may be glorious, but sometimes it's better to get rich quietly—sans fanfare or press. Zhang Rongkun, chairman of Fuxi Investments Holding and sixteenth on the *Forbes* 2005 list, was arrested in connection with improper loans. Even some of China's top moguls cannot avoid scrutiny or allegations of wrongdoing and the much-debated "original sin" (*yuanzui*, or, getting rich in a sneaky way). But it is no accident that many new rich are rising from those industries that have been open to private competition, which is a sharp contrast to the early billionaires in America (Rockefeller, Carnegie, etc.) who were mostly from the oil and steel industries (that China has not yet opened to private enterprise).

Equally interesting, many Chinese who came to study and stay in the U.S. eagerly returned home or started to do business with China from America. From 1978 to the end of 2005, Chinese students studying abroad totaled 930,000, among whom 230,000 have returned. Of the 700,000 Chinese students still living abroad, about 160,000 have finished their studies and begun to work, while 500,000 are still studying. Overseas students, once the much-envied minority, are now jokingly called "sea turtles" because the Chinese pronunciation of "overseas returnees," haigui, sounds like "sea turtles," while the pronunciation of "unemployed returnees," haidai, sounds like "sea weeds."

In less than three decades, millions of Chinese have joined the middle class. Based on per capita income of $6,000 as the middle class criteria for developing countries, the Chinese urban middle class was approximately 250 million strong in 2005 and could reach 400 million by 2010. By a different standard, middle class were those with household incomes over 80,000 yuan (about $10,000) in Beijing, Shanghai, Guangzhou, and Hangzhou, or over 60,000 yuan in smaller cities.

Fixed deposits, stocks, and funds are the three major investment channels for these families, with 56.2 percent holding fixed deposit accounts, 42.9 percent investing in stocks, and 24.5 percent investing in funds. With the boom of the stock market, over 100 milion trading accounts have been established across the country. China currently has more than 320 mutual funds. Investors pumped 387 billion yuan into Chinese funds in 2006, pushing assets under management to 856 billion yuan.

Ninety-five percent of middle class families own their own homes, and real estate remains a major investment sector for them. German, Japanese, and U.S.-brand cars are their favorites, while only 4 percent own a domestic brand. As villa homes, luxury cars, yachts, and other expensive luxury goods like diamonds and gold are commonplace for the new rich, the hiring of not only servants, but wet nurses (young women of childbearing age hired to breastfeed the offspring of the rich—a throwback to the typical trappings of wealth among China's richest families before the Communist Revolution) is increasingly common in China's eastern cities.

According to Merrill Lynch & Co, the more than 300,000 Chinese who have a net worth over $1 million control some $530 billion in assets. The rich also invest in art. A painting by the early twentieth-century Chinese artist Xu Beihong (known for his depiction of horses) fetched 33 million yuan ($4.1 million) at an auction in the summer of 2006. The frenzy was echoed by the gobbling up of Chinese art in Sotheby's auction of contemporary Asian art in New York. The top ten buyers among Hong Kong's auction houses are full of names of mainland investors.

Just five years ago mainland buyers accounted for 1 percent of global sales of luxury handbags, shoes, jewelry, perfume, and the like. Today the Chinese are the third most-numerous high-end buyers on earth, with more than 12 percent of world sales. Goldman, Sachs & Co. predicted that, within a decade, China will likely leapfrog Japan and the U.S. to become the top luxury market in the world.

Many Chinese still observe their traditional love festival on the seventh day of the seventh lunar month, but Valentine's Day has gained unprecedented popularity in China. On Valentine's Day, 2007, a Shanghai banker spent 40,000 yuan on a Cartier watch for his wife, a value twelve times more than the average Chinese farmer earns in a year. JW Marriott Hotel in Shanghai fashioned a 28,888-yuan package, including an overnight stay in either its Chairman's Suite or the Presidential Suite, and a romantic cruise on a luxury yacht along the Huangpu River. In 2006, one hotel offered a Valentine package for a staggering 188,888 yuan.[33] A 2005 survey conducted jointly by AC Nielsen and Tax Free World Association (TFWA) tracked, for six months, 1,500 consumers from Beijing, Shanghai, and Guangzhou who visited Asia and Europe. The survey revealed that each of these tourists spent $987 on average shopping abroad, ranking them first worldwide. On average, their shopping expenses were one-third of their total tourism budget, enough to make store owners willingly gloss over some of the atrocious manners often exhibited by Chinese mainland tourists.

In 2004, twenty-nine million people from the Chinese mainland traveled abroad, a year-on-year increase of 43 percent. About thirty-one million Chinese traveled abroad in 2005, making China the largest exporter of tourists in Asia. While over 90 percent of Chinese tourists visited other Asian nations, more and more are visiting Europe, Australia, North America, Africa, and the rest of the world. In 2005, over 31 million Chinese tourists went overseas, an increase of 8 percent, including 530,000 people who traveled to the United States, up 20 percent. The United States is now the fifth most popular destination for Chinese tourists. By 2025, with a population near 1.8 billion and a rapidly growing middle class, China's tourists heading overseas on holidays may number 100 million.

China is now one of the top four global tourist destinations. In 2005, inbound tourists numbered 120 million, a new record, up from a mere 230,000 in 1978. Applications by foreign visitors for travel visas to China continues to rise. Tourists can be found in every corner of the China, and China's tourism industry is scrambling to meet their needs.

For the culturally inclined, a popular saying goes: "To see 25 years of Chinese history, go to Shenzhen; for 150 years, go to Shanghai; for 500 years, go to Beijing; and for 5,000 years, go to Xi'an."[34] China is projected to become the No. 1 tourist destination worldwide within only a few years. Industry numbers are formidable: total tourist income for 2005 reached $96 billion, an amazing change considering that China's tourism sector hardly existed thirty years ago. The sector now employs over seven million people directly and over thirty-three million indirectly.

The most spectacular change of recent years has been a shift from foreign to domestic tourism. While overseas tourists contributed $29.3 billion to the Chinese economy in 2005, their contribution was far outweighed by that of domestic Chinese tourists, who contributed $66.7 billion. China is already the world's biggest domestic tourism market in terms of sheer numbers.

Naturally, the Chinese tourism boom has attracted interest from big global players like Hilton, Holiday Inn, Shangri-la, Sheraton, and ANA, among others, whose hotels can now be found in most Chinese cities. As the "Sky Train" rides the rails onto the world's highest plateau, Tibet now becomes one of the hottest tourist destinations.

The rise of domestic online travel agents, led by Ctrip.com and eLong Inc., helps boost tourism and the rapid expansion of the otherwise fragmented service industry. The tourism explosion helped Lan Shili's East Star Group quickly emerge from a travel agency to become the best private-owned airliner in China today.

The downside to all this tourism is that most, if not all, of China's most majestic and important cultural and natural sites are being overrun: Huangshan, Taishan, Xishuangbanna, the Shaolin monastery, among many others, are constantly plagued by long lines, overcrowding, litter, and lack of infrastructure.

Recreating the shopping-center model that defined American youth culture in the 1980s is the latest fad and confers a stamp of "authenticity" on the new Chinese suburbia. About 200 malls, with an anchor store, a food court, entertainment, and parking, operate throughout the country. More are on the way as Chinese consumers begin to show mall-rat tendencies.

McKinsey conducted a study on 800 teen-aged consumers across China. They were divided into four types: the fashionable, the well-behaved, the leisured, and the poor. While the total money spent by children came to about 290 billion yuan ($36.5 billion) a year, around $7.5 billion came from the "pocket money" of these (90 million) only children.

To cool down the overheating economy and encourage more domestic consumer spending, the weeks of Chinese Spring Festival, May 1, and National Day, October 1, are now known as "Golden Weeks." When the first golden week holiday was initiated to celebrate National Day in October 1999, China was astonished to see Chinese tourists take 28 million personal trips while spending $1.62 billion.

China's retail sales surged 15 percent year-on-year to 220 billion yuan during the Spring Festival of 2007. According to *Beijing Youth Daily*, consumers in Beijing spent 15.69 billion yuan during the seven-day holiday to shop, dine, and travel, with average expenditures per person topping 1,000 yuan. Department stores in the capital saw sales jump 8.4 percent, spending in supermarkets was up 16.1 percent, and catering industries saw a 19.7 percent increase in sales. Beijing's traditional-food restaurants witnessed a sales surge of nearly 30 percent.

Until the mid 1990s, workers in China put in six-day work weeks and had only one or two long weekends free during the year. Now, when all weekends and holidays are counted, workers can enjoy up to 114 days off, about a third of the year. The increase in leisure time has naturally spurred a boom to the leisure industry. In such major cities as Beijing, Shanghai, and Guangzhou, recreation has become an engine for urban economic development. Tennis courts are available in many cities, and new tennis stars like Li Na have begun to shine in international competitions. Golf courses, 350 built since 1984, can be seen in almost every big city in Eastern China. Though seen by some as "a vulgar pursuit of lucre," some business schools now require students to learn golf to enhance their future careers. Waltzing is set to become compulsory in every high school, where students will be required to take dance classes to stay fit and acquire more social graces.

Dynamics of the China Market

As the world's fastest growing economy with the largest consumer population of 1.3 billion, the largest mobile phone population of over 461 million users, the second-largest internet population of over 137 million users (52+ million with broadband access and on target to overtake the U.S.), and the largest television audience of more than 350 million households and 1.1 billion viewers, the potential for China's future growth is limited only by one's imagination. Currently, China is the world's largest market for refrigerators and mobile telephones, the second-largest market for PCs and automobiles, the third largest for electronics, and the fourth largest for chemical products. Some 470 of the world's top 500 companies from 200 countries and regions have invested in China, and more are heading in.

China's economic boom is powered largely by cheap rural labor, investment in manufacturing, and export-led, low value-added expansion, a mode of crude economic growth driven by high-energy consumption, high pollution, and high input with low output. As this pattern of growth may take some time to phase out, the market force has started to shift toward industries beyond traditional agriculture and manufacturing. Over 20 percent of investment is currently directed into housing, and 30 percent is invested in infrastructure. Construction, service, and high-tech industries now take a bigger share of the economy.

Market competition compels companies to take innovation seriously and to focus more on the domestic market, especially in the country's second- and third-tier cities, as well as China's "Midwest" region along the Yangzi River. While foreign companies want to tap the country's 1.3 billion consumers, some Chinese firms are desperate to be innovative in winning the cutthroat competition at home. It's a myth that Beijing's one-party politics have bred a timid business culture that prevents domestic firms from developing key technologies, hence keeping them dependent on the West. As China's WTO market-opening pledges were completed by the end of 2006, the China market is more wide open for market penetration and deepening of service industries to accompany such growth. Foreign banks now enjoy a level playing field and are able to compete with Chinese banks on better terms. Since December of 2006, foreign lenders, with registered capital of over one billion yuan, can take yuan deposits from at least one million yuan ($127,000), lend to Chinese retail customers, make loans, take deposits in foreign currencies, and provide yuan-denominated services to corporations.

The China Banking Regulatory Commission (CBRC) approved the first group of nine foreign-funded banks to transform their Chinese branches into locally incorporated banks in Shanghai. The nine banks are the Standard Chartered Bank, the Bank of East Asia, the Hongkong and Shanghai Banking Corp., the Hang Seng Bank, the Mizuho Corporate Bank, the Bank of Tokyo-Mitsubishi UFJ, the DBS Group, Citibank, and the ABN Amro Bank. These nine accounted for 34 percent of all branches run by foreign-funded banks in China as of September 2006. Total assets of foreign-funded banks in China totaled $105.1 billion, accounting for 1.9 percent of all banking institutions in the country. The change gives overseas lenders access to China's pool of individual customers for products like mortgages and credit cards.

Telecom operators and broadcasting network operators can now have both telecom and broadcasting operations after China Mobile (Viacom's alliance through MTV China) acquired a nearly 20 percent stake in Phoenix Satellite Television from Rupert Murdoch's News Corp. More than sixty countries, including Australia, Brazil, Argentina, South Africa, New Zealand, and Russia, have recognized China's status as a market economy. Most notably, twenty-one of the thirty-one countries that had once launched anti-dumping investigations into China have also since recognized China's status as a market economy.

Eight years ago China produced no mobile phones, yet by 2005 it had churned out 300 million handsets. Motorola's "Razr" phone is China's biggest seller, a huge feat in a country that has over 461 million cell phone users, whose norm is to pay for both hardware and the service plan. Nearly fifty million new subscribers were added in 2006. Nokia predicts that China will account for nearly a quarter of the estimated 1.3 billion in new global mobile subscriptions over the next five years. China currently has the world's largest mobile phone network.

Text messaging is all the rage among China's mobile-phone users. Even the Intermediate People's Court of Nanjing started delivering, on request, basic information on filing a lawsuit, court notices, and case-specific information to mobile-phone subscribers by text message. Leading internet portals like Sina.com also provide mobile value-added services to their users.

Leading the trend in entertainment, news, and business reports, Hunan Satellite TV, Phoenix Satellite TV, and Dongfang Satellite TV provide various programs with interactive content, which helps fuel the advertising industry and the growing fan base in entertainment markets to a new high. Even Chinese audiences in the U.S. are glued to their Chinese satellite TV variety shows and dramas, so much so that the geographic divide between China and the US becomes a non-issue. Many forget they are actually sitting in their U.S. living rooms watching Chinese television.

IT is making big waves in China. The country's IT industry accounted for one-sixth of China's GDP and one-third of its exports in 2005. Many see China's 800 million rural population as the next big wave of PCs and mobile phone customers.

There are over 13,000 software companies in China. In 2000, $400 million-worth of software was exported from China; in 2005, it rose to $3.59 billion; and $12.5 billion is predicted for 2010.

The cities of Dalian, Chengdu, Shanghai, Shenzhen, and Xi'an have been designated as base cities for China's service outsourcing business. China intends to spur the rapid growth of its service outsourcing businesses while optimizing its export structure. China has just started in this sector; its offshore service outsourcing exports reached only $900 million in 2005. The scale of the global service outsourcing market, which ranges from $300 to $500 billion, is expected to exceed the one-trillion-dollar mark by the year 2008.

China is by far the most frequently cited location for R&D expansion, well ahead of the U.S. and third-place India. The total number of foreign-invested R&D centers in the country has surged to about 750 from 200 four years ago. By the end of 2007, China and India combined will account for over 30 percent of global R&D staff, up from 19 percent in 2004. More than 75 percent of the world's research and development sites to be set up over the next three years will be in China and India.

A survey of 186 companies worldwide found a general trend of innovation moving east, and predicts that China and India are on the verge of overtaking Western Europe as the most important locations for foreign R&D for U.S. businesses.[35] In 2006, China surpassed Japan to rank number two, with over $136 billion in R&D investment (both remain behind Americans' $330 billion). China's 926,000 researchers, rank second following the U.S. count of 1.3 million.

In 1995, China's spending on R&D as a percentage of GDP more than doubled, from 0.6 percent of GDP to over 1.3 percent in 2005 (2.7 percent for the U.S., 0.77 percent for India). China seeks to boost R&D investment to 2 percent of GDP in 2010, and 2.5 percent by 2020. Much of what is spent in China still comes from foreign companies, since less than 25 percent of Chinese midsize and large enterprises have their own science and technology research facilities. Total R&D spending in China (excluding foreign investment) rose from $11.3 billion in 2000 to $29.4 billion in 2005. Nearly 90 percent of China's high-tech exports, valued at $218.3 billion in 2005, were produced by foreign-invested companies.

To China, technology is about both national pride and economic benefit. It plans to replace the DVD format (Digital Versatile Disc—currently the world standard—with its own EVD (Extended Versatile Disc) in 2008, much like replacing CDMA/WCDMA phone technology with its 3G TD-SCDMA, and Wi-Fi technology with its WAPI. It's also possible that China will bypass the 3G standard for mobile phones and deploy its 4G technology by 2010—a technology initiated in 2001 to match optical fiber speed at 100 Mbps, which Samsung is also testing.

Incredibly, many speculate that the internet revolution in China is still in its infancy, with more waves to come. While internet users are saturated at 210 million in the U.S., China's internet users will grow from 137 million to over 210 million within two years. A 137 million online population, however, means that 90 percent of Chinese are still off-line. No wonder people have to fight for a seat in almost every internet café.

There were 60 million bloggers in China at the end of 2006, and the number is expected to reach 100 million in 2007. A survey by Baidu.com shows 36.82 million blog sites in China are maintained by sixteen million bloggers. Star blogs, written by celebrities, attract the most attention. Sina.com is host to one of the most successful blogs. Written by Xu Jinglei, a talented and single female movie star and director, the blog became the first in China to receive more than ten million viewers in the course of a few months. Xu's blog immediately drew the attention of advertisers who had long sought ways of making a profit from blogging. Xu's blog later reached forty million viewers.

Though the blog had its share of detractors, it was estimated on paper to be worth $10 million to advertisers. Advanced Micro Devices worked with Xu to create a TV commercial for its 64-bit processors, and sponsored a show on Hunan Satellite TV. A report by the Internet Society of China showed that 9 percent of bloggers write every day, 29 percent write one to three times every week, and 35 percent write four to six times weekly. The number of websites registered in China reached 2.6 million at the end of 2005 and 1.1 million of the them have the ".cn" domain name suffix. Websites increased by 40 percent and websites with the domain name of ".cn" increased by 154 percent in 2005, becoming the largest national domain name in Asia and sixth in the world. The number of web pages soared 269 percent to reach 2.4 billion in 2005.

In 2006, China's online transactions hit one trillion yuan, a sharp rise from 700 billion yuan in 2005. Over three million small and medium-sized companies will choose online transactions: their investment in e-commerce will rise by 35 percent every year to 100 billion yuan in 2010. At present, 99 percent of China's thirty-one million companies are small and medium-sized, and only 800,000 of them make deals over the internet.

Due to the limited use of credit cards, online "B2C" (Business to Consumer) still has huge potential for growth. The siren song of the internet has called out to companies and investors both at home and abroad, enticing them with visions of riches to be mined from the country's vast online population. The biggest such company right now is Tencent, owned in part by Naspers and running www.qq.com—a B2C platform providing IM (instant messaging) and entertainment services through the internet, and mobile phones for 400 million users.

QQ, a cute penguin, Tencent's official mascot, has been powered into a heavyweight brand name recognized by youngsters nationwide. Launched in 1999 with a focus on text messaging, Tencent is now number one in Asia and one of the world's top three most popular IM service providers. Started in September 2005 with the TenPay online payment system, similar to eBay's PayPal and Taobao's AliPay, Tencent lets users pay on Alibaba and eBay with a C2C (Consumer to Consumer) auction platform called PaiPai.com. The company also launched a new search portal, Soso.com, and joined hands with TCL for the first smart interactive television services in China—iTQQ.

Tencent's virtual money "Q coins" have become so popular for purchasing products and services that China's central bank has expressed concern over the coin's possible impact on the value of the yuan. In terms of commanding dominance in its home market, Ma Huateng's Shenzhen-based Tencent is no doubt the envy of all companies in the world.

At the 2006 Beijing Auto Show, organizers set aside 4,000 square meters of space for luxury cars, where top brands, including Bentley, Mercedes-Benz, Rolls-Royce, Maybach and Spyker, showcased their new models. On the second day of the show, a Rolls-Royce Phantom on display was bought for 6.6 million yuan ($825,000) and a Bentley Arnage Mulliner sold for 6.48 million yuan. British brand Rolls-Royce, owned by German carmaker BMW, sold seventy Phantom vehicles in China (including Hong Kong) in 2006, which enabled the world's most populous country to unseat Japan as the firm's No. 3 single market after the United States and the United Kingdom.

China, once a "bicycle kingdom," is now the second-largest auto market in terms of sales (7.2 million), surprisingly overtaking Japan (5.7 million) in 2006, and it expects to surpass the U.S. (16.5 million) within ten years. With the production of nearly 7 million cars, China overtook Germany to become the third-largest car-producing country in 2006, behind the United States and Japan.

China has about 380 million families, each of which makes every effort to have a furnished house/apartment to live in and a vehicle to drive. That's the simple reason China will never have a "glut" of any big-ticket item like houses or cars—and why the housing and car boom has no end in sight. While every G8 country's consumer base is already at 100 percent market penetration, many segments of the China market remain untapped, even unexplored. The car ownership ratio will rise to forty cars for every 1,000 citizens by 2010, compared with the current twenty-four and a ratio of more than 700 in the United States (world average: 120).

Fifty-five million vehicles will be running on China's roads, while the annual production rate will hit nine million units a year in 2010. By the year 2020, there will be 140 million cars in China, seven times the current level, and the number of cars sold annually will rise from 4.4 million units to 20.7 million. As the government relaxes its control policy, more foreign cars flood into the domestic market, as do auto parts as the government shows flexibility in its regulation of auto part imports. Both the EU and U.S. lodged a complaint in 2006 with the WTO over China's planned auto parts tariffs. China decided to postpone the higher tariffs on certain imported auto parts from July 1, 2006 to July 1, 2008. According to the rules, imported car parts making up more than 60 percent of the value of a car would be subject to a tariff of about 28 percent, the same tariff as on completed new cars. Components making up less than that share of a vehicle's value would be charged only 10 to 14 percent.

Penetration of the auto financing industry in China remains low—less than 10 percent of financing in 2005—compared with rates of 60 to 70 percent in Europe and 80 to 90 percent in the United States. It is nevertheless expected to rise to 30 to 40 percent in 2010. In addition, China's secondary car market is essentially a fledgling one, with a mere 460,000 used cars traded in 2004—equivalent to less than 20 percent of the total number of new cars—compared to international norms of 70 percent, and up to 200 to 300 percent in more developed markets such as the U.S. and Germany.

In the U.S., the $26 billion car parking industry has created one million jobs. Yet there is only one legal parking space for every five vehicles in China. In many cities, parked cars line alleys and every sidewalk, causing problems for normal traffic and pedestrians. The market potential in consumer passenger vehicles and related industries will not remain untouched for long.

In the commercial vehicles market, growth has been driven largely by extensive road projects, increased urbanization, and heavy reliance on public transportation. About 2.5 million commercial vehicles were sold in China in 2005, and sales amounted to over 3 million in 2006. Homegrown manufacturers, such as Beiqi Foto, Dongfeng Motor Group Co. Ltd., and China National Heavy Truck, control the lion's share of the domestic market. According to KPMG, China exported $1.17 billion worth of vans, trucks, and buses to over seventy smaller markets in the Middle East and Africa in 2005, some 120,000 commercial vehicles. Clearly the commercial vehicle market has room for joint ventures and opportunities for foreign companies.

China's appetite for air travel is likely to match that of its appetite for cars. U.S. commercial aircraft manufacturer Boeing predicts that China will be the largest market for commercial air travel outside the U.S. for the next twenty years; during this period, China will buy 2,300 aircraft valued at $183 billion. By 2023, Chinese carriers are expected to fly more than 2,801 airplanes, making China the largest commercial aviation market outside the United States. In 2005, the total turnover of scheduled flights of Chinese airlines rose by 12 percent to 25.7 billion ton/kilometer, pushing China's ranking to second, ahead of Germany and behind the U.S.

The auto and air travel market will increase China's overall demand for oil, having surpassed that of Japan's, to become the second largest in the world. By 2020, China is expected to import 70 percent of its oil needs, compared with 40 percent today. Meanwhile, the growth in U.S. oil consumption, starting from a higher base, rivals China's growth when measured in barrels a day instead of percentages. From 1995 to 2004, U.S. oil imports grew by 3.9 million barrels a day, while China's grew by 2.8 million.

During the last twenty years, China has transitioned its oil imports from concentrating on Asia Pacific and the Middle East to diversifying into all oil-producing areas in the world. In 2006, Angola replaced the world's largest oil producer, Saudi Arabia, as China's main oil supplier. Driven by economic expansion and continued demand from China and India, worldwide demand for oil will climb 47 percent. Total global use is expected to increase 71 percent between 2003 and 2030. Crude oil reached a record high of $80 a barrel in the summer of 2007. Similarly, China's share of global crude steel output in 2010 is projected at 42 percent of 1.55 billion tons, up from 31 percent at the end of 2005.

China has become fully self-sufficient in crude steel, coke, and coal, but it still must import 60 percent of its iron ore to meet its steelmaking needs. Statistics also show the astonishing proportion of China's contribution to the increase in world industrial material consumption. China has become the largest consumer of copper, nickel, and zinc; the second-largest buyer of iron ore, and the third-largest buyer of aluminum. It also buys a huge quantity of Thai rubber, Burmese teak, Congo cobalt, and Indonesian pulp and paper. Its consumption of aluminum increased by 50 percent, iron ore by 84 percent, steel by 108 percent, cement 115 percent, zinc 120 percent, and copper and nickel consumption both tripled. As "Made in China" has flooded the world market, "Bought by China" is seen as the most important "single factor" to drive the commodity boom in years to come.

In 2006, China produced about four times as much energy for each ton of standard coal energy as it consumed in 1978. Yet China's coal demand will double in the next decade. In addition to plans for giant hydroelectric stations, such as the Yangzi River dam, China has nine nuclear plants and will build at least thirty more—more than any other nation over a similar time period. China will invite foreign oil companies to explore oil and gas resources in its northwestern Tarim Basin, which has total explorable crude oil reserves of six billion tons and natural gas reserves of eight trillion cubic meters.

On renewable energy, China is set to spend $200 billion over the next fifteen years, a move that attracts industry players racing to grab a piece of the action. China, now the top annual global investor in renewable energy, is building the world's largest solar power station at the "oasis town" of Dunhuang in the poor but sunny northwestern province of Gansu. Credit Suisse estimates the compound annual growth rate of China's wind power capacity at 39 percent between 2004 and 2010, and 20 percent between 2010 and 2020. China aims to have thirty gigawatts of installed wind power capacity by 2020, up from just one gigawatt in 2005, to power between thirteen and thirty million households at full capacity.[36] General Electric Co., Vestas Wind Systems, Gamesa, Hong Kong's CLP Holdings, as well as homegrown firms China Solar Energy Holdings Ltd., Yingli Solar, Goldwind, and Suntech, are all expanding capacity in the country.

China is looking to change its relatively weak position in the Bio-tech sector as it puts Bio-technology high on the country's R&D strategy. With the government's $600 million annual spending on 200 Bio-tech laboratories and 500 related companies, China is rapidly expanding its capabilities in the Bio-tech sector beyond manufacturing lower-end equipment, reagents, and consumables for U.S. and European markets—hoping to learn from and catch up with the U.S. Bio-tech companies who currently account for 60 percent of all Bio-tech patents.

Chinese scientists are taking full advantage of the country's much less restrictive legal environment in bio-research, and Bio-tech startups are offering experimental therapies unavailable or prohibited in the West.

Unlike Europe, China will not turn its back on genetically modified (GM) or transgenic crops so farmers can avoid applying toxic pesticides (Shenzhen-based Biocentury's "Bt cotton" is the widely cited success). In Europe, proponents of genetically modified organisms (GMO) claim that the end-product is what matters, and that if there are no chemical differences between products that contain GMOs and those that do not, the production method is irrelevant. On the other hand, opponents say the production method is the only relevant measure. Recombinant DNA is invasive and unnatural, and the long-term consequences to the ecosystem and the food chain are unknown.

Nor will China reject stem-cell research, as America might do. Shenzhen Beike BioTechnology Co., for instance, is implanting adult stem cells in patients to treat conditions such as autism, ALS/Lou Gehrig's disease, and stroke.

SiBiono GeneTech Co., Ltd., another Shenzhen-based company, received international recognition in 2003 when it developed the world's first licensed gene therapy medication. China's State food and drug regulatory body granted SiBiono permission to produce the medication, now called Gendicine, after five years of clinical trials. The company receives state and private funding and is now working with New Brunswick Scientific Co., Inc., a U.S. lab equipment supplier, to produce 150 million doses of Gendicine per year.

The number of Bio-tech companies exploded between 1997 and 2002, mostly inspired by China's participation in the Human Genome Project, China's sequencing of the rice genome, an influx of returnees with Bio-tech experience, and more available capital. Operations of certain foreign firms are being established in China, including Pfizer Pharmaceuticals (Beijing), Glaxo SmithKline China (Beijing), Novartis Pharmaceutical (Beijing), and Merck China (Shanghai).

Today, more than 300 companies in China are using molecular biology to create products, provide services, and research new drugs. China's biological product market, which generally includes gene engineering drugs, vaccines, antibodies, and blood products, surpassed $2.5 billion in 2004 and is growing in excess of 13 percent per year.[37]

By 2020, China is set to develop its own frontier technologies, such as pharmaceutical elements, genetic operations and protein engineering, dry cell-based human tissue engineering, and new-generation industrial biotechnology. China is expected to enter the top five countries in the world in terms of biotechnology on an industry scale. The output of China's biotechnology industry will hit two trillion yuan ($250 billion), or 5 percent of GDP, in 2020.

China's pharmaceuticals sector is also poised for significant growth, making it attractive for multinational corporations. The government approved more than twenty biopharmaceuticals and granted more than 130 companies Good Manufacturing Practice (GMP) certification. The nation's biopharmaceutical market is primarily generic, and most players are smaller domestic companies that compete on price. According to Kline & Company's study, the mature markets of the U.S. and Western Europe are growing at 2.3 percent and 2.6 percent, while China's emerging market is growing at 8 percent. As Chinese drug makers replace wet granulation production techniques with the direct-compression method and increase exports, there will be more opportunities for outsourcing as well as increased price competition in U.S. and European markets.

Occasionally, people hear stories from China like a bank putting a global positioning system (GPS) device on every new car to track its location in case the owner failed to make loan payments. Bizarre practices may be powered by technology, but the real problem is the lack of reliable solutions for measuring credit risk. And Chinese "face culture" dictates that trust is personal rather than impersonal, yet banks and credit card issuers see opportunities. China's credit card industry is booming and issuers jump into the market in hopes of tapping growing consumer spending as the government eases restrictions on their operations.

The number of credit cards in China topped twelve million in 2005, up from three million just two years earlier. In 2004, Citigroup Inc.'s Citibank and Britain's HSBC Corp. became the first foreign banks to win government approval to issue credit cards in China, working through local lenders. American Express Co. issued a card in China later in the same year. Chinese banks began issuing their own cards in the 1990s, some with foreign help. Wal-Mart also joined the race for a share of China's growing consumer credit market by issuing its own credit cards—one Visa and one Mastercard.[38]

As China evolves from a nation of savers to one with more borrowers and investors, banks are clamoring over the prospects. But risks loom in a market where consumer credit is a novelty and competition is intensifying. By global standards, China's 1.3 billion people have only dabbled in financial services. While households have stashed away some thirty trillion yuan ($4 trillion) in savings,[39] rates of credit card usage, mortgage loans, and car ownership are among the lowest in the world. Things are changing fast as China's surging economy creates an expanding consumer class. JP Morgan expects retail lending in China, including mortgages, credit cards, and car loans, to grow from $247 billion currently to $1 trillion by 2010. Consumer loans are equivalent to just 14 percent of gross domestic product in China, compared with 59 percent in Hong Kong and 65 percent in South Korea. The market for investment products remains underdeveloped.

The Bank of China, the country's number-two lender, has issued only about one million credit cards, compared with 95 million debit cards. It now expects retail loans to increase by 16 to 18 percent a year—faster than growth in the economy and overall lending. The first dual-currency credit card in China was issued in late 2002, and industry players estimate that the number of Chinese packing plastic has risen to about 25 million.

But unchecked growth in consumer lending can backfire, as South Korean banks learned the hard way from a burst credit bubble in late 2002. Reckless card loans and cash advances led to many card firms seeking bail-outs from shareholders and creditors. In China, individuals are only beginning to embrace the concept of revolving credit. The novelty of consumer lending means banks have access to only rudimentary credit data, although default rates on mortgages and cards are very low.[40]

Foreign financial firms have partnered with China's biggest banks, hoping to use their extensive networks to sell their products in the world's fastest growing major economy. Discover cards are being accepted on China's largest bankcard payment network, China Unionpay, and are expected to be accepted at more than 480,000 merchant locations and 90,000 automated teller machines in China. With 37 percent credit card market share, Industrial and Commercial Bank of China (ICBC) has China's largest network, with over 18,000 outlets. American Express and ICBC have jointly developed credit cards since signing a cooperation agreement in March 2004. China's growing popularity among tourists will help boost the credit card industry. From 2006 to 2010, overseas tourists' Visa card spending in China is expected to soar to $250 billion. Domestic tourists' spending by credit card is also on the rise.

In the financial market, China will soon open its commodities futures markets and its new financial derivatives market to foreigners, through China's qualified foreign institutional investor (QFII) program. China currently has two stock exchanges, in Shanghai and Shenzhen, and three futures exchanges for commodities. The value of open interest on the new exchange, the Shanghai Financial Derivatives Exchange, could reach 120 billion yuan within a year of operation. China's futures brokerage industry, with more than 180 firms—similar to the number in the United States—makes up just 0.2 percent of the country's economy. The new markets will attract trading volume and allow foreign investors to hedge their stock investments.

According to China Security Regulatory Commission, QFIIs earned more than twenty billion yuan ($2.5 billion) in China in the past three years. By August 2006, the QFIIs had invested 55.4 billion yuan ($6.93

billion) in China, while their combined assets had risen to 75.5 billion yuan ($9.44 billion). China has awarded investment quotas totaling $9 billion to forty-eight QFIIs since 2003 when it began to allow overseas institutional investors, such as the UBS, Deutsche Bank, and Citigroup Global Markets Limited, to enter the Chinese capital market. The quotas will be increased to $30 billion as China's stock markets continue to rally.

As industries develop and market competition intensifies, mergers and acquisitions (M&A) will be anything but avoidable. In the retail market, for example, the top 100 retail firms account for only 10 percent of the industry in China. According to Ernst & Young, retailers accounted for 3 percent, or 11.1 billion yuan ($1.4 billion), of the total activity for mergers and acquisitions in China during 2005. M&A transactions are expected to grow in the near future. Similar situations of extreme fragmentation exist in other sectors too. The auto component industry and the pharmaceutical industry, for example, contain thousands of manufacturers. M&A activities by multinationals are a popular strategy for market entry. M&A will likely take hold on industry consolidation for scale of economy as was revealed by the experience of the developed economies, even though Chinese entrepreneur psychology and credit culture may put a check on the scale and swiftness of this process.

China has the largest elderly population in the world. Currently 144 million people are over the age of sixty (16 million are over eighty). That figure will go up to 200 million by 2014, 300 million by 2026, 400 million by 2037, and top out at 437 million in 2051. Only 5 percent of China's population was over sixty in 1982. From 11 percent now it will grow to 17.2 percent by 2020, and 30 percent by 2050. People born during China's "Baby Boom" of the 1950s and 1960s will become senior citizens in the next fifteen years, accelerating China's aging numbers. China expects three overlapping population peaks in the first half of the twenty-first century: the overall population, the working-age population, and the aging population.

The purchasing power and consumption levels of China's 144 million elderly are on the rise. Consumption by seniors will likely reach 1.4 trillion yuan ($175 billion) by 2010 and 4.3 trillion yuan by 2020, accounting respectively for 11.39 percent and 15.43 percent of the country's total, according to the China National Committee on Aging. Industries that serve the aging population, such as pharmaceutical, health care, insurance, and tourism, will begin to feel the impact of this trend. A related trend is a decline in the fifteen-to-fifty-nine year-old working-age group relative to the elderly population.

The one-child policy has created a "1-2-4 pattern" (one child, two parents, and four grandparents) within many Chinese families, with the dependency doubling by the generation. The working-age to elderly ratio will fall from six to only two in thirty-five years (2.5 in the U.S.), making it more challenging for the government to build an effective social security system, and at the same time providing more business opportunities in this area. In the decreasing working-age group, the market impact begins to surface as the lopsided male-female ratio in China caused by sex-selection abortions is being pushed up to 118 men for every 100 women. On average in the rest of the world, 106 baby boys are born for every 100 girls, and the numbers tend to even out by adulthood as more boys die in childhood. By 2020, China will be home to a staggering 300 million more men than women, a number equivalent to the entire population of the United States.

At present, less than 4 percent of China's 1.3 billion people have insurance. Although the Chinese market for insurance has been growing by 15 to 20 percent a year over the past decade, at the end of 2004, it had just a 1.9 percent share of global premium volumes, insurance premiums per capita of $27.30, and a premium-to-GDP ratio of just 2.14 percent—while the global average for premiums per capita stood at $292.20 and the premium/GDP ratio averaged 4.53 percent.

China's life insurance market, now about one-tenth the size of the $540 billion-a-year U.S. market, could grow in the coming years to become the world's biggest market. Since China joined the WTO in 2001, forty-seven foreign insurance companies have set up 121 branches in China, with 135 more establishing 200 representative offices. Revenues of foreign insurance companies in China amounted to 34.1 billion yuan ($4.35 billion) in 2005, nine times more than in 2001.

Foreign insurance companies had a 7 percent market share in China at the end of 2005, up from 5.3 percent in 2001. However, they have 19 percent of the market in Beijing and 17 percent in Shanghai. U.S. insurers accounted for $1.5 billion of the $61.6 billion in life insurance premiums paid in China in 2005. In comparison, foreign companies account for 25 percent of Japan's insurance market and 13 percent of South Korea's. Obviously, there's a fair amount of room for growth, especially when one takes into account the rapid growth of China's middle class.

The government may now look to create tax and other incentives for families to invest in annuities, long-term health care policies, and other retirement services that can provide real help to the working class and the sixty million poorest people.

In July 2006, Standard and Poor's ratings services upgraded its outlook on China's insurance sector to "positive" from "developing," and raised China's long-term sovereign credit rating to A from A minus to reflect expectations that the financial strength of the industry will improve in the medium term. At the close of 2006, foreign investors were able to set up their own insurance agent companies, including insurance brokerages, notary, and appraisal businesses in China. However, foreign investors cannot solely fund a life insurance company, and there is a 50 percent limit on foreign stake in a life insurance company.

Opportunities go with challenges. Even though Chinese firms are increasingly adopting the norms of international business for corporate governance, accounting and auditing, marketing and general management, China remains a heterogeneous, complex, and difficult market to enter. Government regulations and labor laws that empower trade unions will continue to test the nerves of multinational CEOs. While the country is among the most attractive places for executives to take an international assignment, it's also one of the most difficult places for them to succeed, with understanding one another's cultures being the top barrier.[41] According to a recent World Bank survey targeting 12,400 enterprises in China's 120 cities, foreign investment in China has a profit margin of as much as 22 percent. Domestic as well as international competition will keep vying for the China market until the last penny of profit disappears.[42]

3

Authoritarian Laissez-faire: Stories of Super Growth

Revolution from Collusion

What makes China miraculously rise to be an economic superpower, as if wealth suddenly grew out of the earth overnight? How does the Chinese "Cult of Face" or the cultural "Magic Chain" fit into the explanation of its stunning economic growth? The origin of the Thanksgiving holiday is a great episode in the American Experiment for understanding China's initial moves toward economic success:

> Most Americans think of Thanksgiving as a time to gather with family and friends and celebrate with a feast. If they have any idea of the origin of this national holiday, declared each year by presidential proclamation, it's probably confined to the idea that the Pilgrims were grateful for a good harvest in their new land and set aside a day to give thanks. What they may not remember is that things weren't always so good for the Pilgrims, who came to the New World from England to escape religious persecution. Their first winters after they landed at Plymouth Rock in 1620 and established the Plymouth Bay Colony were harsh. The weather was lousy and crop yields were poor.

Half the Pilgrims died or returned to England. Those who stayed in the New World went hungry. Despite their deep religious conviction, the colonists took to stealing from one another.

In the spring of 1623, following three grueling winters and widespread famine, Governor Bradford and the others "began to think how they might raise as much corn as they could, and obtain a better crop than they had done, that they might not still thus languish in miseries . . ." One of the traditions the Pilgrims brought with them from England was something called "farming in common." The colonists pooled the fruits of their labor and rationed the harvest. The idea that "taking away of properties, and bringing them into common wealth, would make them happy and flourishing" was misplaced. Instead, "this community was found to breed much confusion and discontent, and retard much employment that would have been to their benefit and comfort." Young and able men resented working hard for other men and their families without compensation. So after three winters of starvation, Bradford instituted a new policy when it came time to plant in the spring of 1623. He set aside a plot of land for each family, allowing each to "plant for his own particular, and in that regard trust to themselves." For the colonists, the results were nothing short of miraculous. The women now went willingly into the field, carrying their young children with them. Those who previously claimed to be too ill or weak to work, given an incentive, were eager to till their own plot of land. Bradford writes of the new plan: "This had very good success; for it made all hands very industrious, so much more corn was planted than otherwise would have been by any means ye or any other could use, and saved him a great deal of trouble, and gave far better content."

Yet it was no miracle. Without knowing it, Bradford and the Pilgrims discovered what Eastern Europe learned—the hard way—more than 350 years later: socialism doesn't work. Deprived of property rights and lacking economic incentives to work, produce, and save, human beings behave in a predictable manner. It was that way in 1620, and it's that way now. Allowing the Pilgrims to farm their own plot of land and reap the benefits produced a bountiful harvest in the fall of 1623. They set aside "a day of thanksgiving" to thank God for their good fortune. . . . From that day forth, "Any general want or famine hath not been amongst them since to this day," Bradford writes in an entry from 1647, the last year covered by his History. Pretty soon, the colonists had more than enough food for their own needs and started to trade their surplus corn for other commodities, such as fur. After three winters of famine, the Pilgrims viewed their times of plenty as a stroke of good fortune. Today we know fortune had nothing to do with it. The story of the Pilgrims' hardships under a collectivist system and the seeming miracle of capitalism are worth acknowledging. On Thanksgiving, we give thanks for the system of government that allows our market economy to flourish.[1]

Why did the Pilgrims' initial communal system not work? First of all, it is difficult or in fact impossible to measure each person's labor, effort, or contribution. But even had there been measurement, their system did not tightly relate personal contribution to personal reward, as "Young and able men resented working hard for other men and their families without compensation." The problems of "effort measurement," "effort-reward relation," "communal free-riding," and "special incentives" are so hidden and so powerful that people would rather suffer from hunger, take to stealing, give up and go back to where they came from, complain to God, or even face death than do their best to find a quick and effective solution. It took those free minds three difficult years to resolve it.

The interpretation of the Thanksgiving story, however, was heavily influenced by "property rights" economic theory. The truth is, neither fortune nor private property rights have anything to do with it. The Pilgrims' initial communal system was the consequence of a special contract in the early days of capitalism whereby the colony, its products, and the colonists' labor were entirely mortgaged to the London investors, whose loans had to be paid off before any Pilgrim could own free-hold property. Real private property didn't exist for these colonists until 1627, when a small group of colonists bought the debt and the responsibility. At that time, a temporary monopoly on the fur trade was reserved for the "loan purchasers" as compensation for taking on a higher level of personal and financial responsibility.

Therefore, even though the communal system was similar to modern Soviet collectivism, the shift away from it—Governor Bradford instituted a new policy of setting aside a plot of land for each family—did not result in private property change. It was simply a change in the organization of indentured labor, a re-arrangement of the production method. This historical fact thus puts the Pilgrims' success story into a broader context of using efficient "institutions" (formal or informal rules) and "intentionality" (adaptive learning) instead of "property rights" to explain incentives and economic performance.[2]

Setting aside a plot of land for each family is exactly what happened in rural China in 1978. Like the early American experience, the initial re-arrangement of agriculture production did not involve any change of property rights in China. Farmers' land was still collectively owned land, but something did happen and it started the economic miracle overnight.

After Mao Zedong's death in 1976, a number of experiments began: land was assigned to small groups of households. Much of this occurred in Sichuan and Anhui provinces, with the encouragement of the then provincial leaders, Zhao Ziyang and Wan Li, both of whom later reached national power. Some experiments resulted from bribery and collusion with local cadres who permitted a family to farm a plot of land instead of working in a group. But in a tiny village, something very different happened.

One night in November 1978, eighteen villagers of poverty-stricken Xiaogang village in Anhui risked their lives to sign, with their thumbprints, a secret agreement. That year, Xiaogang suffered from a serious drought and its twenty households of some 100 villagers, who were mostly dependent upon state relief funds and loans to ease the financial strain of their continual crop failures, again faced starvation. Two village leaders, Yan Junchang and Yan Hongchang, decided in desperation to find a way out. They called in the household heads and made a radical decision after a short discussion: to abandon the long-practiced communal farming system and divide the land among themselves. They drew up a contract that would fulfill their production quotas for the state and keep whatever remained. "If the trial fails," the contract concluded, "We cadres are prepared for death or prison punishments under the laws, and other commune members pledge to raise our children until they are eighteen years old."

The secret was soon known but surprisingly it went unpunished. Other villages followed suit and the practice spread like wildfire. What started as a secret pact is now considered the first bold move of agricultural reform in China. How come it took the American Pilgrims three years to change while it only took the Chinese farmers the length of a short discussion? After the People's Republic of China was founded in 1949, the state carried out an agrarian revolution by expropriating land from landlords and distributing it to landless peasants. By the mid 1950s, like other socialist countries, Chinese leaders fell hook, line, and sinker for Soviet style collectivization, in which individual farmers were compelled to join the collectively owned and operated "People's Communes."

The result mirrored what happened to the American Pilgrims. In addition to these economic changes, other policies were implemented in the countryside, including the banishing of religious and mystical institutions and ceremonies, and replacing them with political meetings and propaganda sessions. Attempts were made to enhance rural education and the status of women (allowing females to initiate divorce) and end foot-binding, child marriage, and opium addiction. Internal passports (the household registry system, or *hukou*) were introduced in 1956, which forbade travel or relocation without authorization. Central control was unprecedentedly embedded into Chinese society at the grassroots level.

As early as 1956, the household responsibility system appeared in some coastal areas (e.g., Yongjia, Zhejiang province). In 1962, when party leader Liu Shaoqi favored the introduction of incentive-based policies to lead China out of the depths of the catastrophic failure of the "Great Leap Forward," this so-called "household production responsibility system" was widely employed. Because of the threat and affront to Mao of Liu's success and populariy, Liu, unimaginably, was tortured to death during the "Cultural Revolution," which was largely aimed at him by Mao. That's why those farmers saw a risk and needed to "prepare for death."

After Mao's death, reform-minded Deng Xiaoping championed the philosophy of "Touching for the stones while crossing the river," and endorsed the "household responsibility system" in April 1979. Since then, the "household responsibility system" has been the nationwide statutory pattern and has proved a great success. There is no doubt that the system generates incentives for production by giving farmers freedom of land-use rights and decision making, linking rewards closely with performance which solves the above-mentioned problems of "effort measurement," "effort-reward relation," "communal free-riding," and "special incentives." As a result, China's agriculture dramatically revitalized.

After thirty years of stagnation, growth in agricultural output in the first half of the 1980s accelerated several times faster than the previous average rate. Between 1978 and 1984, output of the three main crops— grain, cotton and oil-bearing crops—increased at annual rates of 4.8 percent, 7.7 percent, and 13.8 percent respectively, compared with the average growth rates of 2.4 percent, 1.0 percent, and 0.8 percent per year from 1952 to 1978. Production of grain, China's most important farming product, reached a peak of 407 million tons in 1984, a net increase of more than 100 million tons within six years. The centuries-old fundamental problem of feeding the giant population was basically solved.

One can perhaps argue that these eighteen farmers changed or even saved China. But the argument is better viewed as praise for their courageous move. The truth is: this production change is just an old trick that had to be endorsed by the liberal-minded leader. As a strong supporter of

Liu Shaoqi in 1962, Deng was well aware of the arrangement himself. His strategy was to create a liberal environment to induce changes cautiously and incrementally. In fact, right when the farmers signed the secret pact, Deng and other party leaders were busy in "work meetings" for the historic "Third Plenum of the Eleventh Central Committee" (December 1978), which essentially put an end to the Mao-styled class struggle, re-evaluated the "Cultural Revolution," and set up the beginning of reform and the "Four Modernizations."

This brings up a unique feature of China's reform approach: a gradual "intentional" interactive process that is from both the bottom *and* from the top. What the people at the bottom want are incentives and wealth; what the people at the top want are stability and development within the orthodoxy of Marxism, socialism, and Party leadership, with firm and resolute Party leadership as the ultimate bottom line.

Therefore, reform became a process of "adventurous institutional innovation" with or without bribery and collusion. On one hand, it's a learning process of understanding market economy, free market pricing, property rights, privatization, macroeconomic management, and the global trade system; on the other hand, it's a policy process of maintaining a continuity of ideology by revising Marxism, putting everything into the bucket of socialism, and eventually defending the legitimacy and necessity of strong Party leadership. Since these two parallel processes were induced by a liberal political environment created by Deng, reform was uniquely interactive from the bottom and from the top, and continues to be characterized by balancing the soaring demand of institutional innovation and the lagging supply of appropriate institutions. It's a learn-by-doing or trial-and-error process for both bottom and top, and that's how come China often resembles a huge laboratory where human endeavor and creativity are constantly on display, changing, evolving, testing new waters, and exploring new frontiers in its political, economic, and social development.

China's centralized planned economy carried the logic of "You can't do it when the laws didn't say you can do it." Liberalization and decentralization changed the logic to "You can do it when it's permitted," "You can do it when it isn't prohibited," and "You can do it even when it is prohibited." Therefore, China's economic miracle can be seen as a combined result of "permission-driven" growth, "non-prohibition-driven" growth, and "corruption-induced," "collusion-induced," or even "outright outlawed" growth. Fascinating stories unfold in China every day when supply provided by existing channels falls behind demand, which in turn causes widespread non-conventional growth. This is how the unaccounted-for "underground" economy can account for as much as 15 percent of GDP in China.

From this perspective, the farmers' bold act exemplifies China's "adventurous institutional innovation" in a political sense, and a separation of use rights from collectively owned property rights in an operational sense. This "use rights model" later spread to state-owned enterprises (SOEs) and became an "internal institutional innovation" approach within the collective-state ownership structure, which runs side by side with the "external institutional innovation" approach that involves the establishment of township, private, and foreign-funded enterprises.

The gradual nature of China's reform is therefore especially noticeable within the collective-state ownership structure when privatization is absent in rural areas and in state-owned enterprises. The farmers also liberated millions of laborers from farmlands—since the new system no longer dictated that every farm laborer remain with his land. This is the source of China's huge pool of cheap labor that fueled the shift of production facilities from the U.S. and other countries. Within two decades, between 1978 and 1998, the percentage of China's agricultural workforce fell from over 85 percent to about 60 percent, while a similar transformation in Japan took almost sixty years.

How does it look in Xiaogang village after nearly thirty years? It appears that the household responsibility system had exhausted its benefits by 1985. Even though high-yield hybrid crops were widespread and starvation was no longer a problem, stagnation returned to haunt the village. Today's Xiaogang is not what people expect, given the influence of the village since 1978. Its population of over 470 has an annual per capita income of just 2,000 yuan (about $250). Some fifty-five villagers have migrated to work in urban areas for better livelihoods, and more than half the households are in debt. Many people say that Xiaogang solved China's agriculture problem in one shot, but the village has existed on the margins of wealth for more than twenty years. Today, most signs of prosperity in the town are the result of subsidies. Beautifully designed architecture was paid for by donations. The government funded the building of several houses. No one knows how much money in donations and funds the town has received. But schools are built, roads are paved, and water is tapped—and all tout the town as a "trailblazer" and the birthplace of the new agriculture production system.[3]

The seeming stagnation of Xiaogang is as interesting as the story of its reform. Since the good news came from the change of production method, the bad news has to come from collectively owned property rights. The American Pilgrims began to buy property rights from London creditors only four years after their experiment, yet Chinese farmers are still stuck with their land use rights almost thirty years after their initial move. How come? The biggest secret is, collectively owned land property rights are only rights in name, not rights in reality. In reality, a village cannot collectively sell all its land to anyone except the state; it cannot collectively divide its land and let each member own a share; and it cannot even collectively decide how many years it can lease the land use rights to its members. The state controls all these. This is a classic case of vaguely defined property rights. Collectively owned land property rights, therefore, are only land use rights. When the government abolished state tax in 2006, villages got back another part of their land property rights: rent rights; but the property rights still belong to the State.

What happened in rural China is this: villages distribute their land based on the size of the farmer's family, which has egalitarian claim on land use rights. Given the abundant population and the limited amount of land, the amount distributed to each household is very small. Moreover, farmland differs from plot to plot in terms of fertility, irrigation conditions, location, and so forth. A household usually has to obtain plots from each of the land grades. Thus, a household's land was not only insufficient, it was fragmented and scattered. In an extreme case in the 1980s, a household with seven family members had 128 allocated plots of farmland. Large areas of cultivated land were separated by paths and boundaries that defined each household's holdings, which blocked the possibility of using relatively advanced mechanical equipment and agricultural infrastructure.[4]

According to the system, newborn babies and newly married spouses from other villages are all eligible to share equal amounts of land (subject to whether or not they are in accordance with the "family planning" policy); when a villager dies or divorces, his or her right may or may not disappear, depending upon the situation. As population increases, villages have to re-adjust the distribution structure after a few years, which not only lead to disputes but also further subdivides the farmland. When the selling price of agricultural products can't keep pace with the cost of farming tools and materials, plus heavy taxes and fees from villages and townships, farmers tend to leave their land for non-farm job opportunities. Every major city in China is crowded with job-seeking farmers (who still need to pay fees to keep their land use rights). This results in land use rights transfers or temporary giveaways, partial planting, or even land-sitting, especially when a mutually beneficial transfer is not approved by the village. Currently, only some provinces, such as Guangdong in the south, have started trial sales of rights to use rural land.

Numerous new experiments of scale production within the collective use rights structure have been launched. Examples include fixed responsibility farmland within a contract term (usually thirty years): two-land system with food land for family consumption and contract land for commercial farming: salary-based collective farming: and the promising farmland shareholding cooperative. Still, what rural China faces now is how partial property rights and high contract transaction costs impede efficient scale farming.

Contrary to the situation in manufacturing, low efficiency in agriculture easily takes away the advantage of cheap labor cost. According to Chinese statistics, domestic wheat prices are currently 75 percent higher than those on the international market, the price of corn 63 percent higher, and the price of cotton 12 percent higher. WTO accession will put Chinese farmers in a tighter corner as cheaper foreign agricultural products flood in.

If land privatization is going to happen in China, it is going to be a two-step process: privatization to villages, then privatization to households and individuals. Since privatization may cause rapid land concentration, wealth disparity, massive population migration, employment pressure, public security, and other problems, what the government is doing now is to slow the process, reduce the shock, and keep a balance between efficiency, equality, and stability. China's rural revolution is an unfinished revolution. But it is not a straightforward, simple-minded efficiency issue. The development of grassroots elections and township and village enterprises won't change the social-historical nature of the land ownership problem.

The Forefront of Capitalism

In May 2006, three unrelated events happened almost at the same time in Wenzhou, eastern Zhejiang Province, one of China's most important cities. First, fifty-nine farmers won a land-use lawsuit over the city government after an eighteen-month fight that involved the village committee, the Wenzhou economy and technology development zone, and the Wenzhou municipal government. It is about the farmers again, but this time it concerns blatantly suing the government rather than avoiding the punishment of the government. China's Ministry of Land and Resources admitted that, in some cities, more than 60 percent of the commercial land acquisitions since 2004 have been illegal. In extreme cases, the proportion reached 90 percent.

Second, Kean University, New Jersey's third-largest public university, sealed a deal to open the first full-scale American college campus in China. Under the agreement, the Chinese government will pay 500 million yuan (about $62.5 million) to build and help operate the 300-acre campus in Wenzhou. The Kean campus will enroll 3,500 to 4,000 Chinese students who will be taught in English by western professors from the university. New Jersey students may also spend semesters on the American-style campus. The Chinese students will be charged Kean's out-of-state tuition (about $9,656 a year). The new campus will be led by a Sino-American board headed by a Chinese national. The Chinese government will allow U.S. textbooks and give its overseas students passwords to access the university's U.S. website. That means Kean's Chinese students will avoid Chinese censorship by accessing the internet through the university's U.S. servers.[5] The campus is to open in 2007 and be fully operational by 2010.

Thirdly, thirty-nine private companies in Wenzhou City were planning to buy their own aircraft. Among the twenty-two orders already placed, the most expensive was for more than 60 million yuan ($7.5 million). A Shanghai company held an exhibition of U.S.-manufactured helicopters, and two local businesses placed orders of 3.5 million yuan each. The Leqing Aviation Association was planning to invest some 300 million yuan (about $37.5 million) to build an exclusive airport for these private companies.

Suing a local government, building an American university, and purchasing private aircraft are all big news in China. But some were caught off guard when it all happened in Wenzhou, China's freewheeling city at the forefront of capitalist endeavors. During the era of the planned economy, private property was viewed as the root of all evil. In the early 1970s, the entire economy was nationalized or collectivized, and virtually the only private job remained that of a shoe polisher, which the government somehow felt impossible to bring into its realm.

Now, it's a different story. China's economic miracle started from small villages, the engine of growth. Although small township and village enterprises (TVEs) still boom in the countryside,[6] the driving force of growth since the 1990s are the rise of private enterprises, reorganized state-owned enterprises, and foreign-funded enterprises (joint ventures and wholly foreign-owned enterprises). By the end of September 2005, China had more than 4.19 million private firms registered. Private companies now account for more than 50.5 percent of the country's total. They employ more than 60 million people, which outnumber those working in foreign-funded companies. More than 63 percent of the private companies are clustered in eight provinces and cities, including Jiangsu, Guangdong, Zhejiang, Shanghai, Shandong, and Beijing.

Located in the southeastern corner of Zhejiang Province in eastern China, Wenzhou, now an area (including satellite towns and villages) of 7.4 million people, has been an immigrant city for more than several hundred years. Throughout its history, Wenzhou's traditional economic role relates to its seaport access to the mountainous interior of southern Zhejiang Province. Remote from both imperial and provincial capitals, this small town was ecologically isolated and heavily influenced by the non-orthodox Yongjia school of thought with its more self-dependent philosophy for material gain.

In 1876, Wenzhou was opened to the foreign tea trade. During the Second World War, Wenzhou gained significance as one of few ports still under Chinese control. The city is also known for its emigrants who left their native land for Europe and the United States. A long history of a mobile, sojourner lifestyle nurtured an adventurous spirit. Wenzhou residents were thus equipped with a strong business sense and a commercial culture more dominant than anywhere else in China. Two things stand out for Wenzhou: it was the earliest to launch a market economy, and it has the most active and developed private economy in China.

In many ways, Wenzhou symbolizes the rise of China's private sector. Renowned for its entrepreneurs, it's an economic model for export-oriented manufacturing. The city is the country's largest manufacturer of small-scale goods, such as lighters, eyeglasses, and shoes, which have been exported to almost every corner of the world. Whereas other booming cities in China have relied on foreign investment or government funding to fuel their economies, Wenzhou has done it on its own.[7] The truth about Wenzhou is this: it took to capitalism earlier than the rest of China and now benefits greatly from its head start.

While Chinese leaders were still bickering about private business and free markets in the 1980s and early 1990s, Wenzhou, helped at that time by its remoteness and its relative lack of state-owned industries, allowed private enterprise to flourish. The weakest link of central control turned out to be the epicenter of China's private capitalism. In typical Chinese showcase cities, such as Shanghai and Beijing, well-funded state-owned-enterprises and high-profile foreign investors rule the economy. In Wenzhou, 97 percent of the city's 130,000 enterprises are private, accounting for some 90 percent of its industrial output. From 1978, when China first opened its doors, until 2002, the total FDI (foreign direct investment) into Wenzhou was a mere $600 million.

Wenzhou's manufacturing structure also exemplifies Zhejiang's characteristic local specialization, which takes industrial clustering to a comic extreme. In Zhejiang, there is Datang, also known as sock city. There is

Qiaotou, the button-making town. Shengzhou does ties. Shaoxing produces textiles and dyes. In the outskirt towns, parts of Ninghai are dedicated to electric hand tools, stationery, and pressing and stamping machines. Cixi has become a haven for kitchen equipment makers. With 8,000 international traders living in the city, Yiwu is a place for traders of thousands of consumer products. Many of these manufacturing centers dominate not only the national market for their products, but increasingly the international one too. Datang, for instance, reckons to turn out eight billion pairs of socks a year from 8,000 factories, accounting for one-third of all socks sold per year in the world, and two-thirds of those bought in China.[8] For China as a whole, estimates of the size of the private sector range from the official 33 percent of GDP to private assessments of up to 65 percent. In Zhejiang, even the official figure is as high as 65 percent, although most experts say the true figure is closer to 80 or even 90 percent.

The millions of workers, often as young as sixteen, in Wenzhou's assembly lines also produce 25 percent of China's shoes, 80 percent of its eyeglass frames, 60 percent of its razors, and 65 percent of its electricity transformers. Eighty percent of the world's metallic-shell lighters and zippers are produced here. Wenzhou's thirty or so industrial clusters are each comprised of hundreds of private enterprises. Most are in light industry, and 95 percent of Wenzhou's produce is exported.

A significant component of Wenzhou's success is the development of a cluster model, whereby hundreds of small enterprises work together to produce complementary goods based on a very efficient division of labor. The city's lighter manufacturers, for example, comprised of hundreds of firms, some specializing in particular components, others in final assembly—lead to fast, flexible, and competitive production. Long before assembly lines were used in Western mass manufacturing, sixteenth-century Chinese used assembly lines to produce porcelain. Now it's come back to life in Wenzhou. Clusters affect competition in at least three ways: increasing the productivity of companies based in the area, driving the direction and pace of innovation, and stimulating the formation of new businesses.[9]

One of Wenzhou's many success stories is the Ri Feng Lighter Company, where rows of workers hunch over small desks piecing together lighters of all shapes and sizes. Ri Feng's 600-plus employees produce more than 8 million lighters a year; 90 percent are exported. The company's main overseas markets are in Europe, America, and Japan. Ri Feng is currently trial-manufacturing a product for the U.S. lighter company Zippo. Huang Fajing, the boss of Ri Feng, bragged that almost all major lighter importers buy his products.

Shoemaking has a long history in Wenzhou. As early as the Chenghua Reign (1465-1488) of the Ming Dynasty, Wenzhou boots were sent to the capital as an imperial tribute. In the 1930s, leather shoe manufacturing developed rapidly in the city, and Wenzhou products sold well across the country. In the 1970s, Wenzhou's high-heeled leather shoes dominated the national market, winning it fame as China's "City of Shoes." The development of shoemaking gave rise to an increase in the number of shoe manufacturers in Wenzhou, including a number of frauds. For a time, stories of poor-quality Wenzhou shoes spread around China, causing them to be shunned by Chinese consumers. August 8, 1987, was a day of humiliation for Wenzhou's shoemaking industry. In Wulin Square, Hangzhou, capital of Zhejiang Province, 5,000 pairs of flawed Wenzhou leather shoes were publicly burnt.

"That fire also incinerated Wenzhou's reputation," says Wang Zhentao, then a young Wenzhou shoe dealer doing business in Hubei Province. The debacle kindled his determination to start his own shoemaking business and redeem the reputation of Wenzhou businesspeople.[10] Wang believed that his success would come from design concepts. He traveled to Italy and other countries in Europe every year, visiting his counterparts and studying the market. In 1999, he set up an office and a design and development center in Italy; he hired experienced local designers to ensure his products were in line with world trends. Today Chinese and overseas shoe designers at the Aokang Group in Wenzhou work with advanced CAD systems, pooling their artistry and drawing inspiration from one another. Within a period of thirteen years, Wang's business developed from a rural workshop to a shoemaking group with net assets of 300 million yuan.

Inspired by Aokang's design model, other Wenzhou companies followed suit. Kangnai Group joined SATRA (Shoe and Allied Traders Research Association) in Britain in 2001 to better command the latest shoe technology information and the dynamic state of the shoe industry. Feidiao Electrics Co., Ltd., well-known in the domestic switch industry, bought 90 percent shares of the Italian company ELIOS and brought established Italian designers to its R&D center in Shanghai for products sold in both the U.S. and European markets. In 2002, Fapai Group set up a garment research center in Florence, Italy; Zhuangji also opened a garment and adornment design studio in Milan. In 2004, Hazan Shoes Co., Ltd. acquired Italian shoe maker Wilson and built up its China-Italy Hazan Shoes R&D Center for its overseas production. Delixi Group purchased an electric appliance manufacturer in Bonn, Germany, building its R&D center in "The Kingdom of Electric Appliances."

Today Wenzhou enterprises have established more than thirty overseas R&D centers, making their products more appealing to "the taste" of the international market. Qian Jinbo's Hong Qing Ting is another private shoe manufacturer that emerged from Wenzhou. Qian was a latecomer to the shoe industry in 1995 when he started his company in his hometown, Wenzhou's Yongjia County. He decided to build a corporate image based on quality and on a "shoe culture," an approach none of his predecessors had tried. He was successful, and created a miracle in China's shoe industry within seven years. His company has grown into a group, and the Hong Qing Ting brand has been exempted from inspection by the State Bureau of Quality and Technical Supervision. Its current annual sales amount to 830 million yuan. Today, Wenzhou, the manufacturing powerhouse of Zhejiang Province, is home to nearly 4,000 shoemakers.

Over 1.5 million Wenzhou natives reside outside the city of Wenzhou, and a 500,000-strong expatriate community of "Wenzhouese" lives around the world, not just in places like Hong Kong and Taiwan, but also in Italy, France, South Africa, and America. You can find "Little Wenzhou" in Rome, Paris, and New York—all assisting Wenzhou to look outwards and become an important part of the workshop of the world. In the last few years, the number of enterprises that Wenzhou people invested in abroad, as well as new overseas institutions built by them, are multiplying exponentially in 87 countries and regions.

Before 2002, only 91 Wenzhou companies did overseas business. By 2006, 380 newly approved Wenzhou firms engaged in overseas business: 97 percent are private-owned enterprises. In 1998, Wenzhouese founded China's first specialized overseas market, China Commercial City in Sao Paulo, Brazil. During the following seven years, they built fifteen markets in the major cities of Cameroon, the Netherlands, Russia, the United Arab Emirates, Mongolia, the U.S., Britain, and Finland.

Wenzhou's "clustering mentality" is clearly seen in expanding overseas markets. In ACT market, the largest in Moscow, nearly 2,000 Wenzhouese sell leather shoes, hiking shoes, garments, and sundry goods. Opened in 2003, their Dubai China Light Industry City can accommodate more than 100 stores. Finland's North Europe China Town has more than 10,000 square meters in the first phase of its operation, and will soon expand to 100,000 square meters. Since 1998, Wenzhouese have brought over 1,000 enterprises and vendors to overseas markets. Since China's entry into the WTO, Wenzhou exports have increased by 32 percent annually, reaching $6.18 billion in 2005.[11]

In recent years, however, trade barriers have affected many Wenzhou products, including lighters, eyeglasses, shoes, and small appliances. This development has fired up overseas expansion into the area of production: Wenzhou is offshoring. In 2001, Wenzhou Mingming Optical Co., Ltd. built a factory in Turkey, which boosted its exports to $4 million in the first year. It is now the third-largest eyeglass manufacturing enterprise in Turkey. Wenzhou Hengdi Machinery Plastic Co., Ltd. invested $1 million in Vietnam to transfer its poly-woven bag manufacturing entirely out of Xiaoshan to realize the localization of both production and sales.

In 2004, Wenzhou Hazan Shoes Co., Ltd. built a factory in Nigeria with its equipment and personnel, investing a total of $5 million in two phases, transporting semi-finished products from China and processing them into finished products in Nigeria. Cai Jianlin, a boss from Ruian, set up a shoe company and processed the domestically semi-finished products in Russia. In 2006, Kangnai Group and Heilongjiang Dongning Jixin Industry and Trade Group Co., Ltd. jointly invested 2 billion yuan in Ussurijsk, Russia, to construct Far-East Kangji Industrial Park. When the EU decided to impose anti-dumping duties on Chinese shoe manufacturers in 2006, some shoe companies in Wenzhou quickly shifted their production base to Indonesia.

It seems clear how Wenzhou earned its reputation for being the first to spot new trends in China. Businessmen from Wenzhou piled into property in Shanghai before house prices soared, and started acquiring coal mines well in advance of the commodities boom. Wenzhou speculators have pushed up property prices across the country, taken control of many of China's private coal mines (and thus incurred responsibility for the appalling death rate among miners due to accidents), and made life miserable for taxi drivers by buying up limited licences and reselling them for huge profits.

But what makes Wenzhou citizens especially scary in the public imagination in China is their ability to pool funds and deploy them to capture or—as critics see it—manipulate markets. Many Wenzhou speculators in China's bubble-like property market have been housewives who, at least until the government began attempting to rein in the market during 2006, would team up together to buy entire new residential blocks. Their buying spree would help stimulate markets by creating an impression of strong demand. Even Shanghai, 370 kilometers (230 miles) to the north of Wenzhou and a city hardly short of speculative acumen itself, is somewhat in awe of Wenzhou's home-buying syndicates. The Shanghai media often look for clues that reveal what Wenzhou speculators are doing as a way of predicting market trends. But this attention may well be a product of an increasingly elaborate Wenzhou myth, rather than proof of any real ability of the city's citizens to move markets.

Recently, much attention has focused on the emergence in Wenzhou of two super-syndicates, each comprising several private companies, that pool their funds to make big investments. Members of the biggest, Zhongrui, have a combined capital of several billion dollars. In 2005, they bought a parcel of land in Wenzhou for $185 million, paying a record high price per area-unit for an auctioned lot in the city.[12] Thanks to government measures, the property market in Shanghai and other cities is showing signs of cooling. Yet the real demand for housing continues to soar with the rural migration, the new "gold-rush" of foreign investment, and over 10 million newborns each year, Wenzhou tycoons are waiting to scoop up deals at any sign of market softness.

Today, Wenzhou companies, again leading the trend of "following the workers," are undertaking big investments they hope will be followed by other Chinese manufacturers. In Chongqing, a rapidly growing metropolis in mid-West China, Aokang, the country's biggest shoemaker, is developing an enormous manufacturing complex in the city, while another consortium of Wenzhou businessmen is creating an industrial park for plastic molds used in manufacturing. The two projects are at the forefront of a surge in investment in Chongqing by companies from the coastal areas. The numbers are relatively modest in the context of the investment spree China is undergoing.

Yet, if the process accelerates, these projects will be seen as early example of a big change in the country's economic geography. That is to say: instead of the workers moving to the factories, the factories will move to the workers.[13] Ford Motor Company has a manufacturing facility in Chongqing, which is also home for its motorcycle production base. Intel has a chip packaging plant in the nearby city of Chengdu, Sichuan's capital.

For the past two decades, China's manufacturing success has been concentrated in two regions, the Pearl River Delta just north of Hong Kong, and the area surrounding Shanghai at the mouth of the Yangzi River; both are well-placed for exporting. Millions of workers flocked to factories in the two regions, a large proportion of them from the heavily populated inland areas of Hunan and Sichuan. However, reports began to surface of labor shortages, especially in the Pearl River region, and these complaints have increased over time. In recent years, wages have also been rising at double-digit rates. Employers in the coastal areas often report alarmingly high turnover, sometimes up to 50 percent. Some companies have already decided they need to shift inland to secure more reliable labor.

Many Chinese businesses are looking at moving to Chongqing because the labor supply is plentiful and they feel the coastal areas markets are saturated. The production cost of an air conditioner, for example, is 100 yuan ($12) less than in southern China. Jierda, a large Wenzhou shoemaker that still has all its production in the coastal cities, sees a future when the company moves much of its manufacturing to inland provinces while maintaining a design and marketing center on the coast.

There is another dimension to this process. The companies investing in Chongqing are not just seeking employees, but also new customers. From Chongqing they get better access to several hundred million consumers in the surrounding provinces, where incomes are rising rapidly, albeit from a lower base when compared with the coastal regions. This is of particular interest to companies such as Aokang, which focus on the domestic market as well as exports. The company views Western China as a huge market easily accessed from Chongqing.

In spite of the surge in interest, many questions remain about the viability of doing business in Chongqing. Even though the Yangzi River is opening up to container ships, transporting goods in and out of the region remains costly. There is also a shortage of skilled labor, which requires that high salaries must be offered to attract experienced technicians, and labor productivity is lower. Also, much of the dynamism in Chongqing has been created by a huge inflow of public money, leaving the area vulnerable to boom-bust cycles. Before more companies move so far west, they will want to see stronger evidence of a real consumer base. In retrospect, however, Wenzhou's investment was mainly concentrated in first-tier cities like Shanghai and Hangzhou, then expanded to second- and third-tier cities. Currently, Wenzhou businessmen have covered almost all the big and medium cities in China, leading the way in the competition for low-cost production and market penetration.

Most businesses in Wenzhou began as a family operation. Many believe the expansion of production and China's entry into the WTO will force businesses to make the transition from family orientation to modern management. The Chint Group Corporation is an example of such a transition. Nan Cunhui, chairman of the board, argued that, after fulfilling a certain level of capital accumulation, it was only by transforming from a "family enterprise" to an "enterprise family" that they could make the leap from product to capital management. Nan and his friend Hu Chengzhong started Chint in 1984 with an initial investment of 50,000 yuan. Today it is a shareholding company. Chint has 106 shareholders, a negligible number of whom are family; the largest non-family member owns an equity interest worth tens of millions of yuan.

Neighboring Chint in the city of Wenzhou is the Delixi Group. The two are known as the dual heroes of Chinese private enterprise. They rank fifth and sixth respectively among the top 500 private enterprises in China. After an initial period of partnership, the two enterprises became fully fledged and entered into strong competition. Nan Cunhui describes their relationship as one of friendly rivalry, where both need to be on their toes, and one constantly tries to outdo the other. Delixi goes in for diversified development, while Chint concentrates on specialization. In June 2004, nine private enterprises in Wenzhou were thrust into the limelight as they joined together to form a new entity, Sinorich Consortium (Holdings) Co., Ltd., which will allow them to enter new businesses and undertake big investment projects like road, power plant, and real estate developments without affecting their own daily business operations.

Currently, Wenzhou enterprises with a scale of between 0.1 and 1 million yuan, between 1 million and 5 million yuan, and over 5 million yuan account for 63 percent, 5.8 percent and 1.5 percent respectively. Nearly 200 companies have a capital of over 100 million yuan.

While Wenzhou is looking to grow out of its "shop at the front, factory at the back" model, there are good reasons why Wenzhou's clustering industries would be non-existent without family enterprises. Merger and acquisition-type consolidation and building into public corporations may look inevitable for some, but reality may not always follow ambition. Breaking the family mode and achieving a larger scale of economy comes with a price: sacrificing management and control. When business culture is largely built upon "family-based personal trust" rather than "contract-based impersonal faith," making it bigger can often mean making it ready to crumble (*zhou da zhou kua*). The need to go from "family enterprise" to "enterprise family" may not be wishful thinking, but it may happen later rather than sooner given China's "credit culture" and its dominant interdependent psychology.[14]

Many stories during these years reveal that when private firms managed by non-family outsiders grew to large scale enterprises, only then did they discover that their assets were hollowed out from the inside by mortgage schemes, misappropriation, negligence, squandering, or even outright fleecing of the company's coffers. A "face culture" relying heavily on relational sanctions may see company operations following the rules of modern shareholding logic, yet underneath, enforcement is weak, and those who prosper maintain a familial tinge in terms of personal loyalty, financial control, equity structure, and intelligence organization. Many more realized that making an enterprise specialized and strong (*zhou zuan zhou qiang*) is still the realistic way for the majority of Wenzhou's cluster economy firms to continue to thrive. Business simply cannot grow out of the context of its own culture. Wenzhou is no exception.

The flourishing of private enterprise is the result of the parallel development of attracting foreign investment on one hand, and growing out of small-scale household workshops (*ge ti hu*) on the other. While tax incentives are generally given for the first three years of business operation, capital financing remains a problem. In America, we are all familiar with stories of successful small businesses that started from a small credit card loan. During the Dot Com boom of the 1990s, for example, Jason Olim and his twin brother, Matthew, took a gamble and racked up $64,000 in credit-card debt to expand their online music retailer business called CDnow. The Olims paid off the debt quickly, took the company public, and later sold it to the German media giant Bertelsmann AG for $117 million. In China, the credit card was virtually unknown in the 1980s and was extremely rare in the 1990s. When a bigger loan for some private venture is needed, it becomes a good test for a market economy: is it only a product market? Or is it a full-fledged market with free flow of all production factors, including labor, land, and capital?

In China, the "Big Four" state-run commercial lenders—Industrial and Commercial Bank, Agricultural Bank, China Construction Bank, and Bank of China—usually don't loan to private companies, even when they have collateral. These banks have been so bogged down by state-owned enterprises that they all have a high percentage of non-performing loans (NPL). High private savings keep their businesses going, and they in turn sustain the existence of many near-bankrupt state-owned companies, making them the walking dead of the business world. Today, China's private economy takes more than a 50 percent share of GDP, yet receives less than 30 percent of the total loans extended. This forces many entrepreneurs to go into the informal lending market, which of course carries higher repayment commitments.

The majority of small businesses that begin on a shoestring budget usually launch their startups with their own savings or by borrowing from friends and relatives. But what they usually come up with is not enough. Many small businesses in Wenzhou started from some sort of "rotating money pool" called a *hui*. Here's how it works: Suppose a few people need cash to start their business. The first few would start to network and expand the group to, say, twelve people. Each would then contribute 10,000 or so yuan each month to the pool for a twelve-month period: 120,000 yuan per month. A lottery decides who will take the pooled money from the first to the twelfth month. Other variations exist, with some rotating the period and the way of deciding who gets to go first.

This is a good way to pile up cash among those who know and trust one another. But, there is risk when someone who takes the money in an earlier month and fails to contribute in later months. This individual, whether he is new to the group or not, runs into unexpected money troubles, can end up breaking the pool and ruining the whole deal, especially when multiple *hui* go on at the same time, or when the *hui* evolves into a pyramid scheme. That is, when a "private money house" comes to take preference over a "rotating money pool."

The "private money house" traces back several hundred years in China and first appeared in Wenzhou in 1984. Like a "shadow bank," a money lender usually runs his own business and has a good reputation for dealing with money within a specific community. The lender typically takes in something like 10,000 yuan in deposits from family, friends, and people in the community. He pays them interest, uses their money as working capital, and occasionally extends loans to other private companies. Of course, he gives better returns to depositors than do local state-run banks, and people trust him. As time goes by, these "back-alley banks" become more specialized and even develop into a kind of shareholding structure that challenges both the interest rate cap and the deposit flow monopolized by state-run banks.

Li Qiyou is a good example of how the informal bank works. Li, a forty-five-year-old resident of Wenzhou, grew up in the countryside during the Cultural Revolution and has only a second-grade education. In the early 1980s, he borrowed some $1,000 from friends and relatives for a brewery business—but lost money for three straight years. With Li's background and lack of connections, regardless of how good his ideas are, the odds of his qualifying for a bank loan are extremely small.[15]

There are, of course, some well-known tricks. A common technique used by local entrepreneurs to raise capital from the official banking system is to devise an elusive way to become affiliated with state-owned enterprises or to register as a collective enterprise, even when in truth they are privately owned. Another technique centers on attempts to tap the state-owned banking system via the use of credit guarantees. Often these arrangements are perfectly legitimate and clearly defined, but equally often they rely on murky relationships, and, occasionally, outright law-breaking.

There usually have to be favors, relationships, or interests involving relatives and business partners for one to think about providing a guarantee, even though the notion of providing a guarantee based on family connections rather than sound financial reasons might seem less than wise to some observers. One may lose money this way when companies one guarantees go bankrupt. There are businesses that specialize in providing credit guarantees. In situations where companies fail to meet the requirements of a loan, they turn, in desperation, to more shady practices in an attempt to dupe the loan officers at banks with guarantees of dubious merit. One favorite technique involves related-party transactions. For example, a company sets up a subsidiary with a decent amount of capital, and then uses the subsidiary as the guarantor for its own loans without disclosing the relationship to the bank. Such schemes are widespread, and in many cases can be structured to be legally sound. Nonetheless, these arrangements create trouble for the banks involved.

Another technique to provide short-term liquidity is invoice discounting or receivables financing. Methods such as these have a long and respectable history; companies borrow money from banks or other parties against the strength of their accounts receivable ledger, with the lender charging a fee for the loan. In China, however, the unique nature of the banking system means that such venerable financing ideas are practiced in unusual and sometimes questionable ways.

In one frequently used situation, a company looking to borrow money will arrange a fake transaction with a company it knows well—often an associate firm or related party. The aspiring borrower will take the fake invoice to a cash-rich state-owned enterprise (SOE) and use it as collateral to borrow needed funds for a period of time just shorter than the due date on the invoice. The incentive for the cash-rich SOE is the opportunity to lend money at a better rate of interest than it would earn on deposit in the bank. Sometimes the SOE will demand a pledge of fixed assets, such as land, as additional security. The deal is essentially a formal contract grafted onto a pseudo-trading contract. Needless to say, invoice discounting of this sort touches a gray area in the law, and there are huge risks for participants. Should the borrower go bankrupt, not only does the SOE risk losing its capital, the debtor named on the fake invoice could face charges of financial fraud.

Another twist on the invoice-discounting model arose in response to the government's moves to tighten China's monetary policy in a bid to rein in runaway sectors of the economy. As overheating concerns are prominent in China's eastern coastal cities, banks in this region are under the most pressure to cool the pace of invoice discounting. This created an opportunity for banks from China's slower-moving western provinces to step into the fray. Eastern-region banks face more lax regulation in western China than do banks in eastern coastal cities; and eastern-region banks prefer to keep their business interests in the east, where companies are more dynamic, faster growing, and less likely to go bankrupt. In 2004, the banking system of Shanxi Province lent 115 billion yuan in invoice-discounting deals, an increase of 13 percent over the previous year—against a backdrop of falling borrowing in Shanxi province itself. The trick lies in the fact that, while cross-province loans are highly restricted, cross-province invoice discounting is allowed. More and more private firms in Zhejiang and Jiangsu provinces in the east are turning to banks in western regions to discount their receivables. To attract more business, banks in the west also offer lower interest rates than those in Shanghai or Zhejiang, and are even setting up offices in the eastern provinces to drum up business.[16]

For small business owners like Li Qiyou, all these tricks won't apply. After failing as a brewer, he borrowed more money from local lenders in 1984 and started an electrical-parts company. Since then he has rolled profits over to start a sink factory that employs forty people and built it into a $600,000 business in 2005, exporting to New Zealand, Iran, Dubai, and Turkey. Li has paid off his loans and now helps friends who need a financial boost. Gray-market lenders are doing a better of job investing money than the state-owned banks. Their behavior resembles that of the early days of European banks run by families, where connections were everything. "When you lend to people you know," Li says, "they are going to work hard to return your money." Li is already planning his next corporate expansion. Once he finds a good location, he wants to borrow $400,000 from friends and relatives to triple the size of his factory. Getting the capital, he figures, won't be a problem. "In Wenzhou we've never been able to rely on the government," he says, "so we've learned to rely on ourselves."[17]

Wenzhou's biggest restaurant, the 200-table Golden Fields Village, opened in May 2006 and specializes in shark-fin soup, giant snails, and stingrays. Owner Wu Jianguan started the business by borrowing a home mortgage loan of $100,000 from banks. But that wasn't enough to pay for the floor-to-ceiling fish tanks and staff of 150 hostesses in purple evening gowns. So he borrowed five times more from friends at a higher interest rate. The cornerstones of such informal lending practices are his relationships with family and friends, relationships far stronger than Wu's connection to the bank. "If the bank repossesses my home, I'll have nowhere to live, but I can still do business," he says. "But if I fail to repay my friends, I'll never do business here again."[18]

Zhang Chongchao, a thirty-six-year-old entrepreneur from Wenzhou and owner of three leather factories generating annual sales of over 100 million yuan, is an experienced user of underground finance. A high-school dropout, he started his first business at the age seventeen with a loan of 200,000 yuan from his fellow villagers. In the years since, Zhang has returned to the shadow markets, accessing pools of funds supplied by rich entrepreneurs, smart merchants, and even relatively well-off peasants who have already made their fortunes from China's phenomenal economic growth over the past two decades. "I wouldn't be where I am today without the support of private loans," Zhang readily admits. Typically, he says, a loan of less than 10 million yuan requires just a phone call and an IOU letter to proceed. "You know," says Zhang, "I have money, but when I need a 5 million yuan short-term loan. I come over and sign an IOU and take the money. It's as simple as that." In the past, he has paid annual interest rates of about 13 percent a year, and also had to pledge a property ownership certificate for one of his businesses to secure the loan.[19]

In Wenzhou, private loans generally come with a commitment to pay annual interest, typically twice that charged on official loans. Terms are less than a year, with interest rates ranging from 12 to 30 percent per year, depending on the strength and credibility of the borrower. For lenders, this offsets risk and keeps money flowing. In other regions, especially the northeast and northwest, the interest rates on private loans are significantly higher (sometimes more than 100 percent). If that's a danger in an overheating economy, the root of the problem lies in the dysfunctional, clumsy state sector, not the working private sector. This partially explains why China's economy has resisted official efforts to slow it down.

Wenzhou, now the financial center of eastern China's private enterprises, was the first to challenge the state's interest rate control, and was the first city to allow floating interest rates for bank deposits and loans in early 2003. At the peak of informal finance in the mid-1980s, up to 95 percent of all financial transactions in Wenzhou were occurring outside the formal banking system. Wenzhou's underground credit markets were so vibrant that people withdrew their savings from state banks so they could earn higher interest rates in the underground markets. This in turn led state banks to float their interest rates so they could compete with these markets.

Some of Wezhou's underground banks are open twenty-four hours a day, seven days a week, and interest is sometimes charged by the hour. These are real full-service operations. The central government had seriously considered cracking down on private financing because it might get in the way of the central bank's control of the money supply. They soon recognized that shadow banks are needed to keep the private sector alive. This steady source of finance has given Wenzhou not only China's most vivacious private economy, but also the lowest level of nonperforming bank loans in the country. By the end of 2004, loans in the city's shadow market totaled as much as 42 billion yuan.

Wenzhou's local informal system continues to be the mainstay of capitalism, reinforced, in recent years, by the fact that foreign and private commercial banks (such as Minsheng Bank and Taizhou Commercial Bank) have started to come in and shake up the system across eastern China. In July 2003, nine private-owned enterprises, including Zhejiang Xinhua Holdings Co. Ltd., and Hongqingting Group, became the stockholders of Wenzhou City Commercial Bank. The state's onetime 34.42 percent stake in the Wenzhou Commercial Bank has dwindled to 7.94 percent. Private capital accounted for 67.78 percent of the bank's shareholdings, up from 22.96 percent, and each private shareholder now holds a stake of at least 7.84 percent, up from less than one percent. In June 2004, regulators approved the country's first two private-investment funds. Both plan to invest several hundred million U.S. dollars raised from private firms in Wenzhou. Such funds are still barred from lending, but managers expect approval in the future.

Informal banking in China is an almost "organic" part of society, with deep roots either in the forms of *hui*, private bank houses, credit associations, or a network of pawnshops. The development of Wenzhou's private money houses experienced three distinct phrases: first, prohibition by both the central and local governments, second, prohibition by the central government and non-prohibition by the local government, and, thid, current non-prohibition by both the central and local governments.

Kellee Tsai, a specialist on informal finance in China, notes that only in Wenzhou would the local office of the central bank issue a statement saying that private money houses "are essential for the development of market socialism."[20] There is, however, a bank insurance issue involved. There seems to be little ideological resistance in the communist government toward private banks. But a key sticking point in discussions with state regulators and bankers involves deposit insurance—seen as an essential condition of private banks. The state banks don't think they should have to pay it on the grounds that the government already underwrites their risk. But Fan Jianjun, a researcher at a finance institute under the State Council, believes that the chances of private banks being licensed are very slim. He asks: "What if bank shareholders carry away depositors' money? What if the banks accumulate heavy bad debts? The Ministry of Finance can plug the holes of state-owned banks by injecting money, but who will clear up the mess for private banks?"

Instead of using insurance to take care of the problem and legalize private banks, almost all emerging banks in China now take the form of joint stock ownership, with state control or direct oversight. But the problem again seems to be less an issue of state control than an issue of "credit culture." Private money houses, shareholding banks, and state banks all have their roles in the economy, depending on scale and transaction costs. Building a "contract-based impersonal faith" model in a "relation-based face culture" market takes time.

In the most credit-sensitive finance sector, government institutions provide a necessary control mechanism of external sanction that matches the level of China's current credit reality. For those who have blind faith in a free market, culture is never in their equation, so attacking government intervention is always a moral cause seemingly backed by sound economic reasoning. Yet the Chinese are much more practical than we usually imagine. When government institutions help to reduce uncertainty, take away risks, and ease transaction costs more efficiently, they have no problem leaving it to the government. No wonder the Chinese see market as a means to an end, not a liberal ideal from which perfection is achieved by maximum competition. Culture, however, does evolve over time. More fascinating stories will unfold as the finance sector opens for international competition and more foreign practices are introduced. As preferential tax policies between foreign companies and domestic companies are brought into more equal terms, domestic banks will also benefit.

The Roaring Engine of Export

Like Zhejiang, Guangdong province in the south is also a haven for private enterprise, but its enterprises are characterized by foreign direct investment (FDI) and export oriented growth. In 2002, Zhejiang's export growth totaled $29.4 billion, Guangdong's $118.5 billion; Zhejiang's FDI totaled at 4.7 billion, Guangdong's 13.1 billion; Zhejiang's top 500 largest private companies in China numbered 205; Guangdong's 19; and Zhejiang's number of richest 400 businessmen was 62, Guangdong's 48.

In Guangdong, a second level of rural industrialization is exemplified by activities in the counties lying adjacent to Hong Kong, where enormous investments in rural factories have been made by Hong Kong and Taiwanese corporations. In Chen Village, a community in the Pearl River Delta that encompasses central Guangdong, there is practically no indigenously owned industry today, either collective or private, since the village and the local people alike feel incapable of competing successfully against the experienced, well-capitalized foreign investors. Yet the Party secretary of Chen Village controls sizeable funds by renting out collectively owned land and buildings to foreign companies, and through such fees has been able to construct a new village school and other public facilities, and to develop a substantial personal patronage system. But the village here has become a one-man show, dominated entirely by the Party secretary, since, as a simple rent-collector; he has no need for additional personnel.

There are three recognized models of private sector development in China, namely the "Guangdong Model," the "Sunan Model," and the "Wenzhou Model." In the "Guangdong Model," private enterprises were developed as equipment suppliers for foreign-invested enterprises looking to reduce costs as much as possible. The most common industries are electric appliances, IT-related high-tech equipment, and automobiles. In the backyard of Shanghai, Jiangsu Province is characterized by the development of the agriculture industry with the "Sunan Model" for township enterprises (mixed with private and collective ownership), while Zhejiang Province is famous for its spirit of entrepreneurship, which gave birth to the "Wenzhou Model."

Wenzhou demonstrates a strong focus on sales, a tremendous reliance on comparative advantage, clarity of ownership, and as great a propensity for commercial pricing and market distribution of capital as is possible to realize in China today. The "Guangdong Model" differs from its most obvious domestic rival, Zhejiang, in being much more dependent on outside (i.e., Hong Kong or Taiwan) middlemen, foreign direct investment, and exports. Guangdong also operates with the benefit of generous tax incentives, the Shenzhen reform "laboratory," and various other perks handed out by the central government. It is no surprise that foreign direct investment is channeled primarily to cities with a thriving market and the convenience of sea transportation. Consequently, FDI per capita in the southeastern provinces is $128, which is 1.3, 7, and 25 times as much as in the northeastern, central, and western regions respectively. In Zhejiang, Jiangsu, and Guangdong provinces, foreign enterprise makes up 43 percent of the total gross industrial output value.

Nearly thirty years ago, Hong Kong's small-time manufacturers made a big bet on the rural Pearl River Delta, backed by limited capital—and close personal connections and enormous faith in China. The Delta region offered cheap labor, abundant land, hospitable environment, hard workers, and low taxes. Hong Kong's small-time manufacturers provided production orders, management, quality control, logistics support, marketing, and other value-added services needed to sell to every corner of the world. That synergy is nothing short of electric, making the Hong Kong-Pearl River Delta connection an indispensable part of the global supply chain.

Currently, about 80,000 Hong Kong companies in Guangdong employ about 12 million workers—more than the entire population of Hong Kong itself. Hong Kong has become both a winner and a victim of its success. The migration of labor-intensive jobs to China has transformed Hong Kong from a sweatshop to a leading financial and service industry center. However, the Pearl River Delta has been transformed into not only a giant manufacturing base, but also a growing rival of Hong Kong in the service sector.

Air transport is a great example. In the vicinity of Hong Kong's Chek Lap Kok airport, there are four other international air terminals, in Shenzhen, Guangzhou, Zhuhai, and Macau. Shenzhen, only minutes away from Hong Kong, has taken over much of the low-cost flight business. The newly expanded Baiyun Airport in Guangzhou is even more formidable. Due to its superior location, flights that used to go via Hong Kong or Zhuhai will now go to Guangzhou. From transport facilities to call centers, Hong Kong has to fight off competition posed by its low-cost neighbors.

Feeling the hollowed-out effect, Hong Kong remains ambitious, especially in its finance sector. In recent years, its stock market made numerous IPO deals with mainland companies, mostly snapped up by international investors. Foreign companies continue to see Hong Kong as a gateway to China. Hong Kong-registered firms, regardless of origin, benefit from a pact, the Closer Economic Partnership Agreement (CEPA), signed between Hong Kong and China, effective January 2004. The pact offers duty-free status to 1,087 categories of goods originating from Hong Kong, and easier market access to the mainland market for eighteen types of professional services, including accounting, fund management, advertising, and legal services. Firms can enter the China market with lower capital requirements, as long as they have been operating in Hong Kong for three to five years, and as long as half of their staff are Hong Kong residents.

The Pearl River Delta Economic Zone is Guangdong province's economic hub, accounting for about 85 percent of its GDP. The Economic Zone covers fourteen cities and counties: Guangzhou, Shenzhen, Zhuhai, Foshan, Jiangmen, Dongguan, Zhongshan, Huizhou, Huiyang, Huidong, Boluo, Zhaoqing, Gaoyao, and Sihui. Guangdong's economy leads the country in many ways: it has the largest share of GDP among all provinces and municipalities, accounting for 12 percent of the national total; it has the highest industrial output (13 percent of the national total), the largest export value (32 percent of the national total), and the largest retail sales of consumer goods (12 percent of the national total).

Among the most industrialized "star" cities—Guangzhou, Shenzhen, Dongguan, Foshan, Huizhou, Jiangmen, and Zhuhai—the influence of Hong Kong can be seen almost everywhere. People there speak the same dialect (Cantonese), cherish the same local culture, construct a highly personalized business network, and share the same commercial spirit. In 2006, Guangzhou became China's first city to have a per capita GDP of over $10,000. Japan reached this level in 1984, Hong Kong in 1987, Singapore in 1989, Taiwan in 1992, and South Korea in 1995.

The Pearl River Delta is home to countless manufacturing and assembly workshops. Every year, it consumes almost a quarter of China's total foreign direct investment. About 80 percent of its total export is assembly processing. If anything you own is "Made in China," chances are it was made the Delta. Major products include television sets, fans, refrigerators, microwave ovens, computers and computer accessories, plastics, mechanical and electrical products, refined chemicals, hardware, and other consumer products such as textiles, clothing and accessories, bicycles, toys, and shoes. Not surprisingly, exports of most of these products rank the highest in China due to the Hong Kong factor. In recent years, Guangdong is also moving toward heavy industry and the high-tech industry. The share of heavy industries in gross industrial output increased from 43 percent in 1999 to around 55 percent in 2006.

New and high technology industries in Shenzhen, China's first "Special Economic Zone," for example, accounted for over 40 percent of the city's total industrial output. InfoTech, of course, is the mainstay here. Factories are almost everywhere in Shenzhen. Taiwanese electronics group Foxconn, one of the largest, makes motherboards and other components, and its parts feature in nearly every electronic device, from mobile phones to laptops. Workers at its complex of factories number over 200,000 people; 3,000 pigs a day are needed to feed them.

In 2005, exports from Shenzhen broke the $100 billion barrier for the first time, making it the first Chinese city to do so. The ten biggest exporters in Shenzhen accounted for 28 percent of the city's entire export value, and three of those firms were part of Foxconn. Other big exporters in Shenzhen include the Quanta Computer group, the world's largest notebook PC maker, with Compal Electronics following close behind. Other Taiwanese manufacturers include Inventec, BenQ, and LiteOn, which make everything from servers to mobile phones.[21] Bio-tech and other industries are also on the rise.

Shenzhen's research and development expenditures equate to 3 percent of its GDP, the highest among Guangdong cities, and much higher than the national average at 1.3 percent. Foreign-funded enterprises have generated two-thirds of the city's gross industrial output. Interestingly, foreign-funded companies, especially those of relatively small size, usually have a short operational life. Many have purposely folded to start new businesses as preferential tax policies are given to new foreign-funded companies after their first five years. Under separate laws passed in 1985 and 1991 (expected to be merged and standardized before 2008), the tax rate for domestic companies is 33 percent and that of foreign-invested businesses is 30 percent. But with pre-tax deductions, preferential tax policies, and tax rate differences, the actual rate for foreign firms can be as low as 13–15 percent, compared to about 25 percent for domestic businesses (though it is expected that both foreign and domestic will be brought to 25 percent). It is also common for these new companies to use "round tripping" FDI for their registered capital, a tricky way to move money out of the border and then move it back in as "foreign investment" to take advantage of preferential incentives. No wonder capital from Hong Kong usually totals around 70 percent of Guangdong's total foreign investment: Hong Kong, China's "Special Administrative Region," is still considered "foreign" after its return from British control in 1997.

Many Hong Kong companies, including V-Tech, Gold Peak, Johnson Electrics, Hutchison, and Hopewell, have participated extensively in Guangdong's industrial and infrastructure investments. In recent years, Hong Kong's investment in Guangdong has diversified from manufacturing to the services sector. Hong Kong brands such as Baleno, Esprit, G2000, Giordano, Cafe De Coral, and Just Gold are highly visible in Guangdong's retail sector.

Other major investors in Guangdong come from Taiwan, Japan, South Korea, Singapore, and the U.S. Many leading multinationals—among them IBM, Intel, Hitachi, Samsung, Nokia, Sony, General Electric, Proctor & Gamble, Amway, ICI, Ericsson, Siemens, Panasonic, Bosch, Toshiba, Sanyo, Nestlé, Pepsi, Coca-Cola, and Mitsubishi—have established their presence in Guangdong. Foreign investment has increasingly been channeled into infrastructure, agriculture, property, and capital and technological projects in recent years. Given China's World Trade Organization commitment to further liberalize its services sector, an increasing share of FDI is expected to go into the service sector in the coming years.

Production by Guangdong's vibrant private sector (non-state-owned and non-state-holding enterprises) accounted for around 85 percent of the province's total industrial output. Many local companies have developed a strong brand name in their specialized areas and become market leaders in China, including Galanz, Midea, Macro, Donlim, Kangbao, Gree, and Sunten.

Destructive Innovation

Chen Kai, living in Shantou City[22] of Guangdong province, represents the generation who endured the tough years of China's planned economy. During the 1960s, schools closed due to the Cultural Revolution; he and his peers became young "Red Guards" defending Mao's revolutionary word. In the 1970s, during the middle of the Cultural Revolution, the only "job choice" was to be one of Mao's followers, "going up to the mountain and down to the countryside," the process through which millions were dispatched to rural areas and re-educated through "working the land."

When the Chinese economy started to take off in the 1980s, Chen came back to Shantou from a factory in northern Guangdong and squeezed into an over-employed state-owned company through some back-door connections. The Chinese believe when bad luck strikes twice, it will surely strike for a third time. China's state-owned enterprises began to crumble. After a few bad years, Chen decided to start his own business. He did this in the 1990s, when the private economy was set in motion. Chen's shop was like a boat, rising upward on the water of reform; for the first time, he found himself empowered. The good times didn't last long; the nightmares of the 1960s and 1970s began to haunt him. Chronic gambling took its toll. Addiction was followed by debt, alcohol, more debt, and finally the collapse of his business. While many of his peers sailed with the business boom into the new millennium, Chen Kai, at age 50, was unable to recover from despair.

In a place where a market economy is taken for granted, it is hard to imagine how a planned economy and the enterprises under it had actually worked. Before China's reform started in 1978, the state-owned enterprise was not really a business entity. SOEs can be best viewed as a trio: they are at once an economic unit, a social unit, and political unit. In the sense that an SOE produces goods and provides services, it is a business body. Yet its social functions were performed through the official arrangement of employment, public security, healthcare, retirement benefits, childcare, housing, and even schools in some big "units" (danwei). Political functions were operated by Party branches, through which mass mobilization and ideological control for political agendas were fulfilled. In such a setting, the business of the SOE was militarized in a way that production was executed by top-down commands, and incentives were artificially boosted by ideological propaganda, with "model heroes" and "political celebrations." Product pricing was merely an accounting symbol, not a market signal.

How the SOE trio entity functions under a planned economy is unclear to many outsiders who champion a privatization prescription and a market "shock therapy" with a Western-style prognosis. In fact, even many insiders may be unclear about how the Chinese cultural logic will impact the process of marketization. But the miraculous result of China's "controlled experiment" proves that what it has been doing—"gradualism therapy"—is the best that can be done.

Specifically, "gradualism therapy" employs the Chinese holistic style of systematic treatment to reform the SOE internally and promote private and foreign owned businesses externally; at the same time, with these internal and external innovations, price control gives way to market pricing; and the building of market institutions (labor markets, shareholding banks, stock markets) and macro-economic management are on track with the parallel development of enterprise-level micro-transformations. "Gradualism therapy," essentially, is replacing the old "Massive Militarization" with "Managed Marketization," with authoritarian control as the common theme. SOEs internal innovation cannot succeed without the external support of private and foreign businesses that take over most of its social functions (employment for example). The burgeoning market system as the state-owned enterprise's operating environment, on the other hand, cannot maintain an orderly manner without strong macro-management. Today, it can be securely said that China has passed the marketization test with its gradualist reform approach.

The internal process of reforming the SOEs, however, is still a painful experience for all parties involved. The process can be summarized by the "Four Ds," namely: decentralization, deregulation, desocialization, and depoliticization. Reform of state-owned enterprises began by focusing on increasing efficiency, just like the re-arrangement of production methods in agriculture. Measures included loosening government control and implementing contract responsibility and leasehold systems. Reform in setting up the shareholding system began in the late 1980s, even though the nature of "state-run" anything didn't really change in any meaningful way, even though "short-termism" was rampant among contracted managers.

In 1993, China decided to further reform its SOEs by establishing a modern corporate system and encouraging foreign and private investment to participate in SOE corporatization through joint ventures, mergers, and acquisitions. As a result, SOEs were transformed into mixed ownership companies with different types of investors who could run checks and balances on each other. From the mid-1990s forward, the government proceeded to privatize state-owned enterprises in the name of its policy of "keeping the large and releasing the small" and the "strategic realignment of the state-owned economy" in various industry sectors.

The fact that local government will be able to retain the income from the sale of state-owned assets has become a major incentive for them to promote privatization. In short, four processes were employed for SOE reform: the first is through the contracting or leasing of public firms. The second is the one most often identified with the word "privatization" in policy discussions. The third is a more ambiguous one, whereby government officials and their associates begin to reap such private benefits from their domination of public firms that public firms begin to shade gradually into a form of local elite privatization. It usually proceeds through the closed process of management buyouts or management-employee buyouts. The fourth process occurs when state agencies or enterprises invest public funds in new enterprises that operate independently as private firms.[23]

Although most of the SOEs have successfully sold off company housing to their workers, it has proved much more difficult to lay off employees accustomed to "iron rice bowls" and to unload other social welfare undertakings. Anxiety over mounting labor unrest is holding back some of the largest SOEs from completing the ambitious program of layoffs they began in the late 1990s in an effort to cut costs and boost productivity. With healthcare and social security systems still not in place, the fear of unrest adds to the lingering sense of social responsibility toward affected workers.

In 1978, SOEs generated about 80 percent of China's GDP. As reform moves on, state collectives, private companies, and foreign company businesses have led to the scaling back of SOE input to less than 20 percent of GDP.

During the years 1989 to 2003, the number of private enterprises increased thirty-fold, from 90,000 to 3 million. The number of individual business during the same period almost doubled, from 12.47 million to 23.53 million. The number of foreign-funded enterprises rose from about 16,000 to 226,000. In comparison, the number of collective enterprises fell from 4.16 million in 1992 to 1.63 million in 2003, and SOEs from 1.55 million to 150,000. Only 161 centrally controlled SOEs and 138,000 locally controlled SOEs remain (managed by the State-owned Assets Supervision Administration Commission, or SASAC). And the government still plans to approve the bankruptcy of more than 2,000 SOEs before 2008, which will be the last exception to strictly following a unified corporate bankruptcy law for all 8 million companies in China.

Under such "administrative closure," the money recovered from insolvent SOEs is used to manage the unemployed first, with leftovers going to creditors or the state-owned banks. SASAC defines seven economic sectors that are "vital arteries of the national economy" and in which state ownership (solely owned or majority controlled) is considered essential. The sectors are armaments, electrical power and distribution, oil and chemicals, telecommunications, coal, aviation, and shipping. More than 40 of the 161 large SOEs supervised by SASAC are engaged in these sectors. Their total assets account for 75 percent of all central SOEs, and they rake in 79 percent of the profits. To reorient state capital away from non-critical areas to priority sectors, China will reduce the number of central SOEs by at least one-third to between 80 and 100 before 2010 through various mergers and eliminating of redundancy. China aims to build between thirty and fifty large, internationally competitive companies by 2010.

According to Chinese official statistics, the number of employees working for SOEs in 2003 was 68.8 million, a sharp decline compared with 112.6 million in 1995. By contrast, workers in individual and private enterprises reached 89.5 million in that same year, exceeding SOE employees by about 20 million, and registering a big increase over 55.7 million in 1995. Looking at the breakdown, the number of employees of individual businesses rose steeply from just 2.3 million in 1981 to 46.5 million in 2003, a twenty-fold increase. The number of employees rose even faster in private enterprises than in individual businesses, from 1.6 million in 1989 to 43 million in 2003, a twenty-seven-fold increase in fourteen years.

Foreign funded enterprises employ many workers, even though their share of total employees is less than that of individual and private enterprises. Employees in private enterprises now make up 19.2 percent of total national employees. Currently, SOEs still control 57 percent of the country's industrial assets. They dominate vital industries such as financial services, power, steel, railways, and telecommunications. On average, state-owned enterprises yield a return on assets of 3 percent, well below the 7 percent in the private sector. State-owned company profits represented 3.3 percent of China's GDP and 20 percent of the government's tax revenue in 2005.

But China maintained a "no-dividend" policy for its state assets before 2007. When the majority shareholder doesn't have to be paid a share of the profit, it becomes a lot easier for managers to reward themselves with excessive corporate perks. As a result of government subsidies and "policy loans" to SOEs, the government-reported profit of many SOEs may be less than meaningful. In 1999, China set up four Asset Management Companies: Huarong, Cinda, Orient, and Great Wall, to dispose of 866.34 billion yuan in bad loans accrued by the country's four state-owned lenders, recovering 180.56 billion yuan in cash by the end of March 2006.

To facilitate corporatization, the Shanghai Stock Exchange was founded in 1990, the Shenzhen Stock Exchange in 1991. Many SOEs that had adopted the shareholding system went public, with some of their shares acquired by private capital. SOE managers, many of whom viewed the Chinese stock market as their own personal ATM, were all eager to go IPO. Not surprisingly, only the best-performing or in many cases the best-connected firms could get the green light to make an initial public offering With the economy on an upswing, the country's stock markets were plagued by insider trading, listed companies' bad loans, and illegal asset transfers. The problems prompted an effort to improve market credibility.

In 2004, brokerage houses that had engaged in overly speculative and illegal trading were either cleaned up or blacklisted. Later, bogus loans and asset-stripping of listed companies were declared criminal offenses. State-owned shares in the more than 1,300 listed companies were freed by a "selling to the float" scheme (*gu quan fen zi*), putting $270 billion government-controlled assets into the market. This massive capital-sucking scheme had always been a huge drag on stock prices, but once the news was out, investor jitters were soon replaced by hopes of improved performance given the huge influx of foreign capital. As a result, the stock market almost tripled from mid 2005 to early 2007.

While Zhejiang's economic expansion has been a manifestation of the aggressiveness of family business culture, Guangdong's global supply chain reveals the merit of close-tie cultural connections with Hong Kong and Taiwan—both of which have been in the loop of modern business practices for years. The secret that large Chinese companies are overwhelmingly state-owned lies not only on the legacy of state power but, more importantly, on the Chinese "credit culture" and interdependent psychology (expressed by satisfaction from personal attachment, less aggressive material pursuits, and less ambitious in greatness—the Weberian argument that Confucian ethics are unfavorable for capitalist expansion).

Corporatization revitalizes China's state-owned enterprises, yet a call for total privatization—from insiders with an undigested free market view or from outsiders with a different cultural perspective—can cause a destructive imbalance. Markets will produce sustainable cooperation only to the extent they can ensure that individuals or firms will be responsible for the beneficial and harmful effects of their actions on others. In an interdependent-oriented culture, the sensitivity to external effects is too frequently assumed away either because cultural interdependence is not recognized or because the extent of sensitivity is seen as universally constant. This is why the role of the government in China is often mistakenly attacked. A nation with a relational tradition will have a lot more things than "efficiency" to take care of.

Modern shareholding corporations do provide a better mechanism for family business to scale up and outlive the shareholders. But the evolution of trust and faith takes time and is a dynamic game that involves many factors. In addition to the "credit culture" and interdependent psychology that limits the size growth of private firms, traditional personal indulgences among business elites also plays a part. A Chinese idiom goes: "Affluence will not go beyond three generations" (*fu bu guo san dai*). Gambling is not the only pursuit, though it could be. *Majiang* (the game played with several sets of patterened tiles) is now almost a national sport. Profligacy in the elite culture may include having a "second wife" (*er nai*), drug abuse, squandering the family fortune, and other forms of reckless behavior. The family-oriented mentality sets up a narrow world-view dominated by social connections.

Among the Chinese, there is an endemic detachment from someone they simply don't have a connection to. The Chinese national psychology is so different that it's no wonder Westerners find it hard to understand how come the Chinese government always plays such an important part in society. It is a convenient deduction that an authoritarian regime imperils its capacity for political control if it embraces full economic liberalization. It's also a comforting thought that economic liberalization will eventually produce civil liberties and political pluralism.[24] But one is as wrong as the other because the logic of government dominance is not only the will of the "supply side" from political elites, but also a requirement of the "demand side" from society. As we shall see, such ideas are the major obstacles in understanding the present and predicting the future of China.

Thus, China's strategy, though seemingly unfair to many, is a unified, enforceable, and effective strategy given its political structure. It allows a portion of the people to get rich first, then attempts to solve other problems in the overall reform process. For the same market reforms, others may let the free market work itself out. China's philosophy is to control it rather than to let it flow.

To showcase Chinese companies for foreign investment, for example, the government only lets its first-rate companies go to New York, the second-tier companies go to Hong Kong, and the rest stay in the home market. In China's stock markets, there are strict upper and lower limits for daily fluctuation, both for individual stocks and indices. When the market bubble burst in early 1997, China ordered its banks to stop lending to companies and individuals who used the money for stock investments. In its derivative market for futures and options, the government expedited the process when Singapore "illegally" developed financial products based on China's stocks. Even the number of companies destined to join the *Fortune* Global 500 is carefully planned—the intent is an increase from nineteen today to fifty in the years ahead. The era of planned economy may be long gone, yet the government is always in command. Its marketization is, in effect, a "managed marketization." When China's accession to the World Trade Organization was thought by some to be an inevitable "coming collapse," the Chinese demonstrated unprecedented determination and strength.[25]

The Chinese government imposed tight restrictions on bandwidth for internet traffic entering the country, which makes any website host located outside China run slower than the sites hosted within China—a way to control web content and force companies to invest in the market. To protect the country's diminishing farmland, the Chinese government has banned the building of new golf courses, luxury homes, and racetracks on undeveloped land. New land use for large commercial facilities such as large furniture and building materials facilities, entertainment centers, theme parks, and cemeteries are to be restricted and prohibited on farmland.

When auto exports hit new highs in 2006 (340,000 units), the government established export quotas for 2007 to prevent domestic carmakers from getting too involved with cutthroat competition. When a Shanghai teahouse came up with the catchy name "Qingwa Bao Ernai" ("Frog Keeps a Mistress"), it was immediately considered immoral and in violation of China's advertising law. China's internet is filtered; the news media is in the grip of the government, but, by some bad calculation, the plan to regulate foreign media in China was aborted when the timing coincided with the return of Hong Kong in 1997.

In *One Billion Customers*, former *Wall Street Journal* ex-China-bureauchief James McGregor detailed how excited he was to exploit this miscalculation. However, restrictions made their way back in 2006, during a time when openness suddenly seemed like the norm in China, and free-minded journalists chided China for being both a market player as well as a media regulator. The reality is that the Chinese are not going to surrender control of their vital economic sectors (be it finance or news), or, for that matter, key state-owned companies. China understands how come the U.S. government made such a big deal over China National Offshore Oil Corporation's bid for U.S. oil giant Unocal in 2005.

During the first China-U.S. "Strategic Economic Dialogue" in December 2006, U.S. trade representative Susan Schwab argued that the "Asian model" of basing economics on state control and massive exports was no longer suitable for China. This argument was refuted immediately by Ma Kai (chairman of the National Development and Reform Commission of China) and Wu Yi (deputy prime minister), who said that China's model of mixing state control and free markets was appropriate given China's volatile history. Wu Yi also furthered the discussion by stating: "We have had the genuine feeling that some American friends are not only having limited knowledge of, but harboring much misunderstanding about, the reality in China."[26] The American construct of this logic is "bottom-up" and "straightforward," while Chinese culture is "top-down" and "fame-favor." For example, to state: "You are wrong. You should do this for your own benefit" may be an effective statement from an American point of view. However, the statement: "You are right, *but* can you do *this?*" makes more sense when dealing with China.

Explaining Boom and Bust: "Blame the Cow"

"It's the Investment, Stupid!"

The Chinese "Cult of Face" explains economic behavior only on the level of cultural psychology; it doesn't actually explain economic motivation on the incentive level, which is much more relevant to economic expansion. In the context of explaining economic growth, no other story is more gripping than one told by Michael Fairbanks in his paper, "Changing the Mind of a Nation: Elements in a Process of Creating Prosperity:"[1]

> The Monitor Company worked for the government and private sector leaders of Colombia to study and provide recommendations on how the leather producers in that nation could become more prosperous by exporting to the United States. We began in New York City to find the buyers of leather handbags from around the world, and we interviewed the representatives of 2,000 retail establishments across the United States. The data were complex but boiled down to one clear message: The prices of Colombian handbags were too high and the quality was too low.
>
> We returned to Colombia to ask the manufacturers what low-

ered their quality and forced them to charge high prices. They told us . . . it was the fault of the local tanneries that supplied them with the hides. The tanneries had a 15 percent tariff protection from the Colombian government, which made the price of competing hides from Argentina too expensive.

We traveled to the rural areas to find the tannery owners. . . . "It is not our fault," they explained, "It is the fault of the *mataderos,* the slaughterhouses. They provide a low-quality hide to the tanneries because they can sell the meat from the cow for more money with less effort. They have little concern for damaging the hides."

We went into the *campo* and found slaughterhouses . . . asked them the same questions and they explained that it was not their fault; it was the ranchers' fault. "You see," they said, "the ranchers over-brand their cows in an effort to keep the guerrillas . . . from stealing them." The large number of brands destroys the hides.

We finally reached the ranchers. . . . We had reached the end of our search because there was no one left to interview. . . . They told us that the problems were not their fault. . . . It's the cow's fault. The cows are stupid, they explained. They rub their hides against the barbed wire to scratch themselves and to deflect the biting flies of the region. . . .

There are many different ways to consider the issues faced by our friends in Colombia. Imagine a macro-economist's interpretation of the "blame the cow" story: He might remove the tariff and "let the market find a new equilibrium." The nongovernmental organizations (NGOs) might work to upgrade the barbed-wire fence, and a business strategist might study and segment the consumer market. A sociologist might say that "the level of interpersonal trust" in the community is too low. An anthropologist might say that they are simply at "a different stage in their economic development" and should be left alone to progress naturally. . . . Our challenge is not unlike that of the experts who would attempt to fix the "blame the cow" story: How to merge one set of insights with another, to begin to create a locally owned process for change in developing nations that is so thoughtfully integrated, well guided, and productively discussed that it begins to put nations and peoples on the path to high and rising prosperity.

Blaming non-human factors for human mistakes in all human affairs is almost a universal phenomenon. China's economic miracle presents a different story. But if "Authoritarian Laissez-faire" can be seen only as a cultural interpretation rather than an analytical explanation, then how do we "merge one set of insights with another" so as to decipher China's "locally owned process for change"? Putting it differently, given China's culture, why was economic growth not sustainable before reform?

Economic growth is nothing more than the increase of output in goods and services. To increase output, all you need to do is increase input. That is, to invest with more land, labor, and capital. In the 1960s, such growth theory became more sophisticated by looking at labor, capital, and a residual component called "total factor productivity," which could be determined by population structure, education, human capital, savings, capital accumulation, relative price of resources, geography and climate, economies of scale, trade, knowledge, technology, innovation, entrepreneurship, work methods, management, public infrastructure, and macro-economic policies. But the focus is still the same: input. When a society fails to grow, economists will say: "It's the investment, stupid!"

No one challenged this perception until 1973, when two economic historians, Douglass C. North and Robert Paul Thomas, stated that, while all the factors listed above represent "growth," they are by themselves sources rather than causes.[2] In their book *The Rise of the Western World: A New Economic History*, they pointed out that "if all that is required for economic growth is investment and innovation, why have some societies missed this desirable outcome?"

In 1982, along a similar line of thought in *The Rise and Decline of Nations: Economic Growth, Stagflation, and Social Rigidities*, Mancur Olson further stated that "estimates of the sources of growth, however meticulous, subtle, and useful, do not tell us about the ultimate causes of growth. They do not tell us what incentives made the saving and investment occur, or what explained the innovations, or why there was more innovation and capital accumulation in one society or period than in another. They do not trace the sources of growth to their fundamental causes; they trace the water in the river to the streams and lakes from which it comes, but they do not explain the rain. Neither do they explain the silting up of the channels of economic progress—that is, what I shall call here the 'retardants' of growth."[3]

This, essentially, is merely explaining water by explaining the rain. You can't, however, just "trace the water in the river to the streams and lakes" and stop there. China's economic reform started from incentives. Initial industrialization and rural development in the 1950s were driven by input. But the military-ideological style of mobilization proved to be inefficient and un-sustainable. The problem of planned economy, however, is about "the critical interdependence between market choice itself and the informational content of this process which can only be revealed as the process is allowed to occur."[4]

When incentive-based reform spread from agriculture to other economic sectors, production gradually shifted from planned quota to market demand. To further address the "allocative efficiency" issue, many government-monopolized industry sectors were open for competition, and price controls were gradually removed. State-owned enterprises were privatized and corporatized. Activities of non-state-owned enterprises took hold and private property started to prevail. Free trade and free entry expanded free pricing and the free flow of production factors. Legal reform helped reduce transaction costs. Investment by foreign companies and by overseas Chinese is systematically encouraged. The process is far from perfect, but the right steps have been taken in the right directions.

The institutional changes and favorable enforcement of private property, free competition, and organization rearrangement all induced unprecedented expansion of investment. But these productive efforts alone still didn't explain growth when destructive efforts are not contained. The "Great Leap Forward" from 1958 to 1962 and the "Cultural Revolution" from 1996 to 1976 are examples of politics-related destructive efforts. These disasters happened under an institutional arrangement that reflected the legacy of the traditional autocracy that was prone to "cult of personality" and dynastic political struggles.

In the 1950s, Mao saw grain and steel production as the two key pillars of economic development. "Catch up with Britain and get ahead of America" (*guan ying chao mei*) was the slogan for "Socialist development." Mao was shown an example of a backyard furnace in September 1958 by the first secretary of Anhui Province, Zeng Xisheng. It was claimed to be manufacturing high quality steel while, in fact, the finished steel had been manufactured elsewhere. Mao encouraged the establishment of small backyard steel furnaces in every commune and in each urban neighborhood. To fuel the furnaces, trees were cut down and wood was taken from doors and furniture of peasants' houses. Pots, pans, and other metal artifacts were requisitioned to supply "scrap" for the furnaces so that the wildly optimistic production targets could be met.

On the communes, a number of controversial agricultural policies were promoted, including close cropping, whereby seeds were sown far more densely than normal on the assumption that seeds of the same class would not compete with each other. A proportion of fields were left fallow, and deep plowing was encouraged on the mistaken belief that this would yield plants with extra large root systems. Grain-eating birds were killed, which resulted in a widespread proliferation of insect pests. Large-scale but poorly planned irrigation works were built. Due to the political oppression of the "Hundred Flowers Campaign" and the "Anti-Rightist Campaign" earlier in 1957, those who were aware of the folly of these plans dared not voice criticism, and the plans were only quietly abandoned later when everybody was exhausted.

The "Great Leap Forward" is also known as the "Great Leap Famine" because it caused the death of at least 30 million people, a number that approximates the entire population of Canada. China's GDP in 1961 was a miserable 27.3 percent negative growth. When Liu Shaoqi condemned it as "30 percent natural disaster, 70 percent human mistake," the massive internal battle of the Cultural Revolution was on. Power struggles shifted from between Mao and Liu, to between Mao and his handpicked successor Lin Biao, to between the "Gang of Four" and other party elites, all with large-scale mass involvement.

During this period, millions of teenage "Red Guards" were first used by Mao to purge Liu and other "Capitalist Roaders," who were sent to get educated by the farmers. It shouldn't be too hard to see that the elimination of politically related destructive efforts during the reform era was conducive to the institutional environment of economic growth. In fact, during the thirty years from 1978 to 2007, the only large-scale political unrest was when GDP growth slid to 4.1 percent in 1989, and to 2.7 percent the following year, the lowest in the thirty-year reform period. The 1989 democratic protest carried the institutional shadow of previous mass movements, even though it was for a different purpose. The Tiananmen Square incident revealed that social instability could result when the government has no institutionally accepted way to handle a group of frustrated human beings who mobilize and participate in a mass movement to underscore social change.[5]

The point here is not about destructive efforts,[6] it's about how such destructive efforts are culturally and politically institutionalized. Douglass North has noted that we cannot truly understand economic change until we understand what drove a group of well-educated, middle-class Muslim men to fly planes into the World Trade Center. The same can be said that we cannot truly understand economic change until we can understand what drove a group of teenage Red Guards to mercilessly kill head of state Liu Shaoqi and many others during the Cultural Revolution. If Deng Xiaoping didn't systematically put an end to Mao-styled "class struggle," his reform would certainly be less fruitful. The reality of human affairs is this: it takes so much less effort to destroy than to build, that the pain of construction and reconstruction can easily stall productive efforts when human destructive efforts are not institutionally curbed.

In addition to productive efforts and destructive efforts, there are also efforts related to the wealth distribution and redistribution process. Corporatization reform effectively reduced the political and social welfare functions of state-owned enterprises and made them operate more like business entities. No matter how corrupt the privatization process, the outcome is a substantial decrease in distributional efforts. Deregulation also contributes to this positive process.

China introduced active measures to encourage domestic consumption, including American-style mortgage and credit card systems. Such consumption efforts undoubtedly help investment and growth. Input-driven growth dimension should not be neglected. In the U.S., a 3 to 5 percent growth rate is often called "robust" or "vigorous." In China, the same can almost be called a "recession." During the last thirty years, the U.S. has had three negative growth years (1980, 1982, and 1991), which weren't slow growth years in China. In fact, what we often hear from China is not about economic slowdown, it's almost always about overheating. The "taking-off" from a low-level economic stage effect cannot explain this because the level was much lower before China's reform. Besides those institutional factors that stimulate growth mentioned above, one more drives China's growth: the institutional setting of the fiscal relations between the central and the local government, and the administrative relations between the government and the state-owned banks and firms.

In 1994, China launched a large-scale campaign to reform its fiscal and taxation system from a centralized fiscal planning (before the 1980s) and a contract-based fiscal bargaining, to a tax-sharing system whereby the tax revenue is divided by both the central and the local governments. Central government's taxes include customs duties, consumption taxes, and taxes on centrally controlled companies (railroads, banks, etc). Local government's taxes include corporate income taxes, and real estate and property taxes. Personal income tax and value-added tax revenues are shared by central and local governments (75 percent central, 25 percent local).

But the reform still gave preferential treatment to the vested interests of the former system in various regions. Reform efforts were unable to break through the former distribution structure formed on the basis of one-to-one bargaining. While it strengthens the central government's position for more stable tax revenue, the local taxation system doesn't have a reasonable tax base and stable income source. Central government's share of total government budgetary revenue went from 11 percent in 1979, 38 percent in 1986, 21 percent in 1993, to more than 50 percent after 1994. On the other hand, the central government's share of budgetary expenditure went from more than 50 percent before 1984, 28 percent in 1996, to above 30 percent after 1998. A net "local to central" redistribution of budgetary expenditure was changed to net "central to local" redistribution. The share of local government expenditure (over 60 percent) in total government expenditure now is much higher than the average of industrialized countries (about 33 percent) and developing countries (about 22 percent).

Local governments in China have too many responsibilities and too many mandates (more than 60 percent of the country's fiscal burden), but little fiscal power (can't borrow directly from commercial banks or from issuing bonds). The only way out for them is to raise indirect borrowings via local government-owned firms, and collect not-strictly-regulated non-tax revenue, including extra-budgetary and off-budget funds from various kinds of charges and fees. While the proportion of budgetary funds to GDP went down year by year, the extra-budgetary and non-budgetary fund has grown rapidly, making the government revenue to GDP surpass 25 percent in recent years. These "disguised funds" help relieve local financial pressures and contribute to a boom in fixed-asset investment, seriously undermining the central government's efforts to rein in overcapacity and head off inflation.

In the first five months of 2006, for example, fixed-asset investment rose 30.3 percent year-on-year to 2.54 trillion yuan, despite a hike in interest rates, intensified scrutiny of bank lending, and the announcement in April of new property curbs (more down payments). The growth rate was well ahead of Beijing's target of 18 percent for 2006. Local governments' power over corporate income taxes and property taxes also provides an incentive for them to invest in those most profitable high-priced sectors and to levy taxes and fees on those products from other regions—an institutionalized "local protectionism."

Government's fraternalism to the state-owned enterprises and their "investment hunger" due to distributional demand, asymmetric information, and moral hazard are another aspect of the institutional setting. This so-called "soft budget-constraints" problem evolved from more about direct government budget grants to more about bank loans and non-budgetary funding. The current Chinese banking system has emerged from financing under the planned economy, where banks worked like a cash artery or an accounting department—and funds were used for what is called "policy lending," or loans with socio-political objectives, which resulted in a high level of non-performing loans (NPLs).

The World Bank estimates that, between 1991 and 2000, almost a third of investment decisions in China were misguided. The Chinese central bank's research shows that politically directed lending was responsible for 60 percent of non-performing loans in 2001–2002. Even though nonperforming loans as a percentage of bank assets dropped to about 7 percent in 2006 from 9 percent in 2005, high-risk medium- and long-term loans (mostly without collateral) still account for nearly 50 percent or about $1.5 trillion.

Chinese economic planners revealed in early 2006 that 11 major capital-intensive manufacturing industries were overproducing. For example, the country's steel industry, the world's largest, has 116 million tons (or about 30 percent) of excess capacity. Excessive investment has exacerbated oversupply, and overcapacity still exists in sectors like steel and iron, cement, aluminum, coke, and coal. Production lines with low capacity and outdated technology cause serious pollution and waste, while intensified overcapacity drives more export and further fosters China's foreign trade imbalance. A 2004 survey by the Ministry of Commerce found that of 600 major consumer products, 446 or 74.3 percent were in oversupply. Brazil, Russia, India, and China (BRIC) are all experiencing phenomenal growth in recent years. Distribution-driven over-heating provides the main reason for the diversion of capital efficiency between China and the other three "BRIC Countries," especially between China and India where an investment rate at 50 percent of China's investment rate has achieved a growth rate well over 50 percent of China's growth rate.[7]

Altogether, economic growth is not just about incentives, nor is it just about institutions that favor reducing the gap between social and private rates of return or conforming individual return with individual efforts.[8] It is not just about achieving "organizational efficiency" (efficiency from incentive-sensitive organizational re-arrangement), "allocative efficiency" (efficiency from free market resource allocation) and "adaptive efficiency" (efficiency from intentional learning of how property institutions affect growth).

Here, institutions (as defined by Douglass North) are composed of formal rules, informal rules, and characteristics of enforcing those rules. One possible advantage of this "Effort-based Institutional Analysis" is: its analytical structure provides a categorized conceptual tool to logically combine Douglass North's institutional growth theory and Mancur Olson's "distributional coalition" growth theory.[9] According to Olson, small distributional coalitions have the incentives to form political lobbies and influence policies that tend to be protectionist and anti-technology; since the benefits of these policies are selective incentives concentrated amongst the few coalitions members and the costs are diffused throughout the whole population, the

"Logic" dictates that there will be little public resistance to them; as time goes on, these distributional coalitions accumulate in greater and greater numbers, the nation burdened by them will fall into economic decline.

The analytical structure will go from a first-level structure of "productive-destructive-distributional" efforts, to a second-level structure for each of the different efforts. For example, productive efforts, as shown above, can be input-based, organization-based, ownership-based, allocative efficiency-based, or adaptive efficiency-based. This analytical structure suggests that it is still not enough to trace the water in the river to the streams, lakes, and to regular rain. This doesn't mean that we shall trace forever and find out all roots of the causation. The goal here is to move from "investment" to "institutionally constrained efforts" for explaining growth. It is the difference in institutions that constrain the three types of efforts that makes the difference in economic growth in various countries or regions over the long run. The school of thought following Douglass North points to the insight that economic institutions matter for economic growth, yet it is the "comparative static results"[10]—the three types of institutions controlling the three types of individual efforts—which will allow us to explain why economic performance differs.

One obvious problem in China's economic growth is the sharp contrast between the rich coastal east (China's "First World") and the poor mountain-locked west (China's "Third World"). One may wonder that given the similar institutional arrangements, why there is such big difference and how can it be explained without "blaming the mountain?" In fact, there is a "geography theory" that asserts that geography and climate explains why coastal areas are richer than landlocked areas and temperate areas are more advanced than tropical areas. Like the "National Character" theory or the "Confucian Ethics" theory, it is an adequate explanation on the ecological-psychology level, but is an ad hoc explanation on the economic-motivation level. The ad hoc fallacy is to give an after-the-fact explanation that doesn't apply to other situations. Austria, Luxembourg, and Switzerland are all mountain-locked, yet they are among the richest countries and have been for a long time. Many African countries have long coastlines, and they are poor. Hong Kong and Singapore are tropical, yet they are rich. Eastern Europe and parts of Africa are as temperate as Western Europe and North America, but they are poor. The sharp contrast between South and North Korea provides a great example of how institutions, not geography (and culture), lead to differences in economic performance. A larger scale of evidence beyond the extreme Korean case can be found in European colonial history.[11]

The non-human geographic factor can't explain China's poor mountain-locked west, though it does raise transaction costs related to transportation, communication, and information. If labor and other input costs are not substantially lower, given the same institutional structure, its economic growth tends to be slower. But the point here is not about how geography affects transaction cost, but how, given the geography, what would happen when a more preferential institution is enforced.

A meaningful and relevant theory is one with policy implications. In this regard, traditional "only-input-matters" growth theory is relevant only when it applies to the same institutional settings. The problem is, institutions are never the same in different societies; and even within one society, economic performance not only depends on institutions related to productive efforts, but also depends on institutions related to destructive and distributional efforts. While geography is a stable factor, natural disasters are not, especially the unexpected (diseases) and unrelated to human activities. But like accidents by non-institutional human mistakes, natural or non-human environmental disasters are part of Mother Nature. Their negative effects can lead to economic decline, but their random nature cannot explain the decline. Systemic human behavior patterns cause economic growth and decline, and it is they we need to identify and change. From this perspective, institutions are what help explain why and what physical factors are present and combined in a particular way and time in the production function.[12] But even when everything is measurable, the calculation of a grand production function is a problem for Applied Mathematics, not for Economics.[13] Everything is important in a nation or region's production function, but institutions (formal and informal rules) matter most.

Crouching Bribery, Hidden Embezzlement

The September 2006 sacking of Chen Liangyu, party secretary of Shanghai and one of the top twenty-four leaders in China, was a Chinese political explosion. The drama unfolded two days before the official announcement when he and Han Zheng (Mayor of Shanghai) went to Beijing together to meet Hu Jintao. Only Han came back to Shanghai, proclaiming Chen's involvement in siphoning off Shanghai's social security fund, helping further the economic interests of illegal businesspeople, protecting staff who severely violated laws and discipline, and fostering the interests of family members by taking advantage of his official posts. Chen's case was soon followed by the fall of Qiu Xiaohua, head of China's National Statistics

Bureau; Zheng Maoqing, vice-governor of Hunan; Du Shicheng, deputy Party head for Shandong province and party secretary of Qingdao (Tsingtao), a resort port city and former German concession (and home to Tsingtao beer and appliance maker Haier). But Chen was the highest-level Chinese leader removed from office since former Beijing party secretary Chen Xitong was fired for his role in depriving the city's coffers in 1995. Beijing vice-mayor Wang Baosen committed suicide rather than admit his association in the same corruption case.

A few months earlier in June 2006, Liu Zhihua, a Beijing vice-mayor in charge of the Chinese capital's $55 billion construction preparations for the 2008 Olympics, was fired for alleged corruption. The case was an acute embarrassment for the government, which vowed to "clean up" Beijing. Liu's scandal triggered accusations of widespread corruption surrounding the Games that troubled foreign companies working as specialist contractors on Beijing's Olympic sites. The Beijing Organizing Committee for the Olympic Games hurried to distance itself from the vice-mayor by stating that he held no position in the committee and that his case would not affect the preparations for the hosting of the 2008 Olympic Games. Liu demanded a bribe from a foreign developer for the sale of a piece of land in Zhongguancun, Beijing's version of Silicon Valley to the west of the Olympic site. Liu's fate was sealed when the businessman reported him to the authorities after he failed to hand over the land despite having been paid off.[14] Anti-corruption investigators moved against Liu with unusual speed and Liu was whisked away into "shuanggui" ("double designation")—a Communist Party disciplinary investigation to pressure the target to confess at a designated time and a designated place.

Details of Liu's colorful private, or "dissolute," life began to surface. Liu had built himself a pleasure palace filled with young mistresses in the resort town of Kuangou, part of a resort complex in the hills north of the capital close to the Great Wall. The architecture mixed a classical Chinese courtyard layout with modern glass and steel structures. Nearby was a conference centre with 150 rooms where domestic and foreign companies regularly conduct business meetings. A sports club on the same piece of land offers tennis courts, saunas, and private venues for karaoke. The interior of the buildings aimed to emulate high-end hotels with thick carpets, gilded sofas, and gemstone-bedecked chandeliers.[15]

Liu was known to have a clean image with his peers before he was caught on tape in a six-hour video of him having sex with a string of mistresses. It is not really surprising for China's "new upper class" to keep mistresses, a traditional practice among the rich that has re-emerged with the country's rapid economic growth. It is also no secret that many corrupt officials' private lives are colored by what is known as the "3Gs": girls, golf, gambling, and "three escorts" (*sanpei*): playing, dining, and sleeping with mistresses.

But keeping mistresses proved to be fatal for vice admiral Wang Shouye, one of five navy deputy commanders and a member of China's parliament. One of his mistresses blew the whistle after he refused to give in to her demands for money in June 2006.[16] Wang became the most senior People's Liberation Army (PLA) officer ever convicted of the crime of accepting millions of dollars in bribes from contractors.

Earlier in 2005, Major General Liu Guangzhi, who was targeted by Taiwan for recruitment as a spy, was sentenced to thirteen years in prison for accepting bribes from subordinates seeking promotions or transfers. In 1999, a general and a colonel were executed for spying for Taiwan in the biggest espionage scandal of the Communist era. In a more recent case in 2007, Song Pingshun, former chairman of the Tianjin Municipal Committee of the Chinese People's Political Consultative Conference, committed suicide because he "abused his public power to seek benefits for his mistress."

Stories like these highlighted a culture of graft that has bounced to a new high in the wake of economic reforms that have spawned wealth and greed. The Olympics are certainly not the only event onto which China's leaders are particularly keen to "put on your best face." According to the WTO arrangement, foreign banks are allowed to conduct business inside China in local currency starting in December of 2006. The government has been pressing hard to eradicate the taint of corruption from its state-owned banks as it courts foreign capital in a bid to improve management practices.

Unfortunately but unsurprisingly, the worst corruption in China can be found in sectors where state monopoly is strongest. Banking is on the top of the list, along with real estate, power generation, tobacco, financial services, and infrastructure. In 2006, China's National Audit Office announced that an examination of records at the Agricultural Bank of China, one of four state-owned banking giants, uncovered fifty-one cases of criminal wrongdoing involving 157 people in 2004. The state audit also found evidence of $1.8 billion in improperly handled deposits and $3.5 billion in illegal loans.

These recent additions to a lengthy roster of bank-fraud cases, especially those involving medium- and long-term loans, brings to the fore a basic question about the future of China's financial system: are the state disclosures a sign that the government is indeed serious about fixing the troubles, or are they just another indication of the extent of the problems in a fundamentally shaky system?[17] The Agricultural Bank has long been seen as the most flawed of the four state-owned banks—with its deep institutional problems, including a lack of internal controls, and appointing bank leaders based on administrative power rather than on market performance. In 2002, the bank announced plans to embrace consumer finance as a way of weaning itself off more politically motivated lending. The bank moved aggressively into the fledgling business of auto finance, seeking to profit as China's growing middle class adopts the family car. Yet credit-checking systems were still weak in China. So long as would-be borrowers accurately disclosed their addresses and incomes, few applicants would be turned away. The disclosures added to the evidence that the resulting consumer-finance frenzy turned sour: state auditors said that among the biggest areas of fraud in the cases it discovered were car loans and home mortgages.

In China, corruption takes the most straightforward form: power for money. The exchange of power for money is the improper or unlawful use of public power by politicians or civil servants for their private gain through either bribery (relational corruption) or embezzlement (personal corruption; this category includes misappropriation, profiteering, negligence, squandering, privilege seeking, illegal earnings, smuggling, and moral degeneration).[18] It can involve either the procedure or the substance of enforcing any public power. In the first situation, an official is receiving private gain illegally for doing something which he or she is ordinarily required to do by law. In the second situation, it can be abusing or theft of government funds or paying bribe to obtain services which the official is prohibited from providing (selling official posts or appointments, escaping punishment for corruption).

Hundreds of new laws were enacted in China after 1978, but the rule of the game in corruption is to go against laws. Due to the omnipresence of state power and the connection-based "face culture," favoritism in the distribution of legal permits, government grants, special tax benefits, and other privileges is especially widespread in the process of marketization. Such self-serving relationships may, with more Chinese characteristics, come from family ties, old friends, old bosses, old underlings, old colleagues, old classmates, old neighbors, or just old acquaintances.

Bribery is simply seen as a "tribute" to the "local emperor," who could be a mayor, a government agency director, or a high school principal. It is the "rent" or "necessary evil" to get into the game or get ahead of the game in business or in politics.

Embezzlement, on other hand, can be an outright takeaway of state funds or government grants to local programs. While "rule of law" remains the ideal for market economy that the Chinese government works to achieve, enforcement of laws is another story. The Western conception of law is foreign in China. Westerners conceive of the law as something above any person and apart from any person. In China, this is not the case. Respect is not owed to law and abstract principles, but to specific people: mother, father, husband, brother, boss, or friend. Everything is nuanced. Everything is *guanxi*-based. Everything is in the context of a relationship. There is simply an endemic difficulty sticking to formal rules among people who know each other well, much like the ubiquitous difficulty eliciting cooperation from people who don't know one another.

Privatization is a great case in point. It has a good reputation thanks to its association with efficiency under a favorable institutional setting. Yet in China, the process is all too captivating. Traditional state-owned enterprises have low asset value because they perform poorly, but once improved through better corporate governance as a result of privatization, profitability can be expected and their market value will increase. Therefore, when a person can acquire "unlisted" shares in a state-owned enterprise cheaply, he or she can expect to make large capital gains. However, such profits from privatization are inclined to find their way into the pockets of those in power. The shares of many state-owned enterprises are being sold very cheaply to managers, senior party members, and government officials. It is almost like a process of predation, not to mention any bribery and embezzlement involved.

As a result of privatization, many local elites are turning into new capitalists, while many workers are falling victim to restructuring efforts and turning into real proletarians. The percentage of private enterprise owners who were party members rose to 29.9 percent in 2001 from 13.1 percent in 1993. Only 0.5 percent of that figure comprises private enterprise owners who joined the Communist Party after former President Jiang Zemin's 2001 "July 1 Speech" that officially allowed private entrepreneurs to join the party in line with the "Three Represents" theory,[19] which showed that admitting private entrepreneurs into the party was only a confirmation of the fact that many capitalists were already party members.[20] During this "insider privatization" process, the number of state-owned and state-controlled enterprises fell from 238,000 in 1998 to 150,000 in 2003. The state-owned sector reduced their employees from 103 million to 68 million.

The scale of this predatory corruption is so large that even the largest "selling official posts" scandal couldn't match it. In that high-profile corruption case, Ma De, a senior official in Northeast China's Heilongjiang Province, was charged with taking seventeen bribes amounting to more than 6 million yuan ($726,000) between 1992 and 2001. More than 260 government officials are alleged to have connections with Ma's case, including Tian Fengshan, former minister of land and resources, and Han Guizhi, former chairwoman of the Heilongjiang Provincial Committee of the Chinese People's Political Consultative Conference (CPPCC). Ma's arrest sent a shockwave through the city's political class as more than half of the local officials were allegedly involved, and the entire provincial, municipal, and county governments were found to be contaminated. Ironically, the place where China's biggest political scandal occurred is home to about 460,000 people living below the poverty line.

Cases may not be good enough for a picture of China's corruption landscape. We can examine some numbers. China has five levels of government to which all levels of government officials are nominated and appointed from above by the ruling Communist Party. According to World Bank's 2002 data, below the central government are 31 provincial level units (42 million population on average), 331 prefecture level units (3.7 million people on average), 2109 counties (580,000 people on average), and 44,741 townships (27,000 people on average). Furthermore, there are about 730,000 more or less self-governed villages in rural areas below the township level.

In 2005 alone, nearly 115,000 members of China's Community Party (almost 2 percent) were punished for corruption and other offences; 47,306 officials were discipline-punished by Chinese supervision agencies; 8,490 public officers were investigated for taking bribes of over 100,000 yuan or misusing public funds of more than 1 million yuan; 2,799 county-level and above officials (including eight minister- and provincial-level cadres) were investigated for criminal cases; 7,805 officials were investigated for crimes in finance, education, medicine, electricity, land, transportation industries; 9,117 state-owned enterprise cadres were investigated for pocketing, embezzling or misusing public funds; and 1,931 village cadres were investigated for embezzling or misusing public funds or properties.[21] It should be easy math to compare these numbers with the number of government units to see how serious and widespread it is. As an example, on average, about 55 party members were punished for corruption in each county in 2005. According to latest estimate for 2006, 97,260 officials, or 14 percent of all Party members, were subject to disciplinary punishment. Of them, 78,980, or 81.2 percent, were punished because of dereliction of duty or violation of financial and economic discipline; and 3,530 were turned over to judicial departments. Cases of severe disciplinary violations that were turned over to judicial agencies dropped 10.9 percent over the previous year.

Corrupt officials of course are not going to risk waiting at home for arrest. They can't hide, but they can run. An authoritative source registered 703 corrupt officials who were arrested in 2005 while attempting to fly out of the country with cash, 14.5 percent more than in 2004. More than 7 billion yuan ($930 million) was taken back, 62.9 percent more than in 2004. Corrupt earnings continue to account for a significant proportion of the billions of dollars of illegal capital that "flies out" of China every year. Some Chinese scholars estimate that annual capital flight climbed from $10 billion to more than $45 billion between 1991 and 2000.

As the severity of China's crackdown on corruption intensifies, this illegal capital is all the more desperate to flee. Chinese banks found that of the 6 trillion yuan in personal savings accounts, 1 trillion yuan was money shifted out of company accounts into private ones to avoid paying taxes or to engage in unauthorized projects. It is estimated that 50 percent of state-owned companies, 80 percent of township enterprises, 60 percent of joint ventures, and 90 percent of private companies engage in such activities. Much of the foreign direct investment from Hong Kong (up to $64.3 billion in 2000 from $14.7 billion in 1998) is thought to be mainland Chinese money that left the country illegally and was re-invested as foreign capital to get tax breaks intended for foreign endeavors.

Since 2002, more than 100 minister-level and provincial-level officials, an unprecedented number, were sentenced for corruption, according to statistics released by China's Supreme Procuratorate. Big fish that got tangled in the iron net of the law include former vice-chairman of the 9th National People's Congress Standing Committee Cheng Kejie (executed in 2000 for taking 41 million yuan in bribes); former deputy governor of China's Jiangxi province Hu Changqing (executed in 2000 for taking 5.4 million yuan in bribes and possessing 1.6 million yuan worth of property from unidentified sources); and former vice-minister of the Ministry of Public Security Li Jizhou (sentenced to death with a two-year suspension in 2001 for accepting more than 4 million yuan in bribes in connection with the huge Xiamen smuggling case).

Others include former Party secretaries of Hebei and Guizhou provinces, Cheng Weigao and Liu Fangren, former Yunnan Governor Li Jiating, former Anhui vice-governor Wang Huaizhong, and former Minister of Land and Natural Resources Tian Fengshan. The blacklist also includes Wang Xuebing, former president of China Construction Bank, and Tian Fengqi, president of the Liaoning Provincial Higher People's Court.

Compared with these big fish, the vice-major of a regular city even as famous as Wenzhou can be considered a mere minnow. In June 2005, the Chinese media reported the arrest in the Netherlands of Yang Xiuzhu, a former vice-major of Wenzhou who was wanted in connection with what officials described as the biggest-ever official corruption case in the province of Zhejiang, to which the city belongs. Yang and a dozen other former officials in Wenzhou were accused of embezzlement and bribe-taking to the tune of more than $30 million in the late 1990s. In March 2005, the Wenzhou authorities blew up a $4.2 million twenty-two-story bank office tower that was never used and was deemed unsafe after bank officials accepted bribes to hire shoddy contractors.

An annual survey recently conducted by the Hong Kong-based Political and Economic Risk Consultancy further corroborates initial suspicions that the situation on the mainland has grew worse between 2005 and 2006, with its corruption index rising from 7 points to 8.33, on a scale where 10 represents the worst possible score. "Graft is endemic in China: according to the most conservative estimates, the magnitude of corruption ranges from 3 to 5 percent of GDP," the report said.

As if it were something to be proud of, it can at least be said that China is not the most corrupt country in the region: Indonesia topped the list (9.33), with India (9.3) following close behind.[22] A recent survey of thirty leading exporting countries ranked India, China, and Russia as the top three for bribing when doing business abroad. India was the worst offender of the Bribe Payers Index 2006.[23]

You go to a restaurant, you finish your meal, you pay the check, and leave a tip. It's an enjoyable experience, everybody gives tips, no questions asked. This is a custom, a convention, a way of treating people, and a part of the restaurant culture here in the U.S. In China, bribery is just like tipping. The Chinese have a problem tipping in restaurants because it is simply not part of their culture. When doing business with the government it is customary to take the officials out to an expensive dinner. Here, it is the cadres who are tipped, not the waiters. When tipping the cadres becomes a part of the culture, it is no longer seen as a problem among the Chinese.

Americans who have done business in China know the importance of *guanxi,* or connections. Many American businessmen, including those from IBM, Lucent,[24] and Wal-Mart, feel very much challenged by *guanxi*. And of course, some get their shoes wet when walking too close to the river. Despite laws like the International Anti-Bribery Act of 1998, a survey launched by Anbound, a Beijing-based information consultancy, shows that foreign companies were involved in 64 percent of the 100,000 corruption scandals that have been investigated in China over the past ten years, and the number may keep rising.[25] Businessmen often need to "find the connection" (*zhao guanxi*) to get business done. Another Chinese slang for it is called "getting to the right person" (*tou ren, tuo zhao ren*). When you can't "get to the right person," chances are you're out of luck. In China, the problem usually is not paying the rent for your business. The problem is, rather, you can't "get to the right person" so that you can give them the rent. Just like "rent seeking," "rent giving" can also be an art.

China also has some kind of lobbying in its capital. The Government Offices Administration of the State Council plans to reform the offices of the local governments in Beijing—an estimated 52 offices of the local governments above the vice-provincial level, 520 offices of local governments at city level, and 5,000 offices of county level governments. Thousands of associations, enterprises, and universities across China have also opened offices in the city, with intent to exchange information and attract investment. However, the offices are blamed for many corruption cases in recent years. The offices spend an unconfirmed 20 billion yuan (about $2.5 billion) each year to establish relationships with the departments of the central government.[26]

All the cases and numbers mentioned above expose a system that breeds corruption at every level. One can say corruption is so pervasive in China that it would be hard to find a leader whose associates and family members are beyond suspicion. When they are not too greedy, not going too far, and just playing by the rule of mutual benefit, nobody is going to single them out. Problems occur when they go beyond simple bribery and favoritism into theft, extortion, embezzlement, and outright predation. Of course, there is sometimes no clear line between them.

Nevertheless, Chinese-style cronyism is not a "rule by thieves" type of kleptocracy at the central or provincial levels, though it appears to look like that at the county and township level in some areas. A kleptocracy is a government with no pretense of honesty, one devoted to taxing the public to amass personal fortunes. In China some redistribution schemes, made possible under the institutional settings of power decentralization in the reform era, may be used to keep local rulers in power and benefit the cronies. Yet, as will be addressed in the next chapter, Chinese top leaders are simply not self-enriching leaders under the current institutional constraints.

At a mid-January 2004 national meeting on clean governance, the Central Commission for Disciplinary Inspection (CCDI), the CCP's highest anti-corruption watchdog, announced eight new regulations for party cadres. For example, in addition to being extra careful about conflict of interests, senior officials must keep a close watch on the business activities of their spouses and kids. Leaders at all levels must ensure the probity of their subordinates. Cadres, including top level officials, must "never be dictatorial, soft, and lax about discipline, or indulgent toward their underlings." The new rules also institutionalized the rights of ordinary CCP members to blow the whistle on the assorted "economic crimes" committed by senior officials such as ministers and party secretaries. Moreover, the CCDI must within a reasonable period compile a report on every graft-related complaint or petition filed by party members and other citizens. More recently, there have been "Strike Hard" (*yanda*) campaigns, "morality exams," as well as joining the United Nations Convention against Corruption for more international cooperation.

Yet for all the tough words and occasional high-profile sentencing and executions, in the minds of many officials, the potential gain from corruption far outweigh the risks. When everybody benefits from the reform, there is no reason to expect them to be left out. They have the power, and they need incentives to work for reform. It would be bizarre if they remained poor and clean while everyone else got rich from a successful reform that they all worked hard for. People constantly argue that Chinese leaders won't institute effective measures because those measures are going to come back to bury them and the one-party system altogether. As mentioned above, this is a "culture-empty" argument. Laws and media exposures are not going to be effective when enforcement is a problem. While democratic India, Mexico, and Taiwan have all failed to get out of the trap, Singapore and Hong Kong present a different picture. One can't just argue for democracy, or simply blame the culture with a belief in fatalism. It's about institutional design. Effective measures must target the psychological complex of "shame-honor," "fear-power," and "guilt-righteousness" all at the same time.

No official is not greedy (*wu guan bu tan*). When institutions channel incentives more toward corruption, such institutions will ultimately exert a negative effect on economic growth. In textbook theory, corruption is bad for economic growth because it adds rent and negotiation costs to producers' income statement. The granting of privilege may protect firms from competition and sustain inefficient firms by lowering compliance with construction, environmental, or other standards.

Although corruption may reduce costs by cutting red tape and reducing wait time, the expectation of bribes can induce officials to engineer new rules and delays. Corruption shifts resources from productive use due to increases of countermeasures and litigation. Bribes may also result in capital flight and investment moved overseas. Equally important, since decisions are weighed in terms of money rather than social need, corruption and its demonstration effect poison the social environment and cause "morale declines."

Corruption may also produce a "knowledge depreciation effect" since getting educated and being innovative may become less attractive than getting the direct benefit of bribe money. Honest officials may be threatened or even blackmailed in the corrupt environment. Corruption is the best way to lower people's respect for the government, which in turn can lead to objective failures by the government and even a legitimacy crisis, which is the top concern of the Chinese government.

A Most Expensive Death

On May 18, 2005, Wang Wenhui, a retired high school teacher, was sent to the Second Affiliated Hospital of Harbin Medical University in China's northeast Heilongjiang province. A payment of 180,000 yuan ($24,000) was submitted over the first two days. Yet almost every morning for the following two months, Wang's family got phone calls from the hospital for more payments. On June 1, Wang was transferred to the Cardiology Intensive Care Unit in the same hospital. Within sixty-seven days, Wang's family paid a total of 1.397 million yuan ($186,000) to the hospital, an average of 21,000 yuan per day (the average annual income of a college graduate is less than 20,000 yuan). In addition, more than 4 million yuan was spent during this period for extra medicines suggested by the hospital. Still, Wang didn't survive the sixty-eighth day and died on August 6. As if it were not sad enough, Wang's family got two more medical exam reports after his death, and the hospital further claimed that they undercharged a total of 1.3 million yuan. Even more shocking to Wang's family was their finding, in the medical records, that the hospital used medicines that Wang was allergic to. This was not the end of it. On a medical bill for July 31, the hospital used the outrageous amount of 10,000 milliliters of blood and charged for it a total of 22,197 yuan (approx. $3,000).

After the whole story was reported to a newspaper, the hospital provided its explanation. The doctor in charge said that Wang was in critical condition when admitted into the ICU. Expenses for such care and the drugs used are usually much higher. As for the medical record for July 30— at least 94,000 milliliters of blood was used, (more than twice the amount of blood in a normal adult body)—the doctor said he was not sure and should ask the nurse in charge. The nurse said she couldn't remember the details, but that everything was carried out under the doctor's order. Wang's son, a fairly successful businessman, almost went bankrupt from paying the medical bills. According to his investigation, the whole story was caused by the hospital's over-examinations, over-counts, over-charges, and over-use of drugs. All medical records and reports were full of unmatched numbers, contradictions, confused signatures, and dubious stamps. He also found that the extra medicines he bought were not used on his father and were most likely stolen.[27]

An extreme case best reflects what goes wrong with the existing health-care system. Before the reforms got underway, healthcare, like everything else in China, was taken care of by the state's planned economy. From 1952 to 1982, the centralized healthcare system shone with its tremendous achievements. Infant mortality fell from 200 to 34 per 1,000 live births, and life expectancy increased from about 35 to 68 years. China was well on the transition of infectious diseases giving way to chronic diseases (e.g., heart disease, cancer, and stroke) as leading causes of illness and death. Smoking-related diseases are serious as China's smoking population is the largest in the world: 360 million smokers of which nearly 60 percent are men.

When the market gained momentum, change was naturally seen as going from one end to the other. And here is what went wrong. The central government essentially decentralized the healthcare system, and at the same time unloaded its financial burden. It transferred much of the responsibility for funding healthcare services to provincial and local governments, reducing its share of national healthcare spending from 32 percent to 15 percent during 1978 and 1999. Each province, no matter how rich or poor, was more or less on its own to provide healthcare funding. State-owned hospitals were gradually given the right to function much like for-profit organizations, focusing heavily on the bottom line. While government price controls remained in effect for basic care, many areas—including new drugs, new tests, and new technology—were marketed, and physicians' incomes started to link to their performance on the top line. When Chinese physicians were rewarded for providing high-tech services, they did exactly what U.S. doctors have been doing for decades.[28] The result was an explosion in sales of expensive pharmaceuticals and high-tech services, and rapid overall increases in healthcare prices and spending.

There is nothing wrong for the hospitals to behave like other business companies. The problem is that their welfare function was removed too soon and too fast, and without the build-up of a functioning medical insurance system. "Whoever gets the healthcare pays the bills" became the unquestionable yet unfortunate market doctrine. What's more devastating is that government regulatory agencies failed to work as effective watchdogs, all of them busy with revenue-generating activities (*chuan shou*) and leaving medical cost, especially drug cost, totally out of control. Of course, corruption is also part of the story. In July 2007, the former director of the State Food and Drug Administration (SFDA) Zheng Xiaoyu was executed on charges of taking over $850,000 worth of bribes. Zheng reigned as China's chief drug and food chief between 1997 and 2006, during which China suffered from a bad reputation in the pharmaceutical industry. All of a sudden, China joined the other countries of the world that spend the highest percentage of health dollars on drugs. China's drug expenditures accounted for more than 50 percent of total health expenditures. While the increase in physicians' salaries is relatively small, they are overwhelmingly drawn to sell and use more drugs for kickbacks, rebates, and other benefits offered by domestic and foreign drug makers.

Improper marketing basically rips apart the health care safety net for most people, both in urban and rural areas. In 1998, the central government required all private and state-owned enterprises to offer their workers medical savings accounts combined with catastrophic insurance. In late 2002, the government established the New Rural Cooperative Medical System (NCMS). Still, more than 70 percent of Chinese people currently have no health insurance. The health insurance market has gradually opened for domestic and foreign competition. Yet many employers refuse or simply cannot afford to comply with state mandates, and many others don't cover dependents of their employees. Millions of workers have been dismissed when officials shut down or sold state-owned enterprises to investors. They now join many retirees and most of the 800 million farmers who are uninsured and have no way to pool risks for healthcare expenses. Many people rely on relatively low cost traditional Chinese medicine; some simply give up seeking medical care. Stories abound of families forced to stop treatment for dying seniors and children because they are bankrupted by healthcare costs. Television and newspapers are full of such reports; some assist by appealing to readers and the TV viewers and for donations.

Using the analogy of game playing, the key here is the government's role as a rule maker, a judge or regulator, and a player of the game. Before reform, government made the rules, judged, and play all the games. Now it needs to overhaul the rules (provide the legal framework), learn to judge new games (maintain market competition, redistribute income, correct for externalities, and stabilize the economy), and play only some of the games (provide public goods and services, support key industries).

The most important hidden issue here is: as reform enforcers, government agents (rule makers, judges, or game players) need incentives to do what they are supposed to do. There is no reason to expect them to involve themselves wholeheartedly in a game where other participants take away all the benefits. A healthcare system that involves care delivery, payment and financing, accountability and regulation requires a high degree of learning, adaptation, and coordination.

Yet with all the budget constraints, knowledge constraints, organization constraints, and political constraints, problems and distortions in the healthcare reform process shouldn't come as any surprise. This "incentive to enforce reform" logic is also exemplified, as discussed above, in the corruption case.

But as reform is on an over-reaching national scale, this logic is carried into almost every function of the government: from security, to justice, and to general welfare. "Bureaucratic commerce" (*guanshang*), in which officials in almost all government branches engaged in business, is one of the many results of this logic. In 1997, Hu Jintao, who became party leader in 2004 and is the first of China's leaders to have grown up in the communist era, had to take responsibility for implementing the decision to eliminate business interests within the Police, Army and Judiciary in an effort to ensure the purity of the state apparatus.

China's healthcare story underscores a much more fundamental question on government functions in a modern society. Generally speaking, government is supposed to take care of security (national defense, internal security—police, fire, traffic), justice (economic, judicial, and political justice), and welfare (humanitarian, educational, environmental, scientific, and infrastructural welfare). In terms of economic functions, governments provide the legal framework, maintain market competition, provide public goods and services (benefits of nonrivalry-nonexclusion), support key industries, redistribute income, correct for externalities (unintended-uncompensated-for damages like pollution), and stabilize the economy. For a government with an autocratic tradition and an imported legacy of planned economy, its reform efforts and outcome deserve much commendation. Yet, in the practice of a gradualist approach characterized by "doing whatever is easy and whatever costs less," what's challenging remains challenging. China's lack of a comprehensive health insurance system is now forcing many households to save more and spend less (the logic is the same for its pension system), contributing to the country's high savings rate. Low domestic consumption is in turn hampering the country's ability to transform its economic growth from an export-driven to a domestic-driven path.

Tracking the Top Problems in China

The top problems in China today are: corruption; banking-State Owned Enterprise inefficiency; distribution-driven overheating; intellectual property violation/piracy; healthcare crisis; the decline in social mores; crime and social unrest; unemployment and income disparity; environmental degradation, and vulnerability to international economic shock.

A young American teaching English in China shared his experience of taking buses in Beijing:[29]

I'll never forget my first experience on a bus. When the bus arrived at the bus stop, there was a crush of people getting off and another crush boarding it. Forget manners and waiting politely for everyone to disembark—we had to literally shove our way on board and pay for our tickets. There was barely room to breathe as we were packed in like sardines—literally. I remember one of the other teachers telling me to be careful with my money because of pickpockets. Purses weren't recommended and I soon learned to deal with using just a wallet or a billfold tucked into an inside pocket of my jacket (during cool weather). I was always amazed at the ladies who took the bus fare, they had to remember so many faces and know who had paid and who hadn't. They were constantly busy taking money, giving change and little paper receipts. I wondered how they could keep track and if they knew when someone was trying to get a free ride. Unfortunately for me, I found out not too long after starting at the university that they did.

One day another teacher and I were going back to the university (the main branch) from a shopping excursion. We took the bus from the subway, as we still had quite a way to go, when all of a sudden there was a lot of yelling going on in the bus. A passenger was arguing with the lady who took bus fares. The bus stopped and everyone on one side of the bus had to get off while the floor was searched, then everyone re-boarded. Apparently, that passenger hadn't paid for their ticket or if they did, they had lost their receipt. It resulted in a very long wait for us, which concerned us since we both had a class to teach soon. Finally the police arrived and had that same end of the bus disembark, and this time the other teacher and I pushed our way off of the bus and took off for the university, which was still quite a good distance away. We shakily made it in time to get our teaching materials and go off again to the other side of campus for our classes.

It was an experience I'll never forget, and I never let go of the ticket stub again—to prove my fare had indeed been paid!

"The outside world is so entertaining; the outside world is so discouraging." This is how a pop song in China goes. It is really amazing how the songwriter captures the reality, including the "bus culture" in the story above, with such accuracy. This is a relationship-centered society and respect is owed only to someone they know. People outside of their relationships are all strangers whom they have been taught from young to watch out for. If "social capital" is about the cultivation of good will, fellowship, sympathy, and social cohesion for a society to be cooperative and to sustain prosperity, then the "social capital" in China is a personal and exclusive one with norms of narrow reciprocity and trustworthiness. This is a society with isolated individuals that is rich in "relational civic virtue" yet poor in impersonal "social capital." The Chinese have demonstrated extreme warmth and courtesy to foreigners and guests, or within their circle of family and friends, but have no problem being rude and offensive to strangers.

China's city streets are jammed with cars. More than 600 lives are lost and more than 45,000 people are injured on China's roads every day, the highest mortality count in the world. Pedestrians, bike and motorbike riders, and low-income coach passengers suffer most from traffic accidents. Losses caused by traffic accidents from 2000 to 2004, over $12.5 billion, accounted for about 3 percent of China's GDP. The amount is higher than the country's budget for public health services and rural compulsory education. Tougher traffic law enforcement proved to be effective. In 2006, the number of road traffic deaths in China was down 9.4 percent to 89,455—the first time below the 90,000-benchmark since 2000. The number of traffic accidents fell 15.9 percent to 378,781, among which major traffic accidents or accidents with more than ten fatalities dropped 30.9 percent to 38—the lowest since 1991.

If the "bus culture" story reflects how the Chinese interact with each other in public, then "wall culture" demonstrates how the Chinese do their best to prevent undesirable interactions in the community. When Chinese students come to study in the U.S., one of the things that puzzles them is that universities are not surrounded by walls. There is usually no separation between a university and the town or city where it's located.

When Chinese buy a house in the U.S., they have an uneasy feeling about how a regular American house is structured with so many glass doors and windows that outsiders can easily see through, or worse, break into. In their mindset, there should be a solid wall to separate and protect them from strangers. Even when the wall is not really safe enough, they need it for peace of mind. This "Great Wall psychology" costs a lot economically, but it does lower the potential for intruders.

In China, almost every university, company, government agency, or "organization unit" is encircled by walls. Almost all new residence buildings, single-family houses, and luxury villas are secluded by walls. Windows and doors are further armored by iron or steel protectors, and security guards are employed at every community unit (*xiaoqu*). A sign of economic prosperity in every community may be a scene of isolation. Culturally, the Chinese are really not "aggressive overseas expansionists;" otherwise they wouldn't bother to build and re-build the Great Wall in almost every dynasty.

Any regular urban Chinese can say that the overwhelming majority of criminal offenders are people from rural areas. China used to have more than 1 billion people in the countryside. Over the last thirty years, near 300 million (the current population of the U.S.) migrated to cities for employment and to grab a piece of the economic action.

One of the most notorious crimes in China is the so-called "motorcycle-based robbery." The crime is most often committed by gangs who coordinate their effort to rob pedestrians and disappear on their fast vehicles, usually stolen ones. In the southern province of Hunan, four members of a motorcycle-based gang committed 130 robberies in less than four months, robbing an average of a few thousand yuan each time. They were given prison terms ranging from two and a half years to fourteen and a half years. In Nanning, the capital city of Guangxi province, 2,298 cases of motorcyle-riding thievery happened within two years, a record that stunned both local and central governments. A more recent example near the Olympic site in Beijing involved fourteen farmers who committed as many as 300 robberies within 18 months, by far the biggest "motorcycle-based gang" activity in China.

These gangsters started by robbing pedestrians from their cars and speeding away. For ease of escape, they robbed from a motorcycle and used a car as a diversion to help the motorcycle get away if there was a problem. They usually rumbled out at night and targeted female pedestrians. As many as four robberies could be done per night, and the "top dollar" in one case amounted to more than 30,000 yuan. This quick-and-easy money came to an end when one of the gangsters used a cell phone he had just robbed for a few quick calls. The numbers were traced when the victim reported them to the police.

Criminals get caught often when they enjoy too much success and become cocky. A burglar in Shanghai broke into a luxury apartment during the summer of 2006 and relaxed by cooking, watching TV, and sleeping. The burglar, named Ma, was a college graduate who'd just spent a year in jail for stealing before he decided to hole up in this villa home. On the third day, the homeowner returned and caught Ma sleeping soundly in the owner's bed. Another comical case is called "Two dollars for eight years in prison." A farmer from north China's Hebei Province, identified as Shi, lived in Leting County and lost money in a shrimp-cultivating business. He decided to commit robberies to generate a prison sentence to avoid paying his debts. Shi went to neighboring Luannan County and robbed a fifty-year-old woman of 15 yuan (near $2) at her home, then broke into her neighbor's home. The woman reported him and police rushed to the scene and caught Shi. The farmer was later sentenced to an eight-year prison term and fined 5,000 yuan.

A more shocking case involved prostitution by teenage high school girls. In Kunming, capital of southwestern Yunnan province, as many as fifty high school girls got mired in an informal prostitution scheme. What caused the most shock is that the girls, described as good students, apparently took part voluntarily, with friends introducing friends. Many said they were impressed by the wealth and power of their clients, mainly local businessmen and officials, who took them to luxurious hotels and gave them relatively large sums of money—paying even more when the girls were virgins.

In a nation where teenage sex is considered appalling, the case brought pain to the Chinese society and aroused far greater outrage than cases like poor rural girls being forced into prostitution. In China, taboos about sexual matters mean children actually receive little education about either sex or morality, as most girls in this case were motivated either by poverty or by curiosity. The case also provoked rare criticism of the men involved, in a society where many men with money and power see visiting prostitutes as normal behavior.

China's criminal code does include the crime of buying sex from an under-age girl, but this applies only when the girl is under fourteen.[30] A more recent survey of 2,300 high school students in Beijing gave the Chinese another surprise. More than half of those polled said there was nothing wrong with a one-night stand, and some 200 said they were willing to do it when an opportunity arose. About 6.2 percent admitted they already had a sexual encounter. The average age when they first had sex was about fifteen (the global average: 17.3). Of the 1,300 girls asked if they would agree if their boyfriends sought sex with them, only six gave a definite "no."

The typical answer: "As long as he loves me, it's OK." About 30 percent believed that teen sex is fine as long as it is consensual, and 55 percent said it depends on how much the two love each other. Those in a more serious relationship said they would most likely have sex after graduation from high school. More than 40 percent of those who had sex didn't use contraceptives the first time. This matched the fact that underage girls account for about a quarter of the 1.5 million abortions in China each year.[31]

While criminals are getting younger and targeting juicier goals (richer people, better cars), criminal cases happen more often in public spaces where there is no wall. The streets are becoming less safe than they used to be. Murder, rape, arson, bombings, robbery, burglary, and assault and battery are still common, but they are old-fashioned now. New types of criminal activities are emerging: blackmailing, elaborate cons, drug-trafficking, weapon-smuggling, human-smuggling, the formation of triads, and prostitution via the web. There is no fancy way to put it, but when government officials loot with public power, ordinary people loot with physical power (when they can't encroach upon or penetrate into the local authorities). A Chinese saying goes: "While Tao is as high as a foot, the demon is as high as a yard." The authorities continue to step-up the fight against crime, but with cases in the millions every year, public security remains a daunting task.

In the past few years, China has also experienced rising social unrest, including protests, demonstrations, picketing, and group petitioning. Such "public order disturbances" have grown from 8,700 incidents in 1993, 24,500 in 1998, 58,000 in 2003, to 87,000 in 2005. The average size of protests and demonstrations grew from 8 persons in 1993 to 52 in 2003. Recent protest activities have escalated not only in size and scope, but also in frequency and severity. Environmental disputes and large-scale protests increased 30 percent in 2005 compared to the previous year. Over 50,000 incidents were documented: 50.6 percent were about water pollution, and nearly 40 percent were related to air pollution.

In July 2006, a riot by rural migrant workers took place in Guiyang, the capital of southern Guizhou province. Hundreds of protesters overturned police vehicles and threw bricks after a migrant worker was beaten up for refusing to pay for a resident's permit. During the morning rush hours of July 20, 2006, a fifty-three-year-old from the central province of Hubei set himself on fire in Beijing's Tiananmen Square. The farmer came to Beijing to appeal to higher authorities to help him get back-pay. Security was tight there and the flames were soon extinguished before the man was rushed to the hospital. In 2001, a similar self-immolation story happened to five Falun Gong practitioners. The most serious case after the 1989 Tiananmen crackdown happened in Dongzhou village, Guangdong, in December 2005. Armed police opened fire on a large group of protestors, causing several deaths at the climax of escalated tensions over seizing local farmers' fields with insufficient payment for construction of a power station.

This clash between villagers and police in Dongzhou reflected the depth of anger of those with grievances and the inability of the authorities to resolve disputes peacefully. Growing disparities of income, unemployment, official corruption, illegal taxation, forced abortions, illegal seizure of land for development, illegal land grabbing by renting rather than by buying (*yi zhu dai zhen*), ethnic tensions (in Tibet and Xinjiang), and the lack of channels for resolving problems are likely to continue to fuel social unrest.

However, through policies that mix accommodation, growth opportunities, and violence, the government is likely to be able to contain such social unrest. There is no reason to expect such protests to evolve into a national crisis because it is unlikely that other disaffected social groups, particularly the middle class, intellectuals, and students, would join the protests. If the Dongzhou incident is the biggest unrest since 1989, it in fact suggests that the situation is well under control.

While poverty is behind many cases of crime, many believe unemployment and income disparity contribute much to the problem. Unemployment in China is due to the closing-down of many state-owned companies and excessive labor from rural migration. To be fair, unemployment is a "necessary evil" for improving the structure and efficiency of the economy as a whole. It's a matter of either "idle at work" or "idle at home." But those who become idle are certainly unfortunate and need to be treated well accordingly. The reality is, with the massive domestic and foreign investment in the county, unemployment in China still amounts to about 20 percent of the labor force, or approximately 170 million workers. When more than 50 percent of state-owned companies were shut down and millions of workers got laid off, many couldn't get the compensation and training they were supposed to get, not to mention healthcare and other benefits.

In a recent survey of 10,000 respondents, the following pattern of social divisions was identified for the class structure of the Chinese society:[32]
Senior government officials: 2.1 percent;
Senior business executives: 1.6 percent;
Private business owners (with eight or more employees): 1 percent;
Professionals (academic or technical, including teachers): 4.6 percent;

Private business owners (with 7 or fewer employees): 7.1 percent;
Clerical workers (including lower level officials): 7.2 percent;
Service industry workers: 11.2 percent;
Industrial workers ("workers" in the traditional definition): 17.5 percent;
Farmers: 42.7 percent.
Urban and rural unemployed and underemployed: 4.8 percent.

This list gives a picture of a pyramid-like structure, with the three classes at the bottom making up as high as 65 percent of the whole population. Here is the income disparity issue behind the scene: the annual disposable income of the average urban Chinese was $1900 in 2006, more than three times that of the average farmer (up from 2.5 in 1978), just $592. The top 10 percent income earners receive a wage 9.2 times higher than those in the bottom 10 percent (up from 8.9 in 2005). In rural China, the multiple was 7.3, compared with 6.9 one year before. The poorest 20 percent of China's 1.3 billion citizens account for only 4.7 percent of total income, while the richest 20 percent account for more than half.

The United Nations standard for poverty is an income of less than $1 per day. China now has 26 million people with an annual income of less than 668 yuan (about $84) and 70 million people have an income of less than 948 yuan (about $119) a year. Both are well under the poverty line. In sum, about 200 million people in China live below the poverty line. An international measurement of income disparity is known as the Gini coefficient. A Gini coefficient of 0.3 or less indicates substantial equality. A coefficient of 0.3 to 0.4 is generally considered an acceptable normality, 0.4 or higher is considered too large. A value of 0.6 or higher is predictive of social unrest. In 2005, the official level of the coefficient was 0.45 in China, up from 0.389 in 1995 and 0.417 in 2000. The level is considered as hazardous as that in the U.S.: 0.428 in 1990, 0.462 in 2000 (the highest among the industrialized countries).

China's income disparity has its own structural twist. The high salaries in China are found in the electricity, telecommunication, finance, insurance, tobacco, and other government monopoly industries. Recent statistics show that the real income of people working in profitable sectors is seven to ten times higher than in other industries. In the manufacturing sector, wage increases lagged GDP growth by five percentage points every year between 1998 and 2003; some factories have not given ay meaningful pay raise for up to five years. Employees of profitable state-run companies and foreign-funded companies get the biggest share of income gains. Despite all these facts, China is actually doing a better job of spreading the spoils when comparing with countries like Russia. The *Forbes* 2004 rich lists shows that China's top 100 wealthy control $29 billion, or just 2 percent of national income, while Russia's fat cats (mainly oligarchs whose riches came from state assets) control $137 billion, or more than 25 percent of Russia's national income.

At the end of 2006, a survey by China Youth Daily and Sina.com showed that 90 percent of Chinese believe the gap between rich and poor is "serious," and 80 percent agree that the government must take action to redress the inequity. Measures taken by the Chinese government to tackle income disparity included the scrapping of the agricultural tax in 2006, extending an experimental health-care insurance scheme to 40 percent of counties, and the elimination by the end of 2007 of tuition and other fees for rural students receiving compulsory education. The central government spending on rural areas for everything from healthcare to subsidies for grain producers increased by 14.2 percent to 340 billion yuan ($42 billion) in 2006. Government spending on infrastructure will be shifted toward rural areas. More will be spent on projects, such as rural roads, water and power supplies, schools and hospitals. Central-government spending on the countryside will still amount to only 8.9 percent of total government expenditure, up from 8.8 percent in 2005, but down from 9.2 percent in 2004. Abolishing the agricultural tax and other fees imposed on peasants save each rural dweller an average of 156 yuan ($19) a year—about 4.8 percent of net income.

In his 1968 essay "The Tragedy of the Commons," Garrett Hardin extended a parable (introduced by Wiliam Foster Lloyd in 1833) of a pasture shared by local herders. The herders wish to maximize their yield, so will increase their herd size whenever possible. The individual herder gains all of the benefit from each additional animal to the pasture, but the "external effect" or cost is shared among all herders since the overgrazed pasture is slightly degraded over time. The logic here is that individual's gain is always greater than the cost distributed to each individual. Consequently, degradation of the pasture from over-exploitation is its long-term fate. Because this sequence of events follows predictably from the behavior of the individuals concerned, Hardin described it as a tragedy. As such, it illustrates how the self-interested "invisible hand" approaches to resource problems need not always provide the expected optimal solution and promote public good. Hardin argued against the reliance on conscience for the use of unregulated resources and favored solutions by privatization and regulation.

This "pasture fable" is not really hypothetical in China. In its northern grassland, the number of livestock grazing had mushroomed since the late

1970s, and, with little regulation, the number of sheep and goats jumped to more than 300 million, compared with about 7 million in the United States. The result is the largest conversion of productive land to desert in the world, and Beijing is now plagued by sandstorms every spring. In some area where soil erosion is serious, a poisonous grass flourishes. Once sheep eat the grass, they become addicted to it and refuse to eat good grass. After a few days, they all die.

Perched more than 10,000 feet above sea level, Lake Qinghai is China's largest expanse of inland water. Declining rainfall and desertification partly caused by overgrazing during the past three decades have caused water levels to drop almost thirteen feet, and a large area has been turned into dry land. Despite recent expansion caused by thawing glaciers and abundant rainfall, the number of rivers feeding it has halved in the past fifty years and salinity has risen markedly. Other Chinese lakes face similar problems, such as Poyang in the southeastern province of Jiangxi.[33] In fact, nearly 1,000 lakes have disappeared over the past fifty years, an average of twenty lakes per year. According to the State Environmental Protection Administration of China, 75 percent of China's 20,000 natural lakes and thousands of artificial lakes suffer from algae pollution caused by an influx of wastewater containing nitrogen, phosphorus, and other harmful substances.

Over the past centuries, China's environment has been deteriorating due to overgrazing, deforestation, desertification, soil erosion, and air and water pollution. Rivers run black, deserts advance from the north, and smoky haze covers the country.[34] The Yangzi River, China's longest, cuts through the country's most heavily populated regions, sweeping along with it 40 percent of all wastewater produced. With roughly 25 billion tons of wastewater a year, less than 20 percent is treated before it flows into the river. Agricultural runoff and industrial waste make up the bulk of the pollution, followed by domestic sewage, and oil residue and sewage from the 210,000 ships that ply the river each year. The effects of pollution have reduced of the number of animal species living in the river from 126 in the mid-1980s, to just 52 as of 2002.

Of China's total farmland of about 1.2 million square kilometers (nearly five times the size of England), about 100,000 square kilometers is contaminated. A further 21,677 square kilometers was irrigated by polluted water, and more than 1,300 square kilometers have been illegally turned into dumping sites. Among the twenty most severely polluted cities in the world, sixteen are located in China. Linfen, a city in western Shanxi Province, holds the dubious title of most polluted city in the world. Factories in Linfen continuously release waste gas and sewage that make the whole city smell and cover it in smoke. Nearby trees are withered. Polluted water is like thick oil, and polluted rivers have caused a higher incidence of cancer among area citizens. "Send you to Linfen" is now one of the worst curses for the Chinese.

The government's "Go West" effort is running into an environmental stop sign. E-waste is also a big problem in China. A study by China Home Electronics Association showed that around 150 million home appliances and an unknown amount of other electronic items are discarded every year. According to a report by the Beijing-based *Science and Technology Daily*, an astounding 80 percent of the home electronics thrown out by developed countries ends up on container ships bound for Asia, 90 percent destined for China. Only 10 percent of this discarded e-waste gets recycled. In Gui-yu, the e-waste processing center west of the Southern seaport Shantou, 80 percent of local children suffer from lead poisoning. Thousands of tons of plastic waste shipped from Britain and elsewhere every year are dumped in Linjiao, another recycling hub nearby.

With only one-fifth the size of the U.S. economy, China is now the largest emitter of greenhouse gases. According to a 2007 report released by the Netherlands Environmental Assessment Agency, China overtook the U.S. in emissions of carbon dioxide by eight percent in 2006. While China was 2 percent below the United States in 2005, insatiable coal consumption and rapacious cement production caused the numbers to rise swiftly. It also burned nearly 6.5 million barrels of oil per day, releasing vast quantities of heat-trapping carbon dioxide into the atmosphere. Pollution—a dangerous brew of soot, toxic chemicals and climate-changing gases from the smokestacks of coal-burning power plants—can become an export item. In April 2006, a dense cloud of pollutants over northern China sailed to nearby Seoul, South Korea, sweeping along dust and desert sand before wafting across the Pacific. A U.S. satellite spotted the cloud as it crossed the west coast of the U.S.[35] Dust from sandstorms originating in overgrazed and desert-like Northern China has been followed all the way to the United States and Canada. Hong Kong and Taiwan are also complaining about pollution from the mainland. The Taiwan-controlled island of Jinmen (Kinmen) off the southeastern coast of China witnessed tons of garbage washing up on its beaches in recent years.

According to China's State Environmental Protection Administration, about 12 million tons of crops have to be destroyed each year because of contamination by heavy metals. A UN study issued in 2005 warned that a deteriorating environment, including encroaching deserts, could drive about 50 million Chinese away from their homes by 2010. Desertification, according to officials at China's State Forestry Administration, is causing direct economic losses of about 54 billion yuan ($6.7 billion) a year. The sulfur dioxide produced in coal combustion poses an immediate threat to the health of China's citizens, contributing to about 400,000 premature deaths a year. It also causes acid rain that poisons lakes, rivers, forests, and crops. Estimates maintain that 7 percent annual growth is required to preserve social stability. China's pollution problems are costing the country more than $200 billion a year, roughly 10 percent of the country's 2.26 trillion GDP.

On the surface, China's myriad environmental problems seem to be caused by wars, power struggles, overpopulation, and recently by policies that favor economic growth. Yet as the "pasture fable" suggests to us, the real culprit is not the growth policy, it's the technically and institutionally unrestricted free access to natural resources. Unrestricted access leads to a distorted incentive structure that favors an individual's gain over his share of cost; this, in turn, leads to over-exploitation, which ultimately dooms the resource.

What's worse is: parallel with this "entry incentive," the "exit incentive" is just as discouraged. "Entry incentive" is the incentive to pollute, "exit incentive" is the incentive to stop polluting. An individual's cost to organize and combat the polluters usually far outweighs his gain from a cleaner environment. Once again—the "free-riding" problem. Everybody is rationally expecting someone else to fight either the polluters or the bureaucrats who failed to enforce the law effectively. This exact same logic applies to anti-corruption: it is usually not enough to give people rights to report violations Incentives should also be given to reporters so as to raise the violators' potential costs.

Pollution and corruption exemplify an institutional problem that can be called "selective infringement"—an act that disregards or undercompensates public or private rights. "Selective infringement" can arise because of actors' unequal power potential (corruption, land seizure, predatory privatization), asymmetry of information (opportunism), and asymmetry of transaction cost (pollution, piracy). A transaction cost theory of "selective infringement" may be developed because all cases can be reduced to the problem of transaction cost. They represent a troubled trade-off with either positive or negative outcomes related to the hold-up or speed-up "external effect of property rights" in the process of economic development.

A similar case involved waterpower in the history of American development. Building mill dams required a dam site and a flowage area to back up water. To facilitate the growth of much needed waterpower, many states chose to empower private persons to acquire land at its agricultural value rather than at its unique value for waterpower, a measure that was applied later to canal and railroad development. Clearly, a policy in favor of the flowage owners rather than the mill entrepreneur could well have slowed down the American westward movement of settlement.[36]

People need an incentive of a spiritual nature rather than a material nature to fight. This is why we have environmental advocates. In *Time* magazine's "The People Who Shape Our World" for 2006, a Chinese named Ma Jun appeared in the "Scientists & Thinkers" section for the list of 100. A journalist turned environmental advocate, Ma's 1999 book *China's Water Crisis* sounded the alarm for the potentially catastrophic consequences of the enormous water resource crisis—floods, water scarcity, and pollution—confronting China today. Of greatest concern to Ma is the condition of China's two major rivers, the Yellow and the Yangzi. The very existence of the Yellow River is threatened by massive reductions in water flow caused by a variety of man-made programs and the growing abuse of aquifers for industrialization. Chronic soil erosion resulting from deforestation together with dam construction has led to a cycle of flood and drought in the Yangzi River basin.

Effort by environmental advocates and journalistic coverage wakens ordinary people and raises the polluters "moral cost" at the same time. Still, the war needs to be won by getting both the "entry incentive" (over-exploitation) and "exit incentive" (under-engagement) right, and by effective enforcement of environmental laws. Spending money to clean up the mess rather than preventing it is not enough. The Chinese government realized this and is putting together a comprehensive package for its eleventh Five-Year Plan (2006 to 2010) to invest 1.4 trillion yuan, more than 1.5 percent of its total GDP, to deal with matters in six areas, such as water pollution, atmospheric environment, and solid waste management, including:

• Investing 180 billion yuan to install equipment that can treat 40 million tons of polluted water per day in the cities and towns across ten large river basins, and will invest 200 billion yuan in industrial wastewater treatment. It plans to build thirty-one province-level hazardous-waste treatment centers. It is going to take 15 billion yuan to handle collective treatment of hazardous wastes, 20 billion yuan to comprehensively reuse disused resources and industrial solid wastes, and 30 billion yuan to build non-hazardous treatment facilities for urban refuse.

- Focusing on improving the air quality of 113 important cities. It will take as much as 300 billion yuan to fight sulfur dioxide pollution, and a further 200 billion yuan to control car, smoke, and dust emission within these cities.

- With desert covering one third of its land mass, will invest 150 billion yuan to control soil and water erosion, and to reclaim the land in mined areas, of which 24.8 billion yuan will be used for an environmental protection project for rural areas.

- Spending 3.1 billion yuan in nuclear safety and environmental radiation protection.

The Five-Year Plan requires energy consumption per unit of GDP to decline by 20 percent from the previous planning period. Currently, 3.56 million square meters of land in China suffer from soil erosion and 1.74 million have been transformed into desert. During the past five years, China improved 540,000 square kilometers of soil eroded fields, and will improve another 200,000 square in the next five years. The proportion of eroded land in the country's total territory will drop from the present 36 percent to 34 percent by 2010.

At the end of the last century, areas affected by desertification in China were expanding at an annual rate of 10,400 square kilometers; this has slowed to about 3,000 per year. Discharges of industrial wastewater, sulfur dioxide, smoke, and dust per unit of GDP have decreased by double-digit percentages from 1995. By the end of the Five-Year Plan, the total amount of major pollutants discharged will be reduced by 10 percent, and forest coverage will be raised from 18.2 percent to 20 percent. The biggest increase in China's commitment to environmental protection occurred in the past decade. Between 1996 and 2004, China's investment in pollution control totaled 952.27 billion yuan ($118.7 billion). In 2005, investment amounted to 238.8 billion yuan, 1.3 percent of GDP.

The State Ministry of Land and Resources, along with the administration, is carrying out eight projects, including surveys on China's pollution situation for further research and prevention. The projects, costing 1 billion yuan, are scheduled for completion in four years. Starting from 2005, Pan Yue, vice-minister of China's State Environmental Protection Administration (known as "Hurricane Pan" for his tough stand), endorsed a program called "Environmental Protection Storm" targeting economic projects nationwide for compliance with environmental regulations.

In the book *The Changing Face of China* (2006), John Gittings made a case that China's spectacular economic growth over the past two decades has dramatically depleted the country's natural resources and produced skyrocketing rates of pollution. The nightmare scenario for China is not a collapse of the Party, the banks, or another uprising by the rural masses. It is that China will run out of water.

While more than one-third of China's population lives in the northern part of the country, and the region accounts for roughly one-third of its GDP, only 7.5 percent of its naturally available water supplies are in the north. Hence the "North-South Water Diversion project" attempts to pump water from the south to the north. Drought-plagued China compels the government to create "the world's leading force" in artificially seeding clouds and inducing rain to relieve droughts, and fight fires by burning chemicals such as silver iodide using an arsenal of rockets, artillery, and aircraft. Rain was induced in Beijing in early May 2006 to help cleanse the capital after a series of sandstorms. Government agencies provided $4.7 million for the Green Olympics project. A public campaign has been under way to reduce the amount of coal burned and to clean up polluting factories. To clean China's environment, the government not only has to be clean, but also needs to be strong. Balancing local economic interests with the encompassing environmental interests, however, remains a daunting task. In 2006, China ranked 100 out of 118 countries in terms of environmental protection—the same level as in 2004.

On May 14, 1997, the baht, Thai's currency, was hit by massive speculative attacks, which came seemingly out of nowhere. It dropped swiftly and lost half of its value after Thailand's administration was forced to abandon the baht's 12-year-long peg at 25 to the dollar on July 2. It reached its lowest point of 56 to the dollar in January 1998. Even more devastating, the Thai stock market dropped 75 percent within a few months, a free fall even after IMF's $19.9 billion rescue package. The largest Thai finance company, Finance One, collapsed. This was the initial shock of the 1997 East Asian Financial Crisis. Hong Kong, Indonesia, South Korea, Malaysia, Laos, and the Philippines were all hit by the slump in the value of currencies, stock markets, and other assets. On August 15, 1998, Hong Kong raised interest rates overnight from 8 percent to 23 percent, and at one point, to an unimaginable 500 percent. The powerful negative shockwave also sharply reduced the price of oil to a low of $8 per barrel at the end of 1998, which in turn contributed to the Russian financial crisis. After losing $4.6 billion in four months in its international operation, Long-Term Capital Management in the United States collapsed. Emerging economies like Brazil and Argentina also failed to escape the disaster.

China's fixed rate and non-convertible yuan at that time protected it from being attacked by currency speculators. That foreign capital was mostly in direct investment rather than securities investment also helped insulate it from problems related to capital flight. While relatively unaffected by the crisis, China's GDP growth slowed to 7.8 and 7.1 percent in 1998 and 1999 due partly to foreign trade and investment contraction. Structural problems related to non-performing loans within the banking system have drawn greater attention since then.

After joining the WTO and under constant pressure by the U.S., China began to liberalize its currency regime toward managed free float and greater convertibility. With its increasing dependence on foreign markets and energy resources, plus a more open policy on foreign investment in the securities and property markets, China has become more than ever before vulnerable to international influence. It may have to issue new regulations to control foreign capital in its sizzling property market.

But a sharp rise in oil and basic material prices, an unexpected slump in foreign consumer markets, and any sudden move of foreign capital out of its domestic markets will have a greater impact on its economy in the future. The continuing weakness of the U.S. dollar will eat away much of its hard-earned foreign reserves. In the early 1990s, China was a net exporter of oil; today, it imports nearly half its oil and nearly a fifth of its natural gas. But the major risk for China's growth is less related to its increasing reliance on oil imports than to crude and gas prices. If prices surge and remain high, China's annual growth could fall by up to 2 percent.

The Asian financial crisis of 1997 is a microcosmic example of the challenges and dangers involved in globalization. China's "export dependency," "energy dependency," and "foreign capital dependency" all call for a vigilant macroeconomic policy against various external risks, especially external financial risks. Since the bottoming-out of the stock markets in mid-2005, the Shanghai Index soared from 1,000 to over 5,000 in two years. Overseas investors pumped in funds to increase their holdings of Chinese A shares from 34.7 billion yuan in 2005 to 97.1 billion yuan at the end of 2006. The Shanghai and Shenzhen 300 index was valued at 36 times earnings in early 2007, the highest among other regional benchmarks. If, without control, the stock market continues to go crazy like Japan's Nikkei in the 1980s and America's Nasdaq in the 1990s, it could be forced into a prolonged consolidation in the 2010s.

Meanwhile, expanding its domestic market by encouraging domestic consumption has more relevance now for avoiding the so-called "Japan disease," an economic downturn plagued by sluggish domestic consumption. Anti-dumping practices and all sorts of trade barriers to Chinese exports by the EU and the U.S. will become severe should these countries be hit by economic slowdown. It is a positive move for China's Ministry of Commerce to expand its national early warning system on imports and exports to protect industries and companies from unfair competition. The industry security database will increase monitoring indicators from the current 27 to 142, widen company coverage from 500 to 30,000 by 2008, and expand product coverage to include products under all 7,614 customs tax file numbers.

As initial yuan appreciation starts to pressure the export sector, job security and business competition may get increasingly rough. Chinese yuan gains value from the growth of its economic strength, yet floating the yuan and freeing the yuan to fully-convertible may be too hasty a step, and making the appreciation of the yuan more predictable will be pointless. When the results of joining the WTO and further marketization reaches a point of no return, a lack of sensitivity to external surprise could easily result in an unprecedented domestic shock.

China Meltdown or Doomsayers' Whimsy?

The top problems in China, to be sure, are all serious, and more can be added to the list. For example, mine accidents occur almost daily. China's coal-mining industry is the deadliest in the world. In 2005 alone, the year of China's worst mine disaster (203 fatalities), nearly 6,000 miners died in 3,300 blasts, floods, and other accidents as mine owners pushed production beyond safety limits in the rush for booming demand and soaring profits. China's second-worst mine disaster occurred in August 2007, resulting in over 180 casualties.

Epidemic disease (HIV/AIDS, SARS, bird flu, rabies) is another frequently cited problem. It is estimated that near 1 million Chinese are HIV-infected and the disease is expected to grow at an annual rate of about 20 percent. The associated annual reductions in China's GDP growth, due to cost of treatment and productivity loss, could be as high as 2 percent. In central Henan province, thousands of poor farmers sold blood and have been infected with HIV by re-using contaminated needles. For his painstaking efforts to help stop the spread of AIDS there, Gao Yaojie received the Vital Voices Global Women's Leadership Award in March 2007. A documentary film "The Blood of Yingzhou District" also won the 2007 Academy Award for "Best Documentary: Short Subject."

There are reasons to be pessimistic. But the obvious questions here are: How do we reconcile China's "economic miracle" with its "social problems?" Is China's rise hype? Will China's problems cause a social meltdown or a government collapse? To put it differently: If the Chinese government is so corrupt, economic development is so unsustainable, and things are getting so ugly ("government dysfunction," "governance deficit," "weak political mobilization capacity," "regime decay"[37]), how come China keeps on growing with considerable stability? The answer to this question, from a historical-analytical perspective, is actually more optimistic than pessimistic.

By putting an end to the internal "class struggle" (1949–1976, after the "war century" of 1839–1949), creating a high level of national security in a relatively peaceful international environment, and developing a stable Party-based political system from a dynastic family-based polity, the current Chinese regime has been extremely successful in laying down a solid foundation for China's social economic development, which institutionally discourages politics-related and war-related "destructive efforts."

After 140 years of social turmoil (1839–1978), China is back on the trail of social prosperity. Those who personally experienced the turnaround in 1978 and 1992 won't have any problem expecting more to come after the first thirty years of its economic boom (1978–2007). By dismantling its planned economy, opening the door to private entrepreneurs, and inviting participation from the international community, the Chinese government has been equally successful in promoting organizational efficiency (family responsibility system, SOE corporatization), allocative efficiency (a greater degree of free entry to formerly monopolized sectors, a greater degree of free market pricing on products, labor, and capital), and adaptive efficiency (improved enforcement of business laws and property rights protection) which institutionally encourages organization-based, allocation-based, and ownership-based "productive efforts."

Through implementing the tax-sharing system, opening the Party and government's door to private actors, and strengthening the new "socialist authoritarianism" ideology, the "Three Represents," against foreign and domestic political pressures, the central government has been particularly successful in gaining greater fiscal and political power. In this regard, the 1989 democratic movement became a historic watershed as both sides showed their "hold cards" and the Party was repositioned to abandon the "state ownership doctrine" of the old ideology and shifted to boost the "legitimacy function" of the new "Three Represents" ideology.

The Party's legitimacy is now coming from a meritocracy that "represents the development trends of advanced productive forces, the orientations of an advanced culture, and the fundamental interests of the overwhelming majority of the people of China." In the sense that the 1989 tragedy (the Tiananmen Square crackdown) shifted the nation's attention from political strife to stable social economic development, it is not a bad omen for the Chinese people. Deng Xiaoping's mistake is not so much on the crackdown, but more on the softness toward anti-corruption, the hastiness of price system reform, and miscalculating the loyalty of Party leadership.

On the other hand, by devolving authority to local officials, phasing out the "discipline function" of its ideological control (not to mention that lenient Party discipline often replaces severe law punishment), and continuing its negligence on the negative sides of traditional culture, the Chinese government has fallen short of building a functional system that draws an adequate line between government functions and market functions.

In the process of reform and decentralization, the government continues to regulate what should be further deregulated, and worse, it fails to regulate what should be regulated. This reflects the fact that the booming economy pushes government agents toward an incentive-based culture (rather than a service-based culture), a culture that echoes its connections-and-power-oriented tradition and weak "relational control." Such a social environment fails to institutionally discourage "destructive efforts" related to crime, social unrest, environmental degradation, and social mores degeneration (traffic culture, drug abuse, prostitution, addictive gambling), and fails to build enough disincentives to institutionally discourage "distributional efforts" related to corruption, budget-based overheating, local protectionism, healthcare distortion, and intellectual property rights violation.

Overall, "distributional efforts" are institutionally rising along with "productive efforts," but "productive efforts" outweigh "distributional efforts" and positive institutional developments on restraining "destructive efforts" outweigh negative institutional developments on inducing "destructive efforts." We see this mixed but upbeat picture in the 1990s as well as in the beginning of the new century with all the similar factors working in the background. The fact that China didn't melt down and still manages to enjoy encouraging growth in the beginning of the new century suggests that the seemingly weakened central government is in fact adding power in degrees (financially, organizationally, and militarily) while scaling back in terms of magnitude. The central government is in firm control and there is simply no sign it will lose its grip.

The symptom of "good economic growth with bad local governance" means the central government is too busy focusing on creating a bigger pie and too busy bolstering the legitimacy of its political position—while at the same time failing to combat forces that work against making the pie bigger. This political strategy mirrors the one embraced for economic development: setting the priority, getting the business going, then dealing with associated problems later. In the government's words: "Problems arise from reform will be solved in the process of further reform."

Take "selling official posts," for example, a common practice throughout Chinese history. But the practice is mostly a "central government phenomenon" when the dynasty is near the end of its fate. This, in China now, is a "local government phenomenon." When the central government got stronger financially and politically under the leadership of Hu Jintao and Wen Jiabao, it started to shift more focus from economic growth to social development. Currently, anti-corruption campaigns, "harmonious society" ("eight pride and eight shamefulness," *ba rong ba chi*), "scientific development concept," and the Party's "advanced nature" promotion started to take Chinese connection-relation culture into account, though it is still necessary to effectively institutionalize and operationalize what needs to be done.

By appealing more to an after-the-fact "fire alarm" mechanism rather than a before-the-fact "police patrol" system, its social crisis management remains passive rather than proactive, and the official image remains predatory rather than accountable. "Anti-rule psychology" leads to "weak enforcement of rules," and "weak enforcement of rules" in turn shores up "anti-rule psychology." This mutually reinforcing circle is the Chinese "cultural trap" that is responsible for most of the current problems discussed above. There are, nevertheless, two possible ways out of this "cultural trap": one is the democratic "Taiwan model," the other is the authoritarian "Singapore model"—both belong to Chinese culture.

Even though the Party has the strongest legitimacy motivation, the most powerful moral incentive, and the political clout to get China out of the "cultural trap," the task remains challenging. The good news is: a "first push" by a strong central government does make a difference. Lessons to be learned are mainly on building the "authority of institutions," be it Hong-Kong-style anti-corruption institutions or Singapore-style authoritarian measures in transforming civic culture. It won't take too long for the central government to realize that its current solutions lack the "shock and awe" effect. The central government is strong, yet it needs to be stronger and tougher to get China out of the "cultural trap." It is widely known that there is a "Law of penalty reduction by official ranks"—the higher the rank of the corrupt official, the fewer penalties (sentence) he will receive for the same case. A "shock and awe" measure is one that's going directly opposite to this law. China's problems are deeply rooted in its culture and in its institutional legacy. It is not the form of government (authoritarian-democratic) but the degree (strong-weak), scope (wide-narrow), and scale (deep-shallow) of government that matter to Chinese society.

To remain optimistic on the Chinese central government, consider its growing strength, evolving institutional formality, and its ability to adapt to challenging environment. The government has commendably put an end to the blaming games (blaming specific political leaders) regarding the "Cultural Revolution" and the "1989 Tragedy." Only by institutional state building can China avoid events that occurred in its destructive past and guarantee the nation's focus on market building.

As we will see, China's recent tragedies are a price the country paid to transform its political institutions. It is unfair or even useless to always blame the past on leaders like Mao or anyone else and lose the bigger picture of institutional design. The leadership succession system, key to the strength of the central government and the overall stability of the country, has been radically transformed over the last decade. This silent revolutionary "institutional change" to its central government is arguably vital for China to avoid falling again into the "Dynastic Cycle." The dynastic inheritance-succession system failed every single time to rein in the "distributional efforts" and "destructive efforts" in Chinese society. No dynasty in Chinese history could get itself out of the vicious circle of the "productive rise—distributional predation—destructive fall."

To fully understand why the Chinese government is not collapsing, we need to know why China cyclically collapsed in the past. There is a growing tendency in the West to plunge into a different cultural trap of conveniently deducting from cognitively biased concepts instead of thinking in terms of China's cultural-historical reality. When the diagnosis is from some "conceptual movement" in the head rather than "interactive movement" with reality, an "electoral democracy" prescription and an "either-collapse-or-democratize" prognosis are then taken from granted.

A typical example can be found in British commentator Will Hutton's *The Writing on the Wall: Why We Must Embrace China as a Partner or Face It as an Enemy* (2006), in which comforting deduction is done by a context-independent universal truism of Enlightenment. Given no analytical explanation, Will Hutton asserts that China's $300 billion nonperforming bad loans can well go over Ernst and Young's withdrawn estimation of $900 billion. And "China, with its projected $1 trillion of foreign exchange reserves, could not afford to restructure and pay down bad debts of that magnitude. It would be overwhelmed, the growth process would stall, and social unrest could rise to unmanageable proportions."[38] A similar prognosis can also be read from Bruce Gilley's *China's Democratic Future* (2005) or James Canton's *The Extreme Future* (2006), in which economic liberalization to plural democratization is seen as a Hegel-style linear process for all human history.

In her book, *China: Fragile Superpower: How China's Internal Politics Could Derail Its Peaceful Rise* (2007), Susan L. Shirk argues that China's leaders face a troubling paradox: the more developed and prosperous the country becomes, the more insecure and threatened they feel, and that this fear motivates many of their decisions when dealing with the U.S., Japan, and Taiwan where potential conflicts may not be avoidable. But what she fails to answer is: throughout the history of China, every regime has always been afraid of its own citizens and top leaders have always been haunted by the fear that their days in power are numbered. In *Capitalism Without Democracy* (2007), Kellee S. Tsai offers a convincing critique of the common perception that privatization is leading to democratization in China. James Mann's *The China Fantasy: How Our Leaders Explain Away Chinese Repression* (2007) also discusses a "third scenario" that Chinese capitalism continues to evolve and expand but the government fails to liberalize, which is beyond the "Soothing Scenario" (capitalism will gradually bring about democracy) and the "Upheaval Scenario" (the contradictions in Chinese society will eventually lead to a revolution). Mann didn't provide any reasoning for his argument yet he proposed tough actions be taken now by the U.S. government to replace the active engagement and integration approaches.

Imaginative whimsy is a symptom of lacking a culturally defined cognitive self-consciousness. In the following pages, we will see why the Western democratic solution, so fervently championed by those who predict calamity in China at every chance (be it corruption, bad debts, social unrest, the Three Gorges Dam collapse, bird flu, or pollution), is in fact a wrong solution to China's problems; we will see how China is more institutionally constrained to have a "Singaporean Lee Kuan Yew style" leader rather than a "Soviet Mikhail Gorbachev style" leader; and we will see why China stands a chance for the first time in its history to avoid the "Dynastic Cycle"—and sustain its economic growth and "peaceful rise."

To solve the "China puzzle," it is necessary to wade through game theory and Chinese political culture to explain why China failed to "fit through" electoral democracy in its modern history, and draw on cognitive cultural psychology and American experience to elucidate why China isn't "fit" for electoral democracy. The real issue, however, is more about diagnosis and less about prognosis, more about the "fit" and less about the "pro and con" of electoral democracy.

5

Two Tigers Can't Share the Same Hill: Decoding Political Culture

The Feast at Hong Gate

Three aspects of Chinese political culture are of particular relevance to the issues of China's continuing prosperity and China's political future: first, the inter-dynastic fight for domination; second, intra-dynastic power wrestling; third, the "inheritance-succession" system and the logic of the Chinese "Dynastic Cycle."

The Chinese Empire started with the Qin Dynasty (221 BC to 207 BC), which was preceded by Xia, Shang, and Zhou dynasties. The Zhou Dynasty (1022 BC to 256 BC) was the longest dynasty in Chinese history, and Zhou rulers were the first to legitimize their rule by invoking the "Mandate of Heaven"—the divine right of the ruler granted by Heaven— to justify the demise of the Xia Dynasty and the Shang Dynasty (the first Chinese dynasty with written historical records).

The Zhou instituted a Chinese-style feudal system of vassal states, delegated to royal family members with titles (dukes, ministers, and knights), and fiefdoms.[1] As Zhou rule and central power weakened, each state saw itself as an autonomous kingdom—the origin of Chinese prolonged local-ism. These kingdoms entered a period of "Warring States," when all kinds of ideas and philosophies of state-building flourished to an extent unmatched by any other period in Chinese history (Legalist, Confucian, and Taoist). The state of Qin employed legalist ideas and became the first to centralize its state power by setting up a non-hereditary bureaucratic system and a county system to replace feudal fiefdoms.

China opened its 2,000-year imperial chapter when the Qin defeated all other warring states and Qin Shi Huang declared himself the "First Emperor" in 221 BC. After only twelve years of centralized "legalist rule," however, the Qin crumbled when the first rebellion in China's imperial history, led by Chen Sheng and Wu Guang, evolved into widespread revolts by peasants, prisoners, soldiers, and descendants of the nobles of the warring states.

Among these states, the strongest was Chu; Xiang Yu as army chief won popular support following his heroic Battle of Julu with the Qin. According to the promise made by King Huai of Chu, the nominal leader of all states, whoever occupied Qin's heartland Guanzhong first would be rewarded with the kingdom of Guanzhong. King Huai of Chu then sent "Duke of Pei" Liu Bang for this mission. When Xiang Yu was busy fighting the main force of the Qin, Liu Bang raided Guanzhong, and the last Qin ruler, Ziying, surrendered in 207 BC.

From this came the well-known story of "The Feast at Hong Gate" (*hongmen yan*). Xiang Yu was afraid that if Liu Bang was made the King of Guanzhong by the promise, he would lose too much face because destroying and conquering the Qin was perceived as an honor reserved only for him. When his army finally arrived at Guanzhong in 206 BC, his advisor Fan Zeng suggested that he get rid of Liu Bang in the coming meeting and take over the surrendered Qin ruler and Guanzhong with his overwhelmingly strong forces.

Xiang Yu's uncle, Xiang Bo, a general in his army and a close friend of Liu Bang's military strategist, Zhang Liang, knew about this secret plan. Xiang Bo, concerned about Zhang Liang's safety, sneaked into Liu Bang's camp the night before the meeting. Xiang Bo met Zhang Liang and persuaded him to go over with him to Xiang Yu's side. As a loyal advisor to Liu Bang, Zhang Liang thanked Xiang Bo for the tip, but refused to follow his suggestion. Instead, he arranged for Xiang Bo to meet with Liu Bang. Known for his people skills, Liu Bang buttered up Xiang Bo with sincerity and vowed to respect and follow Xiang Yu. Apparently moved by Liu Bang's sweet talk, Xiang Bo became convinced and promised to go back and plead with Xiang Yu to give up his secret plan. That night, Xiang Yu, a man with a strange combination of ruthless cruelty and petty kindness, began to hesitate, so affected was he by Xiang Bo's persuasion.

The next day, Liu Bang arrived at Xiang Yu's camp at Hong Gate and found an elaborate feast waiting for him. During the feast, Liu Bang was deliberate in showing respect to Xiang Yu and apologetic for stealing the glory of overtaking Guanzhong. Xiang Yu was not pleased getting his face back this way, even when Liu Bang eulogized his heroism in battling the Qin.

While Xiang Yu was casually chatting with Liu Bang, Xiang Yu's advisor Fan Zeng became anxious. Xiang Yu still couldn't make up his mind as Fan Zeng signaled with his eyes and hands. After several failed attempts, Fan Zeng decided to not let this opportunity slip away. He hurriedly summoned Xiang Yu's cousin Xiang Zhuang and instructed him to entertain the feast with a sword dance—and stab to kill Liu Bang during the dance.

Xiang Zhuang soon showed up and offered to do a sword dance. Xiang Yu approved, as it seemed like a good idea to add some fun to the feast. Xiang Zhuang's swordmanship was nothing short of marvelous, but it was even more breathtaking for Xiang Bo when he saw Xiang Zhuang aim to strike at Liu Bang at a distance, again and again. Xiang Bo realized the sword dance was a plot to kill Liu Bang and quickly rose to join the dance and blocked Xiang Zhuang's from getting close to Liu Bang.

By then, everything was clear to Zhang Liang, who accompanied Liu Bang to the feast. He came out of the scene to find Liu Bang's chief guard and brother-in-law, Fan Kuai, who raced into the tent. Xiang Yu was impressed by Fan Kuai's audacity. Knowing Fan Kuai was Liu Bang's guard, Xiang Yu gave an order that Liu Bang be given wine. Fan Kuai wasted no time in giving a speech about Liu Bang's contribution to overthrow the Qin and how he—Liu—would respect Xiang Yu's leadership. As Fan Kuai went on about how unfair it was to hurt Liu Bang, Xiang Yu stopped him and invited him to join the table for more wine. Zhang Liang, who had kept his cool all this time, developed a plan to help Liu escape. When Liu Bang was excused to relieve himself, Fan Kuai remained at his side and was able to take a single horse on which Liu made his escape.

After a while, Zhang Liang figured Liu Bang should be far away and safe. He went up to Xiang Yu to apologize on Liu Bang's behalf for the unannounced leave due to over-drinking. He also presented a precious jade tablet for Xiang Yu and a pair of jade cups for Fan Zeng as gifts. Seeing the perfect chance to kill Liu Bang slip away, Fan Zeng furiously threw the jade cups on the ground and cut them into pieces with his sword. He grumbled with deep disappointment: "Liu escaped, peril follows."

"The Feast at Hong Gate" became a well-known Chinese proverb implying a back-stabbing trap during a joyful event. Another idiom coming out of this historic incident is: "Xiang Zhuang's sword dance is aimed at the Duke of Pei" (*Xiang Zhuang wujian, yi zai Pei Gong*), meaning a person's act is intended as a veiled attack on another. Xiang Yu took over Guanzhong and only awarded Liu Bang as king of Han. Soon Liu Bang took Guanzhong back and launched the "Chu-Han War" from there against Xiang Yu. As Fan Zeng predicted, Liu Bang crushed Xiang Yu after four years of fighting.

Liu Bang then started the Han Dynasty, which lasted for more than four hundred years. The "Han," the majority ethnic group in China, got its name from this dynasty. Today, Chinese Chess is known as a game of "Chu-Han Contention." The red side of the chessboard is Han, the green side is Chu, and the middle division is called "Chu River and Han Border." Legend has it that when Liu Bang's wife and father were taken hostage, Xiang Yu threatened to kill and eat them unless Liu Bang agreed to a duel. Liu Bang rejected the offer, saying, "Killing my father and my wife will be unfilial because we both had sworn into brotherhood. But if you still decide to kill and eat them, please share a bowl with me."

The moral of the whole "Feast at Hong Gate" story, nevertheless, isn't limited to these two idioms. As temporary superiority of strength and resource may not guarantee final success, anyone in Xiang Yu's position may want to act more decisively than Xiang Yu did against his potential opponents, especially when they revealed their ambition for power. Some may contend, on the other hand, that even if Liu Bang had been killed at the feast, Xiang Yu would have had one less obstacle, but still might not have been able to conquer China. Xiang Yu's military brutality (murdered Emperor Yi of Chu and slaughtered 200,000 surrendering Qin soldiers) and political incompetence mirrored the Qin's legalist approach—which failed miserably to attain the "Mandate of Heaven" in a relation-based society. In fact, in all post-Qin dynasties, while legalist measures and institutions were still enforced, almost all rulers incorporated the more humanistic Confucianism, at least in name, to treat their subjects. Though it seems like an "after the fact" notion and is not institutionally guaranteed, the "Mandate of Heaven" is not simply "might is right." Being a virtuous or sagacious emperor was still an aspiration of many rulers.

In any case, the "Chu-Han Contention" started the Chinese political tradition of "Two tigers can't share the same hill." In Confucius's words, "Just as there are no two suns in the sky, there can be no two kings on the land." This is a zero-sum game; it's a matter of either you getting killed or me getting buried. Were there a tie like that in the Chinese chess game, it would be a chaotic situation. In pre-Qin Chinese history, there were five rulers in the Spring and Autumn period and seven kingdoms in the Warring States Period; in post-Han Chinese history, examples include the Three Kingdoms (220–280), the Eastern Jin Dynasty (317–420), the Southern and Northern Dynasties (420–589), the Five Dynasties and Ten Kingdoms (907–960), and the Southern Song dynasty (1127–1279). This is why in China the art of relationships in general, the art of ruling, and the art of war in particular, developed far ahead of the art of managing business (economics) or physical objects (science and technology). Ancient Chinese Legalists produced numerous writings that are far more Machiavellian than the works of the celebrated Renaissance Italian scholar—eighteen hundred years earlier.[2] The art of medicine and the art of cooking developed well partly because there was great demand from the royal family and local officials.

During the years of interdynastic struggle, the "tiger fight" could be within the same camp with potential contenders more dangerous than those in the competing camp. After Liu Bang besieged Xiang Yu near the Wu River and ordered the besieging troops to sing Chu songs to squash the morale of Xiang Yu's soldiers, the overlord Xiang Yu was forced to bid farewell to his beloved concubine Yuji and committed suicide. Now came the turn of his own chief commander, Han Xin, who defected from Xiang Yu's camp and helped him defeat Xiang Yu. Once Liu Bang became the Han emperor, he felt threatened by his powerful generals. He directed his own version of "The Feast at Hong Gate" to capture Han Xin. When Liu Bang was out to crack down on another rebel general, his wife Empress Lü executed Han Xin for fear of his involvement with that rebel. One of Liu Bang's generals concluded: "When the fast-running rabbits are all hunted down, then the hunting dogs shall be broiled. When the highflying birds are all caught, then the strong bow shall be put into storage. When the enemy states are all conquered, then the ministers shall be executed."

Hiding one's ambition became an important lesson for the art of ruling. At the end of the Han Dynasty, the "Yellow Turban Rebellion" broke out. Liu Bei, a descendant of the royal family, joined a local government's force. After some successful battles, he was made governor of Pingyuan, and later governor of Xuzhou. As regional warlords went into territory-claiming civil war, he was defeated by Lü Bu and had to seek help from Cao Cao, who held the emperor under his control. During his stay in Cao Cao's home, he attempted to hide his ambition by doing random housework and backyard planting. One day, Cao Cao invited him to drink, during which Cao Cao turned talkative and turned to the topic of real heroes among the warlords. Liu Bei became very nervous and failed to hide his reaction when Cao Cao commented that the true heroes were "you and I." The cup on his hand fell down to the floor at Cao Cao's comment, but he managed to "cover his face" by blaming a boom of distant thunder. After this incident of "Talking about heroes while warming up the liquor" (*zhu jiu lun yingxiong*), Liu Bei soon ran away from Cao Cao, and both of them later became two of the three rulers of the Three Kingdoms.

Lü Bu, who once defeated Liu Bei with strong martial arts skills, was known in Chinese history with a reputation of betrayal. In the Chinese "36 Strategies," his story with Diao Chan was a classic example of "Strategy 31: The Beauty Trap." Diao Chan, one of the top beauties in Chinese folktales (like Xiang Yu's concubine Yuji), was sent to seduce him so as to make him fight with his adoptive father Dong Zhuo (who held the Han emperor hostage before Cao Cao did) over Diao Chan's beauty. In the same way he betrayed his former master Ding Yuan, Lü Bu fell into the trap and killed his adoptive father. Later, when he requested to serve the warlord Yuan Shu, Yuan Shu turned him away for fear of his fickleness. He then served under another warlord Yuan Shao, but was tied up by his own soldiers while sleeping and brought to Cao Cao. When asked by Cao Cao how to deal with Lü Bu's pledge for service, Liu Bei casually talked about Ding Yuan and Lü Bu's adoptive father Dong Zhuo. Cao Cao quickly got his point, and that was the end of a betrayer's life.

"Accompanying the emperor is just like accompanying the tiger." But not all dynasty creators treated their generals like Liu Bang, even when they sensed potential challenge. Coming out of the chaos of the Five Dynasties and Ten Kingdoms (907–960), the Song Dynasty (960–1279) led the Chinese Empire to a new high when Zhao Kuangyin—the emperor's guard of the old dynasty—dethroned a baby emperor through a palace coup. The new emperor, also known as Song Taizu, set up a well acclaimed event in Chinese history called "Feast for Power Handover" (*bei jiu si bingchuan*). Song Taizu was a master of disguise. He pretended to be modest and reluctant when his soldiers put the emperor's dragon robe on him. At the "Feast for Power Handover," he vividly described to his generals how miserable he was after he became the emperor. He couldn't eat much at every meal. He couldn't sleep well every night. He couldn't enjoy what he was doing every day. His generals were all puzzled (this was what he wanted). He professed with tears that he was so worried that his generals would do the same to dethrone him. The generals at the feast were shocked by his open and straight words. Soon, their shock was elevated to sympathy, and they asked how they could help (which is exactly what he was looking for).

Song Taizu masterfully tricked his generals into the belief that only wealth led to happiness. He could choose to play nice in this way because he knew that the risk of the game is low when one is well in control. Not every potential new emperor had the luxury of such an option. Zhu Yuan-zhang, the founder of the Ming Dynasty (1368–1644), whose rulers made China enjoy both the highest GDP and per capita GDP in the world during that time, came from a humble origin and was once a monk before he joined the "Red Turban Army" to rebel against the Mongolian Yuan Dynasty. After he was trained and had positioned himself in the army, he murdered the army leader Han Ming'er (a potential new emperor). He took the advice of the Confucian Zhu Sheng to "Build high walls, stock up supplies, and be slow to be a king." By cleaning up smaller and weaker rebels in southern China, he turned north, attacking his main enemy with the motto of "Expelling the Mongols and Restoring China." Under the iron rule of the Zhu family, the Ming Dynasty pushed the Chinese Empire to its all-time high with overseas sailing explorations, glorious arts and culture, and advanced commerce ("Silk Road" from China's north-central to far west, "Tea Road" and "Salt Road" from southeast to north, and "Medicine Road" from southwest to north-central).

Deciphering the "Dynastic Cycle"

During the 2,132 years of imperial history (221 BC to 1911), China experienced twelve major dynastic periods. All were a result of military confrontation:

1. Qin Dynasty (221 BC–206 BC)
2. Han Dynasty (206 BC–AD 220)
3. Three Kingdoms Period (220–280)
4. Jin Dynasty (265–420)
5. Northern and Southern Dynasties (420–589)
6. Sui Dynasty (581–618)
7. Tang Dynasty (618–907)
8. Five Dynasties and Ten States (907–960)
9. Song Dynasty (960–1279)
10. Yuan Dynasty (1279–1368)
11. Ming Dynasty (1368–1644)
12. Qing Dynasty (1644–1911)

With a few chaotic exceptions mentioned above, the majority of the time—about 75 percent—China was united under one single authority.

No other civilization in the world has sustained such a long period of continuity and unity over an area the size of China. However, continuity was characterized by a pattern of the so-called "Dynastic Cycle," while unity was underscored by constant hereditary power struggles. Compared with the interdynastic military conflicts, the hereditary succession struggle—the "tiger fight" political culture in an intradynastic setting—was only more intriguing due to the relationships of the players involved.

At the beginning, instead of from father to son, the title of emperor was passed to the next person considered by the community to have the highest virtue. According to legend, Yu, the first emperor (king) of the first Chinese dynasty, was given the throne by Shun because of his ability and merit in flood control. However, Yu's son Qi happened to be very capable himself and was recommended to be the next ruler, which marked the beginning of rulership in China based on heredity. This was also known as "Family Rulership" (*jia tianxia*). The tradition of "Family Rulership" also went along with the tradition of patriarchy and polygamy in the royal family. The emperor usually had more than one wife, with one of them as empress and others as concubines. Polygamy served two purposes: one was obviously the personal desire of the emperor; the other was the need to make sure there was a son to inherit the throne. Polygamy was also common among the feudal upper class in the Zhou Dynasty, and was later supported by Confucianism with the belief that death without an heir was an unpardonable sin (*wu hou wei da*).

The birth number, the age, and the ability of the emperor's son are not the only factors for hereditary succession. There were examples when the emperor's brother or even the son of the emperor's brother was proclaimed to succeed the throne, just like there were examples when the crown prince (*taizi*) was not necessarily the eldest son born to the empress (*di zhangzi*). Other factors shaping a smooth succession included the possibility of a powerful external competitor, the strength and merit of the current ruler, the power of those who were close to the emperor, and other unexpected events (death of the emperor or his son). The key to the problem, however, is not only about hereditary succession, or polygamy, it is also about how certain individuals wanted to have the absolute power of the emperor. "All land under heaven belongs to the King, and all people on the shores are subjects of the King." When the stakes are so high, it requires great skill to hold it, pass it, steal it, and take it over. It consumes a lot of resources, takes a lot of learning, involves a lot risks and decisions, and entails a lot of relationships and reputation—all determinants of a political game.

The fascinating story of hereditary succession begins in the Qin Dynasty. The first emperor, Qin Shi Huang (260 BC–210 BC), simply didn't want to die and hated to even mention death. Of course he left no will that dictated which son would succeed the throne. Obsessed with the secret of eternal life, he consulted with alchemists and witch doctors and took "pills of immortality" made from mercury and cinnabar. He even traveled to Eastern China in search of the legendary Islands of the Immortals, even at the risk of assassination.

On one tour, accompanied by his second son Huhai, he suddenly died of mercury poisoning. Under the advice of the Imperial Secretariat Li Si and chief eunuch Zhao Gao, Huhai forged the emperor's will, taking the throne for himself and forcing Qin Shi Huang's first son Fusu to commit suicide. Chief eunuch Zhao Gao, who set the precedent for eunuchs meddling in the emperor's rule, gradually took control of the situation and killed not only the generals who had supported Fusu, but also Imperial Secretariat Li Si. He once devised a loyalty test by bringing a deer to a formal official meeting and called it a horse. The emperor Huhai thought he was just joking. But later Zhao Gao got rid of those who followed the emperor and called the deer a deer. This was the origin of the Chinese idiom "calling a deer a horse" (*zhi lu wei ma*). At that time, the whole country was plagued by widespread rebellions. Fearing that Emperor Huhai might blame him for the disorder, Zhao Gao took preemptive action, forcing Huhai to commit suicide and replacing him with Fusu's son Ziying, who later managed to kill Zhao Gao and surrender to Liu Bang.

Han Dynasty Emperor Liu Bang (247 BC–195 BC) attempted to change the Qin's ruthless oppressive policies. After Liu Bang's death, however, Empress Lü became Empress Dowager (*huang taihou*), who reigned for fifteen years—setting the first precedent of regency by an empress dowager in Chinese imperial history. Her son Emperor Hui (210 BC–188 BC) was simply too young to avoid her control and influence; he indulged himself in drinking and women, and died at age twenty-two without a designated heir. In fact, Emperor Hui and Empress Zhang had no son of their own. Emperor Gong (deposed by Lü later) and Emperor Hong were believed to be sons of Emperor Hui's concubines. After the death of Lü, the Lü clan was punished by Liu Bang's old ministers, who denied Emperor Hong's royal blood for fear that he might be a descendant of the Lü clan. Liu Bang's other son was therefore put onto the throne and the Han Dynasty started the golden age of the "Rule of Wen and Jing."

Yet the fight among the emperor's sons and concubines seemed to have just gotten started. Emperor Jing (188 BC–141 BC) and Empress Bo also didn't have a son. Emperor Jing therefore declared his eldest son Liu Rong the crown prince, but didn't make Liu Rong's mother Consort Li the empress, even after the disposal of Empress Bo. Emperor Jing's sister Princess Piao was fond of selecting beautiful women for Emperor Jing, an act that aroused much jealousy from the arrogant Consort Li. When Princess Piao tried to make it up by giving her daughter Chen Jiao as wife to Prince Liu Rong, Consort Li saw it as an attempt to kiss up, and turned down the offer. Princess Piao quickly worked out a backup plan by giving Chen Jiao as wife to Liu Che (156 BC–87 BC), the son of Emperor Jing's other favorite concubine. Then she started to work on Emperor Jing, and made him believe that Consort Li would eventually follow in the steps of Empress Dowager Lü and kill all his concubines. Emperor Jing soon replaced Liu Rong with Liu Che, and Princess Piao set her own precedent for power-dealing in future Chinese history. Before his death, Emperor Jing was very much concerned about young Liu Che's ability to survive the baby emperor's fate under Empress Dowager Lü. However, Liu Che, later Emperor Wu, turned out to be one of the top four greatest emperors in Imperial China (with Tang Taizong, Ming Cheng Zu, and Kang Xi).

All these stories underscored an attempt by someone to choose a future emperor to that someone's advantage. A close relationship to the present emperor—be it eunuch, empress, concubine, minister, brother, or sister— carried a lot of weight in tilting the balance toward favoritism for rather than ability or merit of the future emperor. This was the institutionally constrained common theme in all imperial successions when future emperors were not in control by themselves, which also underlined the fragility of instituting the emperor's will.[3] When a future emperor turned out to be strong by chance, then everything was fine; otherwise, the "tiger fight" would go on.

The story of Qin Shi Huang's first son, Fusu, became a historic lesson and was repeated with different twists numerous times in later history. Emperor Wu of Han's Prince Ju failed to secure the throne before his father's death; Emperor Wen of Wei (Cao Pi) would have killed his brother Cao Zhi but for Cao Zhi's poem on their fraternal relationship; Emperor Yang of Sui killed all four of his brothers and father (Emperor Wendi) for the throne; and Tang Taizong killed his elder and younger brothers during the "Palace Coup of Xuanwu Gate."

Hereditary succession in imperial China proved to be institutionally problematic, not only from fights—over favoritism, legitimacy, capability, and merit—that were all subject to heavy tactical or even biological manipulations, but also because the institutional arrangement of "Family Rulership" installed lifetime rulership and limited the continuity of power to a small, single-family "gene pool" that was unable to meet the skill set required of an imperial ruler.

The institutions of "Family Rulership," with problematic lifetime tenure, hereditary succession, and limited "gene pool," sustained the "tiger fight" political culture in the intradynastic setting on one hand, and became the root cause of the "Dynastic Cycle" on the other. The royal family was the key player in the "dynastic game." But it was not the only one. Other players were peasants, bureaucrats, soldiers, bandits, and nomadic invaders. All these players were potential power competitors (political entrepreneurs): the royal family could never trust any of them.

"Family Rulership" was institutionally always under severe internal and external competition and pressure, which explains why so many emperors in Chinese history chose to indulge themselves and abdicate power one way or another. When an emperor couldn't even swallow royal-court power politics, there was no way he could stomach the pressure of external crises. Peasants were the productive force in agriculture-oriented China. Bureaucrats represented the distributional force. Bandits, invaders, and to some extent soldiers, were destructive forces. It was the dynamic interaction of all these players in imperial China that determined the course of the "Dynastic Cycle": productive rise—distributional decay—destructive fall.

The state's predation and unprotected property rights were the main reasons science and technology (including agriculture technology) stagnated throughout the centuries. In plain and simple Chinese, "There is no stable mind when there is no stable property." According to Douglass North's *The Rise of the Western World*, the effective enforcement of property rights protection was the key reason for the modern industrial revolution—it reduced the gap between social and private rates of return so that private return could be brought in line with private efforts.

China's bureaucratic system was one of the earliest and largest in the world. Imperial bureaucrats were selected from intellectuals who passed the grueling civil service exams that tested for mastery and application of the Confucian classics. They typically included political history, policy application, and individual and social moral principles. Civil officials, directly appointed and paid by the state, owed their primary loyalty to the emperor. Patronage and nepotism, however, were widespread within the connection-based bureaucracy.

Even though the salaries of bureaucrats were low, the positions usually offered great opportunities for personal enrichment—through explicit bribery or implicit embezzlement. When the dynasty was on the rise or the emperor was strong, the bureaucratic system tended to function relatively cleanly. Nonetheless, corruption developed and spread over time, especially when the central government was too busy power-wrestling and lost control of local bureaucrats who saw that "the sky is high and the emperor is far away."

According to Mancur Olson's *The Rise and Decline of Nations*, stable societies with unchanged boundaries tend to accumulate more collusions and organizations for collective action over time; small distributional coalitions have the incentive to form political lobbies and influence policies that tend to be counterproductive; since the benefits of these policies are special incentives concentrated among the few coalition members and the costs are diffused throughout the whole population, the "Logic" dictates that there will be little public resistance to them; as time goes on, these distributional coalitions accumulate in greater and greater numbers, and a nation burdened by them will fall into economic decline.[4] In early 2007, many people enjoyed the intriguing TV series "The Ming Dynasty 1566" on Hunan Satellite TV. Dramatized corruption stories easily fit into any time period in Chinese history because the logic of "distributional coalitions" was in every dynasty the same. The problem, however, is not about any specific emperor; it is "Family Rulership" that shaped the corruption pattern. "Good Emperor" was institutionally a scarcity under "Family Rulership." In this sense, the Jiajing Emperor and the upright official Hai Rui were both victims.

The moral nature of the relationship between the emperor and his officials required a strong and skillful emperor to keep officials under control. When the officials (agents) had different interests and an informational advantage, the emperor (principal) had to employ effective measures of selection, evaluation, rotation, monitoring, and investigation to get officials to act in the right direction. These actions proved costly considering the constraints of transportation and communication techniques in a large country.

Despite continuous efforts to better manage the officials throughout Chinese history, the lack of top-down accountability and separation and balancing of government power ultimately lead to the decay of bureaucracy. Trust was always an issue. The emperor had to appeal to favoritism to cut costs, and the officials had to seek patronage for favorable appointments and self-protection in case of upper-level misjudgment, information inaccuracy, cover-up, and other misbehavior.

In terms of modern principal-agent theory, this is a typical control problem whose solution relies on incentives and sanctions for its effectiveness. Both power and art are involved in the process. A weak emperor simply couldn't handle it. This system lacks Western-style top-down accountability and a social feedback mechanism, and relies too much on the strength and stability of the emperor and regime performance. It had to appeal to violence or "tiger fight" to resolve conflicts. Social disorder was always a crisis in the sense that it posed both a threat to the rulers and provided opportunities for potential contenders. This is the source of the Chinese "fear it and like it psychology" for disorder.

Nomadic invaders in northern China were a problem throughout imperial history. The Huns posed the major threat to northern China in the early dynasties. During the Southern and Northern Dynasties and the Song Dynasty, some of the ethnic minorities managed to set up their own kingdoms. Later, the ruling of the Yuan and Qing Dynasties by the Mongols and Manchus respectively reached a national scale in China. The swift speed and mobile nature of the nomadic lifestyle were often cited as their predatory advantage over agrarian culture during the pre-industrialized era—known as the advantage of "wolf culture" over "dragon culture." Yet the horse-riding troops of the Han Dynasty did decisively defeat the Hun cavalry. The same was also true for Emperor Yongle of the Ming Dynasty who defeated Mongol rule. Later dynasties that lost their wars to nomadic invaders did so because "Family Rulership" happened to be at its weakest. This explains the mystery that northern nomadic tribes, though much less developed, could still manage to sweep through central China again and again. The same "weakest link" logic applies to the success of soldiers and bandits who rebelled against royal power. The external challenges were always there. The internal institutional flaws created the "tipping point."

The Chinese "Mandate of Heaven" legitimized "Family Rulership" through both power and merit. Merit had to be based upon power, but power couldn't last long without merit. The "Mandate of Heaven" provides at best an ad hoc after-the-fact explanation and fails to apply in all situations. An institutional explanation for the "Dynastic Cycle" puts the royal family in the center of the "dynastic game"— surrounded by peasants (who comprised 90 percent of the population in any given Chinese society), bureaucrats, soldiers, bandits, and invaders. Peasants, bureaucrats, and the royal family were the key blocks in China's "pyramid social structure."

Based on the tradition of polygamy and hereditary succession, "Family Rulership" set the institutional stage for constant struggles over power, the emperor's supremacy. Favoritism won over ability or merit when tactical or biological manipulation was involved. Over time, the small family "gene pool" eventually failed to produce a viable emperor, so the "tiger fight" political culture moved on.

But the royal family was not the only crumbling block. Subjected to the state's predatory activities and the customs of early marriage and partible inheritance, peasants and even landlords were doomed by technological stagnation and population pressure. The intellectual meritocracy degraded into "greedy officials and corrupt bureaucrats" (*tan guan wu li*) by patronage and nepotism, and principal-agent relations gradually decayed from their own internal logic. Peasants became bandits, soldiers turned into rebels, bandits joined rebels, and invaders showed up for the hunt. With all the "natural disasters and human devastations" (*tian zai ren hou*), a dynasty's productive rise gradually gave way to distributional prey, decay, and ultimately, to destructive fall.

Reasoning Democracy

No other figure in the last two hundred years could compete with Yuan Shikai (1859–1916) for the title of "blatant opportunist" as he played out the political game in late Imperial to early modern China. Born in Henan province, the heartland of Imperial China, Yuan learned the classics of Confucianism and the art of Chinese politics when he was very young. After he failed a second attempt in the imperial civil service exam in the 1870s, he saw the only way to climb the social ladder was to join the Qing Army, which he did and moved up quickly. Under the patronage of Li Hongzhang, China's senior statesman and the Governor of Zhili, he was sent to Korea in the 1880s, when Japan was making every effort to set foot on China's doorstep. During 1894 and 1895, China lost the First Sino-Japanese War. Yuan, who luckily avoided Japan's attack in Korea, was appointed commander of the Qing's first "New Army." During that time, Sun Yat-sen, the "National Father" of Republican China, transformed himself from a reformist to a revolutionary, and started to plot popular uprisings against the Qing court.

Yuan's first major opportunistic play came in 1898 when Emperor Guangxu was desperately seeking military support for a series of reforms to counter his aunt, the Empress Dowager Cixi, and the restoration of her regency. Seeing Cixi remain in control with strong support from Manchu generals, Yuan cunningly pledged loyalty to the emperor, but sneakily gave away the emperor's plan, which resulted in the ill-fated "100 Days of Reform" and the exile or execution of reformers such as Kang Youwei and Tan Sitong. Guangxu was put into confinement and served as a mere puppet under Cixi's reign. Yuan's political gambling proved fruitful with the emperor out of the game and Cixi on his side. The turn of the century, however, was a disastrous one for the Empress Dowager. Shamed by the bullying of Western powers, Cixi first used the anti-foreign Boxer Rebellion to counter Western expansion in China. The Eight-Nation Alliance acted decisively to defend their interests, and Cixi was forced to flee the capital disguised as a peasant. Yuan, then governor of Shandong, was ordered to crack down on the Boxer Rebellion. After the death of Li Hongzhang, Yuan was appointed to replace him in 1902. Yuan's "New Army" was renamed "Beiyang Army" and soon became the most powerful and well-equipped military force in China.

Cixi returned to Beijing, and ironically, with the emperor still in seclusion, started to implement her own reforms. Furthermore, many liberalized measures could only raise the public's appetite on one hand, and induce changes that later helped topple the Qing Dynasty on the other. Guangxu never forgot Yuan's betrayal, but he failed to outlive Cixi, who, aware of her own impending death, allegedly ordered he be poisoned on what turned out to be the day before her own demise in 1908. Avoiding the emperor's revenge, Yuan, still in control of the army through his subordinates, was sent home for treatment of a foot disease by the new Prince Regent, and Pu Yi, the baby emperor.

Sun Yat-sen, though in exile, continued his uprising plots; he aimed to oust the Manchu rulers and establish a republic. His supporters' effort in the "New Army" of Wuchang in central China resulted in a successful uprising in 1911. Opportunity called Yuan Shikai yet again. In control of China's most powerful "Beiyang Army," he knew that both the revolutionaries and the Qing court wanted to win him over to their side. To Yuan, this was a simple decision. The Chinese saying "never release the eagle to attack until the rabbit is in sight" was his action plan. He simply "sat aside and watched the tiger fight" and waited for the best offer. The crumbling Qing court's initial inaction to the uprising snowballed into a widespread declaration of independence by most provinces in southern China.

What was the Qing court doing? It was literally and repeatedly begging Yuan to return to power. There was no hurry. Yuan waited and calculated. He declined the "Governor of Huguang" offer because, according to him, his foot disease was still not recovered. Then came the "Prime Minister" offer. Still, no hurry. Of course his "Beiyang Army" was artfully mobilized and ready for action. The desperate Qing court pleaded again. Seeing he could be in total command in the Qing court, Yuan finally took the offer.

Yuan promptly got the Prince Regent out of his way and his troops swiftly crushed resistance all the way to Wuchang. The new "Republic of

China," founded on the first day of 1912 with Sun Yat-sen as provisional President, was forced to negotiate with Yuan. To Yuan, the Qing court was nothing more than a baby emperor that could be thrown away like a toy in his hand. He was nonetheless shocked at Sun's willingness to compromise: the presidency of the Republic for him in exchange for his promise to end Qing rule. For Sun, this "Great Compromise" was for the good of the new Republic; for Yuan, however, the reward for his easy betrayal of the Qing court was simply too good to be true. Initially, obsessed with the art of dynastic power-wrestling, Yuan couldn't believe the offer. He had no frame of reference for Sun's outright concession.

It didn't take Yuan long to realize that nothing less than the "Mandate of Heaven" had fallen squarely upon his shoulders. But the game was not over. Sun Yat-sen reorganized the Revolutionary Alliance into the the Chinese Nationalist Party (Kuomintang, or KMT) in 1912—and won 269 of the 596 seats in the Lower House, and 123 of the 274 seats of the Senate, in China's first and only popular election of a national government. Yuan was further outraged by prime minister candidate Sung Chiao-jen, the KMT leader closest to Sun. Yuan gave the order to have him murdered, and started, blatantly, to bribe and crack down on the KMT. After replacing the National Assembly with the State Council, Yuan reorganized the provincial governments and installed military governors, essentially instituting warlord politics in China. Yuan surprised the nation one more time by declaring himself the "Emperor of the Chinese Empire" in 1915. This time, he miscalculated. He had created too many enemies, and even his subordinate generals felt betrayed. Faced with widespread opposition, Yuan died in agony in 1916. China soon fell apart into a territory-claiming civil war—an oft-repeated pattern in Chinese history—until Chiang Kai-shek established his KMT national government in 1927. China's first democratic attempt showed that democratic ideas were helpful in bringing down an old regime and instituting a new one, but making the new regime function according to democratic design was a totally different story. In this new political game, nice guys like Sun Yat-sen still finished last. Playing nice proved to be a sign of weakness and Sun (always criticized for this though he is perhaps the only figure respected on both the Chinese mainland and on Taiwan) was easily exploited.

Examining the origins of democracy was an important subject in political studies long before the modern field of political culture emerged. Aristotle traced the origins of democracy and other forms of government to the distribution of wealth and to the relative strength of classes. Montesquieu connected the conditions favoring democracy with the love of equality, frugality, and temperate climate. The "climate theory" outlined in his *The Spirit of the Laws* is similar to the "climate theory" on economic growth discussed earlier. Tocqueville continued the tradition of relating democracy to the equality of conditions, but he also emphasized the significance of suitable laws, ideas, customs, and civic culture.

Austrian Economist Joseph Schumpeter, a giant in the history of economic thought, is one of the first scholars to believe that modern democracy rose along with market capitalism. But contemporary research on the origins of democracy trace primarily to the pioneering studies of Daniel Lerner and Seymour Lipset. Lerner hypothesized that urbanization starts modernization and is followed by increased literacy, media exposure, economic and political participation—and thus democracy.

Lipset's hypothesis is more straightforward: the more well-to-do a nation is (measured by the level of wealth, industrialization, urbanization, and education), the greater the chances it will sustain democracy. Many researchers have empirically tested these hypotheses, and the results have usually supported them: there is a strong positive correlation between democracy and economic development. However, there are anomalies. Democracy exists in countries with low-level economic development, and doesn't exist in all economically developed countries. Is the relationship between democracy and economic development been caused by something only indicated by economic development? Adam Przeworski authored one of the most comprehensive studies: *Democracy and Development: Political Institutions and Well-Being in the World, 1950–1990*. Like Schumpeter, Przeworski gives a minimalist definition of democracy with "contested election." He sees "rule of law democracy" as grounds for "contested electoral democracy" and concludes that economic development in fact does not generate democracies, though democracies are much more likely to survive in wealthy societies.

More recent research, "Income and Democracy,"[5] points out that existing studies establish a strong cross-country correlation between income and democracy, but do not typically control for factors that simultaneously affect both variables. This research shows that controlling for such factors removes the statistical association between income per capita and various measures of democracy. Furthermore, it reconciles the positive cross-country correlation between income and democracy with the absence of a causal effect of income on democracy by showing that the long-run evolution of income and democracy is related to historical factors. The challenge to "growth determinism" (or "economic growth leads to democracy") has pointed to at least four other important directions of further research.

First, both Robert Dahl and Samuel Huntington argue that many factors (economic, historical, social, external, and cultural) appear to be associated with the emergence of democracy. Yet no single factor appears sufficient to lead to democratic development or to be relatively more important at any time and place. They find it impossible to present strict hypotheses, so they present tentative propositions.

In *The Third Wave*, Huntington attempts to explain why, how, and with what consequences a group of transitions to democracy occurred after the 1970s. Though he still believes that the distinction between order and anarchy is more fundamental than the distinction between democracy and dictatorship, he puts more emphasis on the values of democracy. His primary thesis is that transitions in the 1970s and 1980s were produced by common causes, parallel developments, and the impact of early transitions on later ones.

Five changes play significant roles in bringing about the third-wave transitions: the deepening problems of legitimacy and performance legitimacy; unprecedented global economic growth that expanded the middle class; striking changes in the doctrine and activities of the Catholic Church; changes in the policies of external participants; and snowball or demonstration effects. He also proposes that no single factor is sufficient or necessary to explain the development of democracy in a single country or in all countries, and that the combination of causes are different in different waves, stages, and countries.

The second direction points to the fact that the relationship between democracy and economic development does not actually present an answer in itself. It is argued that economic development produces democracy only insofar as it alters favorably such intervening variables as class structure and civil society. In *Capitalist Development and Democracy*, the authors[6] contend that capitalist development facilitates the rise of democracy because it transforms the class structure, strengthening the working and middle classes and weakening the landed upper class. In *The Silent Revolution*, Ronald Inglehart identifies a powerful cultural factor mediating the relationship between economic development and stable democracy: a civil culture syndrome consisting of interpersonal trust, life satisfaction, and political moderation. Robert Putnam's *Making Democracy Work* is another effort in this direction, though it is more about how civic culture influences government performance (degree of government) and economic success.

The third direction is reflected in Edward Friedman's edited book *The Politics of Democratization: Generalizing East Asian Experiences*. Friedman contends that democracy is not determined by economic preconditions.

History has shown that "unique culture" has nothing at all to contribute to democracy. Democratic cultures are the consequences, not the causes, of democratization. There are no unique historical, cultural, and class preconditions for democracy, and there is nothing in Europe or the West that was peculiarly conducive to democracy. What leads to democracy is politics. Politics themselves, however, have no preconditions at all; for politics lie in a contingent realm. Politics are the only preconditions of democracy. He concludes that it has always been the simple truth that democracy was humanly attractive and it is possible to democratize governments, anytime, anywhere, with the right politics. Friedman's "universal political approach" appears to be a tautology because he uses "politics" to explain democracy which in itself is a type of politics. It is the "contingent realm" that needs to be explained.

The last type of research is exemplified by Tatu Vanhanen's *The Process of Democratization*, Daron Acemoglu and James Robinson's *Economic Origins of Dictatorship and Democracy*, and Przeworski's *Democracy and the Market*, which go beyond economic development to seek the preconditions of democracy. Vanhanen presents an evolutionary theory of democracy based on the idea that all species have a species-specific behavioral predisposition common to all members of the species, and that a common factor must account for the major part of the variations in democracy. He assumes that political structure has evolved in the struggle for existence and reproduction. He then hypothesizes that a democracy will arise under conditions in which power resources are so widely distributed that no group is able to suppress its competitors or to maintain its hegemony. According to this "well-tested" explanation, the level of economic development is not the ultimate causal factor behind democratization because various power resources are usually more widely distributed at higher levels of development. The anomalies in Lipset's theory can now be explained; important power resources can become widespread in some poor countries, and remain highly concentrated in some rich countries.

In *Economic Origins of Dictatorship and Democracy*, Daron Acemoglu and James Robinson apply game theory to argue that different social groups prefer different political institutions because of the way they allocate political power and resources. In developing a framework for analyzing the creation and consolidation of democracy, they trace the process of democratization to the strength of civil society, the structure of political institutions, the nature of political and economic crises, the level of economic inequality, the structure of the economy, and the form and extent of globalization.

In mapping the four different paths of political development, however, they assume a linear path to democracy as historical destiny and fail to take more cultural content into account, which coincides with the fact that this ambitious project doesn't even address China. Przeworski's *Democracy and the Market* also delves into the problem of consolidation in the process of democratization. It argues that democracies last only when they evoke "self-interested spontaneous compliance" with fair and effective institutions from all political forces. To evoke such compliance, a democracy must simultaneously offer to all such forces a fair chance to compete ("contestation open to participation") and make losing under democracy more attractive than a future under non-democratic alternatives.

So the central question concerning transitions is, do they lead to a system in which political forces subject their values and interest to the "uncertain interplay" of democratic institutions and comply with the outcomes of the democratic process? Przeworski does not further indicate the specific conditions or reasons for this "spontaneous compliance" when democracy is not yet established, but it examines all possible outcomes in terms of whether the relationships between all forces are known or balanced when democratic institutions are being adopted. It shows that when the relationships of relevant political forces are known ex ante to be balanced (or in Vanhanen's terms, "power resources are more widely distributed"), anything, including civil war, can happen, not just the formation of a democracy. Those who can gain from democracy will always be its most reliable promoters, and who have the most to lose will resist it. Analysis of the roles of hardliners, reformers, moderates, radicals, and "opportunists" who join under the slogan of democracy presents a more vivid picture than those who concentrate on class.

The simple message from all these studies is: economic development doesn't lead to democracy. There is simply no specific per capita number by which we can determine that a country will evolve into democracy.

The preconditions for "spontaneous compliance" to the "uncertain interplay" of democratic institutions are in fact stricter than what has been imagined: wide distribution of power resources, civic culture, elite's efforts, external influence, and the diffusion of democratic ideas. Since "wide distribution of power resources" had consistently led to "warring states" or warlord-type civil wars in Chinese history (including the civil war between the Chinese Nationalist Party and the Communist Party of China), suggests that external influence and the diffusion of democratic ideas didn't really matter: political culture seems to be the single most important factor (though in itself insufficient) for democratization in the Chinese context now, which goes back to the "tiger fight" autocratic legacy. Huntington is correct when he says that no single factor is sufficient or necessary to explain the development of democracy in a single country or in all countries, and that the combination of causes are different in different waves, stages, and countries. In China's case, the call for a strong and meritocratic government from the demand side, as discussed earlier, is also an important factor. But does political culture change over time?

The Neglected Revolution: From Family Rule to Party Rule

Political culture does change over time. In fact, the twentieth-century cultural change in China proved to be the most dramatic of the past three thousand years (beginning in 1022 BC when the Zhou Dynasty and the use of the "Mandate of Heaven" began). The most important change in political culture, though frequently underestimated, is the transformation from "Family Rulership" to "Party Rulership," or from family-based autocracy to party-based meritocracy. This transformation and other related changes will put an end to the "Dynastic Cycle" that crippled the Chinese empire for the last two thousand years. One implication of the discussion here is: business opportunities in China and doing business with China can flow with a long-term perspective without constant worry about China's cyclical political instability.

Underground organizations with or without religious background existed in China long before modern time. Yet, to China, "political party" was a foreign import. The Whigs (with the Tories) are often described as one of two political parties in Great Britain from the late seventeenth to the mid-ninteeenth centuries. While the Whigs' origins lay in constitutional monarchism and opposition to absolutism, neither group could be considered a true political party in the modern sense. Party politics did not begin to grow until at least 1784, with the rise of Charles James Fox, leader of a reconstituted "Whig" Party, who raged against the governing party of the "Tories," under William Pitt the Younger. According to Richard Gunther and Larry Diamond, political parties can be elite-based, mass-based, or ethnicity-based, and they can be electoralist parties and movement parties. As an elite-based revolutionary "vanguard" imported from Russia in 1921, the Communist Party of China (CPC) radically transformed China's political landscape by instituting a stern ideology that far outweighed that of the Kuomintang. Compared with the corrupt ideology of the two failed peasants' uprisings at the end of the Ming and Qing dynasties, CPC ideology proved highly successful in mass motivation, discipline enforcement (reining in the culture of "weak relational sanction"), and transaction-cost reduction.

Under the setting of party politics, the rules of the game, the expectation of gameplaying, and the action plans and behavior patterns of players are all institutionally different from those under dynastic family politics. Succession system, term structure, and power-exercising schemes are some key aspects of this institutional change. Mao Zedong found it extremely hard to act willfully as had previous autocrats, and the result was the "Cultural Revolution" which got rid of his rivals. But the institutional change from "Family Rulership" to "Party Rulership" has been so taken for granted that its far-reaching implications are mostly ignored or unrecognized.

In the current regime under the Communist Party of China, the long-practiced hereditary succession in dynastic politics came to an end. This is common sense, plain and simple. Yet party politics means succession had been institutionally transformed from a genetics-driven to a merit-driven arrangement. The logic here is that the merit-driven arrangement would inevitably evolve from reliance on revolutionary credentials for the first generation leaders, to reliance on regime-building credentials for later generation leaders. In other words, dynastic politics appealed to the "Mandate of Heaven" and genetics for legitimacy; party politics appealed to "Mandate of Merit" and performance for legitimacy. The genetics factor is gone, the patronage factor still helps, and the merit factor is of overwhelming importance.

After the death of Mao Zedong in 1976, his hand-picked successor Hua Guofeng had to give way to Deng Xiaoping due to Hua's lack of merit, meaning both political loyalty and ability to perform. In Chinese officials' words, merit means "both red and capable" (*youhong youzhuan, de cai jian bei*). While it can be tricky, political loyalty depends not only on top level personal allegiance and coalition building, but also on protecting Party power status. In spite of his success in getting rid of the left-wing "Gang of Four" after Mao's death, Hua Guofeng lost power because he failed to grasp the consensus shift from Mao's "class struggle" to economic development. Hua's successors Hu Yaobang and Zhao Ziyang, on the other hand, went too far to the "right side," jeopardizing the Party's power potential, and, therefore, both Hu and Zhao were purged by Deng.

The "Mandate of Merit" is one of two aspects in the new succession game; the other is the character of the succession process. In contrast to dynastic succession, there is now no more baby emperor, ailing emperor, or old and incompetent emperor. There is also no more worry about succession fights among the emperor's sons and brothers, or favoritism manipulation by eunuch, ministers, the empress, the empress dowager, relatives of the empress, and the emperor's sisters. Deng Xiaoping successfully employed a mechanism similar to "Retired Emperor" or "Grand Emperor" (*Taishang Huang*) to smooth the succession process.

After Deng retired, he kept the title of "Chairman of the Central Military Commission (CMC)." When he gave up the position in 1989, he could still manage to "rule from behind the curtain" due to strong revolutionary and state-building credentials. During his policy-making "Southern Tour" to Shenzhen in early 1992, his remaining official title was "Honorary Chairman of the Chinese Bridge Association."

As the leader of a non-revolutionary generation, Jiang Zemin didn't enjoy Deng's informal authority. But he still followed Deng's footsteps by holding the Chairman of the Central Military Commission title from 2002 to 2005 for the leadership transition to Hu Jintao. The transition from Jiang to Hu was often hailed as "the first orderly and institutionalized transition of power in the history of the People's Republic of China." The smooth succession that required no death or purge of an incumbent had in fact been institutionally built in to the merit-driven arrangement, which evolves from reliance on revolutionary merit to reliance on regime-building merit, from individual authority to norm formation, from cult of personality to consensus building, and from strong-man politics to collective leadership.

The merit-based logic puts the nepotism legacy and the credential requirement into a delicate balance. On one hand, blood ties, school ties, regional identities, bureaucratic affiliations, or patron-client ties still matter. The "Shanghai Gang," the "Princelings' Party" (*taizidang*), "the Qinghua Clique," the "Fellow Provincials" (*tongxiang*), the "Chinese Communist Youth League (CCYL) Officials" (*tuanpai*), the "Personal Secretary Clusters" (*mishuqun*), and the "Returnees from Overseas Students" (*haiguipai*) also play a part in leadership selection.

On the other hand, educational background, experience, skills, and performance are increasingly important in elite recruitment. Evidence of the merit-based logic can clearly be found in the credentials and educational background of Politburo members of the most recent 16th Party Congress. None of the twenty-five members in the 1982 Politburo under Deng had a university education. Of the twenty-four members in the 1997 Politburo under Jiang, seventeen held university degrees. By contrast, among the twenty-five members in the new Politburo under Hu, twenty-two have a university education, which makes the new leadership the best-educated group in communist China's history.

The autocratic legacy as a manifestation of cultural inertia went away with the passing of the revolutionary leaders. As the merit-based logic matures, collective leadership takes hold; and there is no more paramount leader and no more "core" in the Party leadership. Power-sharing, regional representation, and diversification of political connections become the trend. Rules of "regional representation" on the Central Committee were instituted to ensure all provinces have two full members in the central leadership.

The voting mechanism is also at work. The most emotion-stirring sideshow is the practice of "plurality-at-large bloc voting" or "multiple-winner approval voting" (cha'e xuanjiu, or simply "elections with more candidates than seats") adopted after the Thirteenth Party Congress in 1987. This rule is for electing both the Party Congress and the Central Committee. When the number of candidates is 12.5 percent more than the available seats, candidates chosen by favoritism rather than by merit now face a serious threat of elimination, since large-scale vote-buying is practically impossible.

Voting as a way of expressing objection is also becoming aggressive. In 2003, for example, one-tenth of delegates voted against Jiang Zemin staying on as Central Military Commission chairman. The narrow dynastic family "gene pool" was quietly replaced by a much wider range of Party elites. Smooth succession and top-level political stability were institutionally installed by rule-building and the elimination of inheritance clashing, dynastic favoritism manipulation, and personal overindulgence.

The "Mandate of Merit" therefore leads to regime legitimacy, as there is increasingly reliance on both leadership performance and institutional rules. Performance legitimacy and institution legitimacy in turn stabilize leadership succession. Fragile, dynastic "hereditary succession" was revolutionarily replaced by more orderly "meritocratic succession."

Several critical institutional developments underscore the orderly "meritocratic succession." First is "age limits" for leadership positions. The 1997 Politburo regulations stipulate that, except in extraordinary circumstances, all top leaders in both Party and government must retire by age seventy. All ministers of the State Council, provincial chiefs, and top military officers must retire by age sixty-five, and their deputies at age sixty-three.

The immediate effect of this rule is a relatively young Politburo. Hu Jintao's Politboro has an average age of sixty; Jiang in 1997 had an average of sixty-three, and the average age of Deng's in 1982 was seventy-two. One other interesting result is a new two-tiered hierarchy within the Politburo: the Politburo Standing Committee with senior members, and a group of other regular Politburo members with junior status. This two-tiered arrangement can be seen as an innovation intended to institutionalize a process of promotion for a future orderly "meritocratic succession."[7] Leadership positions are now also subject to "term and year limits." Top Party and government terms are limited to five years, and no more than two terms are allowed. According to new rules in 2006, there is also a fifteen-year limit for holding different positions with the same rank.

These "rule of law" elements of "appointment limits" on age, term, and year have been so taken for granted in the West that their institutional innovative nature was ignored by almost all Western observers. The "tiger fight" culture persisted throughout China's history because no institutional mechanism under "Family Rulership" could internalize political competition into self-reinforcing cooperation.

When the prospect of ruling was defined by lifetime tenure, political competition would externalize into brutal contestation or internalize into suspicious cooperation. The emperor had to be vigilant: potential rivals surfaced within and outside of his court. The ministers had to avoid being framed into a rebellion scheme.

Deng Xiaoping's greatest political wisdom was the will to institutionally put an end to this "life-term" tradition. Clearly, family-rulership couldn't install a "term limits" mechanism on the emperor due to the unchallenged political culture and "commitment problems."[8] Only under Party rulership (partyocracy) could such innovation be made possible in China. The merit-based succession that replaced heredity-based succession has evolved from relying more on individual-heroic nation-building credentials to relying more on widely distributed state-building credentials.

The Chinese culture of reciprocal meritocracy enabled China to go the "economy first" approach and install the term-based mechanism in due time (compared with the former Soviet Union). Innovations of "term limits" and "intra-Party elections" miraculously maintain the Chinese family-centered, interdependent-oriented, and harmony-minded national psychology—and at the same time draw on virtues from Western individual-centered, self-dependent-oriented, and contest-minded cultural psychology.

The Party is like a big family, membership is open to the whole society, and consultative cooperation is cherished; competition is about merit, and an anti-corruption mechanism can be worked out in a stable political environment. The government intends to set up a "National Corruption Prevention Bureau" that follows effective anti-corruption practices overseas. It will be directly under the State Council instead of under the prosecutors' offices, and will also be established at the provincial level. In retrospect,

Deng's unshaken determination to crack down on the 1989 turmoil was well-grounded and fully justified. And the 2002 orderly "meritocratic succession" became China's historic milestone.

However, if this "rule of the game" change is not viewed from a historical-institutional and paradigm-shift perspective, it may not be all that clear as common sense or conventional wisdom. H. Lyman Miller, a longtime China specialist, for example, is confused by what he chooses to define as "creeping institutionalization": "I cannot escape the feeling that, after thirty-one years of following Chinese leadership politics on a day-to-day basis, that I know a lot less about how leadership politics work than I used to."

Because "the imposition of institutionalized processes, complemented by a higher premium in the post-1989 period on public displays of leadership unanimity, means that leadership competition and conflict have become embedded and submerged within the framework of institutions and their associated schedules and routines. This has meant that they are less visible and harder to dissect. Many major events in leadership politics seem frustratingly explicable in terms of alternative realities."[9]

As another example, Chen Liangyu was believed by Western media to be a protégé of former President Jiang Zemin, and his dismissal was widely considered a victory for President Hu Jintao in the continuing power struggle between Hu and Jiang. This again reflects an outdated framework for analyzing Chinese politics. The problem is not if it is true or not; the problem is, even if it *is* true, the term-based mechanism has an "interest-encompassing effect" that crushes nested special interests—all because when the term-based leadership replaced lifetime tenure, political expectation and behavior patterns would also change accordingly.

Term-based party rulership eliminates the following uncertainties under "Family Rulership": leaders' lifespan uncertainty, leaders' ability uncertainty due to aging, limitation of successor selection, and uncertainty about the successor's ability, the successor's support system, and the successor's lifespan. The reason Mao ruled to have autocratic traits is exactly because the term-limit rule was not installed, which in turn made "meritocratic succession" impossible. The two most important characteristics of autocracy are absolute power and life-term. Constitutional Monarchy transforms autocracy by limiting absolute power. Chinese reformed meritocracy transforms autocracy by installing term limits, which in turn also limit absolute power. Once put under the microscope of institutional examination, it's all common sense. But only a paradigm shift of institutional analysis can make the murky water clear.

The implications of China's "rule of the game" change are much more far-reaching than what has been recognized. As political competition internalized into self-reinforcing cooperation under Party rulership, the advantages of policy-making efficiency, succession cost-saving, gaining experience, and talent retention over those in Western style electoral democracy are all hard to deny. Most importantly, Party elites may now be much more confident in China's own political institutions and less weak-minded in resisting Western democracy, especially as they gain more understanding of how Western democracy actually evolves and works.

In parallel with these institutional changes is the increasing professionalization of the Chinese military. The military depoliticization was in fact part of the main event in the recent leadership succession. There is no strong military man in the new generation of leadership, and decreasing representation of the military on the central committee and the Politburo is now a sure trend. The Party, however, is in good control of the military through the Central Military Commission, where the Party General Secretary is also the Chairman. The structural change from Military Regions to Group Armies also facilitates the Party's grip.

The Party is essentially putting aside the "exploitation" issue and opening its door to the admission of private entrepreneurs and other "outstanding elements" from the emerging layers of society. The institutionalization of this radical change (along with the other radical change: legalization of private property rights protection in 2007) sends a clear message: the CPC's "advanced nature" is not only reflected in its merit, it's also reflected in its provision of an institutional mechanism of "upward mobility" for the whole Chinese society. Since the Party is now open to everyone, and there is a "Political Consultative System" available for multi-party cooperation, the CPC sees no need to pursue political reform that would result in a Western style multi-party election. The new system therefore echoes the "Mandate of Heaven," which is totally Chinese and radically different from the European Social Democrat style characterized by participation in the bourgeoisie parliament. In 2007, two non-Communists were appointed into the cabinet: Chen Zhu, former vice president of the Chinese Academy of Sciences (CAS), is China's Minister of Health, and Wang Gang is the Minister of Science and Technology.

In any case, the current Chinese regime is no longer the stereotypical autocracy, dictatorship, or guardianship as discussed in Robert Dahl's *Democracy and Its Critics*. In fact, the "Mao era" was only a transition period before the institutional logic of the transformation from "family politics" to "party politics" runs its full course. It is simply a myth that

Chinese communist leaders are ineffective, incompetent, politically rigid, narrow-minded, and shortsighted. It is also a wishful thinking that a vicious power struggle is going on among various factions, especially among the top contenders of the fourth generation, thus leading to a major internal crisis.[10] Those who stick with the autocracy mental model are going to be disappointed if they expect a traumatic political crisis in future China. And the most disappointed of all will be those who expect China's "coming collapse."

One other far-reaching effect of top leadership stability in institutionalized "party politics" is the structural impact on the Chinese "social pyramid" that used to produce the "Dynastic Cycle." As concluded earlier in this book, dynastic "hereditary succession" was the ultimate cause of the shaky top of a periodically crumbling pyramid. "Meritocratic succession" totally changes the political landscape. But the change at the top is not the only institutional transformation happening in China. It's part of the ongoing "triple transition": from a planned economy to a market economy, from an agricultural society to a modern industrial society, and from an autocratic "Family Rulership" to an authoritarian "Party Rulership." Marketization forces the government to function in a different way from its traditional undertaking. The separation of government and the status of law are two of the most important aspects. According to Autocratic Tradition and Chinese Politics,[11] the following features are typical in the traditional dynastic setting:

1. Traditional law had never been conceived of as having a divine origin. It was simply commands handed down by the autocrat to rule over his subjects. There was never a provision in Chinese law that constrained and checked the power of the emperor and his state.

2. From its very inception, Chinese law was perceived as a tool wielded by the ruler to maintain his authority. Laws were seen as punitive and coercive measures used by the imperial state for social control.

3. There was no legal provision for the protection of individual rights against encroachment by the state, and that's why no lawyers even existed in Chinese imperial history.

4. The autonomy of the judicial court had never existed in China. Both legislative and judicial powers had been subordinated under and merged into the imperial administration.

5. Laws emanate from the state vertically down to the subject rather than mediate horizontally between subjects. In Chinese legal tradition, there

was neglect of civil matters such as contract and property rights. Social activities were mainly regulated by customs and personal relationships.

6. Traditional legal practices in China also include the use of physical torture, the implicit assumption of "guilty until proved innocent," punishments that extend beyond the culprit to relatives and even neighbors, corporal punishments not provided by formal law, and arbitrary imperial decisions overriding existing law.

During the last thirty years of reform, most of these features have undergone significant changes. Laws and the legal enforcement of contract and property rights are now part of business life. Working as a lawyer is increasingly an important career choice for many people. A quarter century ago, China had some 3,000 lawyers. Today China has a bar of some 150,000, reflecting a fifty-fold growth in the legal profession in a single generation.

There is similar growth underway in the court system, in the legislative process, in legal education, and in many other aspects of the legal system. Suing government agencies is no longer sensational news. Legislative and judicial powers are no longer subordinated under and merged into the administrative function. State power is more and more constrained and checked by public opinion and the society. The 1989 Administrative Litigation Law and the 1994 State Compensation Law limit state action by providing redress after the fact, while the 1996 Administrative Penalties Law and the 2004 Administrative Licensing Law introduced the "due process" concept and imposed procedural constraints on government actions.

The base of China's economic pyramid has been radically changed by agriculture reform and China's market economy. The shrinking agriculture sector, the expanding manufacturing and service sectors, and the emerging middle class, will continue to reshape the economy toward a more manageable pyramid base. "Family planning" and "collective ownership" of land certainly weaken the "partible inheritance" tradition that fragmented private property; the modern shareholding system provides a counter-partible mechanism, and non-agriculture industries provide new opportunities. The players on the field have changed from the old "Emperor, peasants, bureaucrats, bandits, soldiers, invaders" to "Party leaders, peasants, bureaucrats, middle class, soldiers, external stakeholders." The most important change is the relative strength of players with intra-institutional and extra-institutional power. The unprecedented dominance of intra-institutional power, due in part to the development of technology, ideology, and political internalization, provides the ultimate source for China's social stability.

Social unrest remains unavoidable, but "peasant uprisings" will be a thing of the past.

Strong and stable top leadership effectively keeps under control the deep-seated fear of disorder in both the bureaucracy and the society. The Chinese usually call their failing governments "corrupt and incapable" (*fubai wuneng*). The theory for the current regime is: it is "corrupt locally but capable centrally" (*fubai youneng*), that is, the government is capable of handling corruption due to the institutional change of "meritocratic succession."

Applying the Western experience to China and predicting democratization are symptoms of cultural-historical naïveté. There is simply no "China puzzle:" If everything in China is so bad, why is China still rising and the government not collapsing? The "China puzzle" exists only when we conceptualize the Western experience and use these context-sensitive ideas to view China, only to find that China refuses to conform to our abstractions. A seeming "bad" may not be really "bad" when put into China's own cultural-historical context. But psychological law dictates that it's easier for one to maintain their cognitive mental process when seeing something that conflicts with it. Hence, there is always something wrong with reality.

The importance of institutional change from "Family Rulership" to "Party Rulership" cannot be overemphasized. If contesting for power is in fact human nature, then the nature of contestation could determine the stability of a regime. The contested factors in "hereditary succession" are genetic purity, favoritism, forces, and merit. The contested factors in "meritocratic succession" are merit and connection. Clearly, fewer factors and therefore less uncertainty operate under "meritocratic succession."

One other key difference between "meritocratic succession" and "electoral succession" is, "meritocratic succession" explicitly forbids multi-party elections for government, making citizen's rights subject to this restriction. Taking this perspective, if democracy means "election" and "equal liberty," the Chinese government has actually been doing a great job in spreading "equal liberty" within the past thirty years. Even though the "old tradition" (state power and lack of top-down accountability) still has vigor, the "new tradition" (state-ownership and planned economy) has been thoroughly reformed. To avoid bureaucratic corruption efforts from pitching the system into the "dynastic circle," it is important to keep central authority institutionally strong in political, financial, and military control, which is what has happened and what needs to be ensured. Can multi-party democracy gradually evolve by itself, or can single-party meritocracy slowly transition to multi-party democracy?

Why China Won't Adopt Western Democracy

Cars in most countries drive on the right side of the road and have steering wheels on the left side of the cars. This rule of the road is by no means universal. Cars in the UK, Australia, New Zealand, India, Indonesia, and Japan drive on the left rather than on the right side of the road, steering wheels are on the right. About 34 percent of the world population drives on the left side of the road, and 66 percent on the right. The initial choice to drive on the left could be random, but once it became a convention, it is too costly to change even when right-side driving appears to make more sense.

The English keyboard for typewriters and computers took its present standard form in 1874 when E. Remington & Sons shipped a commercial typewriter with the QWERTY keyboard invented by Christopher Sholes. The Dvorak keyboard, patented by August Dvorak in 1936, was claimed to be a better alternative. Yet the first-to-market standard created a "lock-in" effect both on user habit and vendor expectation which made the QWERTY keyboard universally used.

The 4-foot-8.5-inch gauge (the width between the rails) for railway tracks has been the most common standard since the late 1820s. This gauge was adopted more than two hundred years ago for horse-drawn coal-cart tramways serving a small group of mines near Newcastle, England. British engineer George Stephenson, known as the "father of railways," happened to have experience designing the old tramways. Instead of creating a technically better and more cost-effective gauge, he simply continued his prior practice. Other standards with wider or narrower gauges to fit traffic conditions appeared elsewhere, yet his standard remains widely used throughout the world.

These three illustrious stories are classic examples of a historical phenomenon known as "path dependence"—the dependence of an outcome on the path of previous events rather than on current conditions. In this process, initial choice has an enduring influence. Choices made on the basis of transitory conditions can persist long after those conditions change. Many people's career paths turn out to be an unintended outcome of their initial jobs. The simple logic here is: "History matters." This applies not only to technical standards and career choice, but also to rules and institutional arrangements.

In ancient times, Europe and China had a somewhat similar "feudal system" that governed the relationships between kings and their vassals.

Yet European feudalism's contractual focus and the presence of a separate religious authority led to the path of pluralism and individualism, whereas Chinese feudalism's kinship-oriented and hierarchical nature landed the Chinese on a different path into autocracy and statism. The feudal origin may be traced to a much earlier in time, and ecological and cultural factors may need to be considered, but somehow somewhere, contingent choices seem to set a specific trajectory of institutional development and consolidation that is over time difficult to reverse. This is much like a "chain reaction" where initial events in the "reactive sequences" set off a temporally linked but causally tight chain of events that is mystically uninterruptible.

Economists like to associate "path dependence" with efficiency, market failure, costs, and remedies. The problem is, efficiency is not always objectively measurable, externally observable, or independently determinable. Preference and uncertainty play a role, especially in institutional "path dependence" related to politics. The design of the American Constitution provides some good examples. The president of the United States is not elected directly by the people but by the "electoral college." The representation of the senate in the U.S. congress is by an equal treatment for each state rather than by a proportional criterion. These two "unfair" designs create serious problems for American democracy. Yet due to the historical lock-in effect from vested interests, constitutional reforms for the good of democratic equality have proven almost impossible.

The reason China fails to adopt "electoral democracy" or "multi-party democracy" can be found in this "path dependence" argument. Preference for a non-confrontational political organization connotes a way of life that is so enduring that change or simply talk of change may cause nervousness and panic. There is not only a psychological price that needs to be paid, there is also a cognitive cost associated with a potential change of "mental model" or "way of thinking." Uncertainty, therefore, comes into play. Given the fact that the Chinese way of thinking focuses more on results than on process, and more on context than on isolation, Chinese people will judge overall personal welfare against the change from their reformed meritocracy to Western democracy. Uncertainty arises when each member calculates and reconfigures his or her "cost-benefit matrix" in the expectation of preparation for change, transition to the new system, and actual performance of the new system. In these processes, costs will go beyond the psychological and the cognitive, to both those who have the most to lose and the most to gain.

In discussing China's "tiger fight" legacy from the "game theory" perspective, we know the democratic "spontaneous compliance" and "contestation open to participation" have been proved impossible in Chinese modern history. In China, "contestation open to participation" is going through an electoral process in an intra-Party rather than inter-Party setting. This "political culture" argument is almost like the other side of the coin along with the "path dependence" argument. The "political culture" argument also explains why a war between mainland China and Taiwan won't happen: it will happen only when both sides are "tigers;" if one is not strong enough to claim itself a tiger, there is simply no fight.

These are not the only two arguments for China's failure to accept Western democracy. Suppose, the majority of the Chinese people were quite certain that "electoral democracy" would be better for them than meritocracy, but there is still a "collective action" issue. Common sense says that when everyone in a group has common interests, then everyone will act collectively to achieve them. This is too obvious to many who feverishly champion overthrowing the current regime for a democratic future in China. Such ideas have been floating around the internet for quite some time. Unfortunately, the obvious is again obviously wrong.

Recall the "free-ride" problem in the Thanksgiving story. On one hand, there is a tremendous organization cost for those who propose violent political change; on the other hand, those who feel they may benefit from the change have an incentive to let other people bear the cost of change, or to take a "free ride" on the efforts of others. In "The Logic of Collective Action," Mancur Olson pointed out that individuals will not "ride free" only in group actions that provide benefits exclusively to active participants, they will ride free because no one can prevent them from benefiting from the "public goods," and their taking the benefit will not affect another's benefit anyway. Therefore, unless there are "selective incentives" or special incentives to motivate participation, collective action is unlikely to occur even when large groups of people with common interests exist.

Olson's insights didn't stop here. A violent political change in China will inevitably involve a large group of people. Yet a large group will face relatively high costs ("increasing cost of scale") when attempting to organize for collective action, while a small group will face relatively low costs in collective action. Moreover, individuals in a large group will gain relatively less per capita compared with the potential cost they may pay for successful collective action ("decreasing proportion of benefit"); individuals in a small group (the existing regime) will gain relatively more per capita through successful collective action.

In short, when there are no strong special incentives for the majority of the participants, common interest won't guarantee successful collective action. And even strong special incentives won't guarantee success when the organizational cost is simply too high. When the Manchu crossed over the Great Wall and occupied the heartland of China in 1644, the Manchu population was only about 2 million. With a population of over 120 million, or 60 Han Chinese to 1 Manchu, the Han Chinese still failed to expel the invasion when the special incentives were obviously strong. The same was also true for the 1937 to 1945 China-Japan war, which proved Chiang Kai-shek's government was corrupt and incapable. The logic of collective action ("free riding," "increasing cost of scale," and "decreasing benefit of scale") worked then as it works now; saying the majority of Chinese prefer democratic change is by itself a very risky statement. In fact, with the rapid economic growth in the past thirty years detailed in the previous chapters, the "performance" argument against uncertain democratic change is as persuasive now as the "logic of collective action" argument.

Can democratic change come from within the current regime at a lower cost, just like what Mikhail Gorbachev did in the former Soviet Union in the 1980s, and what Lee Teng-hui did in Taiwan in the 1990s? When the "external approach" doesn't seem to work, the "internal approach" has great appeal. In the case of the former Soviet Union, Gorbachev's political openness contributed to the rise of Boris Yeltsin. When Yeltsin became the elected president of Russia in June 1991, a special political situation emerged where Russia, the largest republic in the Soviet Union, could stand by itself without the Union. The unsuccessful coup by hardliners against Gorbachev in August 1991 accelerated this process, and Russia finally took over the Soviet Union. Similar to the Soviet Union where democracy was growing out of "contending power," democracy in Taiwan developed from the weakening Chinese Nationalist Party, the Kuomintang (KMT), and a strategic independent attempt from mainland China. After the KMT lost the mainland to the Communists, its international status became increasingly isolated, and native Taiwanese began to challenge its authority. When Lee Teng-hui, a native Taiwanese, took over the leadership in 1988, the Democratic Progressive Party surfaced in the political arena and transformed itself into both pro-democracy and pro-independence. Lee was widely believed to intentionally encourage the independent movement that led to Chen Shui-bian coming to power during Taiwan's free election in 2000.

The cases of the Soviet Union and Taiwan are not only examples of "democracy from within" by elite's efforts, but also examples of contending powers leading to democratization instead of civil war. In the Soviet Union's case, civil war was avoided because the left wing was too weak. In Taiwan's case, the "wide distribution of power resources" that avoided civil war was aided by mainland China's external pressure and the American influence. It may be true that any country can choose democracy (as if culture doesn't matter). Yet enforcement is a totally different story (culture still matters in a hidden way). Russia's democracy is now known as "One step forward, two steps back" (Like India, Russia's regional leaders are appointed rather than elected). Taiwan's story is no better.

Many can still recall the 1989 democratic movement in Beijing, when party leader Zhao Ziyang attempted to play the game like Gorbachev did. Superficially, Zhao was simply too weak in character to overpower Deng Xiaoping; in fact, the patronage relationship between Deng and Zhao dictated the situation. The Chinese political history detailed earlier in this book showed that a contending power either fails to emerge or fails to avoid a civil war. More importantly, the power man always prefers political order over "election." With the collective leadership and diversification of political networks in the current Chinese regime, any political force that buys the "election" ideology won't be able to gain control, not to mention achieve consensus. A rational leader simply won't embrace the "election" ideology in exchange for his political future, and if he does, he simply won't be able to build a coalition powerful enough to challenge the meritocratic system.

The claim of the "advanced nature" of the Chinese Communist Party is not an idle one. Joining the Party itself is a tough process; only the best among their peers get selected. It's a long process to become a regular cadre, and to get promoted first to local leadership, then to a national position. This process, even when patronage is inolved, still largely bases on merit. There are also elections within the Party and in the increasingly important People's Congress. It is simply too difficult to understand the organizational logic of meritocracy when one is not personally involved in the process. In China's "democratic centralism," the key principle is that the minority yields to the majority, the subordinates listen to the superior, and the whole Party follows the Central Committee. Organizational loyalty controls every aspect of the Party. Any centrifugal attempt is prohibited. The political context is such that one will readily feel ashamed, guilty, and self-condemned for one's extra-institutional action even when one thinks one is fighting for a "just cause." A rational leader cannot afford even a small mistake. Under this political setting, "electoral democracy" can be viewed only as a "fast track" attempt for political opportunists who favor avoiding the long meritocratic process.

In fact, the "rational choice" argument has been more and more reinforced by a recent development in Taiwan where its first freely elected president, Chen Shui-bian, was buried deep in the political chaos caused by his own corruption scandal. The truth is that "electoral democracy" simply can't guarantee a clean government. On the contrary, it may stir up more social confrontation as more people get involved in the political process.

The support rate for Chen Shui-bian was only 18 percent in August 2006, much less than the 29 percent for President George W. Bush, deep in the Iraq mess. But within less than a month, the support rate for Chen tumbled to only 10 percent (27 percent for Bush in early 2007). When the leader lost all face, the society inevitably fell into disorder, and electoral democracy could not maintain its abstract promises.

Democracy in Taiwan amps up people's expectation for the top leader's morality, which is by itself from a "sage ruler" tradition. Democracy, on the other hand, gives people more freedom to protest and potentially contribute to social disorder. One of the greatest tragedies for electoral legitimacy is the illegitimate result of the institutionalized self-interested proceduralism. The best example of this was the 2006 "Down with Bian" movement in Taiwan. Millions of Taiwanese took to the streets to show their disappointment at their elected president. Yet Taiwan's legislators, out of pure self-interested motives, didn't support the effort to impeach Chen for fear of a legislative re-election. The institutional rigidity of proceduralism prevents a government that is losing its legitimacy from being deprived of its electoral legitimacy in a timely manner, which demonstrates the means-oriented procedural democracy failing to react to some pressing ends-oriented demands from the people.

If Taiwan presents a "negative demonstration" argument, then Singapore, like Taiwan, also a Chinese-derived culture, offers a "positive demonstration argument. Like Hong Kong, Singapore was colonized by Great Britain in the nineteenth century. After it gained independence in 1965, Singapore quickly raised itself to first-class global city status under the leadership of Lee Kuan Yew's People's Action Party, which dominated in its unicameral parliamentary government.

As Southeast Asia's financial and high-tech center today, Singapore is well known for its clean government and high standard of living: No. 1 in Asia and No. 11 in the world; GDP per capita is at No. 22 among all nations. With a 77 percent Chinese population of its nearly 4.4 million total, Singapore champions Chinese Confucian values and emphasizes stable family life by a policy of encouraging more children. It has a great system of public housing, public education, public infrastructure, and unsubsidized public transportation (high tax for car ownership). Its seaport, airline, and civil service are the most efficient in the world. It also enjoys a low unemployment rate, minimum racial tension, and low pollution levels. Gambling was legalized in 2005, and it remains one of the most attractive tourist destinations in the world.

Singapore's culture is yet underlined by its "law and order" legalist approach. It is ranked No. 140 out of 167 countries for "press freedom" in 2005, and has the top per capita execution rate in the world. However, it has a low crime rate and has been constantly ranked No. 2 in the "Index of Economic Freedom," behind Hong Kong. A Singaporean's answer to the critique of low "press freedom" is: the Philippines' press policy has long been one of the most liberal in Asia, yet its modernization and economic progress remain challenged; the U.S. free press has become more and more aggressive during the last few decades, yet during the same period has had increasingly bad government. There is simply no causal relation between a liberal free press and a good society.[12] Singapore may not be seen as a "model" that can be applied anywhere else. Its micro-management, social engineering, and mini-control measures may not fit China's situation, but it is indeed the best example of how any country can have its own version of government according to its own historical context.

The sage-ruler supported by honest officials was the ideal for a nation without a clear state-society boundary and a society with less differential economic strata. Western "partisan politics" simply has no social basis for existence in China because the concern for encompassing interests has always been stronger than that for special interests in China's inter-dependent culture. The Chinese harmonious egalitarian tradition with its absence of "partisan politics" makes the "harmonious egalitarianism" argument against Western "electoral democracy" in China.

Today, the much-acclaimed grassroots-level village elections in China are tainted by bribed voting by the rich, paid attendance, and disrespected leaders. Zhang Yingping, a Chinese journalist who has written a book called *Democracy in Zhejiang*, tells many stories about grassroots democracy as practiced in east China's Zhejiang Province countryside. One is about a local farmer who had enjoyed twenty-seven free lunches in the summer of 2002, when candidates for the leadership of his village held free banquets for all voters during the election campaign. He was disappointed that village heads were elected only every three years.

Zhang reports many specific innovations designed to make supervision of the government more effective and make officials more accountable. They include the pledges of prospective local government leaders to set up community welfare funds; legislators directly contributing columns to newspapers; and requiring elected officials to take out special insurance policies to guard against mistakes. He concludes that, "Despite so many things happening in modern China, the grassroots level government still has to accommodate, if not rely on, the traditional definition of moral authority."

Chinese people see it a joke to make politics resemble a talent contest or a beauty show. But even in non-political contests like the Chinese "Super Girl," popular election is not the only way to determine winners, as in "American Idol." While popular votes are needed for commercial purpose (charged through voting by phone calls), judges enjoy the right to select candidates for the next round even in the final stage. In the 2007 "Happy Boy's Voice," the face-saving game is played to the extreme and the voting scheme for the top singers becomes so complex that no one admits to understanding it. Judges' decisions are respected, and sometime carry a lot more weight. In another singing contest called "Just the Two of Us," judges can give up to ten points to the singers, each point openly calculated to carry the same weight as 1,000 votes from viewers. The tradition of meritocracy is deeply appreciated in the popular culture, and the apparent increase of pluralism in China now won't reduce much of its sustaining impact. In short, when the election mechanism is used in China, the multi-party element is absent in political contests and the authority element is sustained in non-political contests.

There is obvious reluctance to even mention the overseas "Chinese Democratic Movement" in this regard. But what has happened since 1989? If it has to be reduced to two words, it is "a mess." The movement is anything but democratic. "Electoral democracy" becomes a clown in a circus. There are fewer than 100 Chinese democratic activists around the world, and most are part-time. Yet there are more than thirty-five democratic parties or organizations among them—averaging fewer than three members in each "party." None has the ability or merit to unite the rest, and when they manage to do that for a short time, they fight for power and financial control. They put electoral procedures into a garbage can. They corrupt; they grab external funding and run. They attack each other, and they call one another communist spies.

None of this comes as a surprise. The most amusing thing, however, is that they do anything but "democratic movement."[13] To survive, they need funding; to get funding, they need to have their own organizations that they can control by themselves; and if they can get funding from Taiwan, they have no problem supporting Taiwan's independence. Of course, the Chinese government is happy about this. You want democracy, great, now you have it among you. China not only exports inexpensive goods, it also exports cheap dissidents, and the U.S. government imports them, only to discover they are not worthy of support, unless for useless moral statements. "Give them democracy" here became a curse. The decency and respect meant to be embedded in "electoral democracy" have been blemished. No wonder many withdraw from it completely. They tried to "fit through" democracy but simply failed to fit within it altogether.

The arguments against "Western democracy" in China so far are more in a "positive sense" than a "normative sense." They present more of the logic of "what it is" than the logic of "what it should be." That is, it doesn't involve a "value issue" or a "moral issue." Electoral democracy can be proved politically, socially, and economically infeasible and impractical in China, but can the infeasibility be proved morally justifiable? In other words, can one still argue "Western democracy" is morally superior and "Chinese meritocracy" is morally inferior? The "nationalism" argument, the "subjective morality" argument, the "rule of law" argument," and the "cultural morality" argument will be presented in the discussion of the ideological clash between China and the U.S. In all, there are twelve arguments for the question of "Why China won't adopt Western Democracy:"

1. "Political Culture" Argument
2. "Path Dependence" Argument
3. "Logic of Collective Action" Argument
4. "Performance" Argument
5. "Rational Choice" Argument
6. "Negative Demonstration" Argument
7. "Positive Demonstration" Argument
8. "Harmonious Egalitarianism" Argument
9. "Nationalism" Argument
10. "Subjective Morality" Argument
11. "Rule of Law" Argument
12. "Cultural Morality" Argument

Each of these arguments may seem isolated standing by itself. But when they come together, they become a mutually re-enforcing whole. In *The End of History and the Last Man*, Francis Fukuyama argued that "capitalist liberal democracy" is the "end point of mankind's ideological evolution" and the "final form of human government." To China, Western democracy is like Samuel Beckett's play "Waiting for Godot," a play that spoke without interpretation and confounded many assumed rules by which actors looked for motivation and critics looked for storyline. Yet nothing happens and Godot doesn't appear:

Vladimir: Well, shall we go?
Estragon: Yes, let's go.
They do not move.

China's rise is regarded by some as hype rising faster than China itself. What about "China democracy" hype? Is that the one rising faster than China in some people's minds?

6

Ideological Clash: China vs. America

Human Rights and Human Wrongs

When Seung-Hui Cho turned the campus of Virginia Tech into a hunting ground on April 16, 2007, thirty-two people were killed before Cho turned the gun on himself, marking the worst shooting rampage in U.S. history. The reactions from people in China and America to this tragedy were sharply different, yet the cultural implication went largely unrecognized. Many Chinese and even the Chinese government felt extremely nervous when it was first reported that the gunman was possibly from Shanghai. When it was clear that Cho was of Korean origin, the Chinese were greatly relieved and some started to post inappropriate and irresponsible comments on the web. In the much-heated discussion, commentators from the Hong Kong news media pointed out harshly that the Chinese as a whole are immature and weak-minded while the Americans are calm and mature—a reflection of a confident and strong-minded nation. Is this really true?

On October 31, 1991, University of Iowa Chinese physics student Lu Gang dashed into a faculty office and shot his adviser and several fellow students and then killed himself. Lu had lost his academic job and failed in his appeal before he took the action that traumatized the whole campus. Two psychology graduate students from the University of Michigan observed a sharp contrast between American and Chinese newspaper accounts of the causes of this incident, and decided to conduct research. They did a systematic content analysis of reports in the *New York Times* and the Chinese-language newspaper the *World Journal*. As it turned out, American reporters blamed the perpetrator's character problems ("very bad temper," "sinister edge," and "belief in guns for redressing grievances"), while Chinese reporters attributed it to contextual factors ("didn't get along with people," "rivalry with slain students," and "victim of Chinese top student education policy"). Did the Chinese reporters simply attempt to protect one of their own?

Only two weeks later, a stunningly similar story occured at a post office in Royal Oak, Michigan, where an unemployed postal worker named Thomas McIlvane shot his supervisor and several fellow workers and then committed suicide. Those Michigan psychology students did exactly the same analysis of the same newspapers, hoping to find a clue to the suggested bias in the Chinese reporters. Again, American reports paid attention only to McIlvane's personal attitudes and traits inferred from past behavior, such as "repeatedly threatened violence," "had a short fuse," and "mentally unstable"—while Chinese reporters focused on situational factors like "being fired recently," "supervisor was his enemy," and "availability of gun."

This result prompted them to carry out a follow-up survey. They provided descriptions of the two murder cases to American and Chinese students and asked them to rate the importance of personal attributes and situational factors. American students responded by emphasizing the presumed character in both cases, and Chinese students stressed situational factors whether the murderer was American or Chinese. They found their answer: the "bias" was not about the "subjects," it was about the perceived cause, the difference in "causal attribution" by the Chinese and the Americans. To further test this finding, they gave a list of situational factors to the survey participants and asked if the murder cases might not have occurred under different circumstances. American students mostly believed tragedies would happen anyway, while Chinese students tended to answer that the murders might well have been avoided. In a separate survey, participants were asked to rule out factors irrelevant to establishing a motive for the slaying. Asian students regarded only 37 percent as irrelevant, American students considered 55 percent irrelevant, showing a different tendency toward the belief of complexity and a holistic worldview.

This is one of many studies recorded in the 2003 book *The Geography of Thought: How Asians and Westerners Think Differently . . . and Why*. It also reveals how mistaken it is for the Hong Kong commentators to be ignorant of the difference in cultural psychology—the Chinese nervousness has everything to do with their relational "causal attribution" (much like the reaction from the Koreans), while the American calmness has nothing to do with their strong-minded confidence but about their field-independent perceived cause. The author of this book, Richard Nisbett, is a distinguished professor of social psychology and co-director of the Culture and Cognition program at the University of Michigan at Ann Arbor. By continuing traditional "National Character Studies" through direct tests both in America and in Asia, Nisbett delivers this message: human cognition is not everywhere the same; Asians and Westerners have maintained very different systems of thought for thousands of years, and these differences are scientifically measurable and culturally explainable. He wrote to answer these questions: Are human characteristics really "hardwired?" Do all human groups perceive and reason in the same way? Are the patterns of differences we all experience a consequence of using different "tools" to understand the world?

Nisbett's laboratory tests show that the differences in perceived cause in the study above happen not only in explaining human behavior, but also in explaining animal behavior and causality in the physical world. He found that the casual attribution difference mirrors the attention difference by the Chinese and the Americans. While there are, in fact, no major differences in the conception of "personality trait" between the two cultures, Westerners rely more on personal disposition to explain the cause or causes of a situation because they are less likely to notice situational factors and to realize their relevance in producing behavior.

This so-called "fundamental attribution error" reflects the fact that Westerners are prone to attend to "salient objects" rather than "context." In a related test involving teaching history in Asia and America, American teachers typically start with outcome and spend less time setting the context with initial events or catalysts. Events are usually presented in effect-cause order rather than chronological order, showing a preference for "looking-backwards" reasoning or "goal-oriented" reasoning. Nisbett sees goal orientation and "causal modeling" as characteristics of Westerners' sense of "personal agency," a trait of being free to act and in control of one's own actions. Tests for "predicting events" show American participants are less likely to fall into the "hindsight fallacy" and be less surprised when predictions turn out to be wrong. This is due to their habit of "explicit causal modeling" embedded with various potential outcomes, which suggests that

Westerners' success in science and their tendency to make "hard to recognize and correct" mistakes in causal analysis are derived from the same source: modeling goal objects and its properties, rather than its context.

Nisbett recognized that "the idea moves West" and showed that the West is no monolith concerning issues of independence (object) and interdependence (context): from the Babylonians, the Israelites, the Greeks, the Romans, the Italians, the Protestant Reformation in Germany, the Calvinist subcultures of Britain, to the United States, "The further to the West a given country lies, the greater, in general, that country's endorsement of independent values. Moreover, these differences among European cultures are reflected in their successor subcultures in the United States . . . it is the white Protestants among the American participants in our studies who show the most 'Western' patterns of behavior and that Catholics and minority group members, including African Americans and Hispanics, are shifted somewhat toward Eastern patterns."[1] Their intellectual history shows this exact same pattern: Big-picture social thought is more often found on the European Continent than in Anglo-America. While Anglo-American philosophers concerned themselves with atomistic language analysis, European philosophers were inventing phenomenology, existentialism, structuralism, poststructuralism, and postmodernism. Marxism is a German product, and sociology was invented by the French Auguste Comte and refined by the German Max Weber.

In a study regarding the "nature of change," graphs with positively and negatively accelerated growth trends were shown to the participants. Nisbett found that Americans made more predictions consistent with the trend than did the Chinese. These differences were much greater for the positively accelerated trends than the negatively accelerated trends. This linear versus cyclical thinking seems to match the long line of Western creations from Plato's *Republic*, Puritanism, Shaker communities, Mormonism, Thomas More's *Utopia*, the American and French revolutions, Democracy, Communism, and Fascism. All are different from the Chinese conviction that the perfect world exists in some pattern of the past and the future only repeats the pattern in a higher level (note that Communism is more an ideology for power rather than a belief system for Chinese). These Western utopias share the same characteristics: linear progress, a permanent state once attained, human effort rather than fate or divine intervention, and egalitarian and extreme assumptions about human nature.

In some job-related studies involving middle managers, more than 90 percent of Westerners preferred jobs in which personal initiatives are encouraged and individual initiatives are achieved, whereas more than 50 percent of Asians chose jobs in which everyone works together and no one is singled out for personal honor. More than 90 percent of Westerners thought their jobs would have a limited duration; only 40 percent of Asians agreed. More than 60 percent of Westerners rejected the idea of status being based on age: 60 percent of Asians didn't have a problem with that. In terms of the importance of previous job record in the consideration of dismissal, more than 75 percent of Westerners believed the employee should be let go based on current performance; only 20 percent of Asians thought universal rules should be applied to specific situations. The preferences of some European participants scored between American and Asian scores, indicating again, "The idea moves West."

In a three-word set of "panda, monkey, banana," which two of the three are more closely related? Nisbett found that American students showed a marked preference based on "taxonomic category" (panda and monkey both are animal), while Chinese participants made their choice based mostly on "thematic relationships" (monkey eats banana). Such a preference difference also proved true for American and Chinese children in a separate test. Nisbett believed there must be socialization factors working behind this different perception and reasoning. Categories denoted by nouns are obviously easier for kids to learn than are verbs, which imply relationships. Since verbs are highly reactive and nouns tend to be inert, it should be a universal phenomenon that kids pick up nouns much faster.

Yet developmental psycholinguists found that, unlike Western children, East Asian children learn verbs actually at about the same rate as nouns. Asian mothers tend to teach their kids social routines, while American mothers are found teaching their kids to name objects, which prompts them to focus on categories from object features. Category names in English are marked by syntax ("a duck," "the duck," "the ducks," "ducks") and it is obligatory to indicate either an object or a category. In Chinese, only context and factual cues help discern the difference, and the generic category is usually less used and learned at a later stage.

English is "subject-prominent" while Chinese is "topic-prominent." In English, one asks "More tea?" because drinking is obvious and the object (noun) is more relevant. In Chinese, one asks, "Drink more?" because tea is obviously in the context and the action (verb) is more relevant. In the Western tradition, objects have essences composed of abstract qualities for categories. These stable essences allow for confident linear predictions about behavior independent of context. Rules governing objects can be learned, and, therefore, the objects' behavior can be controlled. In the Eastern tradition, objects have concrete properties that interact with the environment to produce behavior. Abstract properties are not really constant and do not reflect a reality other than a characteristic of a particular object. Context sensitivity suggests that objects and their relationships are complex and less controllable.

Which group of the proverbs makes more sense? "Half a loaf is better than none" and "One against all is certain to fall," or, "Too humble is half-proud" and "Beware of your friends, not your enemies?" Nisbett's studies show that Chinese students had a preference for the proverbs with contradictions and the Americans had a preference for proverbs with straight meaning. Yiddish proverbs were later used to control the bias of familiarity with proverbs, but the result was the same.

Nisbett believes that a preference for contradiction indicates that the Chinese dialectical style of traditional thinking focuses on how to transcend conflicts and find the truth in each side. It reflects the belief in a constant change of positions, opposites completing or making up each other, and a holistic view of interdependence. Since "the opposite of a great truth is also true," finding the "Middle Way" between extreme propositions is the essential tenet of thought. It is also much less "aggressive" than the "thesis-antithesis-synthesis" line of thought by Kant, Fichte, Hegel, and Marx, because the effort is about accepting and transcending rather than eradicating the contradictions. And it certainly runs against Western logical principles, including "law of identity" (a thing is itself and not some other thing, or "cross situational consistency"), and "law of non-contradiction" (a proposition can't be both true and false in both abstract and concrete senses).

Nisbett cautions that these generalizations do not apply to all members of each culture where variations exist. But, on average, real differences are substantial. In East Asia, Japanese are found to have less involvement in immediate family and more commitment to the corporation. Though social constraints are in general greater on both Chinese and Japanese than on Westerners, the constraints come primarily from authorities for Chinese, and chiefly from peers for Japanese. "My claim is not that the cognitive differences we find in the laboratory cause the differences in attitudes, values, and behaviors, but that the cognitive differences are inseparable from the social and motivational ones. People hold the beliefs they do because of the way they think, and they think the way they do because of the nature of the societies they live in."

This is further proven by the fact that people from different cultures can move toward the other side of thinking after they are "primed" by a different environment, though they will never fully assimilate it.

Cognition differences in various cultures make sense when we trace them to ecological origins. But does it make sense if we trace internally into the function of the human brain? One of the findings by Nisbett is that causal attribution differences mirror the attention difference in different cultures ("attention and filter theories"). One of the findings in neuroscience shows that cognition is not merely a passive but rather an active process of seeing and creating our world of experience. The process involves the ability to focus mental effort on specific stimuli while excluding other stimuli through our senses, and involves using only a part of the available data and creating the remainder from our minds.[2] It suggests that the "rational economic principle" not only applies to human social behavior (cost and benefit calculation), but also applies to human brain behavior (ignoring and taking-in mechanism). We can "see" without any visual input because the brain can fill in the details from past experience. We can "reason" without forming any new routine because the brain can fetch the tools from the available mental deposit. It is evolutionarily economical for our brains to have a relatively stable "mental model" to process things in our world. A stable "mental model" makes economic sense, and the difference in the "mental models" between the Chinese and the Americans makes cultural-cognitive sense.

Studies from cognitive science and neuroscience are also echoed by modern physics and philosophy of science. Modern physics shows that the nature of objects in the micro world often depends on the tools it uses to study them. Philosophers of science find that revolutions in the history of science actually involved, in many instances, changes in tools. They further discovered that results of scientific observations depended, to a great extent, on the background knowledge of the scientists and the theories they employed. In other words, observations are always "theory laden" even when inter-subjectivity is also at work. Theories decide what observations we look for. The concepts we use to make sense of the world are usually theoretical. And theories are eventually used to verify observations according to our objectives. It is no wonder that, in many areas, there are in fact more wrong facts than wrong theories.

In linguistics, the Sapir-Whorf hypothesis asserts that there is a systematic relationship between the grammatical categories of the language a person speaks and how that person understands the world and behaves in it. The hypothesis argues that the nature of a particular language influences the habitual thought of its speakers, and that different patterns of language yield different patterns of thought.[3] Nevertheless, social scientists, especially political scientists who believe democracy and democratic values are universal truth, see the cultural influence on the choice of specific political systems as "cultural nonsense." They think human nature is everywhere the same, and Western democratic values are equally cherished in the West as in the East. The fundamental basis of this universal idea (or the "non-cultural nonsense") goes largely unchallenged even until today.

According to an NBC news report on Dec. 13, 2005, the U.S. Defense Department had been secretly collecting information about U.S. citizens who opposed the Iraq war and secretly monitoring all meetings for peace and against the war. According to a report by the *New York Times*, in recent years, the FBI has been collecting information on large numbers of non-governmental organizations that participated in anti-war demonstrations in the United States through its monitoring network and other channels. The volume of collected information is stunning. Among it, there are 2,400 pages of information on Greenpeace, an environmental group. On Jan. 9, 2006, a spokeswoman for the U.S. Bureau of Customs and Border Protection announced that, in the anti-terrorism fight, U.S. customs has the right to open and inspect incoming private letters, which again sparked protests. On Jan. 17, 2006, the American Civil Liberties Union and the New York-based Center for Constitutional Rights separately filed suits in U.S. district court for eastern Michigan and a federal court against the U.S. president and heads of security agencies for spying on U.S. citizens.

The *New York Times* reported on March 13, 2005, that the United States is in "a new age of prepackaged TV news." The federal government has aggressively distributed prepackaged news reports to TV stations. At least twenty federal agencies, including the Defense Department and the Census Bureau, have made and distributed hundreds of television news segments in the past four years. The U.S. military pays Iraqi newspapers and journalists for the so-called information operations campaign. The *Los Angeles Times* reported on November 30, 2005, that U.S. military troops have been writing articles burnishing the image of the U.S. mission in Iraq, sending them to a Washington-based firm, which translates them into Arabic and places them in Baghdad newspapers. It said the military also has purchased an Iraqi newspaper and taken control of a radio station "to channel pro-American messages to the Iraqi public."

Other reports said that U.S. army officers created an outfit called the Baghdad Press Club that pays members as much as $200 a month to churn out positive pieces about American military operations. The *Washington Post* in an editorial called these activities against freedom of the press as "planted propaganda." On November 22, 2005, British newspaper the *Daily Mirror*, citing a "top secret" memo on April 16, 2004, from Downing Street, said the U.S. government wished to bomb the headquarters of Arabic TV station Al-Jazeera in Doha, Qatar, during the Iraqi War to block information about the real situation of the war and remove its negative influence on the U.S. side; the revelation resulted in protests by all Al-Jazeera staff members in more than thirty countries and criticism from the International Federation of Journalists.

Offices of the Al-Jazeera network in Baghdad and Kabul have been bombed by the U.S. military, and its journalists had been detained, threatened, abused, and harassed by the U.S. military during the Iraq war. On April 8, 2003, cameraman Jose Couso of the Spanish Telecino television station was shot dead by U.S. soldiers. After Couso's death, the Spanish court issued warrants for the arrest and extradition of three suspected U.S. soldiers. On Aug. 28, 2005, U.S. forces opened fire on a team of Reuters reporters; one Reuters sound man, shot several times in the face and chest, was killed on the spot. Two Iraqi reporters who rushed to the area were also arrested and endured forced exposure to the scorching sun.

According to the Committee to Protect Journalists, the United States is holding four Iraqi journalists in detention centers in Iraq and one journalist of Al-Jazeera at the United States Naval Base at Guantanamo Bay, Cuba. None of the five have been charged with a specific crime. In July 2005, *New York Times* reporter Judith Miller was sentenced to jail for refusing to disclose her source. Covering the aftermath of Hurricane Katrina, a photographer for the *Canadian Toronto Star* daily was hurled to the ground by New Orleans police. The police grabbed his two cameras and removed memory cards. When he asked for his pictures back, the police insulted him and threatened to hit him. A reporter for a local New Orleans newspaper was also attacked while covering a shoot-out between police and local residents. The police detained him and smashed all of his equipment on the ground.

Racial discrimination in America's justice and law enforcement is serious. William J. Bennett, former U.S. Secretary of Education, once said that the only way to lower the crime rate in America was for all African-American women to have abortions. According to the State of Black America 2005 issued by the National Urban League, blacks who are arrested are three times more likely to be imprisoned than whites who are arrested; blacks are sentenced to death four times more often than whites; and a black person's average jail sentence is six months longer than a white's for the same crime.

A December 2005 study by the University of Maryland indicated that blacks who killed a white victim were two to three times more likely to be sentenced to death than those who killed a non-white; but black offenders who killed white victims were nearly 2.5 times more likely to be sentenced to death than white offenders who killed white victims, and 3.5 times more likely to be sentenced to death than black offenders who killed black victims. Although blacks are just 12.2 percent of the American population, 41 percent of American prisoners detained for more than one year are blacks, and 8.4 percent of all black men between the ages of twenty-five and twenty-nine are behind bars.

According to reports issued by the Human Rights Watch and other organizations, following the 9/11 attacks, at least seventy people, all but one Muslim, were held as "material witnesses" under a narrow federal law that permits the arrest and brief detention of "material witnesses." One-third of the seventy confirmed material witnesses were incarcerated for at least two months, some were imprisoned for more than six months, and one actually spent more than a year behind bars. According to a report by the *Washington Observer* weekly in its forty-second issue in 2005, Chinese-American Muslim chaplain James Yee was charged with crimes of espionage and mutiny, which potentially carry the death penalty. Because there was no evidence to support the allegations, the charges were later quietly dropped. The case was quoted by the media as one of the most serious judicial wrongs in American history.

Women in the United States have a higher unemployment rate than men, and lower pay for the same work. A survey by the U.S. Census Bureau said the median earnings of women and men in 2004 were $31,223 and $40,798, respectively. The female-to-male earnings ratio was 77 percent. Yearly earnings of women business owners were only 49 percent of that of their male counterparts. In 2004, the U.S. Equal Employment Opportunity Commission received 24,249 charges of sex-based discrimination, and 4,512 charges of pregnancy-based discrimination.

Poverty rates are highest for families headed by single women. In 2004, 28.4 percent of households headed by single women were in poverty. More and more women and children became homeless. In the city of Pasadena, California, the number of homeless women and children reached 701 in 2005, increasing by 42.7 percent over 2003, and accounting for 57.6 percent of the homeless population of the city. Homeless women and children form largest homeless population, surpassing that of single men for the first time. U.S. women often fall victim to domestic violence. Statistics from the American Institute on Domestic Violence showed that each year in the United States, 5.3 million women are abused, and 1,232 women are killed by their partner.

The FBI reported in October 2005 that during 2004, approximately

94,635 females nationwide were victims of forcible rape, which means that 63.5 out of every 100,000 women suffered forcible rape. Women are sexually harassed while at work. In 2004 the U.S. Equal Employment Opportunity Commission received 13,136 charges of sexual harassment, 84.9 percent of them filed by women.

According to an investigation by the Pentagon released on Dec. 23, 2005, up to 6 percent of the women at the Army, Navy, and Air Force academies said they experienced sexual assault during the 2004–2005 school year, and about half or more said they were sexually harassed. In the Reserve Forces and National Guard units, 60 percent of women and 27 percent of men were sexually assaulted or harassed during their service, and 11 percent of the women were raped.

U.S. prisons saw a surging number of female prisoners who had received bad treatment. A report by the U.S. Bureau of Justice Statistics on April 24, 2005, said by the end of June 30, 2004, the number of female prisoners reached 103,310, an increase of 2.9 percent from the previous year. In 2004, female prisoners in federal and state prisons accounted for 7 percent of the total, up 4 percent from 2003, nearly twice the increase rate of male prisoners. Almost 50 percent of female prisoners said they were sexually assaulted. A total of 8,210 allegations of sexual violence were reported in U.S. correctional facilities during 2004, and correctional authorities substantiated nearly 2,100 incidents of sexual violence, the majority of them female.

These above examples appear in "The Human Rights Record of the United States in 2005"[4] issued by the State Council of China on March 9, 2006, one day after the U.S. Department of State released its 2006 "Country Reports on Human Rights Practices." From 1993 to 2007, China has issued annual reports on American human rights abuses, summarizing information available openly in the American media. It claimed that the U.S. State Department pointed the finger at human rights situations in more than 190 countries and regions, including China, but kept silent on the serious violations of human rights in the United States; and that to help people realize the true features of this self-styled "guardian of human rights," it is necessary to probe into the American human rights abuses related to crime and armed violence, infringements upon human rights by law enforcement agencies, political rights and freedom, economic, social and cultural rights, racial discrimination, rights of women and children, and the U.S. government's violation of human rights in other countries.

The China report on America is definitely much less comprehensive and less detailed than the U.S. report on China, which encompasses denial of the right to change the government; a politically controlled judiciary and a lack of due process; increased restrictions on freedom of speech, publication, assembly, association, travel, religious rights; severe government corruption; trafficking in women and children; societal discrimination against women, minorities, and persons with disabilities; cultural and religious repression of minorities in Tibetan areas and Muslim areas of Xinjiang; forced labor, including prison labor; and use of forced abortions.

Nevertheless, the China report argued that "The U.S. government ought to first clean up its own record of human rights before qualifying itself to comment on human rights situations in other countries, let alone arrogantly telling them what to do . . . No country in the world can claim to have a perfect state of human rights, nor can any country stay outside the course of human rights development. The issue of human rights should become a theme of social development in all countries and of international cooperation, rather than a slogan for exporting ideologies or even a tool of diplomacy to fix others out of one's own political needs . . . an act that fully exposes its hypocrisy and double standard on human rights issues."

At an international conference on "Human Rights in the Pacific Rim: Imagining a New Critical Discourse" on April 4, 2003, Edward Friedman, the Hawkins Chair Professor of Political Science at the University of Wisconsin, Madison, delivered a keynote address titled "Right and Wrong Ways to Question Human Rights Universalism."[5] Friedman's answer is:

What is obvious is that Europeans, Arabs, and Chinese alike, indeed, all of us, are parochial. In love with ourselves, it is not easy to clearly see the other . . . A self-wounding self-love impedes learning when openness to borrowing from the advances of others is the key mechanism of continuing human progress . . . All of us are socialized to uncritical, prejudiced notions about reality, wrongly imagining our unexamined biases as the source of 20/20 vision, as the only true perspective on truth and justice. . . . To truly stand with the forces of democracy and human rights in fact means standing against the cultural prejudice that insists on the uniqueness and centrality of some unique people, the error of treating the "Anglo-Saxon world" as uniquely the home of the liberal . . . to discuss human rights in useful ways, one should have nothing to do with an alleged binary pitting of the good against the bad; individualism against collectivism; Europe against Asia; the Anglo-Saxon West against all the rest. . . . The one universal is parochialism. . . . You all know about American human rights abuses such as police brutality, arbitrary action by the INS to immigrants, or cover-ups of sexual abuse, or institutionalized discrimination in jobs, bank lending, and promotions in America. . . . Even in democracies, because their leaders exercise a monopoly over the forces of legitimate state violence, governments are criminals and hypocrites; they (we?) all act in terms of double standards. The beginning of wisdom in trying to make progress on human rights is . . . not based on a moral self-righteousness declaring that I am good and you are evil. We are all guilty. The way to argue for human rights is with deeds, not words . . . If it does not, all others will see its preachings as empty words—as self-serving politics with no ethical content. This is a problem for the George W. Bush administration and its proclaimed ideals. . . . To behave as the Bush administration does is to lose the argument over human rights. American behavior costs America its credibility on human rights . . . my voice is silenced or cancelled by the deeds of my government. . . . Forgive me. For me to have any credibility in arguing for human rights, I have to first prove my bone fides by my work at home in America for that cause which my President has abominated. Not having done enough of that, I must be silent and admit failure. I cannot tell others how to argue for human rights.

Friedman's point is: "The cultural approach is all politics and prejudice. . . . The way to argue for human rights is with deeds, not words." Words of moral self-righteousness and deeds of unethical self-serving politics create a credibility and qualification problem that makes human rights avoidance easier for China and human rights criticism of China more difficult. While Friedman's honesty and courage are highly commendable, he is unfortunately being candid for a wrong reason. The U.S. government's unqualification doesn't negate an independent intellectual's credibility. You don't need to comment on the American situation every time before you comment on China's situation as long as you are sincere and self-conscious.

Unfortunately, Friedman failed to recognize that parochialism and cultural prejudice include not only the claim of uniqueness of certain values, but also the claim of the universal nature of certain beliefs. The "cultural approach" to democracy may come from a certain type of parochialism and cultural prejudice that promotes uniqueness, yet a different type of parochialism and cultural prejudice that promotes universalism may also be a hidden "cultural approach." When the claim of uniqueness of human rights and democracy is indeed parochial and culturally prejudiced, how can one logically conclude that the claim of the universal nature of human rights and democracy is not parochial and culturally prejudiced? It seems like Edward Friedman was very sensitive in his attempt to avoid "wrongly imagining our unexamined biases . . . as the only true perspective on truth and justice," but he still saw universalism as self-evident and beyond demonstration. He therefore failed to be conscious of the cognitive "mental trap" that leads him only halfway to "parochialism is universal" rather than all the way to "universalism is also parochial." Maybe "human rights universalism" is obvious to Friedman, but "cultural psychology" (as demonstrated at the beginning of this chapter) shows it is in fact "even more obvious that the obvious is not really so obvious."[6]

Due to the exact same cognitive "mental trap," Friedman used selfishness to define individualism and asserted that individualism is as universal as collectivism in China, and that Asian uniqueness cannot be argued on the basis of collectivism. Asian uniqueness is in fact not based on the abstraction of collectivism. Individualism in China does not have a source of legitimate authority like that in the West that can repudiate all forms of social obligation. Individuals can rarely choose to revolt against their families and the web of social ties into which they are born.

The Western abstraction of collectivism can only blind anyone from the cultural richness of personal (not impersonal), relational (interdependent), in group-sensitive (not group-insensitive), and contextual (not object-isolated) social orientation addressed by the Chinese "Cult of Face" and *The Geography of Thought*. It is "relationalism" rather than collectivism that defines the Chinese. Contrary to Friedman's guess, "Politically conscious Chinese actually" do not believe that "The real American purpose is, as the CCP claims, to undermine stability in China so that Chinese society will fracture and suffer chaos such that the Chinese people will be stymied in their rise and in their return to glory and dignity and international stature."[7] But the Chinese actually believe that "moral universalism" implies a self-contradictory conception, and that what Friedman views as America's "good intention" could be a worse kind of disaster.

There is a Chinese story in the Zhou Dynasty about a man selling shields and spears. He first advertised the shields: "My shields are so strong; they cannot be penetrated by any weapon." Then he promoted the spears: "My spears are so sharp; they can pierce any shield." A bystander asked curiously: "If your spear is thrown at your shield, what would happen?" The Chinese word for "contradiction" was derived from this story and literally means "spear and shield."

Two of the basic assumptions of Western liberal democracy are: "One knows what's best for oneself" and "to treat another with respect and equality requires that one refrain from imposing one's views on that person." But deep in their bones, moral universalists actually hold that "they know what's best for others" and "to treat another with respect and equality requires that they not refrain from imposing their views."

Promoting universal human rights is exactly like promoting shields and spears. "If your spear is thrown at your shield, what would happen?" Of course, this is exactly the question they don't want to hear. It would be a big surprise if moral universalists were not at the same time military imperialists when they move into power.

Regrettably, rational self-interested foreign policies and self-proclaimed "guardians of human rights" often result in hypocrisy and double standards. At times when self-interest and self-proclamation are at odds, universal human rights and democratic values are frequently the first to be given up, especially by the U.S. government. No wonder China appears to have a tradition of receiving foreign guests and then utterly ignoring what they say, especially about human rights. Because the Chinese know that, too frequently, Many Western politicians simply use human rights as "a slogan for exporting ideologies or even a tool of diplomacy to fix others out of one's own political needs." In fact, this is why it is hard to blame the third world countries when the hypocritical self-contradiction gives the "nationalism" argument against parochial Western-style human rights and democracy promotion.

One should not stop at uniqueness vs. universalism for human rights and pause at "We are all guilty" for "human wrongs." In the light of "the way to argue for human rights is with deeds, not words," the specific "democratic values" as well as the actual democratic practices need to be carefully examined so as not to fall into extreme relativism. The purpose of this examination is twofold: to reveal the moral nature of the "democratic values" that are in the middle of the cultural-ideological clash between China and America; and, more importantly, to find out how American democracy has been institutionalized to encourage or hold back individual productive, distributional, and destructive efforts, which in turn will eventually determine the strength of American capitalism at the time of China's rise.

Moral Choice or Public Choice?

On May 25, 1787, fifty-five men gathered at Philadelphia to revise The Articles of Confederation and Perpetual Union that were adopted by the

Second Continental Congress in 1777. Although American independence was gained on the premise of "All men are created equal" in 1776, the new nation was in the middle of a crisis due to the rapid growth of anarchy in the Federal System: failure to deal with foreign and interstate commerce, no power to tax, noncompliance of each state for funding contributions, unpaid foreign debts to France and the Netherlands, mounting cost for fighting Indians in western lands, unmet promises of bounties and land grants for wartime service, animosity kindled among the states by their conflicting regulations, riots by unpaid Pennsylvania veterans, and Shays' Rebellion caused by the elite's political monopoly in Massachusetts.

The summer of 1787 was torrid in Philadelphia. In the Pennsylvania State House (Independence Hall), doors and windows had to be closed when delegates discussed and debated. James Madison, known as the "Father of the Constitution" for his role in creating the Virginia Plan, "chose a seat in front of the presiding member" during the Convention, which resulted in the most valuable "Notes of Debates in the Federal Convention of 1787." Also from Virginia, George Washington saw Shays' Rebellion motivate him from retirement to work for a stronger central government. Thomas Jefferson and John Adams were on diplomatic missions in Europe. Patrick Henry didn't attend because he "smelt a rat in Philadelphia, tending toward the monarchy." Rhode Island delegates also refused to attend.

The delegates came from a variety of social backgrounds. Most were Protestants. All took part in the War of Independence and were distinguished figures in their states and in national affairs. Forty-one were or had been members of the Continental Congress. Many had more than one career at the same time. Thirty-five were lawyers or had legal experience. Thirteen were businessmen and merchants. Six were land speculators. Eleven traded securities. Fourteen owned slave-operated plantations or small farms. Nine held public office positions. Three were physicians and three others had retired. Two were scientists and one was a university president. A few were very wealthy. Most varied from good to excellent. Most were natives of the thirteen colonies. Only eight were born elsewhere. After the Constitution was drafted, sixteen of the fifty-five delegates refused to sign. Two of the thirty-nine who did sign, Jonathan Dayton and William Blount, were charged with treason later. Richard Dobbs Spaight was killed in a duel in 1802, as was Alexander Hamilton in a duel in 1804 with Aaron Burr, who was later charged with treason (with Dayton).

The constitution that resulted from the convention was characterized by a radical break from traditional Western monarchism with three legendary compromises: the Connecticut Compromise (the Great Compromise), the Three-Fifths Compromise, and the Massachusetts Compromise.

The Connecticut Compromise involved the creation of legislative bodies in the new federal government. At the time of the convention, there was a consensus for a bicameral system since all thirteen states except Pennsylvania had that system. In a five-hour marathon speech, Alexander Hamilton detailed a plan largely based on the British form of government, with an elected president and senate serving for life, and a house of representatives elected for three year terms. Due to the shadow of monarchy, his plan was never seriously discussed during the convention. As a response to the Virginia Plan, which favored representation based on population, the New Jersey Plan voiced concern for the under-influence of the smaller states. Delegates from small states argued that three largest states could out-vote the rest of the country. James Madison contended that the fear was not supported by staple productions of those big states, and that large states did not necessarily share common interests.

Delaware delegate Gunning Bedford, Jr., however, warned forcefully that small states might have to find some foreign ally if equality and justice were not served. On the concluding vote, states that favored equal apportionment in the senate represented only one third of the nation's population. But the final compromise was a plan by Connecticut delegate Roger Sherman in which the House of Representatives was based on state population and the Senate was based on equal votes from each state. Until the 1850s, equal representation in the Senate gave the South a veto over any policy affecting slavery. Between 1800 and 1860, eight anti-slavery measures passed the House, and all were killed in the Senate. After the Civil War, non-Southern senators were compelled to accommodate the Southern veto to secure the adoption of their own policies. For another century it prevented the country from enacting federal laws to protect the most basic of human rights.[8]

Earlier in the Declaration of Independence, the language of condemning the British crown for sponsoring the import of slaves was compromised at the request of delegates from South Carolina and Georgia. As the author of the Declaration, Thomas Jefferson himself, one of the largest slave-owners in Virginia, inherited and purchased many slaves, at a point owning several hundred. He was also one of the twelve presidents who owned slaves and one of eight who owned slaves while serving as president.[9] Jefferson freed only eight slaves during his lifetime and in his will. All others were sold after his death as he was too far in debt to free all of them.[10] George Washington, the richest man in America at the time, owned 216 slaves, none of whom were emancipated until after he and his wife died.

During the Constitutional Convention, the slavery issue came up again for a more practical reason: how to count slaves for taxation and for determining representation in the House of Representatives. Northern delegates suggested that only free persons should be counted because they saw that Southern states would end up with too many representatives. Even though more tax would have to be paid, Southern delegates wanted slaves to be counted in full. Regarded as the most brilliant legal theoretician among the delegates at the time, James Wilson suggested that each slave be counted as three-fifths of a free person. In the final compromise, slaves were counted as three-fifths of their actual population.

In the Constitution, however, slaves were mentioned as "all other Persons" along with "free Persons" and the excluded "Indians." The "Founding Fathers" clearly knew the moral dilemma here, but how could they do anything beyond their specific historical context? Additionally, there was a provision for the fugitive slave clause (fugitive slaves were to be returned); and Congress couldn't prohibit slave trade for twenty years. In the following decades, before the American Civil War, Southern states dominated all three branches of the federal government with their lopsided representation. The abolition of slavery was ratified by the Thirteenth Amendment to the Constitution in 1865, nearly three years after Abraham Lincoln's presidential order of the Emancipation Proclamation. But the three-fifths clause was not superseded until the Fourteenth Amendment in 1868.

The Massachusetts compromise concerned the Bill of Rights. As active advocates of the Constitution, Federalists (including Alexander Hamilton, James Madison, and John Jay) won approval from George Washington and gained much support nationwide. Anti-Federalists like Patrick Henry and George Mason (author of the 1776 Virginia Declaration of Rights) were gravely concerned with the absence of a Bill of Rights in the Constitution. After the first five states ratified the Constitution (nine states required), anti-federalists John Adams and John Hancock negotiated a compromise that demanded amendments as a way to avoid total rejection by opponents of the Constitution in Massachusetts. Four other states followed Massachusetts's amendments request in their ratification. Though opposing the idea initially, James Madison wanted to avoid a political deadlock or even a total reconsideration of the Constitution, and pledged a Bill of Rights amendment in the first Congress. The Constitution finally went into effect in 1789.

The Constitution of the United States, created in the form of a republic, was the first liberal democracy in the world, and is the oldest federal constitution currently in use. Four crucial factors contributed to the establishment of American democracy. First is the geographical cut-off from European monarchs, which gave rise to the spirit of self-sufficiency and independence. Second is the influence of Enlightenment ideas that cherished individual liberty and advocated Reason as the source of authority and the way to obtain objective truth. Third is the relative balance of power among the thirteen colonies/states that prevented any political monopoly. Last but not least, unlike the Chinese autocracy, English monarchism carried a Roman Law notion that the will of the king could be bound by law, which paid respect to the church and "natural rights" and was clearly reflected in the Charter of Liberties (1100), the Magna Carta (the 1215 "Great Charter of Freedoms"), and the English Bill of Rights (1689).

As we have seen, however, American democracy as well as American independence was by no means a pure moral choice from democratic principles that are taken for granted today. When John Hancock organized a boycott of tea from China sold by the British East India Company, the resentment was toward King George III, who ended the "Salutary Neglect" policy to impose taxes on the thirteen colonies. When Thomas Jefferson declared "All men are created equal," he was delivering the message to the King, not to the slaves, the Indians, or the poor. Neither did Jefferson say "All rich white men are created equal," nor did the "Founding Fathers" use the word "slaves" for the three-fifths clause in the Constitution.

Democratic principles are arguably used throughout American history to advance democratic progress forward from its imperfect state. The Fifteenth Amendment in 1870 gave black males the right to vote—largely a right on paper. Discriminatory practices, poll taxes, and literacy and property requirements not only kept African-Americans disenfranchised, they also kept poor whites out of the loop. New Jersey, the only state that gave voting rights to women, had a property requirement before the Nineteenth Amendment in 1920 afforded women voting rights in all states. The right of Native Americans to vote were not gained until the Indian Citizenship Act of 1924.

The suffrage movement transformed into the civil rights movement, which worked to secure enforcement of everyone's voting rights. In addition to the strength of the civil rights movement, two undercurrents flowed side by side during the 1950s and 1960s: one, condemnation of the hypocrisy involved when the U.S. claimed to defend freedom against Soviet communism abroad while oppressing African-Americans at home; and two, attention focused by party politics on the demographic change that involved the migration of millions of black Southerners to the North. The final result was the Voting Rights Act of 1965 and the spreading of the fair and equal practice of voting rights—almost 100 years after black males got the right to vote on paper. In 1971, the Twenty-sixth Amendment lowered the voting age from twenty-one to eighteen, so that the young men who fought the Vietnam War could speak their minds via the ballot.

History shows that the "equal rights" democratic ideal works only within a particular political context. Once established, government becomes a political machine often manipulated by political elites no matter how democratic the government claims itself to be. Democratic values are a useful weapon for the disadvantaged who believe in them. But they are not universal; the disadvantaged only fight for democratic values when the time comes, and the political elites either don't really believe in these values or simply don't see them as important. Put more specifically, democratic values are not universal because they are "spiritual interests" that need to be weighed against "material interests" by both the disadvantaged and the political elites.

When the U.S. government chooses national interests over democratic values in its double-standard foreign policies, it applies exactly the same logic to its domestic politics. Furthermore, democratic values are only one type of value in people's "spiritual interests." Not everyone in every culture holds these same values. And even if they believe in them, they only see them as part of their welfare functions that need to be balanced with other interests. Those who see democratic values as universal are simply those who happen to put these "spiritual interests" as the most important values in their value calculations or welfare functions, and they want to persuade or even force other people to recreate their value systems or reorder their value priority the way do theirs, and without considering the cultural-historical context. This is the very nature of democratic Universalism.

"Normative theories" deal with "what should be" or the morality of both political institutions and individual behavior. The mainstay of these theories in the West comes from the traditional contractarians represented by Thomas Hobbes, John Locke, Immanuel Kant, and Jean-Jacques Rousseau, and from the "new contractarians"[11] represented by John Rawls (a Kantian) and Robert Nozick (a Lockean), and James Buchanan (a Hobbesian in positive theory and a Kantian in normative theory).

Contractarians, old or new, usually start from an unfalsifiable "let's imagine" or "just-so" story for the emergence of the social contract from a standpoint of pure logic, or "let reason give the world order." In *A Theory of Justice* (1971), John Rawls imagines a "realistic utopia" where rational people start from an "original position" under a reasonably fair "veil of ignorance" without knowledge of social status and individual capacities (preference or ability), and by a risk-minimizing strategy they reach the agreement of an equal claim to basic rights (liberty principle) and an egalitarian claim to limit liberty only to benefit the least-advantaged (difference principle).

Rawls's "Justice as Fairness" or "Distributive Justice" draws sharp criticism from *Anarchy, State, and Utopia* (1974) by Robert Nozick. Nozick contends that wealth is not something coming from the sky, and sources of income not only come from inheritance and endowment, but also come from individual efforts and choices. Forced redistribution of income would treat people as means rather than ends, and violates the principles of entitlement and free exchange. However, Nozick's "minimal State" is derived from a free-market anarchy that is by itself also out of imagination. While Rawls's egalitarian position and Nozick's individualistic position on "substantive justice" may provide two different viewpoints for normative criteria, they nevertheless suggest that there is simply no theoretical certainty for "justice" (the Kantian "Categorical Imperative") that is supposed to take priority over "good."

James Buchanan avoids the pure reasoning for "substantive justice" and takes an institutional approach to focus on "formal justice" or the procedures for justice. In *The Calculus of Consent* (1962, with Gordon Tullock), he sees unanimity as the ultimate criteria for justice for both pre- and postconstitutional stages. But there is a trade-off between unanimity voting and majority voting because unanimity voting has little external costs and large decision-making costs, while majority voting has various external costs and decision-making costs. This suggests that political decisions with high external costs should be made in unanimity or quasi-unanimity. From this normative standpoint, he turns to a positive theory of "public choice" for the political process, where public interests are not seen from a dichotomy of "public vs. private," but are seen as an aggregation of private actors in the government. Public choice thus pushes insights on politics to the deepest level that is humanly possible.

Politics, like the market, is not a mechanism for finding scientific truth or moral justice, but a mechanism for rendering benefits to specific interest groups and imposing various external costs to different groups of people in the society. There is simply no neutral decision-making even when the public goods from the decision are beneficial to the majority in the society. The true nature of politics is an interest-seeking process involving politicians, voters, and bureaucrats, in which, like market transactions, votes can be traded between voters and interest groups and between politicians (log-rolling). When politicians act in the interests of the public, it is simply because they need to win the votes of their constituents, or the public interests at issue happen to accord with their private material or spiritual interests. There is no competition in democracy like in the market that can prevent "government failure" from happening.

The requirement of non-coercion, however, still has strong normative implications. This is why Douglass North's "violence potential" theory of the state,[12] or the "Transaction Cost Theory of Political Entrepreneurship" is a more realistic theory in a positive sense. A state is simply an organization with a comparative advantage in violence, and with the potential use of violence to control resources by the principals with unequal distribution of violence potential. The gains of initial contracting for the state are balanced by the subsequent maximizing behavior of constituents with diverse interest. Constitutional reforms, as suggested by Buchanan, are difficult if not impossible to to achieve for fixing problems in democracy—budget deficit, for example—because the logic of public choice will also apply to constitutional reform. Like the "substantive justice" approach by Rawls and Nozick, the "formal justice" approach by Buchanan proves again the theoretical uncertainty for justice in general and for democratic values in particular. Democracy is an outcome of public choice rather than moral choice.

Further consideration reveals that the difficulty or the unavailability of a theoretical balance point comes from the following empirical or historical fact in various cultures: there are frequently enormous gaps between the normative principles of equal rights and the unequal enforcement of equal rights; between the normative principles of equal rights and the unequal values of equal rights; and between the equal enforcement of equal rights and the unequal values of equal rights. *This is why no democracy in the world can have a clean human rights record.*

Universalists often contend that basic freedoms in democracy imply the right to act freely. This is certainly one step ahead of the idea of seeing freedoms as being free. But it remains shallow because the decision to act one way or another entails different costs, and the exercising of each equal right denotes different relative values to an individual at different times. There is simply no abstract "intrinsic value" (value "for its own sake" or "in its own right") for each of the "equal rights," even though the abstraction of "intrinsic value" may have aesthetic value in theory. You don't need to interview a homeless person on LA's skid row or along the Chicago River to get the point.

Democracy is often seen as a plutocracy (government by the wealthy) rather than a Robert Dahl polyarchy[13] because the value of basic rights weighs much more in the hands of the wealthy few who have the power to impact policy formation. According to Dahl, the fundamental democratic principle is that, when it comes to binding collective decisions, each person in a political community is entitled to have his interests be given equal consideration. A polyarchy is a nation-state that has certain procedures that are necessary conditions for following the democratic principle. When money is not only helpful, but necessary, plutocracy takes over polyarchy.

Universalists also contend that basic freedoms in democracy imply "negative rights" (rights to freedom from interference, such as the right to property or freedom from violence), which are genuine rights, whereas "positive rights" (rights to impose obligation on others, such as "right to subsistence") have no clear duty-holders to back them up without a contract relationship. Yet different cultures may have totally different views on how the state and the society should act (or redistribute) to provide "positive rights."[14] In America, the independent-individualistic culture makes "positive rights" less popular, while in China, the interdependent-relational culture makes "positive rights" more acceptable.

There is, however, one more twist to the dichotomy of negative-positive rights. It all depends on who is the actor and how the actor defines good or bad. When one thinks something is good, he wants obligations from others; when one thinks something is bad, he wants freedom from interference. Human nature is as simple as that. The "Golden Rule" in Western consciousness is: "Do unto others as you would have them do unto you." Confucius says, "*Don't* do to others as you would *not* have them do to you." Confucius is more conscientious. "Do unto others" is fine when people's preferences are the same. Yet Confucius sees this as a risky assumption, and that's why his seemingly passive inaction implies more respect to another person's preferences. What's more hidden is: when people's preferences are known as the same, "*Don't* do to others" carries a positive notion to avoid inaction. For example, when someone is drowning, you hurry to the rescue because "you don't want to see others not offering help" when you are in that situation.

The problem of universalists is that they always assume identical preferences. George Bernard Shaw once observed, "Do not do unto others as you would have them do unto you; they may have different tastes." When one is the action initiator, he can always choose to hold the Golden Rule when he demands involvement in other people's lives, and he can always choose to hold Confucius's "negative" Golden Rule when he wants to retreat to his own private space and leave other folks alone. On the other hand, when he is the action receiver, he can always choose to insist on "negative rights" so as to avoid interference, and he can always choose to insist on "positive rights" so as to oblige others to help. Again, high-minded moral words are not important, only deeds matter; "book culture" doesn't matter as much as "reality culture." Universalists may believe in negative rights, yet that doesn't stop them from behaving according to the positive Golden Rule to step on others' toes. The Chinese may seem prudent to hold Confucius's negative Golden Rule, yet that doesn't prevent them from behaving by positive rights to assume more social obligation.

The unequal values of abstract equal rights are not even a simple result of some "cost and benefit calculation" because the exercising of each right also reflects one's wealth level, one's stake in the choice, one's perception of outcome and the probability of impact, and one's psychological condition *vis-a-vis* one's social status, which logically leads to the distribution issue. That is why the pragmatic Chinese, either in China or in Singapore, see economic liberty of paramount importance. As the American Civil Rights movement and the evidence from cultural psychology show, the enforcement and value of basic rights is not only historical, it's also cultural—hence not universal, and the abstraction of universalism is simply not supported by the theoretical uncertainty of the normative theories from within the same mental model.

By assuming full rationality and perfect reason, universalism fails to realize that the very nature of the scarcity of human rationality and reason is within the constraint of culture and history, and of course the universalist fails to realize that universalism itself is also a product of this limitation. Universalists may still believe in some "super pill" that can cure all physical pains and all moral agonies in the world. This is fantasy. In any case, it is a "rational bias" or "rational irrationality." People choose to be irrational because the private costs of the belief are less than the private benefits. Even when an individual selects a degree of irrationality with high private costs, it only shows that the utility of holding the belief makes it a good bargain. Yet when the costs of irrationality spill over onto other people, serious conflicts and efficiency problems arise.[15]

Using a universalist's view on human rights as an example, the universalist belief to him provides more private benefit (either material or spiritual) than private cost because he feels more natural and logical. Yet when his universalist belief is proved neither natural nor logical, there will be a potential high private cost because he will appear irrational from a different perspective. At this point, he can choose to remain irrational—or change his idea. When he thinks holding the universalist belief makes it a good bargain, he will stand firm. But the costs of his irrationality will spill over onto other people who see human constraints inevitable on rationality, historical context, and cultural cognition, thus creating ideological conflicts and leading to perilous ideological promotion. "Rational bias" persists because a paradigm shift is a social and psychological process in which unlearning may incur much more cost than learning.

Valuing universalism or absolutism, as discussed in last section, can lead to international dictatorship by its own logic. It is by nature ethnocentrism. Interestingly, in *The Law of Peoples* (1999), John Rawls extends his liberal ideas on justice from domestic to international politics, where usually realism rather than liberalism takes hold. This extension allows democracies to tolerate "decent hierarchies." But when they violate human rights, they should be treated as those in the category of "outlaw states," "societies burdened by unfavorable conditions," and "benevolent absolutisms." Although Rawls claims this is by no means ethnocentric, his domestic liberalism is readily turning into an international realism in that international distribution will not consider that endowments of natural resources and foreign aid should have a cutoff point to avoid "moral hazard." While liberals feel it hard to accept his "decent hierarchies," non-liberals find it ridiculous to have the world organized in the Western liberal way by a happy chance out of his imaginary "original position." All dilemmas of universalism in its domestic and non-domestic applications, nevertheless, support the "subjective morality" argument against democracy in China.

An electoral democracy can be defined as "periodic popular elections for key government offices with multi-party rotating contests and equal voting rights." The degree of electoral democracy depends on the specifics of each element in this definition, which is largely determined by political culture and historical context. A liberal democracy is often known as a political system defined by means rather than ends, and defined by accountability with separation of government powers and checks and balances. It combines the procedural element of elections with the republican elements of protection of individual and minority rights to act freely and limit state power. The democratic nature of a decision, however, is decided by rules and processes rather than by the outcome of rules (minority rights hence might not be truly protected). Universalism sees that liberal democracy ("real democracy") encompasses everything from electoral democracy (non-paternalistic proceduralism), human rights (equal liberty), and rule of law, to market capitalism (economic liberty). Yet if universalism is not really self-evident, can its procedures prove to be universally applicable from the American practice?

Electoral Legitimacy and Electoral Corruption

Let me now take a more comprehensive view, and warn you in the most solemn manner against the baneful effects of the spirit of party generally. . . . The alternate domination of one faction over another, sharpened by the spirit of revenge, natural to party dissension, which in different ages and countries has perpetrated the most horrid enormities, is itself a frightful despotism. But this leads at length to a more formal and permanent despotism. The disorders and miseries, which result, gradually incline the minds of men to seek security and repose in the absolute power of an individual; and sooner or later the chief of some prevailing faction, more able or more fortunate than his competitors, turns this disposition to the purposes of his own elevation, on the ruins of Public Liberty. . . . It serves always to distract the Public Councils, and enfeeble the Public Administration. It agitates the Community with ill-founded jealousies and false alarms; kindles the animosity of one part against another, foments occasionally riot and insurrection. It opens the door to foreign influence and corruption, which find a facilitated access to the government itself through the channels of party passions. Thus the policy and the will of one country are subjected to the policy and will of another.[15]

This statement is not from Deng Xiaoping, but from George Washington's Farewell Address of 1796. Washington was not the only one who took an anti-partisan view at that time. In fact, there was a general consensus to avoid political factions in those early years. The Constitution didn't even mention political parties, and Washington himself and the First Congress were not elected on a partisan basis. As mentioned earlier, however, the poor, the women, the slaves, and the Indians were excluded from elections. White male property owners amounted to about 20 percent of the population. The president was elected by the Electoral College or the Presidential Electors instead of directly by popular votes in each state—a design by the framers to have the president be insulated from both popular majorities and congressional control. The Federalist Party created by Alexander Hamilton and the Democratic-Republican Party created by Thomas Jefferson and James Madison in 1792 were more or less along the line of pro- or anti-federalism at first, and pro-France or pro-England in foreign policies later on. Party politics was first put into work in the congressional elections of 1792 and the presidential election of 1796. With the fading of the federalist passion, the defeat of Napoleon in France, and the compromise settlement of the War of 1812 with Britain, the Federalist Party and the first party system gradually disappeared.

The 1824 presidential election was a turning point at a time when voters' property requirement was eliminated in most states. All four presidential candidates were from the Democratic-Republican Party and had a regional base of support. Andrew Jackson's faction later became the Democratic Party, and the factions led by John Quincy Adams and Henry Clay evolved from the National Republican Party to the Whig Party. Policy issues started to separate party lines with the Democratic Party focusing on farming and new frontier expansion, and the Whig Party stressing modernization efforts. The slavery issue gradually came to the front, and the new Republican Party was created in 1854 to oppose the expansion of slavery into Kansas. Abraham Lincoln dropped out of the declining Whig Party and became the first president of the Republican Party in 1861. The two-party system started to take shape on the basis of policy issues, religion, and regional support. While numerous small third parties came and went, the two major parties dominated in federal, state, and even local governments. Elections became so widespread that many states revised their constitutions so that judges were elected to fixed terms. Election campaigns provided rich soil for all kinds of new techniques and for passionate party workers and volunteers who sought patronage for well-paid government jobs. Election campaigns evolved over time into a multi-billion dollar industry today.

The 1896 presidential election was a landmark for the use of new election campaign techniques. William J. Bryan, known for his anti-evolution stance in the 1925 "Scopes Monkey Trial," went so far as to employ the "multiple appeals" technique to run simultaneously as a Democrat, a Silver Republican, and a Populist. Though this technique was later banned by most states, his "national stumping tour" technique is still widely used. Over the years, money, organization, and public image become the "big three" for election campaigns. The modern commercial advertising campaign finds its origin in the same campaign by William McKinley, who became the twenty-fifth president. Candidates seek funding, set up volunteer organizations with a chain-of-command, and use partisan newspapers, speeches, rallies, parades, banners, badges, buttons, insignias, billboards, posters, lawn signs, bumper stickers, personal contacts, private speeches, telephones, televisions, radio, direct mail, and now the internet. In China, the most sagacious course is to follow the power when you want to understand politics. In America, however, it is vital to follow the money.

Vote buying and voter coercion were common in the nineteenth century. Before 1913, Senators were elected by state legislatures whose votes could sometimes be bought. In 1823, the price of a vote in New York City was $5, and $30 for repeat voters. Some elections even used carbon paper under ballots for proof of payment. The Jacksonian era saw the spread of political patronage. As a result, a practice of political assessment required officeholders to contribute an assessed portion of their pay, which provoked passage of the Pendleton Act of 1873 prohibiting political contributions by all civil service workers. Big corporations became a new source of funding, exemplified by William McKinley's campaign. Progressive activists in the early twentieth century came forward to advocate regulating antitrust laws, restricting corporate lobbying and campaign contributions, as well as standardized secret ballots, strict voter registration, and women's suffrage. More comprehensive reforms, however, began in the 1970s and continued on to the Bipartisan Campaign Reform Act in 2002. By this time, the playing field was littered with issues of soft money donations, a limit on hard money, "issue ads," PACs, 527 groups, 501(c) advocacy entities, and reform of public financing.

The most standard method of collecting campaign checks is the pay-to-play fund-raising dinner, invented by Democratic fund-raiser Matthew McClockey to support FDR. Today's seat at a fund-raising dinner with a federal candidate routinely costs the $2,000 legal limit. Richard Nixon's presidential campaign in 1968 took the innovation one step further by linking twenty-two dinners together by closed-circuit television: the campaign was able to raise $4.6 million with one speech and a few thousand plates of stuffed chicken breast.[17] Strategists from both parties estimate the White House race in 2008 could cost each nominee $500 million, far more than the Presidential Election Campaign Fund can afford.[18] It now takes over $1 billion and more than two years to run for the four-year-term U.S. president. Roughly, running for the Senate costs ten times as much as running for the House, and running for president costs seventy times as much as running for the Senate.

Elections have gotten so expensive that it takes a lot of money even to lose. One senator and one mayor each spend more getting elected in the U.S. than all the legislative candidates in Great Britain combined. Political campaigns now function as collection agencies for the media. Political insiders and donors often judge candidates based on their ability to raise money. Not raising enough money early on can lead to problems later as donors are not willing to give funds to candidates they perceive to be losing, a perception based on their poor fundraising performance. Running for office becomes fund-raising for office, and politics and fund-raising are now the yin and the yang of the game. The money chase discourages competitive elections, creates "part-time legislators, full-time fund-raisers," deters talent from seeking office, favors multimillionaires, corrupts legislation, and discourages voting and civic participation.[19]

Most other democracies get more than a 70 percent turnout of eligible voters. In the U.S., it's 50 percent in presidential elections, 33 percent in congressional elections, and often only 20 percent in primaries. The turnout of eligible voters in presidential elections has been around 60 percent since the 1950s. It dipped under 50 percent in 1996. Due to the war in Iraq, voter turnout went back to the 60 percent level, similar to what happened in1968 during the Vietnam War.

Studies show that low turnout may be due to disenchantment, indifference, or contentment. But voting is also a collective action subject to the "free-riding problem." An individual voter can rely on other voters or political commentators to make a choice without making an effort to become informed and to vote. Several factors determine when someone will make the effort to vote: the probability of a single vote's effect on the outcome of an election, the potential benefit from one's favored political party or candidate being elected, the complexity of making the decision, the effort and cost involved, and personal gratification from voting (social obligation, political allegiance, partisan preference or expressive voting, self-perceived political importance, personal enjoyment, going with the flow, and regret avoidance).[20]

As American political history shows, party politics didn't come with democracy when the Constitution was put into work. Rather, party politics started from power struggles by politicians who had different ideologies and policy orientations (federalism, anti-federalism, regional factions, and anti-slavery). The development of political parties and party loyalties turned the electoral college into a way of counting votes—not the framers' initial design. Political parties may not really represent popular interest. Multi-party elections are the result of a power fight, not, as always suggested, a mechanism to put the government in check. The checks and balances system was in fact better provided by the separation of power into three government branches. The power struggle would be in a form of multi-party or one dominant party (the Democratic-Republican Party in the early nineteenth century), how the party system evolves, and if officials are elected or selected (federal judges) are all a result of specific cultural-historical context.

American democracy was based on the Republican idea. What the founding fathers wanted was to check direct democracy rather than to promote it. That's why the framers leaned more toward aristocracy, limited suffrage, the rights of each state, concern for property rights (including slaves as property), and fear of the populace, than toward a popularly based government dependent on the will of the people.

Over the last 220 years, America became more and more democratic by the criteria of equal liberty, yet its basic structure remains unique among all liberal democracies in the world. For example, the president is still elected through the electoral college in each state rather than through direct votes by the people. The number of electors in each state is the sum of its representatives and its senators. When the 1989 proposal for direct election gained 83 percent approval in the House, the Senate failed to pass it from the debate stage to the voting stage because it requires sixty votes. Even were it to move on to the voting stage, it seems unlikely to get passed because an amendment requires two-thirds of the votes in the Senate. Hundreds of similar proposals have died in the Senate. When half of America's people elect eighteen Senators, the other half elect eighty-two. Senators from the small states have every reason to veto any change that will reduce their influence in electing the president and all other issues.

The point here is: just like electoral legitimacy and meritocratic legitimacy are unique to every culture, the specific way of electoral legitimacy is also unique to every culture. A proportional election system is used in countries like Denmark, Finland, Norway, Sweden, Germany, Austria, Belgium, the Netherlands, Switzerland, and New Zealand. A majoritarian election system is popular in Britain, Australia, Canada, France, and Greece. The U.S., Japan, Spain, and Ireland belong to a mixed election system.[21] In fact, the U.S. government not only adopts a mixed election system, but also has a mix of electoral legitimacy (the president and the Congress) and selectoral legitimacy (the Supreme Court). Federal judges are not elected; they are appointed with life tenure and strong partisan bias. They have veto power from the judicial review of acts of the federal legislature, and they have policy-making power from judicial legislation under cover of enforcement of the Constitution. Electoral legitimacy and selectoral legitimacy have different pros and cons. There is simply no moral supremacy from one over the other. Their applications and appropriateness depend on specific public choice and cultural historical context.

But the problems of American style electoral legitimacy are not limited to campaign financing, patronage, protection of the privileged minority, election costs, and voter non-participation (also note that millions of American permanent residents lack the franchise and millions of Americans in the unincorporated territories of the United States—i.e., American Samoa, Guam, the Northern Mariana Islands, Puerto Rico, and the United

States Virgin Islands—also don't have the right to vote for president). Two other serious problems of electoral legitimacy are "partial legitimacy" and "abuse of legitimacy." Like other democracies, electoral legitimacy in the U.S. is derived from fair and open popular elections. For an election to be fair and open, it needs to prevent explicit or hidden structural bias toward any candidate, and voters need to be equally well informed about each candidate. For an election to be popular, the voting method has to be simple, easy, and convenient. For these purposes, the single-winner plurality voting system (also known as "first-past-the-post," "simple/relative majority," or "winner-take-all") is used in the U.S., as in at least forty-two other countries. The fairness requirement and the use of this foolproof voting system are exactly where the "partial legitimacy" problem kicks in.

Even in the U.S., where elections are generally considered relatively fair and open, "equally well informed" remains unrealistic. It neither guarantees the resources needed ("positive rights"), nor specifies the individual's choice to be informed. As was noted by Mancur Olson, public policies as well as knowledge of public policies are both "public goods" subject to the "free-riding problem." The cost spent on this "public good" for any regular voter is likely to be much higher than the potential benefit. Reasonably, voters will simply choose to not be "well informed" unless something big is at stake or some personal preference takes over. Even when a voter chooses to not be "rationally ignorant," he might still choose to be "rational biased"[22] and go with the party line when election issues are too complex.

The beauty of plurality voting is its simplicity; it is easy to administer and less expensive to run. However, under this system, voters are often forced to vote for one of the two candidates favored to win when their preferred candidate is neither. Voters using this kind of tactical voting essentially give in to media influence. The reality is that even when you don't believe in the media, you know pretty well that most people do. Whoever gets the most media attention will end up in the top two—making election campaigns and campaign financing very important. Of course, voters can choose to not vote or still vote for their favorite candidate and accept the fact that their votes might be wasted. Ironically, the logic of plurality voting dictates that any votes for anyone other than the second place are votes for the winner ("spoiler effect"). So one may still help the winner by not voting at all. It is believed that Al Gore lost the 2000 Presidential Election to George W. Bush because some voters who preferred Gore to Bush ended up voting for Ralph Nader. And many of Gore's supporters got discouraged by bad poll conditions and didn't vote or their votes didn't get counted. Clearly, the logic of not requiring a second-round runoff (it's required in France) may well turn the plurality voting system into a game of promoting "voting against someone" rather than "voting for someone." Even more interestingly, Gore gained the majority of the popular votes and still lost the game due to fewer electoral votes (as in the elections of 1824, 1876, and 1888)—the result of the electoral college system that the Senate refuses to change.

The "structural bias" of the electoral college is not only bad for a popular candidate, it is also unfavorable for a third-party candidate. Since electoral votes are also "winner-take-all" rather than proportional, any third-party candidate who can't get the majority of votes in any state will end up getting no electoral vote at all. Of course, one can argue that the electoral college system was not meant for popular democracy in the first place; it was for Federalism or Republicanism. But you can't have arguments both ways. Since the framers intended the electoral college as a device against popular democracy, you won't be able to color it with full "electoral legitimacy." And you can't further neglect the embedded defects in the mix of partial "electoral legitimacy" and "selectoral legitimacy" (federal judges) and pose it as a universal ideal regardless of historical context. The "structural bias" of the electoral college doesn't end here. The "winner-take-all" mechanism further persuades against voting in non-battleground states, since votes in these states will carry much less weight, especially for voters who realize that a single vote carries no weight.

Plurality voting in general has an effect predicted by "Duverger's Law": it is likely to produce a two-party system, while proportional voting favors the emergence of a multi-party system. Historical evidence shows that plurality voting acts to delay the emergence of a new political party, and accelerate the elimination of a weakening party. This happened when the Republican Party emerged only at the expense of the Whig Party in the 1840s. What may also happen is that one of the two parties can dominate for a considerable period of time, or that the two major parties in fact agree on many important issues over time. This can limit the range of the government's perspectives and concerns on one hand, and prevent voters from making a decision based on more choices on the other. Eventually, voters may be compelled to pick a candidate who seems less "evil" and simply fall into political inaction. Voters' indifference in participation is in fact strengthened by something called "safe seats" in some congressional districts dominated by either the Democrats or the Republicans. This also happens in the presidential election. Illinois, for example, is traditionally a state whose majority votes for Democratic candidates. A Republican voter who believes his vote will be wasted will rationally choose to not vote.

Democratic voters, on the other hand, may also choose to not vote because democratic candidates will win anyway.

The problems of plurality voting have deeper institutional roots. According to James Buchanan, "There are also obvious and important differences between market and political competition. Market competition is continuous; at each instance of purchase, a buyer is able to select among alternative, competing sellers. Political competition is intermittent; a decision is binding for a fixed period, usually two, four, or six years. Market competition allows several competitors to survive simultaneously; the capture by one seller of a majority of the market does not deny the ability of the minority to choose its preferred supplier. By contrast, political competition has an all-or-none feature; the capture of a majority of the market gives the entire market to a single supplier. In market competition, the buyer can be reasonably certain as to just what it is he will receive from his act of purchase. This is not true with political competition, for there the buyer is, in a sense, purchasing the services of an agent, but it is an agent whom he cannot bind in matters of specific compliance, and to whom he is forced to grant wide latitude in the use of discretionary judgment. Politicians are simply not held liable for their promises and pledges in the same manner that private sellers are."[23]

The discussion of partial electoral legitimacy here is not intended to embrace or even promote cynicism. In fact, it is intended to expose the "rational bias" of the universal promotion of electoral legitimacy over meritocratic legitimacy without considering cultural context. Just like there is no theoretical certainty for justice on the system level, there is no theoretical certainty for a voting system that can determine electoral legitimacy. In fact, plurality voting only conforms partially to four of the eight popular criteria for a desirable voting scheme. It conforms partially with majority criterion, monotonicity criterion, consistency criterion, and participation criterion—but not with Condorcet criterion, Condorcet loser criterion, independence of irrelevant alternatives criterion, or independence of clone candidates criterion.[24] Other voting systems may also have similar problems. Arrow's Impossibility Theorem demonstrates that no voting system can possibly meet a set of reasonable criteria (including the dictatorship criterion) when there are more than two options to choose from.[25] Therefore, no other illusion is bigger than "Democracy is the only way to express the actual determination of its people."

For the reason of the problems in elections, it is argued that elections are at most only secondary to the "rule of law" and that the "rule of law"—which has a much longer history—is more important. "Rule of law" is the anti-arbitrary principle that governmental authority is legitimately exercised in accordance with publicly disclosed written laws adopted and enforced by established procedures. Hong Kong (before 1997) is often given as an example as it was ruled by an unelected British administrator but was generally considered to be free and open due to its strong legal institutions. The arguments for the rule of law are:

- Commitments to law and to the separation of government power have no inherent democratic significance;

- Legal liberty may easily exist without democratic liberty, and there is no necessary connection between individual liberty and democratic rule;

- The goal of personal liberty is to curb state authority against individuals, whereas the goal of political liberty is to gain power to exercise that authority;

- A non-liberal legal system may adhere to the rule of law requirements better than any of those in liberal democracies;

- The gravest threat to personal liberty is in fact posed by representative democracy;

- Democracy cannot reduce the tension between liberty and equality, while it may contribute to the decline of the rule of law;

- The rule of law has functioned as a check on the expansion of popular democracy;

- And, most importantly, the rule of law can exist without democracy, yet democracy can't even function without rule of law.[26]

Such a line of thought gives the "rule of law" argument against democracy in China.[27] The irony of democracy is that it can be exterminated by votes. Democracies have failed many times in history from ancient Greece to modern France, and to Germany in the twentieth century. Today, most democracies in the third world are unstable and often collapse from military coups or other forms of dictatorship. The paradox here is that the rule of law that is supposed to check and balance government power may also be threatened when democracy collapses. Rule of law cannot rule unless power goes with it. Such devices as limiting the power of an elected body, requiring a certain majority to change the constitution, using plurality voting to slow down the strengthening of new parties, and setting a higher proportion of votes for a party to get into parliament, will be meaningless when law and order are simply removed (as in Iraq now).

While electoral legitimacy has a short history of only a few hundred years and provides liberal democracy for fewer nations and populations in the world, it is claimed to be applicable to every nation and superior to meritocratic legitimacy with its much longer history of a few thousand years. In the view of democratic universalism, all countries in the world are grouped into three categories: "non-electoral and non-liberal" ("not free"), "electoral but may or may not be liberal" ("partly free"), and "liberal" ("free"). According to the Freedom House 2006 report,[28] 120 countries or 64 percent of all countries enjoy electoral legitimacy; only 89 countries or 46 percent are "liberal" (the percentage in terms of population happens to be also 46 percent); 45 countries or 24 percent are "non-electoral and non-liberal," and 103 countries or 54 percent are non-liberal. Interestingly, among those 58 countries that are "partly free," 31 countries or 53 percent are non-liberal. This percentage has been consistent for the last thirty years. In other words, electoral legitimacy cannot deliver an orderly "liberal" society in those "electoral but not liberal" countries when electoral democracy has been hailed to triumph in the world for the last few decades. On the other hand, China enjoys an orderly society and economic prosperity despite its "non-electoral and non-liberal" status.

Compared with partial electoral legitimacy, the abuse of electoral legitimacy is a much more serious problem in liberal democracies. Blind belief in electoral legitimacy overestimates the virtues of humanity in designing a procedural mechanism to control government, while under-estimating the defects of humanity in going through the loopholes in it. The reason the gravest threat to personal liberty can be posed by representative democracy is because elected leaders frequently choose to live in the inflated moral fantasy of absolute electoral legitimacy, which drives them to a degenerate position of self-indulged supremacy.

George W. Bush provides the best example of all throughout the history of democracy. His is also the best case to illustrate how a nation can be readily put in peril when some radical "neo-con" ideology is supported by a democracy's institutional design. No mechanism of popular constraint on or control over the president's war-making power was built into the U.S. Constitution. The requirement of a congressional declaration of war is not observed and is without effect. There is no federal recall. There is no federal initiative. There is no federal referendum. The president needs to make as many as 6,000 appointments in the executive branch of the federal government, which has about 4 million personnel (including 1 million active-duty military personnel). Patronage is a norm in these appointments.

Legislation is unduly influenced by lobbyists in service of moneyed interests, such as that of the military-oil complex. Government deficit spending is institutionally out of control due to the lack of a budgetary mechanism present in modern corporations. At the same time, President Bush easily abuses his power to cut taxes for the super-richtime and time again. The nation is at war, public debt skyrockets, and private debt balloons to an all-time high. Disasters like Hurricane Katrina slip into the government's blind spot. The administration continues to fail to see how terrorists have achieved their goal by simply spreading terror rather than launching real terror in the warfare sense. Yet the terror of another attack before or after Bush leaves office is like a sword above every American's head. American soldiers are dying in Iraq at a rate of nearly 100 per month, the cost of the war can no longer be measured in dollar terms, and the Bush government is still under the illusion that a "plug and play" democracy without rule of law is going to work in Iraq, or that the "surge" of more U.S. troops there will make a military solution more effective than a political-cultural solution.

All this will only lead one to wonder: how on earth did we get into this mess at the dawn of the new millennium?

Ideological Overreach and Military Overstretch

Thousands of years ago, Asian people migrated to North America via the Bering land bridge and became the Native Americans long before Columbus arrived in 1492 and the Europeans set up the first colony in Virginia in 1607. From the First Anglo-Powhatan War in 1609 to the closing of the frontier in 1890, the history of the American Indians became a record of wars, massacres, decimation, extermination, assimilation, land seizure, "Indian removal," forced relocation, and pandemics. The conquest of the Native American is believed by historians as America's first step on the road to imperialism.

The 1803 Louisiana Purchase from Napoleon's France marked the first successful American expansion. The more than half-a-billion-acre new land is near one-fourth of America's current territory and was bought for three cents per acre. What's more amazing is that it cost a total of $15 million, while $10 million was originally budgeted to purchase New Orleans alone. Even the Alaska Purchase at $7.2 million from Russia in 1867 couldn't match this sweet deal. Thomas Jefferson, who condemned the British denial of American self-determination not long ago, soon signed the Louisiana Government Bill to deprive the new territory of its right to self-rule. In 1810, the United States annexed West Florida in spite of the dispute with Spain. The first setback for the expansionists came in the Canadian colonies during the War of 1812 with Britain. But it was balanced by the acquisition of the Red River Basin in 1818 and the Oregon territory in 1846 from Great Britain. In the South, East Florida was ceded by Spain in 1819. The Texas Annexation in 1845 led to the Mexican-American War, which surprisingly resulted in further acquisition of parts of Texas, Colorado, Arizona, New Mexico, and Wyoming, and the whole of California, Nevada, and Utah—for only a $15 million payment to Mexico in 1848. In only seventy years, the United States evolved from a small thirteen-state country on the Atlantic to a big country embracing the Gulf of Mexico and the Atlantic and Pacific Oceans.

American territorial expansion was accompanied by a clear line of thought. The initial idea of a continental nation-state can be traced to the name of the "Continental Congress"—the first governing body for the thirteen American colonies. In 1823, President James Monroe proclaimed the "Monroe Doctrine," warning European powers to cease to colonize the Americas and to not interfere with affairs in the hemisphere. In 1831, Tocqueville used the term "American Exceptionalism" to echo John Winthrop's famous "City upon a Hill" sermon of 1630 and Thomas Paine's notion of beginning the world over again in his 1776 *Common Sense*, a term that later on acquired the meaning of an America-centered view of the world. In 1843, President Andrew Jackson described it as "extending the area of freedom."

As an ideology, continentalism was expressed by the so-called "Manifest Destiny" advocated first by journalist John L. O'Sullivan of the Democratic Party in 1845 for annexing Texas and Oregon. In his words, the claim to overspread and to possess the whole of the continent "is by the right of our manifest destiny . . . which Providence has given us for the development of the great experiment of liberty." Like the American Revolution, the rise of republicanism, the anti-slavery movement, and the development of political campaigns, the American continental expansion was considered another "missionary crusade" roused with moralistic intensity. "Manifest Destiny" became the God-given chance to redeem the Christian world and beyond. The sense of a special world-historical role and opportunity has never deserted the American national self-regard from then on. By the end of the nineteenth century, "Manifest Destiny" gained wider support as a theoretical justification for America's overseas expansion. In the annexation of Hawaii in 1898, President William McKinley claimed that "We need Hawaii as much and a good deal more than we did California. It is manifest destiny." From Matthew Perry's opening of Japan to the West in 1854 to the "Open Door Policy" for equal economic access to China in 1899, American Isolationism faded away away like a dated dream.

The 1898 Spanish-American War was a new chapter in the American expansion, since after the war outright annexation was replaced by putting Cuba as a virtual protectorate (independent in 1902, perpetual lease for Guantánamo Bay in 1903) and colonizing Guam, Puerto Rico, and the Philippines (independent in 1946). America's imperialistic Empire-building was launched from its hegemony mindset after the Spanish-American War. The British poet Rudyard Kipling published the well-known poem "The White Man's Burden" with the subtitle "The United States and the Philippine Islands" in the following year, expressing a mixed message: the euphemism for imperialism and the cost associated with it. As history turned the page to the twentieth century, expansionism was taken by interventionism under the 1904 Roosevelt Corollary to the Monroe Doctrine. As a proponent of a large navy and "Big Stick Diplomacy," President Theodore Roosevelt was inspired by Alfred T. Mahan's 1890 book *The Influence of Sea Power upon History*, which advocated the expansion of U.S. naval power, the building of the Panama Canal, and the establishment of a military post in the Pacific to stimulate trade with China.

When President Woodrow Wilson led the United States into World War I, he made it clear that "This is the time of all others when Democracy should prove its purity and its spiritual power to prevail. It is surely the manifest destiny of the United States to lead in the attempt to make this spirit prevail." Wilson's claim started the American notion of the leader of the "free world," which was self-decorated by the perception of protecting the causes of freedom, democracy, and justice worldwide. Elite Americans, who had thrown themselves out of the shackles of the British Empire in the eighteenth century, were so ready in the nineteenth century, and so comfortable with administering a new one by their own in the twentieth century and beyond. In the New American Empire, there is no more king or emperor, there is no more annexation; there are only interventions, occupations, wars, the pride of the triumph from World War II and the Cold War, the rise of imperialistic ideology, and the decline of ordinary American taxpayers' interests.

In his 1989 book *The Rise and Fall of the Great Powers*, Paul Kennedy surveyed modern history from the sixteenth century forward to examine the relationship among economic, political, and military powers. According to Kennedy, economic power—though not necessarily a military power at the same time—is the source of the other two. But economic wealth and military power are relative in terms of their distribution among nations and relative within a nation over time. There is a tendency for declining economic powers to spend very heavily on the military, as their sense of security decreases. This tendency that leads to "imperial overstretch" is a characteristic of all declining powers. Only those states who can keep the best balance of military and economic strength remain great powers.

Is the American war in Iraq from 2003 a symptom of "imperial overstretch?" All empires in history are "mortal." Yet every empire and every apologist of every empire firmly believes that their empire is different. When the democratic Athenians invaded Syracuse, they insisted they could never be challenged and could never fail. That battle turned out to be the Waterloo of the Athenian Empire. When the Spainish fought the war of empire and tried to maintain Spain's costly presence in Flanders, they repeated the exact same pattern in history. How different is the American war in Iraq? When the democratic Athenians asked the small city-state Melos to give up its neutrality in the Peloponnesian War, the Athenian envoy told the Melians that right is in question only between equals in power and that the strong will do what they can and the weak will suffer what they must. President George W. Bush is of course very different from the Athenian "realpolitik." The military overreach in Iraq is for America's security interests and economic interests, but it is all the while ornamented by a universal moral interest.

After the September 11, 2001, attacks, with his typical non-dialectical true-false, right-wrong, black-white perception, President Bush declared that, "Every nation, in every region, now has a decision to make. Either you are with us, or you are with the terrorists," much the same way as he sees nations either as democracies or as dictatorships. In what came to be known as the "Bush Doctrine," the cold war strategies of deterrence and containment were replaced by the guidelines of military preemption, "military strength beyond challenge," unilateral action, and a universal moral commitment to "extending democracy, liberty, and security to all regions."

This neatly-put wholesale package provides a high-minded justification for the 2003 invasion of Iraq: if the U.S. is threatened by terrorists or by rogue states that are engaged in the production of weapons of mass destruction, the right of self-defense should be extended to authorize preemptive and unilateral attacks against potential aggressors with "military strength beyond challenge" before they are able to launch strikes against the U.S.

For military preemption, President Abraham Lincoln had this to say: "Allow the president to invade a neighboring nation whenever he shall deem it necessary to repel an invasion and you allow him to do so whenever he may choose to say he deems it necessary for such purpose, and you allow him to make war at pleasure. . . . If today he should choose to say he thinks it necessary to invade Canada to prevent the British from invading us, how could you stop him? You may say to him, 'I see no probability of the British invading us,' but he will say to you, 'Be silent; I see it, even if you don't.'"

For "military strength beyond challenge," President Bush is obviously indulging in the fantasy that the U.S.'s sole-superpower status makes it the most powerful international police force. The truth is: it could also make the U.S. the most dangerous world imperialist. More importantly, the new warfare of suicide bombing makes the most advanced American weapons dialectically fragile and useless both at home and abroad. It is not a "strength beyond challenge," but a "challenge beyond strength." President Bush is spending $8 billion every month taxed from ordinary Americans without seeing this simple fact. Sending more troops will only inflate a bigger illusion.

For democratic universalism, President Bush has more to say in his 2002 State of the Union address: "America will lead by defending liberty and justice because they are right and true and unchanging for all people everywhere. No nation owns these aspirations and no nation is exempt from them. We have no intention of imposing our culture, but America will always stand firm for the non-negotiable demands of human dignity, the rule of law, limits on the power of the state, respect for women, private property, free speech, equal justice, and religious tolerance." We can review what cultural psychologist Richard Nisbett said in his *The Geography of Thought* at the beginning of this chapter, but let's look further at how cultural anthropologist Richard A. Shweder from the University of Chicago argues in his "George W. Bush & the missionary position."[29]

Shweder identifies President Bush's weighty and portentous augury as a "missionary moral progressivism" that is governed by a transcendent and righteous crusade force with imperial tones. For religious fundamentalists and American exceptionalists, Bush's statements aroused a jingoistic response that sees the mere mention of moral equivalence as a sign of self-hatred or ethical weakness, as if the American culture isn't only one among many morally decent and rationally defensible ways of life. But is it really possible to formulate a "right and true and unchanging" moral statement that is free of ethnocentrism, parochialism, political self-interest, or denominational prejudice? And how is it that President Bush's arrogance happens to associate with power and wealth such that whatever he desires has to be what all others ought to desire?

Shweder's concern is also supported by U.S. Appellate Judge Richard

Posner: "morality is local, and . . . there are no interesting moral univer-
sals. There are tautological ones, such as 'murder is wrong,' where 'murder' means 'wrongful killing,' or 'bribery is wrong,' where bribery means
'wrongful paying.' But what counts as murder, or as bribery, varies enor-
mously from society to society. There are a handful of rudimentary principles of social cooperation—such as don't lie all the time, or don't break
promises without any reason, or don't kill your relatives or neighbors indis-
criminately—that may be common to all human societies, and if one wants
to call these rudimentary principles the universal moral law, that is fine
with me. But they are too abstract to be criterial. Meaningful moral realism is therefore out, and a form (not every form) of moral relativism is in.
Relativism in turn invites an adaptationist conception of morality, in which
morality is judged . . . by its contribution to the survival, or other ultimate
goals, of a society or some group within it. Moral relativism implies that
the expression 'moral progress' must be used with great caution, because
it is perspectival rather than objective . . . The criteria for pronouncing a
moral claim valid are given by the culture in which the claim is advanced
rather than by some transcultural ('universal') source of moral values, so
that we cannot, except for polemical effect, call another immoral unless we
add "by our lights."[30] In *Whose Justice? Which Rationality?* (1988), Alasdair
C. MacIntyre also argues that the answer to any question about justice depends upon the historical, social, and cultural situation of the respondent
and upon how he sees himself.

Shweder affirms that many "objective order of goodness" moral claims
("We wish for others only what we wish for ourselves," for example) are
just the gift wrapping of theoretically ungrounded and ungroundable
preferences and aversions. Culture- and context-specific preferences can
always produce a sense of mutual repugnance, be it ways of eating, habits of speech, patterns of thought, or sexual customs. There is simply no
universally binding and rational way to prioritize all of the values for all
of the people all of the time in all of the places. Mutual coexistence, therefore, should take hold for the design of a good society culture by culture.
Cultural differences will not evaporate even when missionary monists want
them removed so that people are liberated. Ironically, President Bush's
claim that "We have no intention of imposing our culture" seems to imply
that the "non-negotiable demands" he enumerates may take very different
forms in different cultures. To Shweder, the questions here are: Should his
careful language be taken seriously? Is it just an ambiguous digression? Or
is it simply a calculated rhetorical device to show gentility and to conceal
imperialistic intention?

Consider the rights to freedom of speech about pornography, which is more heavily censored in China. Does censorship of pornography unjustifiably violate freedom of expression with regard to publishers' commercial interests, consumers' interests, and community or third party's interests? The idea that community or the society should maintain certain standards of morality may offend those liberals who see that it is no business of the state to uphold society's morals. Yet the Chinese see it differently.

In Singapore, the right to privacy does not include stopping the police from testing a person's urine for drugs when the person behaves strangely. While liberals with an anti-paternalistic view see individuals' own well-being as a non-factor in determining the limits of rights, the Singaporeans consider this restriction by law as a legitimate trade-off for the value of individual health and public safety.

In Hong Kong, filial piety is widely regarded as a virtue, and tax breaks are given to those who support their parents. Western liberals may see this as violating the principle of neutrality by favoring some virtues or ways of life over others. Yet the Chinese see that the process of making such an abstract right more concrete is not a process of deduction but as a new step in political morality.[31] Westerners are more concerned about the individual's rights in isolation; the Chinese are more concerned with the context of the individual's rights and potential external effects. Even though "externality" becomes a big topic in western economics today, liberals still find it hard to understand its implications in cross-cultural studies. There are large yet neglected differences between the Chinese and the Americans in terms of the scope and scale of their "external sensitivity."

Also consider the rights to choose government, which is often seen as foremost in human rights. The choice of government forms and government leaders, as discussed above, is in the U.S. a "public choice" rather than a "moral choice" process. People's right to choose government is the American way of life. But there is simply no abstract electoral moral goodness that can apply to every cultural context, not to mention that the electoral mechanism in America is flawed in practice. In China, people's right to choose government is not interpreted in "electoral democracy," it is interpreted in "meritocracy" and "political consultation."

Chinese meritocracy is the Chinese way to choose their government. The future of the Chinese government formation is subject to the process of "public choice" that is culturally defined by Chinese rather than being defined by another culture. Multi-party election as the way to choose government is prohibited in China not only because of political self-serving, but also because of political culture, path dependence, negative demonstration, and harmonious egalitarianism. The electoral democratic idea is prohibited in China not only because the "supply-side" (the government) doesn't like it (what government likes to be overthrown?), but also because the "demand-side" (the Chinese people) want a strong meritocratic government and see a political change as risky, costly, and undesirable. The relative nature of moral goods ultimately leads to the "cultural morality" argument against appropriateness of Western democracy in China.

Western democratic values are seen as universal simply because the elites of the current most powerful and wealthy nation in the world happen to embrace them as their own ideals and believe that "Freedom for others means safety for ourselves." This "democratic peace theory" is a children's trick that all adults play: you first define what real democracy is, and then you find yourself explaining away wars fought between democracies, and then you justify wars waged by real democracies against non-democracies; and you may also need to define what a real war is. But after you make "real democracy" and "real war," you finally make "peace," even though democracy is actually a less peaceful choice. Immanuel Kant foreshadowed the theory in his 1795 essay "Perpetual Peace," seventeen years before the War of 1812 broke out between democratic America and Britain. The War of 1812 is precisely the first war that all believers in democratic peace are eager to exclude. "China threat" is the "pure" logical result of such self-deceiving theory. In Edward Friedman's *What if China Doesn't Democratize? Implications for War and Peace*, this theory is refuted (by evidence like the Dutch/English wars, American attempts to overthrow democracies in Guatemala in 1954, Chile in 1973, and Nicaragua in 1979)—yet Sinocentric expansionism is affirmed with a cultural view, while Western democracy for China is viewed from a non-cultural one.

Just like China's current political system is a combined result of realpolitik and cultural tradition, the Bush Doctrine blends realpolitik and a subscription to "democratic fundamentalism" into a single political platform. No wonder his perfectly pitched discourse of military domination and universal morality struck a chord that was music to the ears of interventionists on both left and right. While the hastily hailed third-wave democracy reversed into a political-cultural breakdown in the non-Christian world, and the liberal democracies in the West experience an unprecedented confidence decline,[32] the lessons of parochial electoral democracy and the relative importance of self-determined rule and order remain unlearned. Now that America is buried deep in the quagmire of the Iraqi insurgencies, the delusion of building a scientific, universally applicable democracy in Iraq is still held tight by those who see that the American blunders are due solely to the miscalculation of the Bush administration rather than to the foolhardiness of "Democratic fundamentalism."[33]

Iraq is now viewed as a "coaling station" for the American presence in the Middle East, much the same as the Philippines was a coaling station for the American navy's presence in the Pacific at the beginning of the twentieth century—the "American Century." As the Philippines (America's only colony) is still in the backwater of Asia's economic boom, it is the people there rather than the American-style democracy who are taking the blame. While Baghdad is still burning and Iraq is still exploding on a daily basis, the mutual frustration is also growing. The Iraqi leaders are frustrated that a superpower with its stunning military presence in Iraq has produced weak post-war performance; the Bush administration is frustrated that Iraq's leaders are always divided and could never generate enough political power to rule the country. Of course American taxpayers are frustrated. When a fresh Iraqi democracy that was supposed to be a superior form of governing and the strongest democracy in the world come together, how come they fail miserably in the hands of sectarian violence?

There is an answer to this question that missionary ideologues don't want to face. "Democratic fundamentalism," characterized by both ideological overreach and military overstretch, is now destroying the future of America's empire because it is politically evangelical, intellectually reckless, militarily suicidal, and economically squandering.

Conclusion

The New "American-Chinese" Century

In 2004, China's state television, CCTV, for the first time in history, broadcast the U.S. presidential election through a neutral special live coverage. The chaos surrounding the 2000 U.S. presidential election and the 2003 U.S. invasion of Iraq discredited American-style democracy among the Chinese. More important is the fact that the Chinese government, after the historic 2002 transition of power from Jiang Zemin to Hu Jintao, has become much more confident in its governance and has less to fear about the American model.[1] The psychology among the Chinese is: "It's showtime again." In December 2006, after the first "China-U.S. Strategic Economic Dialogue," China Telecom, China Netcom, and China Unicom signed a $500 million deal with U.S. communications giant Verizon to build an undersea optical cable system that will increase by sixty times overall existing capacity directly linking the U.S. and China. The Chinese government is clearly not afraid of opening. Yet many people in the West are still under the illusion that this economic engagement will drive China toward pluralism and, ultimately, democracy.

It may be alarming, but the real China challenge is looming. Contrary to the Western belief that only liberal institutions will sustain great power, China's meritocratic institutions have evolved into a stable modern stage, into a different "state model" that can sustain rapid economic growth with reasonable political stability. The real China challenge is therefore on a more fundamental "institutional level," not on the secondary level of business, economy, or the military. The challenge of this reality is not how to contain it with military muscle or engage it with one-sided faith. The challenge lies in how to cooperate with and leverage this first-and-largest-of-its-kind superpower in international politics and benefit from it through economic globalization. "Peaceful co-development" should be the main theme. With double-digit economic growth that can overtake Germany and Japan in GDP, China may not be able to effectively challenge the economic supremacy of the U.S. in thirty years; nevertheless, "A hegemon may have his own self-destructive element." The United States can lose its economic dominance by its own fault if it continues to overstretch its military and economic power in decades to come.

Currently, the GDP of the U.S. and China is $12.5 trillion vs. $2.4 trillion; per capita–wise it is $42,000 vs. $1,800. Even if China's GDP surpasses the U.S. GDP in the next thirty years, its per capita GDP will still be far behind—only about 25 percent of U.S. per capita GDP. China lags in education, innovation, and military power, even though the gap may narrow in thirty years. "A skinny camel is still bigger than a horse." The century we are living in now is an "American-Chinese Century." Europe experienced its greatness in nineteenth-century globalization and is becoming exhausted now.[2] America's twentieth-century dominance as a manufacturing powerhouse is fading.

The message from this book is a largely unrecognized boiling concern: while China is increasingly becoming an open society receptive to international business norms and multicultural practices, America is gradually leaning toward a closed society obdurate for political evangelism and resistant to international multilateralism. When American social scientists study China, they focus more on what China should do to be more like America. When Chinese scholars study America, they focus more on what makes the two cultures different and how Chinese can digest only what they need to learn. What's looming on the horizon may not be all that clear. The American capitalist system is the best in the world in terms of its productive forces, and at the same time the worst market system in the world in terms of allocating tremendous liberal resources to promote its parochial democracy to other countries—when in fact these resources should be allocated to study and fix its own problems at home.

Robert Dahl's *Democracy and Its Critics* (1989), carries an unrecognized logical flaw in its cognitive-cultural foundation. Different cultures see democracy and markets differently. When rule of law is preferred, the Chinese still believe that even the best law does not speak to all situations and cannot contemplate all eventualities in advance. They believe that, in many cases, Western procedurism in effect presents a second-best solution or an unrealistic alternative. That is to say, there is only arbitrary rule when rule of law is absent; but when there is only rule of law, legal rigidity may well sacrifice desirable outcomes with seemingly fair procedures. Western democracy is viewed as potentially the rule of the mob that's susceptible to seduction by demagogues with a negative effect on society. A version of this thinking strives to institutionalize a formal mechanism to revive the meritocratic selectoral-electoral mechanism so as to achieve a balance between rule by man and rule of law. In viewing the market mechanism, the Chinese philosophy is also different: a free market is a great instrument of economic efficiency, but free competition or sometimes excessive competition can never achieve perfection; there are always external effects and an imbalances in buyer-seller power that need to be controlled for the benefit of the whole society. In here, as in democracy, the beauty of universal perfection lies only in the eyes of the beholder. Oswald Spengler's argument in *The Decline of the West* (1918) that democracy is driven by money and corruption may need to be revised in the light of public choice.

Many people in the West are passionate about charting "China's path to democracy." They see at least five possible paths: 1) gradual reform and transition from village democracy and rule of law; 2) an overthrow of the regime by the people—"people power" as in the Philippines and, to a lesser extent, South Korea; 3) gradual political reform from above led by the Chinese Communist Party; 4) a reforming coup instituting democracy; and 5) democracy as an outcome of an increasingly explicit federalist system.[3] None of these will happen. The greatest peril of social scientists is to allow their eagerness for "social progress" to override their search for scientific fact and their respect for cultural truth. What we are in fact seeing is: in building its own version of market economy, China is creating a Chinese version of "meritocratic democracy" that is different from Western "electoral democracy."

The myth of democracy is to bundle electoral democracy, rule of law, human rights, and market capitalism into one "democracy package" as if it were a wholesale deal. Democratic fundamentalists used to claim that only members of a democracy could enjoy capitalism—but China now has market capitalism. Democratic universalists used to claim that only democracy can promote human rights—yet this has been falsified by the records of liberal democracies, by the practice of new democracies in the third world, and by the improvement of human rights in non-liberal countries. Democratic truists claimed that only members of a democracy can enjoy rule of law, yet this is only parochially true in the Christian world (30 percent of the world population); electoral democracy in the non-Christian world frequently "enjoys" social chaos and political breakdowns instead. Just as democracy is still not perfect in America because of its republican tradition, rule of law is still not good in China because of its relationship-based culture. But institutional inertia is one thing, binding democracy with rule of law is quite another. Ethnocentrism, a self-centered expression on the national level, is behind the package idea of democracy.

America's closed-eye mindset and cold war mentality are constantly leading to mutual frustration. Nothing is more agonizing for the Chinese government to deal with than an entity that wants a friendly relationship, yet keeps on badmouthing and even backstabbing by supporting forces that undermine China's governance. On the other hand, American elites are angst-ridden while happily dealing with the Chinese in business: a form of "personality split." Canadian conservatives are pursuing a similar risky game. The Canadian government doesn't answer Chinese calls to send back fugitives in corruption cases, and Prime Minister Stephen Harper keeps criticizing Beijing's human-rights record—yet leaves his economic ministers to talk business.

As Richard A. Shweder pointed out, the repugnance is mutual, which is detrimental to the bilateral relationship. Again, a parochial human rights view is hopeless. When the only tool you have is a hammer, you tend to see every problem as a nail. Human history goes from anarchy to monarchy, autocracy, and dictatorship; it does not necessarily go directly to Western democracy. Chinese reformed meritocracy is now far from dictatorship. Western electoral democracy and Chinese meritocratic democracy are both viable government options. In different cultural settings, governments may take a form of constitutional monarch (U.K.), republicanism (U.S.), democracy (France), meritocracy (China), or mixed authoritarianism (Russia). There are, of course, human "common goods" that can be cherished, which best result from a shared vision and an agreed-upon institution (U.N.), not from a parochial yet imperialistic mind.

Empires come and go. The Chinese Empire lost the nineteenth century empire clash to the British Empire through a hot war. The American Empire won the twentieth century empire clash over the Soviet Empire though a cold war. Despite all the self-low-profiling, China's ambition as an emerging empire can hardly hide.

While American business conservatives see China as a business opportunity and see a tough U.S. policy against China as opposed to their desires for trade and economic progress, American neoconservatives tend to see

China as a looming threat to the United States and argue for harsh policies to contain it. Business conservatives' approach is: you are not here to fix China's problems; stay focused on your business motives and calculations. Neoconservatives' ideology approach is a bit different: democratize China, and if you can't, demonize it.

The truth is, if there is any threat from China, the threat is more about re-balancing the power structure in the international political economy. If this is the fear of John J. Mearsheimer in his *The Tragedy of Great Power Politics*, the ongoing economic cooperation won't be able to stop it, for it is inevitably a non-zero-sum game. But unlike the U.S., whose history is that of an aggressive overseas ideological expansionist, China is a defensive border expansionist traditionally, and there is no agenda in its genes for an ideological expansion in the future. Toynbee's "world-unifier hypothesis" about China, then, might have some merit.

It is human desire to "cut loss short" and "let profit run." Yet human institutions may simply shape human behavior to "cut profit short" and "let loss run." China's economic take-off from its institutional productive rise has been seriously cut short by its distributional corruption and incentive-distorted enforcement. Unless stone-hard determination and institutionally effective measures are taken sooner rather than later by the government, the relational effect of its face culture will backfire on its economic progress and international ambition. There is a great need to reinforce the authority of institutions. Chinese civilization has prominence in material, technological, and organizational advantage in its imperial past; to play a genuine key role in the world, it has to further remake its institutional, behavioral, and spiritual "nation-ware." Moving away from the zeal in political agitation to the passion for market economy revitalizes its people, yet there is always a question of "what do you do after you are rich?" Nothing could be worse than a new level of self-indulgence and the hollowing-out of a more broad-minded inner-self in the process of further commercialization. In this regard, in addition to nation building, market building, and state building, there is also a need for spirit building, a necessary step for all great powers.

While China strives for a market empire, the American empire eats its self-planting "bitter fruit" in Iraq—another "let loss run" scheme much like the Vietnam War. American civilization is like a young kid turning powerful in the street, too ready to give lessons and show its muscle; and at times, too carried away in elaborating the ideal in heart and in satisfying the esthetic image in mind for the outside world. Here lies the source of the "American Tragedy": if it doesn't expand itself, it will feel the pain in its heart; if it expands itself and inevitably hurts others, it will have to continue to expand (hence let loss run) to maintain a balance between external control and internal heartache before things turn unsustainable. America's failure, then, hence comes from its success.

Sending more troops to Iraq, or maintaining the current engagement before admitting total failure in the near future, falls into the realm of this tragic logic. There is little doubt about the tragic ending, just like there is little doubt about how this tragedy is fully institutionalized in American ideological norms and legal establishments. According to the 2007 Failed States Index by Foreign Policy magazine and the Fund for Peace, Iraq is now ranked second (after Sudan) and Afghanistan is at eighth place among world's failed states. People are fleeing from Baghdad and the country everyday. According to the United Nations, more than 2 million Iraqis now believed to be displaced inside Iraq and another 2.2 million sheltering in neighboring states, including some 1.4 million in Syria, up to 750,000 in Jordan, 80,000 in Egypt and some 200,000 in the Gulf region. Do we need to build a wall to stop people running away from an imported democracy? Even though the mistake in Iraq is obvious, correcting it remains subject to the logic of collective actions and American institutional rigidity—individual's inaction due to "increasing cost of scale" and "decreasing proportion of benefit" in collection actions, and the excessive check and balance that balance away urgent encompassing interests over time. This is why even the newly empowered Democrats in the Congress can't really do much to end the war. When the Congress is now at one of its lowest approval ratings in a decade, what Democrats can do is asking the American people to understand that they can only accomplish what they have the votes for, and that they need help from Republicans to clear procedural hurdles and override presidential vetoes. A "do nothing Congress" now is nothing better than a Republican rubber stamp. America is now on a stage when ideological and military overreach are so institutionalized that any politician will be easily proved *incompetent* once elected president. President George W. Bush is the biggest victim of this institution so far. The "world police" mindset fails to realize that authoritarianism is not going to work in international politics because international cultures are so different from America's culture in terms of composition, ecology, cohesiveness, and value orientation. When Bush famously announced "Mission Accomplished," he was not only strategically ignorant but also culturally ignorant. The United States is waiting for a wake-up call that has still not been arranged.

Most Americans don't know that their public debt is $8.5 trillion, nearly 70 percent of U.S. GDP, six times the amount of American currency in circulation, and about $28,000 per person. Household debt is about $12 trillion, almost as much as the GDP. Paying interest for both debts alone easily passes $1 trillion. The institutions behind these figures are in fact logically distributional (political campaigns, interest-group politics) and destructive (war-prone), and increasingly undermine its most powerful productive forces. Thanks to President George W. Bush, Americans' tax money is unrelentingly spent on all fronts of the international arena: Iraq, Afghanistan, and of course searching for Osama Bin Laden and Al Qaeda, all with full justification.

Along with this is the domestic front of the sky-high "triple deficits": federal budge deficit ($319 billion in 2005), current account deficit (both trade and capital flow), and the lower and middle class "family budget deficit." Politicians are less constrained (voter pressure, sinking funds requirement) and less responsible in issuing government debt because the specification and identification of liability are institutionally different from those in private debt.[4] American civilization has become too confident in its institutions, too cocky in its future, hence too swaggering for its future generations without a fair intergeneration equality principle. Its commercial culture is driving everybody selling everything—households are lured into overspending and the government sells democracy abroad with massive subsidies. Just like American people are held hostage for the Iraq war by the government, future generations are held hostage by the massive magnitude of the current debt. The American hope is: confidence will never collapse. Yet it could. The recent subprime mortgage crisis is a warning sign.

In the Chinese civilization's top-down orientation, individual liberty often gives way to broader concerns. The transformation of inheritance-based family-rulership to term-based party-rulership replaces special interests with more encompassing interests in governance on one hand, and broadens the bases of individual liberty, the bottom-up office selection and social feedback mechanisms, on the other. The American civilization is one with bottom-up orientation in which individual liberty often takes precedence over public goods. The republic-centric democratic process strengthens national concerns on one hand, and maintains political mechanisms to special interests to infringe on encompassing interests on the other. In the social setting of both countries, there is obviously different tension between individual liberty and public concerns, and between special interests and encompassing interests. One of the conclusions of this book is that Western electoral democracy is not a panacea—it is not appropriate for China and it is appropriate for but seriously flawed in America. China, as well as America, has a lot to fix under its own roof. There are enough mutual interests that require maximum cooperation between the two in the new century.

Electoral procedurism may be a good mechanism for the reconciliation of conflicting social interests, but just like voting schemes (time and methods) and scope of elected offices (judges, executives, and congressmen) need not be the same in every country, the scale of participation and the degree and aspects of contestation need not be the same either. Minimum participation and contestation in China feature a leadership mechanism of merit and connection. Maximum participation and contestation in America characterize a leadership mechanism of money and performance. As the ideal of democracy is logically separated into electoral democracy, rule of law, human rights, and economic liberty; and electoral democracy is analytically split into voting schemes, scope of election, scale of participation, and degree and aspects of contestation, the nature of a country's democracy is in fact more cultural and political than ideological. There is no out-of-context objective good and bad. There is good reason why realism always prevails. Western Electoral Democracy often fails in the non-Christian world not because the non-Christian world lacks the virtues for Electoral Democracy, but becaue the out-of-context ideal of Electoral Democracy is not a virtue by itself. In our culturally defined human world, perfection is impossible, and radicalism is misleading.

There are a lot of things to despise in each political system. But it is always important to rationally separate those deficiencies by cultural judgment, by specific political logic, and by pure knowledge limitation. Among all human fantasies, political fantasy could be the most dangerous. For the Chinese, the fantasy is to see every operational problem in its system as political and attempt to import the Western system without realizing its cultural context and inherent operational problems. For the Americans, the fantasy is to view every cultural problem as ideological and attempt to export the Western system without realizing its parochial nature and historical non-transplantability. For China to stand on its own merit, nationalism is not enough. "Why is democratic fundamentalism groundless" is a bigger question. For America to stand firm as a leading world country, "military strength beyond challenge" is not enough, multilateralism with multiculturism is a better approach.

China Fever is a by-product of the eagle meeting the dragon. Ideological bigotry will continue to be their worst common adversary. Fortunately, the U.S. and China will never become true enemies,[5] for true enemies not only love what they are not, but also hate what they are.

Endnotes

Chapter 1

1. Drawn from a similar idea by Eric Hall in the forward of a KPMG report on "Foreign Insurers in China," http://www.kpmg.se/download/102974/123155/Foreign_insurers_in_China0507.pdf.
2. James Kynge, *China Shakes the World, A Titan's Rise and Troubled Future—and the Challenge for America* (Houghton Mifflin, 2006); C. Fred Bergsten, *China The Balance Sheet, What the World Needs to Know Now About the Emerging Superpower* (PublicAffairs, 2006); Ted Fishman, *China Inc: How the Rise of the Next Superpower Challenges America and the World* (Scribner, 2005); James McGregor, *One Billion Customers: Lessons from the Front Lines of Doing Business in China* (New York: Free Press, 2005); Oded Shenkar, *The Chinese Century: The Rising Chinese Economy and Its Impact on the Global Economy, the Balance of Power, and Your Job* (Wharton School Publishing, 2004); Laurence J. Brahm, *China's Century: The Awakening of the Next Economic Powerhouse* (John Wiley & Sons, 2001); Daniel Burstein, *Big Dragon: The Future of China, What It Means for Business, the Economy, and the Global Order* (Free Press, 1999).
3. "RR Donnelley Agrees to Acquire Asia Printers Group Ltd.," http://capitalmarkets.rrdonnelley.com/media_jun_05_05.cfm.
4. Dominic Gates, "Boeing's new sales maestro," http://seattletimes.nwsource.com/html/businesstechnology/2003286080_dickenson03.html.
5. Kristi Heim, "Boeing stumbles in race for China," http://seattletimes.nwsource.com/html/boeingaerospace/2002307265_boeingchina05.html.
6. David Barboza, "China bank surges 15% on its first trading day," http://www.iht.com/articles/2006/10/27/business/icbc.php.
7. Irene Shen, "Investing, Citigroup likes bricks and mortar in China," *Bloomberg News*, June 7, 2006, http://www.iht.com/articles/2006/06/bloomberg/bxinvest.php.
8. Emily Kaiser, "Wal-Mart poised for major China expansion," http://today.reuters.com/investing/FinanceArticle.aspx?type=businessNews&storyID=2006-03-19T102450Z_01_N19209142_RTRUKOC_0_US-RETAIL-CHINA-WALMART.xml.
9. Kirby Chien, "Caterpillar sees strong China growth," http://today.reuters.com/

news/articlebusiness.aspx?type=ousiv&storyID=2006-11-22T101704Z_01_
PEK153795_RTRIDST_0_BUSINESSPRO-MANUFACTURING-CHINA-
CATERPILLAR-DC.XML&from=business.

10. K. C. Swanson, "Starbucks a China Star," http://www.thestreet.com/_googlen/
    newsanalysis/emergingmarkets/10320402.html?cm_ven=GOOGLEN&cm_
    cat=FREE&cm_ite=NA.

11. Kathy Chen and Jason Dean, "Low Costs, Plentiful Talent Make China a Global
    Magnet for R&D," *Wall Street Journal*, March 14, 2006.

12. Julia Glick, "China Market Puts Mary Kay in the Pink," http://www.washington
    post.com/wp-dyn/content/article/2006/08/02/AR2006080200920.html.

13. James P. Miller, "Joint venture gives Ryerson entry to China," *Chicago Tribune*,
    September 12, 2006.

14. Tamora Vidaillet, "Deloitte to be bigger eventually in China than US," http://
    today.reuters.com/news/articlenews.aspx?type=reutersEdge&storyID=2007-02-
    08T084644Z_01_PEK265053_RTRUKOC_0_US-CHINA-FINANCIAL-
    DELOITTE-Interview.xml&WTmodLoc=PolNewsHome_R3_reutersEdge-2.

15. Carol Chmelynski, "Chinese language instruction getting more popular in public
    schools," http://www.nsba.org/site/doc_sbn_issue.asp?TrackID=&SID=1&DID=37
    191&CID=682&VID=55.

16. "Why you complain?," March 2, 2006, http://www.amazon.com/gp/product/
    customer-reviews/0743257529/ref=cm_cr_dp_2_1/103-6198570-1588652?%5Fen
    coding=UTF8&customer-reviews.sort%5Fby=-SubmissionDate&n=283155.

17. A.B. Maynard, "Outsourcing 101," http://www.cglcomputer.com/softwaredev/
    outsourcing101-1.htm.

18. Kerry A. Dolan, "Offshoring The Offshorers," http://www.forbes.com/free_
    forbes/2006/0417/074.html.

19. United Nations on Trade and Development, http://www.unctad.org/Templates/
    Page.asp?intItemID=2441&lang=1.

20. Frederik Balfour, "Venture Capitalists Catch China Fever," http://www.business
    week.com/magazine/content/04_12/b3875052.htm.

21. Julia F. Lowell, "US-China trade deficit overstated, expert," http://www.chinadaily.
    com.cn/english/doc/2005-10/31/content_489090.htm.

22. Martin Crutsinger, "Labor Group Seeks Trade Case vs. China," http://www.
    truthout.org/issues_06/060806LA.shtml.

23. C. Fred Bergsten, *China The Balance Sheet, What the World Needs to Know Now
    About the Emerging Superpower* (PublicAffairs, 2006), p. 77.

24. US Census Bureau, http://www.census.gov/foreign-trade/balance/c5700.html; The
    US-China Business Council, http://www.uschina.org/statistics/tradetable.html.

25. Mark Drajem, "Hu's Visit Finds US Companies Torn Over Merits of China
    Trade," http://www.bloomberg.com/apps/news?pid=10000087&sid=abeyJBH19BJ
    Y&refer=top_world_news.

26. Peter Morici, former top economist at the US International Trade Commission
    and a University of Maryland professor, argues that the yuan remains undervalued
    against the dollar by at least 40 percent; "Cause of US deficit with China analyzed,"
    http://news.monstersandcritics.com/business/news/article_1232542.php/Cause_
    of_US_deficit_with_China_analyzed.

27. Recent estimates range from 30 percent to 70 percent.

28. Bergsten, *China The Balance Sheet*, p. 90.

29. Ronald McKinnon, "Exchange Rates, Wages, and International Adjustment,"
    http://www.frbsf.org/economics/conferences/0502/InternationalAdjustment2.pdf.

30. Lawrence Carrel, "A Bubble in Beijing?" http://www.smartmoney.com/oneday-
    wonder/index.cfm?story=20050805.

31. Max Fraad Wolff and Richard Wolff, "China's reverse Marshall Plan," http://www.atimes.com/atimes/China_Business/HC08Cb07.html.

32. Repo man: A businessman whose work is to repossess or take back an object that was either used as collateral or rented or leased in a purchase or credit contract, in which the consumer agrees that the seller may repossess the object if the consumer is late or fails in making an installment payment.

33. Mark Drajem, "US retreats from curbs on tech exports to China," http://seattlepi.nwsource.com/money/269237_chinatrade06.html.

34. M. A. Heller and R. Eisenberg, "Can Patents Deter Innovation? The Anticommons in Biomedical Research," *Science* 280, no. 5364 (May 1, 1998): 698–701.

35. Frances Williams, "China's patent progress," http://www.theaustralian.news.com.au/story/0,20867,20592534-36375,00.html.

36. Charles R. Smith, "War with China," http://www.newsmax.com/archives/articles/2001/8/14/174213.shtml; all his war talk can be found at http://www.newsmax.com/pundits/archives/Charles_R._Smith-archive.shtml.

37. "Game theory, the nuclear button," http://members.ozemail.com.au/~jpascal/comp2.htm.

38. William S. Lind, "War with China?," http://www.lewrockwell.com/lind/lind65.html.

39. Avery Goldstein, *Rising to the Challenge, China's Grand Strategy and International Security* (Stanford University Press, 2005).

41. Joshua Kurlantzick, *Charm Offensive: How China's Soft Power Is Transforming the World* (Yale University Press, 2007); Joseph S. Nye, *Soft Power: The Means to Success in World Politics* (PublicAffairs, 2004).

42. Peter Hessler, "Letters From China," http://www.nytimes.com/2006/04/30/books/review/30spence.html?ex=1304049600&en=a3ec356673d52036&ei=5088&partner=rssnyt&emc=rss.

Chapter 2

1. Simon Burns, "EMC China chief 'to quit' in email fiasco," http://www.whatpc.co.uk/vnunet/news/2155655/china-email-embarasses-emc?page=2.

2. "EMC's Email Gate," http://www.shanghaiexpat.com/community/index.php?blog=20&title=emc_s_email_gate&more=1&c=1&tb=1&pb=1.

3. Hsien Chin Hu, *Chinese Concepts of "Face"* (American Anthropologist Association, 1944); Michael Harris Bond: *Beyond the Chinese Face: Insights from Psychology* (Oxford University Press, 1992); Scott D. Seligman, *Chinese Business Etiquette: A Guide to Protocol, Manners, and Culture in the People's Republic of China* (Warner Books, 1999); Wenshan Jia, *The Remaking of the Chinese Character and Identity in the 21st Century: The Chinese Face Practices* (Ablex Publishing, 2001).

4. Ruth Benedict, *The Chrysanthemum and the Sword: Patterns of Japanese Culture* (Mariner Books, Reprint edition, 1989); Francis L.K. Hsu, *Americans and Chinese: Passage to Difference* (The University Press of Hawaii, 1953 [1981 new edition]); Roland Muller, *Honor and Shame* (Xlibris Corporation, 2001); see also Roland Muller's "Honor and Shame in a Middle Eastern Setting," http://nabataea.net/h&s.html.

5. The general ideas about shamed-based and fear-based culture is drawn from Roland Muller's "Honor and Shame in a Middle Eastern Setting," http://nabataea.net/h&s.html.

6. Transaction cost could be narrowly defined as market dealing cost (search, negotiation, and enforcement cost), or broadly defined as to include non-market dealing cost (coordination, control, and management cost). This theory was inspired by Ronald Coase's "Theory of the Firm" (1937), Douglass North's "Violence Potential"

Theory of the Sate in his *Structure and Change in Economic History* (W. W. Norton & Company, 1981), chapter 3, and Mancur Olson's "Stationary Bandit" Theory of the Sate in his *Power and Prosperity* (Basic Books, 2000), chapter 1.

7. Richard Nisbett, *The Geography of Thought: How Asians and Westerners Think Differently . . . and Why* (Free Press, 2003), p. 34.

8. Francis L. K. Hsu, *Americans and Chinese: Passage to Difference* (The University Press of Hawaii, 1981), chapter 12.

9. Lin Yutang has a similar idea in his "the Female Triad of Face, Fate, and Fame."

10. Julia Lovell, *"Wall to wall,"* edited excerpt from *Great Wall: China Against the World 1000 BC—AD 2000* (Grove Press, 2006), http://www.ramagazine.org.uk/index.php?pid=370.

11. Emperor Qianlong reigned officially from October 18, 1735, to February 9, 1796, when he retired in favor of his son, Emperor Jiaqing, a filial act in order not to reign longer than his grandfather Emperor Kangxi. Despite his retirement, however, he retained ultimate power until his death in 1799, which made him actually the longest-reigning emperor of China in history.

12. "Macartney and the Emperor," http://afe.easia.columbia.edu/china/modern/tch_mcem.htm.

13. James Mann's new book *The China Fantasy: How Our Leaders Explain Away Chinese Repression* (Viking Adult, 2007) discusses a "third scenario" that Chinese capitalism continues to evolve and expand but the government fails to liberalize, which is beyond the "Soothing Scenario" (successful spread of capitalism will gradually bring about a development of democracy) and the "Upheaval Scenario" (the contradictions in Chinese society between rich and poor, between cities and the countryside, and between the openness of the economy and the unyielding Leninist system will eventually lead to a revolution). Though along the same line, Mann's ideas are different from those in this book.

14. James H. Mann, *About Face: A History of America's Curious Relationship with China from Nixon to Clinton* (1998), p. 29–32.

15. The stories here are drawn from James Mann's *About Face*.

16. Arnold J. Toynbee, *Change and Habit: The Challenge of Our Time* (Oxford University Press, 1966), p. 158.

17. "2006: Global political and security report" (Chinese), http://news.xinhuanet.com/fortune/2006-01/05/content_4012616.htm.

18. "National Power Composite" (Chinese), http://www.china.org.cn/chinese/zhuanti/296438.htm.

19. "2004: China Sustainable Development Strategy Report"(Chinese), http://www.cas.cn/html/Dir/2004/03/04/2102.htm.

20. Comparing GDP using market exchange rates does not accurately measure differences in income and consumption. GDP can distort the relative size of economies, not only because currencies fluctuate, but also because prices of non-traded goods and services are lower in poorer economies. Therefore, purchasing power parity (PPP), calculated through a price index, is used as an estimate of the exchange rate required to equalize the purchasing power and compare the standard of living of different countries. Of course, just like GDP, the reliability of PPP is also a subject of debate. World Bank 2005 PPP data is available at http://siteresources.worldbank.org/DATASTATISTICS/Resources/GDP_PPP.pdf.

21. United Nations Statistics Division, http://unstats.un.org/unsd/snaama/selectionbasicFast.asp.

22. In 2005, estimated output per worker in agriculture and related sectors was about $800, whereas in industries such as manufacturing, utilities, and mining, output per worker was about $5,900, more than seven times as much. Ben S. Bernanke,

"The Chinese Economy: Progress and Challenges," http://www.federalreserve.gov/BoardDocs/Speeches/2006/20061215/default.htm#f4.

23. Use 1990 constant price (its 2005 GDP mentioned earlier is current price and not inflation adjusted, so the number looks bigger); source from United Nations Statistics Division, IBID.

24. Kishore Mahbubani, *Can Asians Think? Understanding the Divide Between East and West* (Steerforth, 2001), p. 23.

25. Zhang Jiehai, "Cool Reflections on China Fever," http://www.zonaeuropa.com/20060107_1.htm.

26. Remarks by Treasury Secretary Henry M. Paulson on the International Economy Treasury Department Cash Room, Washington, D.C., http://www.ustreas.gov/press/releases/hp95.htm.

27. William E. Odom, *America's Inadvertent Empire* (Yale University Press, 2005).

28. Aileen McCabe, "Face of powerhouse China most visible in Shanghai," http://www.canada.com/topics/news/world/story.html?id=7f35c528-97c1-4771-8029-7c84afec643c.

29. Clifford Coonan, "On the factory floor: Inside China's engine room," http://news.independent.co.uk/world/asia/article358757.ece.

30. Dexter Roberts, Frederik Balfour, Pete Engardio, Joseph Weber: "China Goes Shopping," http://www.businessweek.com/magazine/content/04_51/b3913041_mz011.htm.

31. "The 400 Richest Chinese," http://www.forbes.com/lists/2006/74/biz_06china_The-400-Richest-Chinese_Rank.html.

32. Andrew Yeh, "Woman tops China rich list," http://www.ft.com/cms/s/7a64b676-585a-11db-b70f-0000779e2340.html.

33. Alfred Cang, "China's rich spend big to celebrate Valentine's Day," http://today.reuters.co.uk/news/articlenews.aspx?type=reutersEdge&storyID=2007-02-12T120521Z_01_NOA243408_RTRUKOC_0_VALENTINE-CHINA.xml&pageNumber=0&imageid=&cap=&sz=13&WTModLoc=NewsArt-C1-ArticlePage2.

34. George Zhibin Gu, "The China tourism explosion," http://www.atimes.com/atimes/China_Business/HC07Cb06.html.

35. Chen and Dean, "Low Costs, Plentiful Talent."

36. Alison Leung, "Cashing in on China's Renewable Energy Boom," http://www.planetark.org/dailynewsstory.cfm?newsid=37280.

37. Matthew Chervenak, "An Emerging Biotech Giant? Opportunities for well-informed foreign investors abound in China's growing biotech sector," http://www.chinabusinessreview.com/public/0505/chervenak.html.

38. Joe McDonald, "Wal-Mart, GE Offer Chinese Credit Card," http://www.chron.com/disp/story.mpl/ap/fn/4282916.html.

39. "China to let 9 foreign banks incorporate, in step toward retail business," http://www.iht.com/articles/ap/2006/12/24/business/AS_FIN_China_WTO_Banks.php.

40. Tony Munroe, "Rewards, risks as Chinese embrace credit," http://www.ibtimes.com/articles/20060908/china-investors-borrowers.htm.

41. Wallace Immen, "China most attractive, and difficult, place for ex-pats," http://www.theglobeandmail.com/servlet/story/LAC.20060927.CABRIEFS27-5/TPStory.

Chapter 3

1. Caroline Baum, "Pilgrims Respond to Incentives and Give Thanks," http://www.r21online.com/archives/2002_11.html.

2. Douglass C. North, *Understanding the Process of Economic Change* (Princeton University Press, 2005); *Institutions, Institutional Change and Economic Performance*

(Cambridge University Press, 1990); *Structure and Change in Economic History* (W. W. Norton & Company, 1981); *The Rise of the Western World: A New Economic History* (Cambridge University Press, 1976).

3. Tang Yukai, "Xiaogang: The First Mover of China's Rural Reform." http://www. bjreview.com.cn/En-2005/05-40-e/china-3.htm.

4. Fu Chen, Liming Wang, and John Davis, "Land reform in rural China since the mid-1980s," http://www.fao.org/sd/LTdirect/LTan0031.htm.

5. Kelly Heyboer and Deborah Howlett, "Kean University and Beijing ratify plan for campus in China," http://www.nj.com/news/ledger/jersey/index.ssf?/base/news-3/1147153521232060.xml&coll=1.

6. China's township and village enterprises have developed on the basis of the handicrafts industry and the processing of agricultural products and by-products. They have flourished since 1978, becoming the mainstays of the rural economy. In 2001, there were 125 million employees in 21.15 million township enterprises, which increased by 19.63 million compared with that in 1978. The proportion of nonfarming industries in rural economy climbed up from 30.5 percent in 1978 to 67.2 percent in 2001. Township enterprises are involved in industry, agriculture, and transportation, along with building, commerce, and catering trades. They produce a variety of goods, from products needed in agriculture to daily necessities, foodstuffs, sideline products and light industrial materials. Many of these products are exported. Currently township enterprises generate one third of the GDP, one fourth of the financial revenue, one third of foreign currency earned, half of the added value of industry, two thirds of the rural social added value, and one third of farmers' income (the line between township enterprises and private enterprises is vague). According to the plan of the Ministry of Agriculture, township enterprise zones will be formed in the future, and in these zones township enterprises will have their own chains of coordination in production, supply, and marketing. These zones are expected to produce around 80 percent of the business income of township enterprises by the year 2015. Township enterprises will focus on the development of high-tech, high value-added, named brand and characteristic products in the coming years. Such products will account for 45 percent by 2015, and the number of rural enterprises boasting an annual export value of more than $1 million should reach 60,000. Agriculture accounted for about 30 percent of GDP in 1978, now it only takes about 15 percent.

7. James Whittington, "Wenzhou lights the way for China," http://news.bbc.co.uk/2/hi/business/4328341.stm.

8. Joe Studwell, "Zhejiang: at long last, capitalism," http://www.theceq.info/ceq2003q3_sec2_07_zhejiang.pdf.

9. Michael Porter, "Clusters and the New Economics of Competition," in Jeffrey Garten's *World View: Global Strategies for the New Economy* (Harvard Business School Press, 2000).

10. Zhan Ni, "Wenzhou's Success Story," http://www.chinatoday.com.cn/English/e20033/wenzhou1.htm.

11. Zhang Mei, "Wenzhou merchants adapt to foreign customers," http://www.symall.com/classifieds_read.cfm?ClassifiedAdID=715.

12. "From rags to cigarette lighters," *Economist* (June 2, 2005), http://www.economist.com/world/asia/displaystory.cfm?story_id=4034226.

13. Geoff Dyer, "Companies following the workers," http://archive.gulfnews.com/articles/06/05/25/10042241.html.

14. Those Chinese who already use credit cards usually have a good record; this is true both in China and in the U.S.—a case that can be explained by formal legal constraint, "face culture," and relatively high income.

15. Craig Simons, "The People's Bank," http://www.msnbc.msn.com/id/6595383/site/newsweek/from/RL.1/.
16. Zhou Xiaojie, Yang Jian, "Shadow Market," http://www.cfoasia.com/archives/200507-02.htm.
17. Simons, "The People's Bank."
18. Matthew Forney, "China's Shadow Banks," http://www.time.com/time/asia/magazine/article/0,13673,501041122-782173,00.html.
19. Zhou Xiaojie and Yang Jian, "Shadow Market," http://www.cfoasia.com/archives/200507-02.htm.
20. Kellee S. Tsai, *Back-Alley Banking: Private Entrepreneurs in China* (Cornell University Press, 2002).
21. Clifford Coonan, "On the factory floor, inside China's engine room," http://news.independent.co.uk/world/asia/article358757.ece.
22. On the backdrop of China's stellar economic growth, Shantou's underdevelopment—one of the only "Special Economic Zones" that fails to blossom—puts the city into the backwater of the on-going globalization, which is a clear sign that a region's economic development simply can't rely on the boost of some overseas big-name individuals' one-time effort or of some preferential policy's short-term effect. As will be detailed in chapter 4, only institutions with inducive efficiency can provide long lasting impact on economic growth.
23. Andrew G. Walder and Jean C. Oi, *Property Rights and Economic Reform in China* (Stanford University Press, 1999), p. 11–12.
24. Minxin Pei, "The Dark Side of China's Rise," *Foreign Policy*, March/April 2006, also available at http://www.carnegieendowment.org/publications/index.cfm?fa=view&id=18110.
25. Like its predecessor organization, the General Agreement on Tariffs and Trade (GATT), the WTO is founded on two core principles: non-discrimination and national treatment. The non-discrimination principle dictates that China cannot impose one level of barriers (e.g., tariffs) against one member country and another level for others. National treatment requires China to treat foreign firms the same way that domestic firms are treated in the Chinese market. These agreements provide for both increased market access and substantive rules. They vary in content but generally require "transparency": open publication or dissemination of measures affecting trade and investment, including not only tariffs and quotas but also subsidies, licensing requirements, and other measures. In China's case, barriers and distortions are numerous and interconnected. Although privatization is proceeding, quantifying the residual thicket of subsidies, price controls, local protectionism, and other forms of state interference will be extremely difficult (SOEs are still being subsidized, especially through the banking system). China will participate in the WTO's dispute settlement system, a big step toward the rule of law. Participation is mandatory and if one WTO member is accused of violating the rights of another—and if negotiations fail—it must submit to a dispute settlement process. Under the WTO accession agreement, specifically, China agreed to reduce the average tariff for industrial goods and agriculture products to 8.9 percent and 15 percent, respectively (with most cuts made by 2004 and all cuts completed by 2010); limit subsidies for agricultural production to 8.5 percent of the value of farm output and eliminate export subsidies on agricultural exports; within three years of accession, grant full trade and distribution rights to foreign enterprises (with some exceptions, such as for certain agricultural products, minerals, and fuels); provide non-discriminatory treatment to all WTO members (foreign firms in China will be treated no less favorably than Chinese firms for trade purposes); implement the WTO's Trade-Related Aspects of Intellectual Property Rights (TRIP) Agreement upon accession;

accept a twelve-year safeguard mechanism available to other WTO members in cases where a surge in Chinese exports cause or threaten to cause market disruption to domestic producers; and fully open the banking system to foreign financial institutions within five years (joint ventures in insurance and telecommunication will be permitted, with various degrees of foreign ownership allowed).

26. Steven R. Weisman, "China and U.S. clash at trade talks," http://www.iht.com/articles/2006/12/14/business/trade.php.

Chapter 4

1. Michael Fairbanks, "Changing the Mind of a Nation: Elements in a Process for Creating Prosperity," in *Culture Matters*, ed. Lawrence E. Harrison and Samuel P. Huntington (Basic Books, 2000), p. 268.

2. Chris Bramall, *Sources of Chinese Economic Growth, 1978–1996*, (Oxford University Press, 2000). Bramall argues that a combination of state-led industrial policy and the favorable legacies of industrialization, human capital (health and education), infrastructure, technology, and capital stock during the socialist era produced China's growth. He shows that industrialization was the key source of growth, and that foreign trade and foreign investment (Open Door policy) were less important than usually thought. Growth was not a result of trade liberalization, the end of socialism, unleashing the productive powers of capitalism, or backwards initial conditions at the end of the Maoist era. Bramall claimed that despite numerous positive influences (such as a restructured incentive system, foreign trade, R & D spending), the release of labor from agriculture reduced labor productivity and did not have a positive impact on China's economic growth (as if the release of labor won't increase total production).

3. Mancur Olson, *The Rise and Decline of Nations: Economic Growth, Stagflation, and Social Rigidities* (Yale University Press, 1982), p. 4.

4. James M. Buchanan, *What Should Economists Do?* (Liberty Fund, 1979), p. 86.

5. Samuel P. Huntington, *Political Order in Changing Societies* (Yale University Press, 1968).

6. In Yi Feng's *Democracy, Governance, and Economic Performance: Theory and Evidence* (The MIT Press, 2005). Political instability and policy uncertainty are believed to reduce economic growth, and political freedom causes economic freedom, not the other way; but the book presents a non-institutional causal analysis and a roseate view of democracy as if democracy is boundless and flawless.

7. Peter Engardio, ed., *Chindia: How China and India Are Revolutionizing Global Business* (McGraw-Hill, 2006), p. 29.

8. The conformity of individual return with individual efforts may not always result in a narrow gap between social and private rates of return. In addition to bad economic institutions that widen this gap, distributional and destructive efforts can also lead to a wide gap between social and private rates of return.

9. This "Effort-based Institutional Analysis" is inspired by Douglass North and Mancur Olson. Douglass C. North, *Understanding the Process of Economic Change* (Princeton University Press, 2005); *Institutions, Institutional Change and Economic Performance* (Cambridge University Press, 1990); *Structure and Change in Economic History* (W. W. Norton & Company, 1981); *The Rise of the Western World: A New Economic History* (Cambridge University Press, 1976). Mancur Olson, *Power and Prosperity: Outgrowing Communist and Capitalist Dictatorships* (Basic Books, 2000); *The Rise and Decline of Nations: Economic Growth, Stagflation, and Social Rigidities* (Yale University Press, 1984).

The central ideas of Douglass North's growth theory are: institutions affect economic performance by determining the cost of transacting and producing (the costliness of measuring performance, fulfilling personal/impersonal exchanges, enforcing rules, and exercising ideology, systems of belief, or "mental models"). Institutions are composed of formal rules, informal constraints, and characteristics of enforcing those constraints. While formal rules can be changed over night by the polity, informal constraints change very slowly. Both are ultimately shaped by people's subjective perceptions of the world around them; those perceptions in turn determine explicit choices among formal rules and evolving informal constraints. In North's framework, where institutions are the rules of the game, organizations are the players. While players seek to alter the game, there is no reason why successful groups will want to make changes that lead to a more productive economy. Institutional path dependence exists because the individuals and organizations with bargaining power as a result of the institutional framework have a crucial stake in perpetuating the system. Paths do get reversed, but it all depends on such factors as network externalities, economies of scope, and complementaries that exist with a given institutional matrix. In many societies, rulers and their political organizations profit not through promoting economic growth but through giving rewards to key constituents who keep them in power. Bureaucracies, too, benefit not by spurring production but rather by controlling allocations of resources. Businesses, meanwhile, prosper if they gain a monopolistic position, even though competition in the marketplace fosters a country's overall economic performance. Through history societies have generally tended to cling to institutions aimed at redistributing wealth—which helps their rulers gain supporters rather than boost production—with the common result of poor economic performance.

Olson's central idea is: small distributional coalitions have the incentives to form political lobbies and influence policies that tend to be protectionist and anti-technology; since the benefits of these policies are selective incentives concentrated amongst the few coalitions members and the costs are diffused throughout the whole population, the "Logic" dictates that there will be little public resistance to them; as time goes on, these distributional coalitions accumulate in greater and greater numbers, the nation burdened by them will fall into economic decline. Olson's idea is compatible with North's institutional path dependence, but Olson's logic is more "natural" incentive-driven while North's logic is more institution-driven. Olson extended his ideas to the notion of "stationary bandit" and "market-augmenting government" in *Power and Prosperity* which is very similar to North's ideas.

10. In Daron Acemoglu, Simon Johnson, and James Robinson's "Institutions as the Fundamental Cause of Long-Run Growth" (Philippe Aghion and Steven N. Durlauf, *Handbook of Economic Growth* [North Holland, 2005]), the authors trace these "comparative statics" to checks on the use of political power, broad group holding political power, and power holders' profit and power potential. Like other neo-institutionalists, their analysis of the impact of economic institutions on growth only implicitly covers all three types of efforts—productive, distributional, and destructive efforts (good economic institutions are defined as "those that provide security of property rights and relatively equal access to economic resources to a broad cross-section of society," "efficiency and distribution cannot be separated"). The "comparative statics" developed in this book can be called "front-end comparative statics" because these institutional statics interface with performance result directly. They focus on motivation level individual efforts and capture the institutionally induced destructive effort (a type of violent and lawless distributional efforts) throughout the Chinese history, which are culturally richer than the generalization of "property protection" on one hand, and provide a more structured analytical framework on the other). Acemoglu's political analysis can be called "back-end

comparative statics," which is supported by their "theory of political institutions"—the distribution of political power (de jure power determined by the political institutions and de facto power determined by the distribution of resources) shapes future political institutions and existing economic institutions that decide the rate of economic growth and the commitment-sensitive resources allocation and economic efficiency. Interestingly, even in the political "back-end," politicians' individual efforts are also constrained by institutions to be either productive, distributional, or destructive. Chapter 5 in this book addresses this topic under China's political setting. Regional growth comparison within a country is a promising topic for future research using the "front-end comparative statics" framework for the political and economic performance of political and non-political actors.

11. Acemoglu, Johnson, and Robinson, "Institutions as the Fundamental Cause" in Aghion and Durlauf's, *Handbook of Economic Growth*.
12. A. Alan Schmid, *Conflict and Cooperation: Institutional & Behavioral Economics* (Blackwell Publishing Limited, 2004), p. 88.
13. James M. Buchanan, *What Should Economists Do?* (Liberty Fund, 1979).
14. Rowan Callick, "Beijing Games building boss sacked," http://www.theaustralian. news.com.au/story/0,20867,19465039-25658,00.html.
15. Oliver August, "Sacked Olympics chief had 'pleasure palace' full of concubines," http://www.timesonline.co.uk/article/0,,25689-2222095,00.html.
16. Benjamin Kang Lim, "Mistress turns in corrupt China vice admiral," http:// in.today.reuters.com/misc/PrinterFriendlyPopup.aspx?type=worldNews&storyID =uri%3A2006-06-14T175742Z_01_NOOTR_RTRJONC_0_India-254643-1.xml.
17. Peter S. Goodman, "China Discloses $1.1 Billion Bank Fraud," http://www. washingtonpost.com/wp-dyn/content/article/2006/06/27/AR2006062700584. html.
18. Yan Sun, *Corruption and Market in Contemporary China* (Cornell University Press, 2004); Melanie Manion, *Corruption by Design: Building Clean Government in Mainland China and Hong Kong* (Harvard University Press, 2004); Yang Dali, *Remaking the Chinese Leviathan: Market Transition and the Politics of Governance in China* (Stanford University Press, 2006, new edition).
19. The Party represents the development trends of advanced productive forces, the orientations of an advanced culture, and the fundamental interests of the overwhelming majority of the people of China.
20. Chi Hung Kwan, "Privatization of State-owned Enterprises Gathering Pace—Whither Chinese Socialism?" http://www.rieti.go.jp/en/china/03092601.html.
21. "Figures of China's Corruption," http://chinadigitaltimes.net/2006/05/figures_of_ china_corruption_people_net.php.
22. "China's Corruption Crackdown," http://www.friedlnet.com/news/03031602. html.
23. Steven Ross Johnson, "India, China, and Russia lead in a corporate corruption list," http://www.boston.com/news/world/asia/articles/2006/10/05/india_china_ and_russia_lead_in_a_corporate_corruption_list/.
24. In April 2004, Lucent fired the president, chief operating officer, a marketing executive, and a finance manager at its Chinese operations following a company investigation into the use of bribery by Lucent executives to secure contracts. The U.S. Securities and Exchange Commission (SEC) later warned Lucent Technologies to expect an "enforcement action" over violations of the Foreign Corrupt Practices Act (FCPA).
25. "Commercial bribery—foreign companies adapt to local market in wrong way," *People's Daily Online*, November 17, 2006, http://english.people.com.cn/200611/ 17/eng20061117_322599.html.

26. "China to reform local governments' offices in Beijing to check corruption," September 4, 2006, http://www.china-embassy.org/eng/gyzg/t270135.htm.
27. Yang Buyue and Wang Xi, "Wong's son exposed detail of the medical bill," http://www.southcn.com/news/community/shzt/550wan/investigate/200512050146.htm.
28. David Blumenthal and William Hsiao, "Privatization and Its Discontents—The Evolving Chinese Health Care System." http://content.nejm.org/cgi/content/full/353/11/1165.
29. M.L., "An American's Experience—Teaching in Beijing, China," http://www.asianinfo.org/asianinfo/issues/teaching_in_beijing.htm.
30. Duncan Hewitt, "Teenage prostitution case shocks China," http://news.bbc.co.uk/1/hi/world/asia-pacific/1775221.stm.
31. Nie Peng, "Student survey stumps sex specialists," http://news.xinhuanet.com/english/2007-01/11/content_5591461.htm.
32. *China Daily*, October 28, 2004, Hong Kong edition, p. 18.
33. Ben Blanchard, "China struggles to stop its largest lake shrinking," http://www.boston.com/news/world/asia/articles/2006/05/24/china_struggles_to_stop_its_largest_lake_shrinking/.
34. Elizabeth C. Economy, *The River Runs Black: The Environmental Challenge To China's Future* (Cornell University Press, 2005).
35. Keith Bradsher and David Barboza, "China's toxic brew hits its neighbours," http://www.smh.com.au/news/world/chinas-toxic-brew-hits-its-neighbours/2006/06/16/1149964736774.html.
36. In "An Institutional Economics Perspective on Economic Growth," A. Allan Schmid proposed a "selective confiscation" hypothesis that "entrepreneurs can tolerate a certain amount of 'confiscation' of rights, and in fact uncompensated change in rights is essential for development of new products." He believed this is contrary to the general message of Douglass North. http://www.msu.edu/user/schmid/institutional%20perspective.htm.
37. Minxin Pei, *China's Trapped Transition: The Limits of Developmental Autocracy* (Harvard University Press, 2006).
38. Will Hutton, *The Writing on the Wall: Why We Must Embrace China as a Partner or Face It as an Enemy* (Free Press, 2006), p. 153.

Chapter 5

1. According to *Autocratic Tradition and Chinese Politics* (Cambridge University Press, 1993), p. 24, by Zhengyuan Fu, "The ties between lord and vassals under Western feudalism were based on mutual obligations and, hence, were more contractual and voluntary, whereas under the Zhou system the relation was more hierarchical and one-directional, stressing the authority of the king versus the obligation of the vassals. Western feudalism developed into a system separate from kinship, whereas Zhou feudalism was essentially based on kinship and regulated by patrimonial norms. Western feudalism had a separate religious authority and a hierarchy independent of the political system, whereas Chinese traditional political system never tolerated an autonomous church independent from the authority of the state. Western feudalism contained seeds of pluralism, whereas Chinese feudalism was impregnated with monistic autocracy from its very inception."
2. Zhengyuan Fu, *China's Legalists: The Earliest Totalitarians and Their Art of Ruling* (M.E. Sharpe, 1996), p. 7.
3. The institution of emperor's will could be a fascinating subject not only because of the unwillingness to make one due to the self-curse implication but also because of

the uncertainty of the emperor's health and ability, and the reliability and enforcement of the will.

4. Holding productive and destructive efforts constant, small distributional coalitions have the incentives to form political lobbies and influence policies that tend to be protectionist and anti-technology; since the benefits of these policies are selective incentives concentrated amongst the few coalitions members and the costs are diffused throughout the whole population, the "Logic" dictates that there will be little public resistance to them; as time goes on, these distributional coalitions accumulate in greater and greater numbers, and the nation burdened by them will fall into economic decline. However, if we think beyond the "natural" cost-incentive structure of Olson's "collective action logic," there are then four possible directions:

i. Intentionality from the knowledge of this logic results in certain institutional design that prevents the negative effects of the distributional coalitions;

ii. The dynamics of distributional coalitions may be changed by political or economic factors, e.g., globalization may affect the formations of the distributional coalitions so that the power of the protectionist coalition is now balanced by a coalition of big importers;

iii. If a society has positive economic growth while distributional coalitions in fact have a negative impact on it, or if a society has negative economic growth while distributional coalitions in fact have a positive impact on it, then we should further look at how a society's institutions favor or disfavor its productive and destructive efforts;

iv. Distributional coalitions may be formed by the pure "logic," they can also be formed by institutional incentives; they could be "natural" due to the free-riding logic, but they are more likely to be "institutionally induced."

The explanation power of distributional coalitions comes from the strength of its "internal logic," we could be easily overwhelmed if "external logic" is neglected. Still, Olson's contribution is his offering of a powerful marginal explanation for the academic world.

5. Daron Acemoglu, Simon Johnson, James Robinson, Pierre Yared, "Income and Democracy," http://www.nber.org/papers/W11205

6. Dietrich Rueschemeyer, Evelyne Huber Stephens, John D. Stephens, *Capitalist Development and Democracy* (University Of Chicago Press, 1992).

7. H. Lyman Miller, "China's Leadership Transition," http://media.hoover.org/documents/clm5_lm.pdf#search=%22Politburo%20with%20new%20people%20in%20effect%20creates%20a%20new%2C%20two-tiered%20hierarchy%20at%20the%20top%20of%20the%20party%22.

8. "Commitment problems" dictate that groups with political power cannot commit to not using their power to change the distribution of resources in their favor; or in a narrower notion, those with power can't commit to their promise that benefit other social groups. Refer to Daron Acemoglu, Simon Johnson, James Robinson, "Institutions as the Fundamental Cause of Long-Run Growth," in Philippe Aghion and Steven N. Durlauf, *Handbook of Economic Growth* (North Holland, 2005).

9. H. Lyman Miller, "Leadership Analysis in an Era of Institutionalized Party Politics," http://chinavitae.com/reference/conferencepapers/Miller.pdf

10. Cheng Li, "China's Political Succession: Four Myths in the U.S.," http://iicas.org/english/Krsten_24_05_01.htm.

11. Zhengyuan Fu, *Autocratic Tradition and Chinese Politics* (Cambridge University press, 1993), p. 105.

12. Kishore Mahbubani, *Can Asians Think? Understanding the Divide Between East and West* (Steerforth, 2001), pp. 63–65.

13. "The Tragicomedy of the Overseas Chinese Democratic Movement," http://www.zonaeuropa.com/20050912_3.htm.

Chapter 6

1. Richard Nisbett, *The Geography of Thought: How Asians and Westerners Think Differently . . . and Why* (Free Press, 2003), pp. 69–71.
2. Jerry Wind, Colin Crook, Robert Gunther: *The Power of Impossible Thinking* (Wharton School Publishing, 2004), p. 242.
3. The idea here is a version of "moderate contextualism"—we operate within contexts and are able to reflect on our contexts and broaden the scope of our contexts so as to embrace and enter other contexts. For a more indepth discussion, see William A. Dembski's "The Fallacy of Contextualism," http://www.arn.org/docs/dembski/wd_contexism.htm. Also refer to Dudley Shapere's *Reason and the Search for Knowledge* (Springer, 1984, 2001); Larry Laudan's *Beyond Positivism and Relativism: Theory, Method, and Evidence* (Westview Press, 2001); and Paul A. Boghossian's *Fear of Knowledge: Against Relativism and Constructivism* (Oxford University Press, 2006).
4. The Information Office of the State Council of the People's Republic of China, "The Human Rights Record of the United States in 2005," http://english.people.com.cn/200603/09/eng20060309_249259.html.
5. Edward Friedman, "Right and Wrong Ways to Question Human Rights Universalism," http://www.pacificrim.usfca.edu/research/pacrimreport/pacrimreport31.html.
6. This quote is from Eric Dowling's book review on Edward Friedman, ed., *The Politics of Democratization: Generalizing East Asian Experiences*, http://www.hartford-hwp.com/archives/55/098.html.
7. Friedman, "Right and Wrong Ways."
8. Robert A. Dahl, *How Democratic is the American Constitution?* (Yale University Press, 2003), p. 53.
9. Rob Lopresti, "Which US Presidents Owned Slaves?" http://www.nas.com/~lopresti/ps.htm.
10. Paul Finkelman, *Slavery and the Founders: Race and Liberty in the Age of Jefferson* (M.E. Sharpe, 2001), pp. 105, 107, 129.
11. Gordon, Scott, "The New Contractarians," *Journal of Political Economy* 84, no. 3 (June 1976): pp. 573–90.
12. North, *Structure and Change*, chapter 3.
13. Robert A. Dahl, *Polyarchy: Participation and Opposition* (Yale University Press, 1972).
14. Stephen C. Angle, *Human Rights in Chinese Thought: A Cross-Cultural Inquiry* (Cambridge University Press, 2002).
15. Bryan Caplan: "Rational Ignorance vs. Rational Irrationality," http://www.gmu.edu/departments/economics/bcaplan/ratirnew.doc.
16. George Washington, Farewell Address (1796), http://usinfo.state.gov/usa/infousa/facts/democrac/49.htm.
17. Mark Green, *Selling Out: How Big Corporate Money Buys Elections, Rams Through Legislation, and Betrays Our Democracy* (ReganBooks, 2002), pp. 2, 4, 47.
18. Jim Kuhnhenn, "White House race may cost hopefuls $500M," http://news.yahoo.com/s/ap/20060916/ap_on_el_pr/presidential_money.
19. Green, *Selling Out*, chapter 5.
20. Anthony Downs, *An Economic Theory of Democracy* (Harper, 1957); William H. Riker and Peter C. Ordeshook, "A Theory of the Calculus of Voting," *American Political Science Review* (1968): pp. 25–42, 62, http://zeus.econ.umd.edu/cgi-bin/conference/download.cgi?db_name=MWET2006&paper_id=84#search=%22Riker%20and%20Ordershook%20in%201968%22; Ming Li and Dipjyoti Majumdar, "Voting to Avoid Regret," http://alcor.concordia.ca/~mingli/research/regretm.pdf.
21. G. Powell, *Elections as Instruments of Democracy* (Yale University Press, 2000).

22. Bryan Caplan, *The Myth of the Rational Voter: Why Democracies Choose Bad Policies* (Princeton University Press, 2007).

23. James Buchanan, "Keynesian Economics in Democratic Politics," *Collected Works of James Buchanan*, vol. 8, *Democracy in Deficit: The Political Legacy of Lord Keynes* (Academic Press, 1977), pp. 98–99.

24. Voting system, http://en.wikipedia.org/wiki/Voting_system.

25. Kenneth Arrow's *Social Choice and Individual Values* (John Wiley & Sons, Inc., 1951) was seen by James Buchanan as having an objective bias in methodology.

26. Brian Z. Tamanaha, *On The Rule of Law: History, Politics, Theory* (Cambridge University Press, 2004), pp. 37–38.

27. A similar argument can be found in Pan Wei, "Toward a Consultative Rule of Law Regime in China," in *Debating Political Reform in China: Rule of Law vs. Democratization*, ed. Zhao Suisheng (M.E. Sharpe, 2006).

28. http://www.freedomhouse.org/uploads/pdf/Charts2006.pdf.

29. Richard A. Shweder, "George W. Bush & the missionary position," *Daedalus*, Summer 2004.

30. Richard A. Posner, *The Problematics of Moral and Legal Theory* (Harvard University Press, 1999), pp. 6–8.

31. Joseph Chan, "Asian Values and Human Rights: An Alternative View," *Democracy in East Asia* (The Johns Hopkins University Press, 1998), pp. 32–33. Also see Stephen Angle's *Human Rights in Chinese Thought: A Cross-Cultural Inquiry* (Cambridge University Press, 2002).

32. Larry Diamond and Marc F. Plattner, eds., *The Global Divergence of Democracies* (The Johns Hopkins University Press, 2001).

33. Larry Diamond, *Squandered Victory: The American Occupation and the Bungled Effort to Bring Democracy to Iraq* (Times Books, 2005).

Conclusion

1. Daniel A. Bell, "Teaching Political Theory in Beijing," http://www.dissentmagazine. org/article/?article=418. Daniel A. Bell made some interesting points against Western democracy in China in his new book *Beyond Liberal Democracy: Political Thinking for an East Asian Context* (Princeton University Press, 2006).

2. Mahbubani, *Can Asians Think?*

3. David Bachman, "China's Democratization: What Difference Would It Make for U.S.-China Relations?" in *What if China Doesn't Democratize? Implications for War and Peace*, eds. Edward Friedman and Barrett L. McCormick (M.E. Sharpe, 2000), p. 196.

4. Buchanan, *Collected Works*, vol. 8, "The Old-Time Fiscal Religion," p. 19.

5. In his novel *Dead Lagoon*, Michael Dibdin says, "There can be no true friends without true enemies. Unless we hate what we are not, we cannot love what we are."

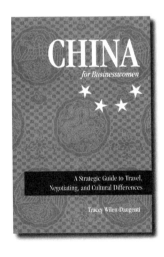

DATE DUE